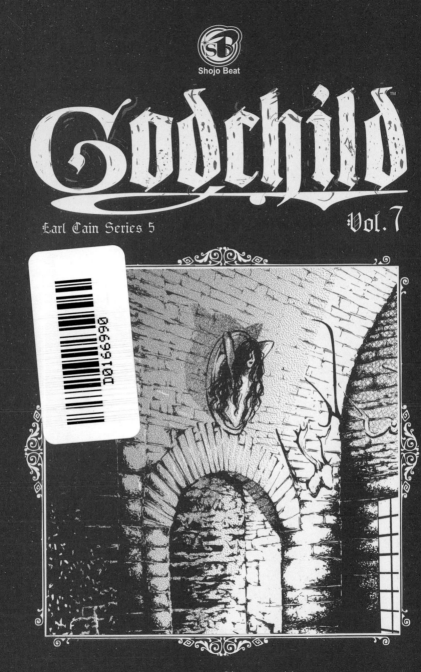

Shojo Beat

Godchild

Earl Cain Series 5

Vol. 7

Story & Art by **Kaori Yuki**

Contents

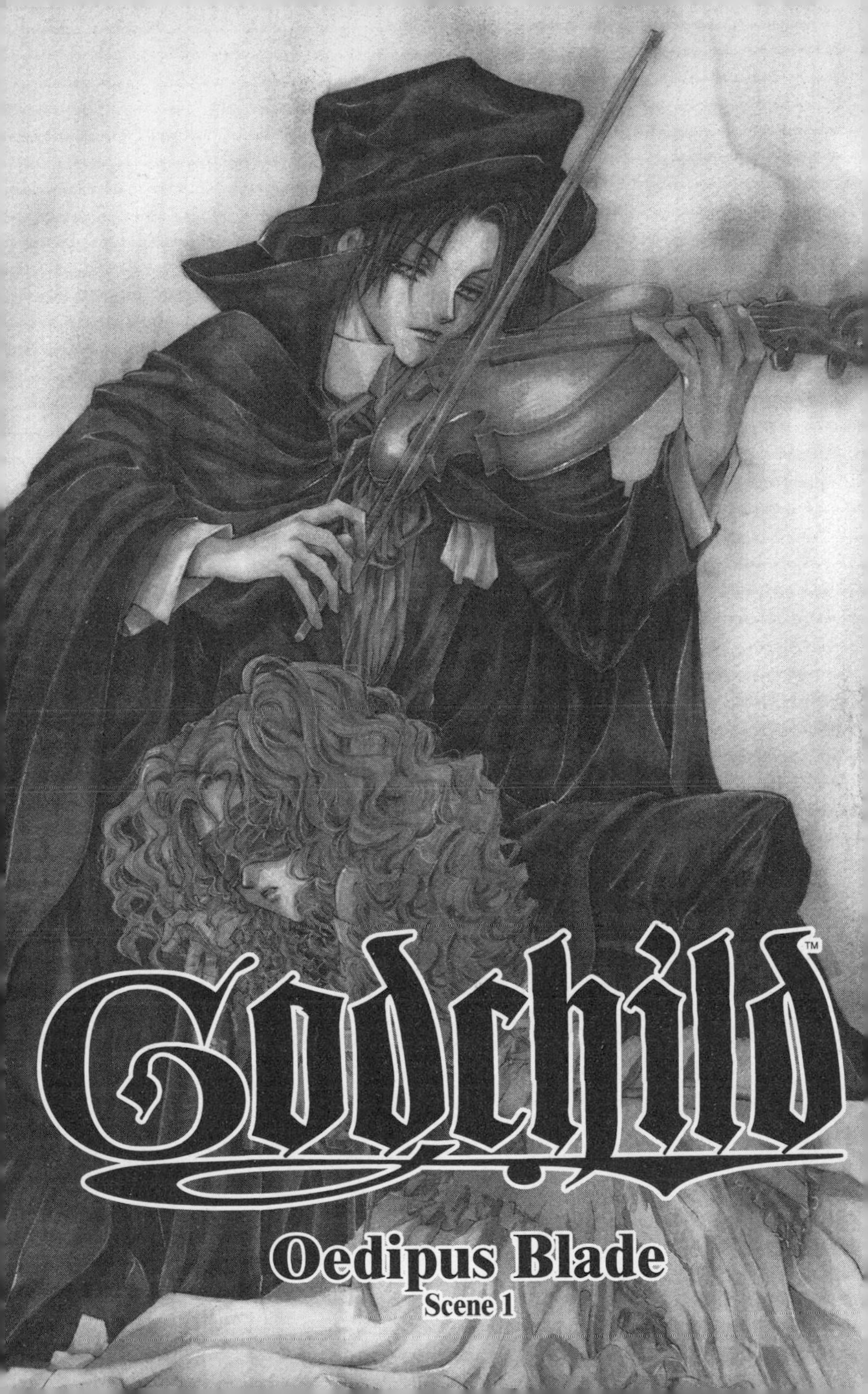
Godchild™
Oedipus Blade
Scene 1

IN THE LATTER PART OF THE NINETEENTH CENTURY, VICTORIAN-ERA ENGLAND CENTERED ON ITS CAPITAL OF FOG, LONDON. THE YOUTHFUL EARL CAIN, A COLLECTOR OF POISONS, CHALLENGES HIS FATHER'S SECRET ORGANIZATION DELILAH, ADDING TO THE GROWING DISCORD BETWEEN ESTRANGED FATHER AND SON. CREHADOR, A FORMER ENEMY, CHANGES SIDES WHEN HIS LOVER IS MURDERED AND NOW IS ASSISTING CAIN. MEANWHILE, THE HARGREAVES' FRIEND OSCAR FALLS UNDER SUSPICION. BUT ALL IS MADE CLEAR AT THE COMMEMORATIVE PARTY FOR THE COMPLETION OF THE 12 ANGEL STATUES AND THE MEMORIAL TEMPLE. IT TURNS OUT THAT CAIN'S CONSTANT COMPANION RIFF, WHO HAD UNTIL NOW BEEN A LOYAL SERVANT, IS ACTUALLY ALEXIS' HIDDEN WEAPON, THE TOWER CARD. HE BETRAYS CAIN AND DISAPPEARS WITH ALEXIS. CAIN FIGHTS TO OVERCOME HIS HEARTACHE FROM THE ULTIMATE DECEPTION, AND TOGETHER WITH HIS FRIENDS ISSUES A FINAL DECLARATION OF WAR... CATCH UP ON THE STORY BY READING THE REST OF THE *EARL CAIN SERIES*, INCLUDING *THE CAIN SAGA* VOLUMES ONE TO FOUR, AND THE EARLIER VOLUMES OF *GODCHILD*.

CAIN
—17-YEAR-OLD EARL HARGREAVES. HIS BIRTH IS SHROUDED IN MYSTERY.

MARY WEATHER
—10 YEARS OLD. CAIN'S SISTER.

DOCTOR JIZABEL DISRAELI
—APPARENTLY, CAIN'S FATHER'S ILLEGITIMATE CHILD. HE HATES HIS HALF-BROTHER CAIN AND WISHES TO ADD HIS EYES TO HIS MORBID COLLECTION.

RIFF
—A YOUTHFUL MANSERVANT FOR THE HARGREAVES FAMILY WITH A BACKGROUND IN MEDICINE.

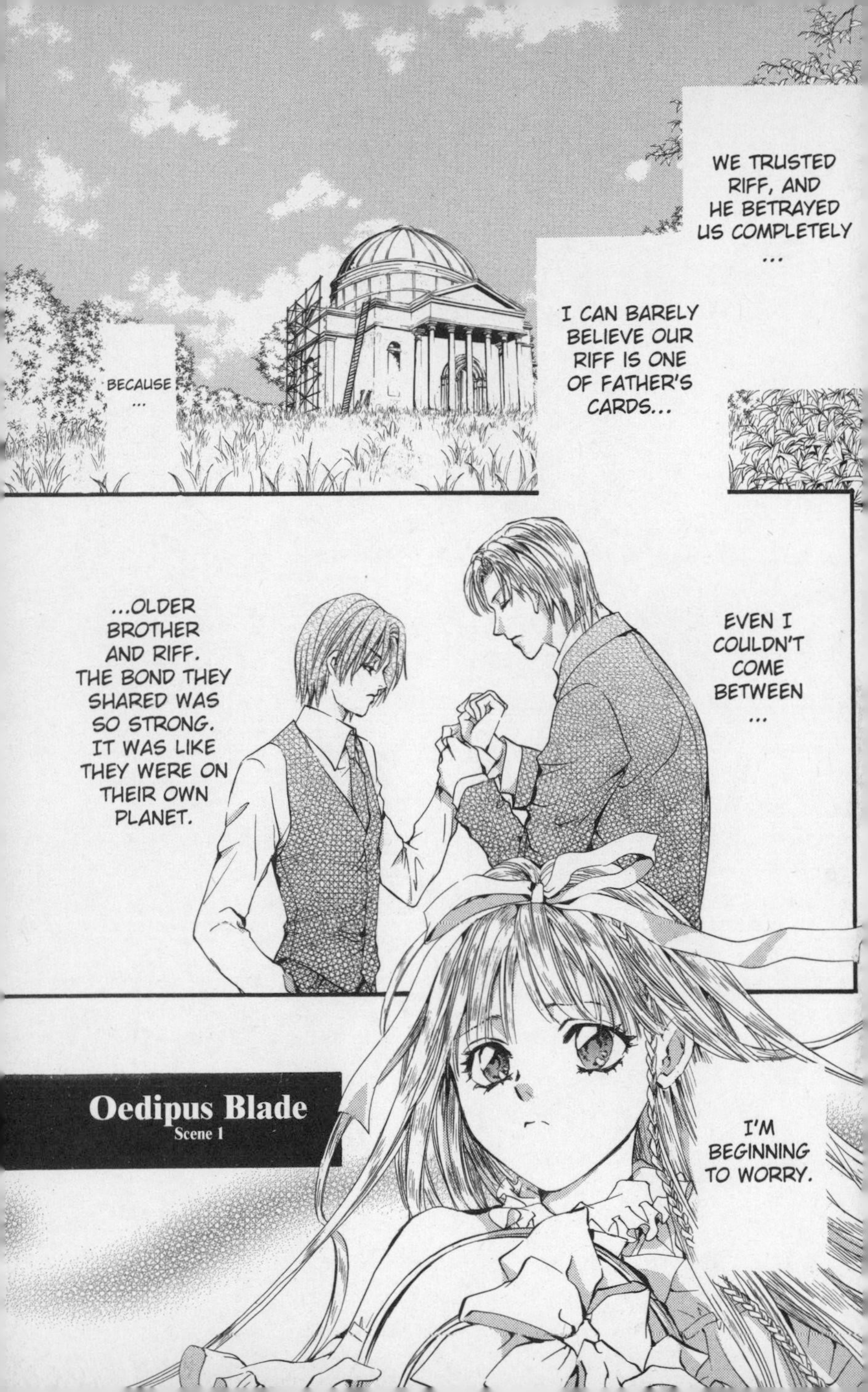
WE TRUSTED RIFF, AND HE BETRAYED US COMPLETELY...
I CAN BARELY BELIEVE OUR RIFF IS ONE OF FATHER'S CARDS...
BECAUSE...
EVEN I COULDN'T COME BETWEEN...
...OLDER BROTHER AND RIFF. THE BOND THEY SHARED WAS SO STRONG. IT WAS LIKE THEY WERE ON THEIR OWN PLANET.
I'M BEGINNING TO WORRY.
Oedipus Blade
Scene 1

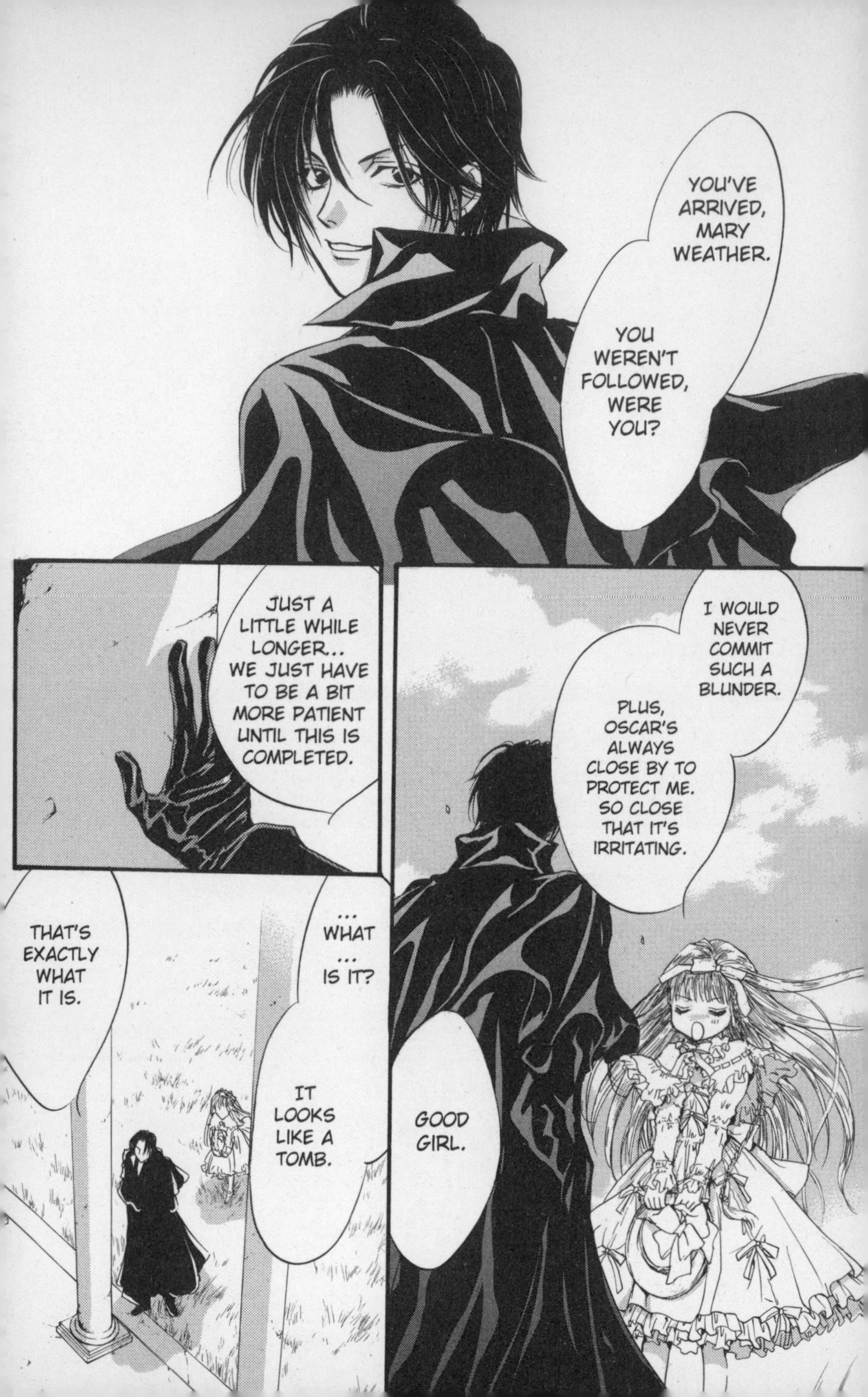
YOU'VE ARRIVED, MARY WEATHER.
YOU WEREN'T FOLLOWED, WERE YOU?
I WOULD NEVER COMMIT SUCH A BLUNDER.
PLUS, OSCAR'S ALWAYS CLOSE BY TO PROTECT ME. SO CLOSE THAT IT'S IRRITATING.
GOOD GIRL.
JUST A LITTLE WHILE LONGER... WE JUST HAVE TO BE A BIT MORE PATIENT UNTIL THIS IS COMPLETED.
... WHAT ... IS IT?
IT LOOKS LIKE A TOMB.
THAT'S EXACTLY WHAT IT IS.

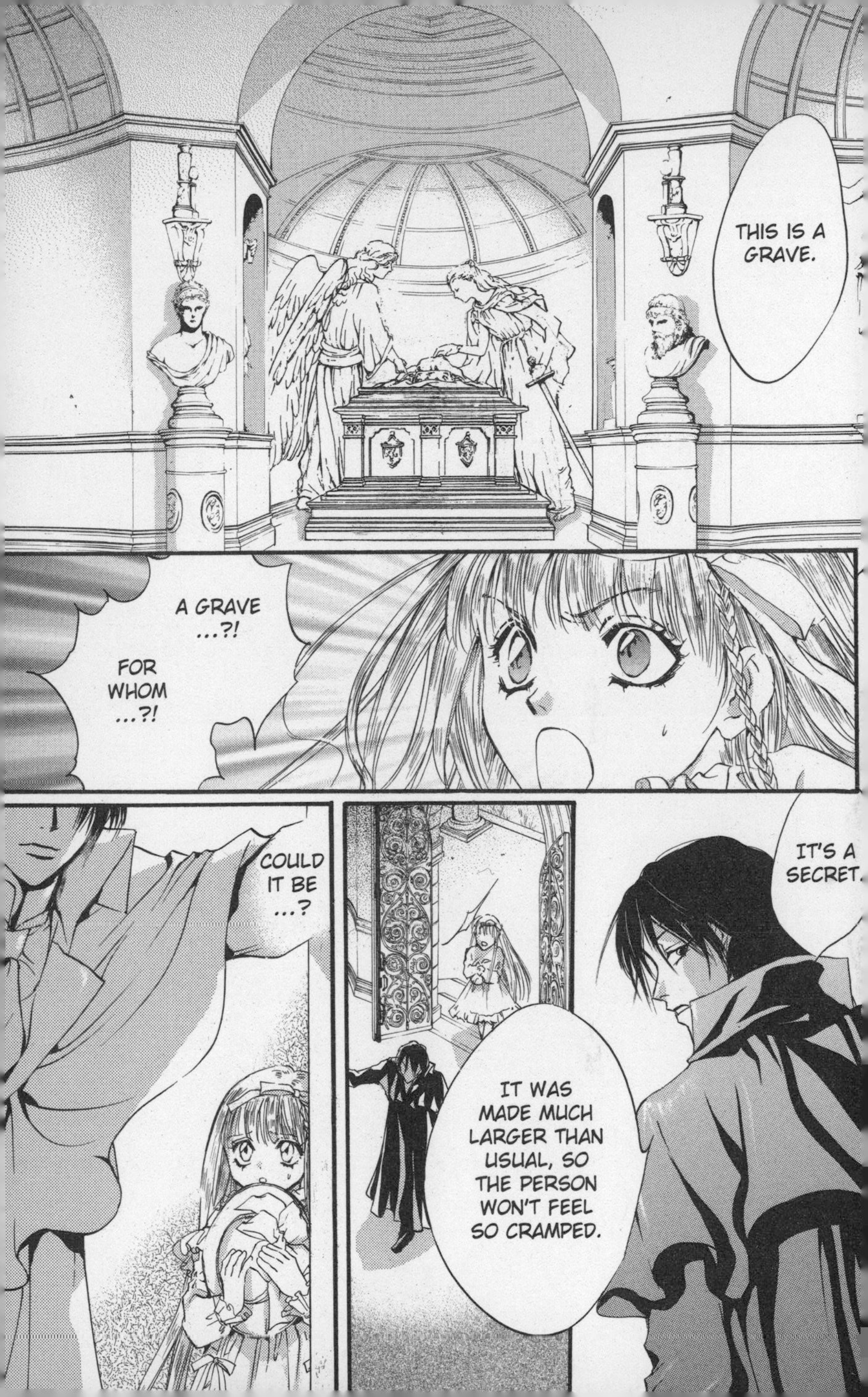
THIS IS A GRAVE.
A GRAVE ...?!
FOR WHOM ...?!
IT'S A SECRET.
IT WAS MADE MUCH LARGER THAN USUAL, SO THE PERSON WON'T FEEL SO CRAMPED.
COULD IT BE ...?

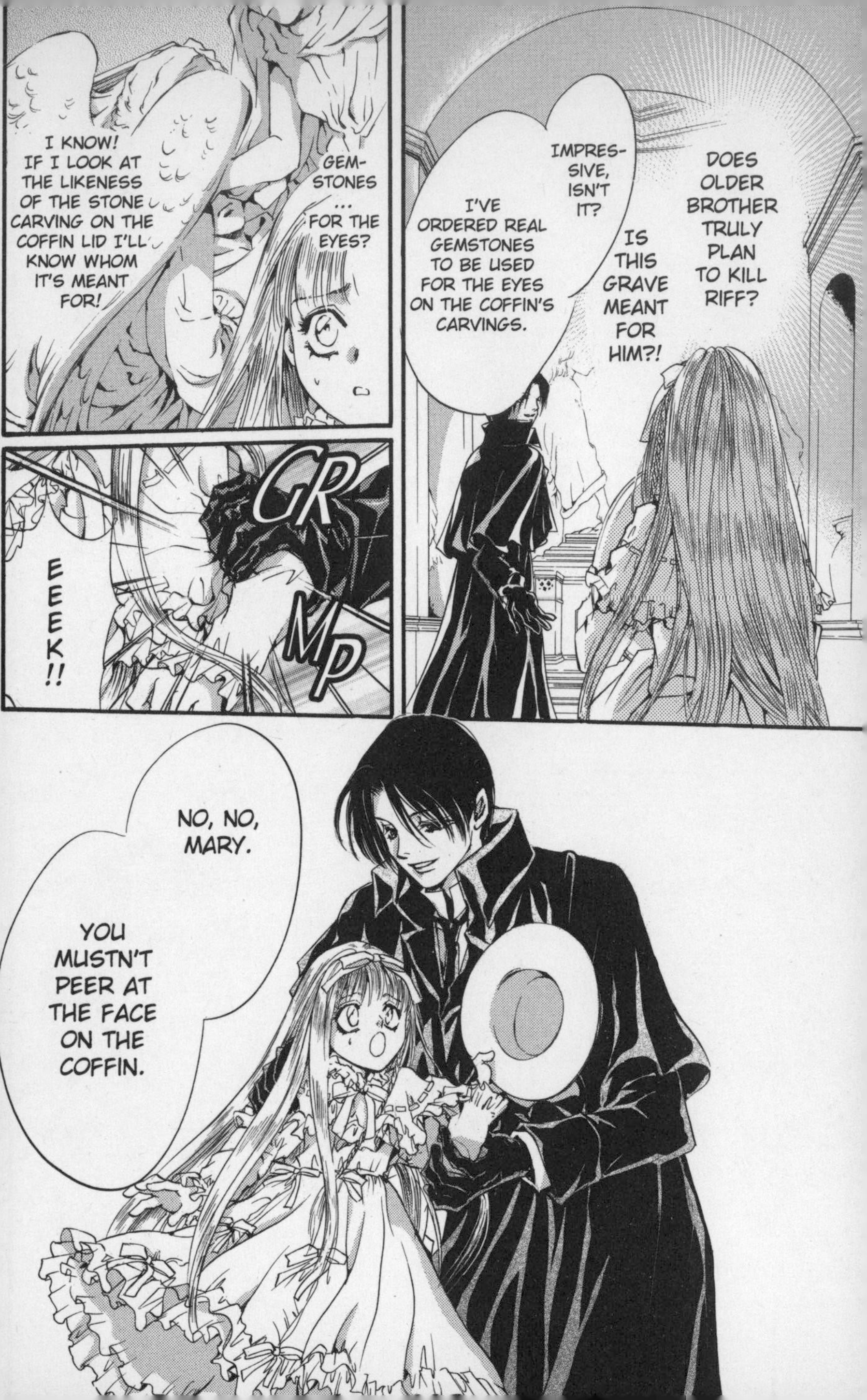
DOES OLDER BROTHER TRULY PLAN TO KILL RIFF?
IS THIS GRAVE MEANT FOR HIM?!
IMPRES-SIVE, ISN'T IT?
I'VE ORDERED REAL GEMSTONES TO BE USED FOR THE EYES ON THE COFFIN'S CARVINGS.
GEM-STONES ... FOR THE EYES?
I KNOW! IF I LOOK AT THE LIKENESS OF THE STONE CARVING ON THE COFFIN LID I'LL KNOW WHOM IT'S MEANT FOR!
GRMP
EEEK!!
NO, NO, MARY.
YOU MUSTN'T PEER AT THE FACE ON THE COFFIN.

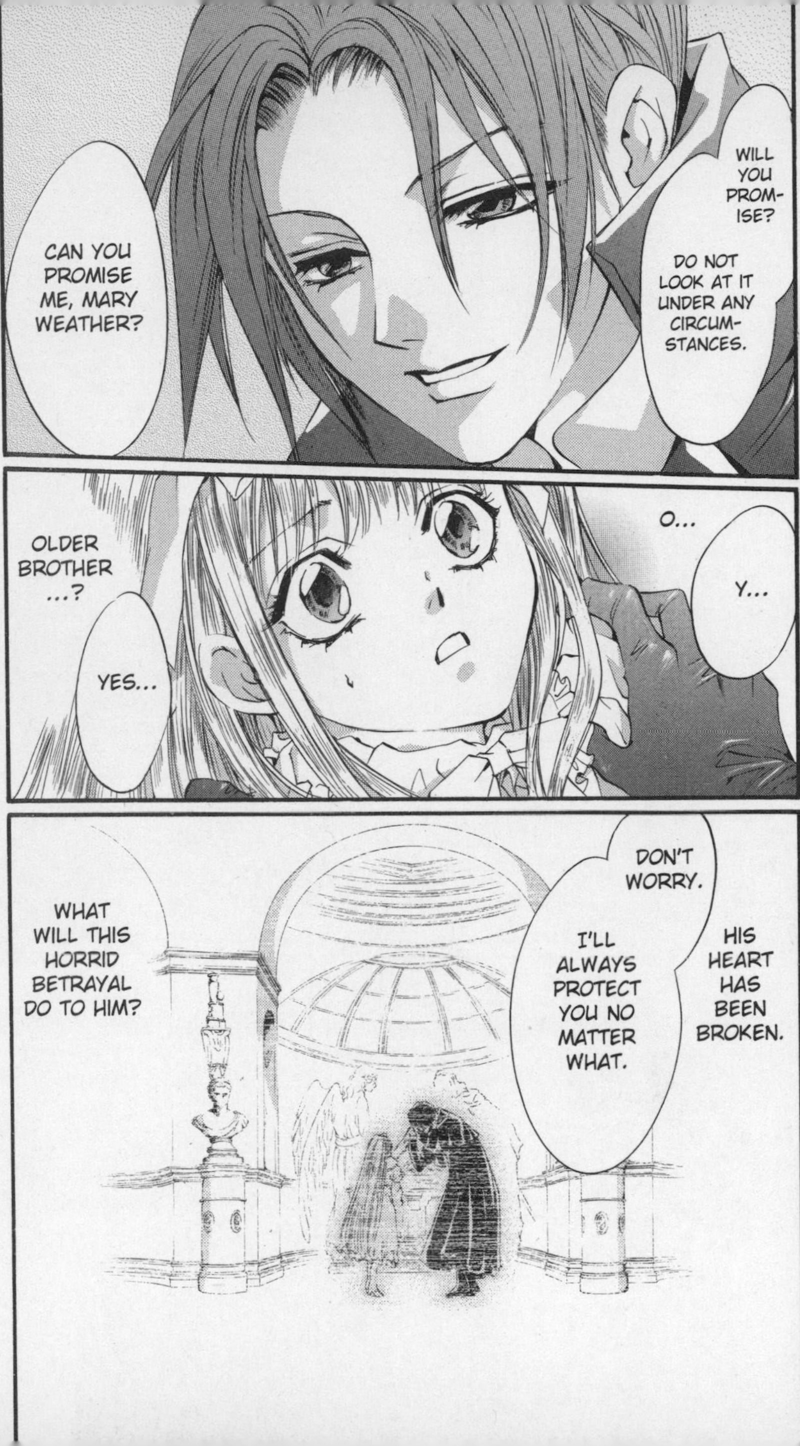
WILL YOU PROMISE?
DO NOT LOOK AT IT UNDER ANY CIRCUMSTANCES.
CAN YOU PROMISE ME, MARY WEATHER?
O...
Y...
OLDER BROTHER ...?
YES...
HIS HEART HAS BEEN BROKEN.
DON'T WORRY.
I'LL ALWAYS PROTECT YOU NO MATTER WHAT.
WHAT WILL THIS HORRID BETRAYAL DO TO HIM?

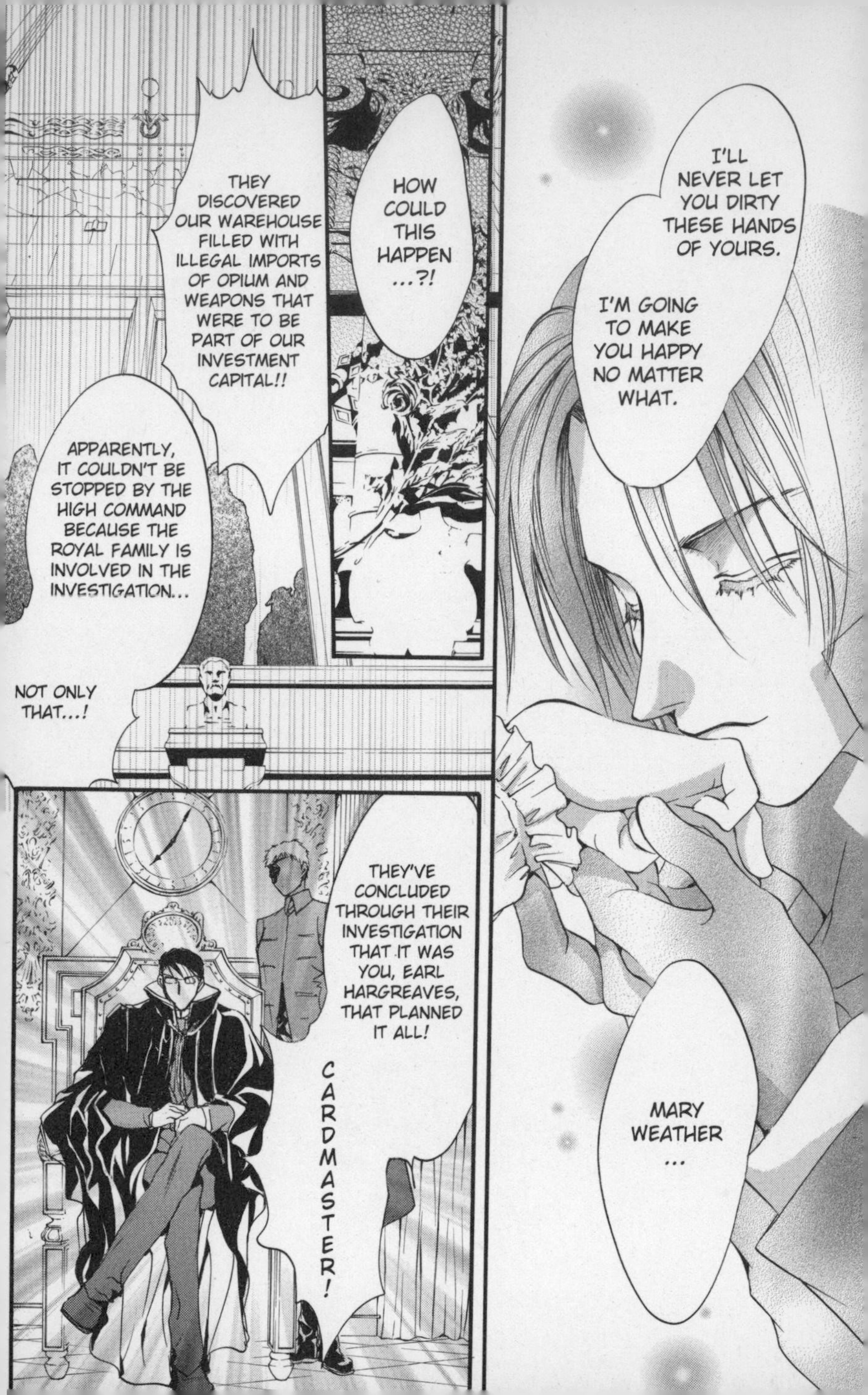

I'LL NEVER LET YOU DIRTY THESE HANDS OF YOURS.
I'M GOING TO MAKE YOU HAPPY NO MATTER WHAT.
MARY WEATHER ...
HOW COULD THIS HAPPEN ...?!
THEY DISCOVERED OUR WAREHOUSE FILLED WITH ILLEGAL IMPORTS OF OPIUM AND WEAPONS THAT WERE TO BE PART OF OUR INVESTMENT CAPITAL!!
APPARENTLY, IT COULDN'T BE STOPPED BY THE HIGH COMMAND BECAUSE THE ROYAL FAMILY IS INVOLVED IN THE INVESTIGATION...
NOT ONLY THAT...!
THEY'VE CONCLUDED THROUGH THEIR INVESTIGATION THAT IT WAS YOU, EARL HARGREAVES, THAT PLANNED IT ALL!
CARDMASTER!

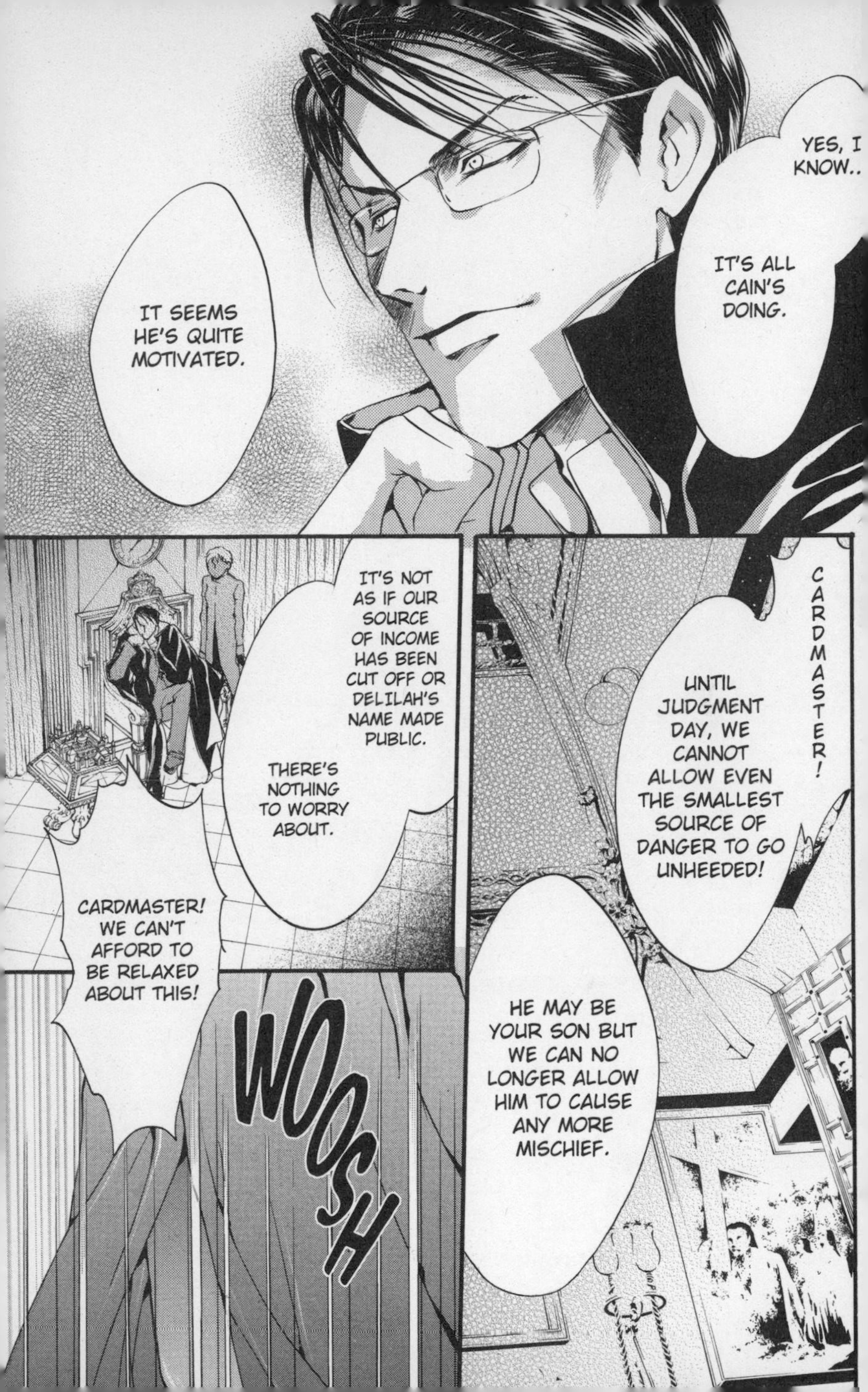
YES, I KNOW..
IT'S ALL CAIN'S DOING.
IT SEEMS HE'S QUITE MOTIVATED.
CARDMASTER!
UNTIL JUDGMENT DAY, WE CANNOT ALLOW EVEN THE SMALLEST SOURCE OF DANGER TO GO UNHEEDED!
HE MAY BE YOUR SON BUT WE CAN NO LONGER ALLOW HIM TO CAUSE ANY MORE MISCHIEF.
IT'S NOT AS IF OUR SOURCE OF INCOME HAS BEEN CUT OFF OR DELILAH'S NAME MADE PUBLIC.
THERE'S NOTHING TO WORRY ABOUT.
CARDMASTER! WE CAN'T AFFORD TO BE RELAXED ABOUT THIS!
WOOSH

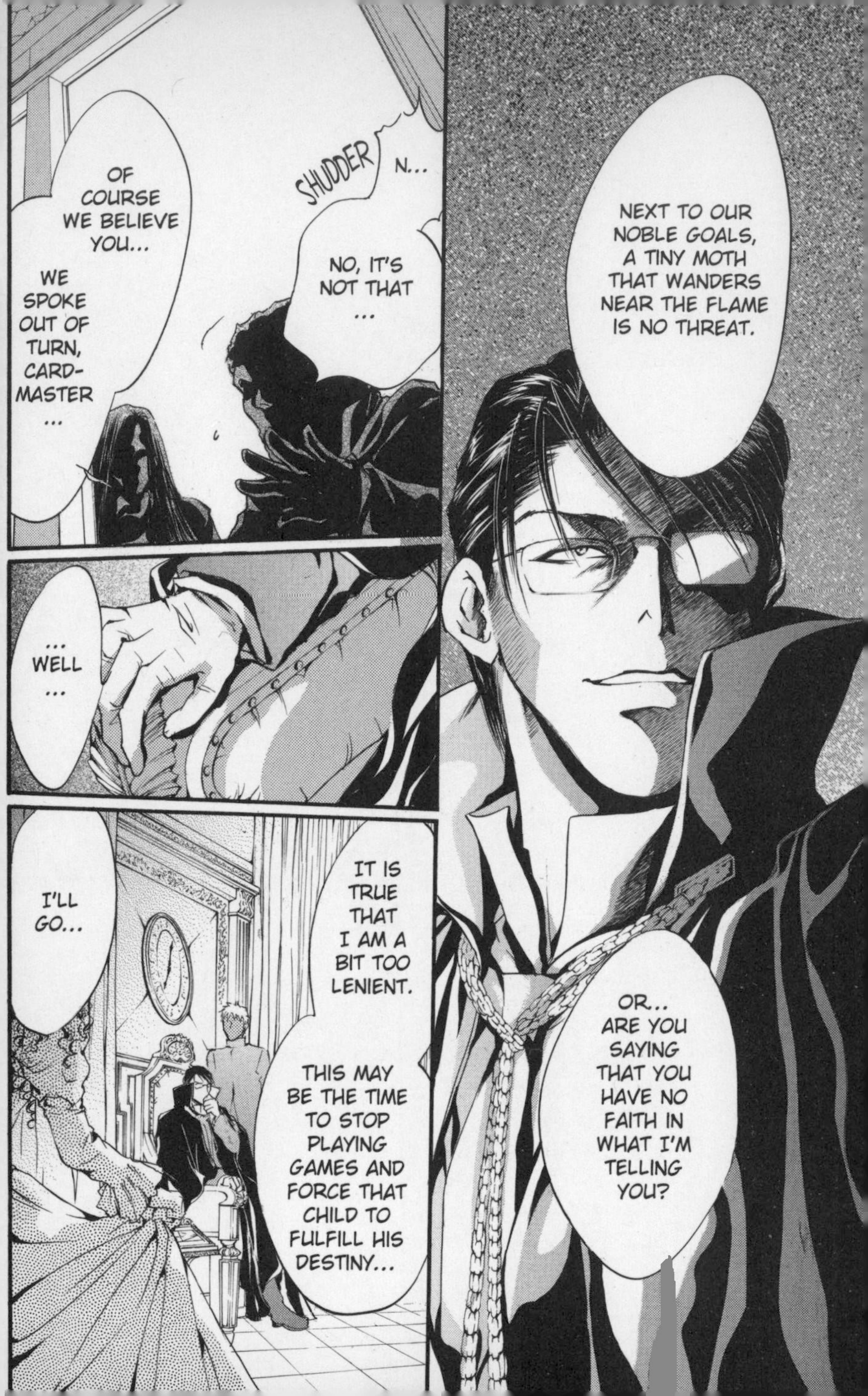
NEXT TO OUR NOBLE GOALS, A TINY MOTH THAT WANDERS NEAR THE FLAME IS NO THREAT.
OR... ARE YOU SAYING THAT YOU HAVE NO FAITH IN WHAT I'M TELLING YOU?
SHUDDER
N...
NO, IT'S NOT THAT ...
OF COURSE WE BELIEVE YOU...
WE SPOKE OUT OF TURN, CARD-MASTER ...
... WELL ...
IT IS TRUE THAT I AM A BIT TOO LENIENT.
THIS MAY BE THE TIME TO STOP PLAYING GAMES AND FORCE THAT CHILD TO FULFILL HIS DESTINY...
I'LL GO...

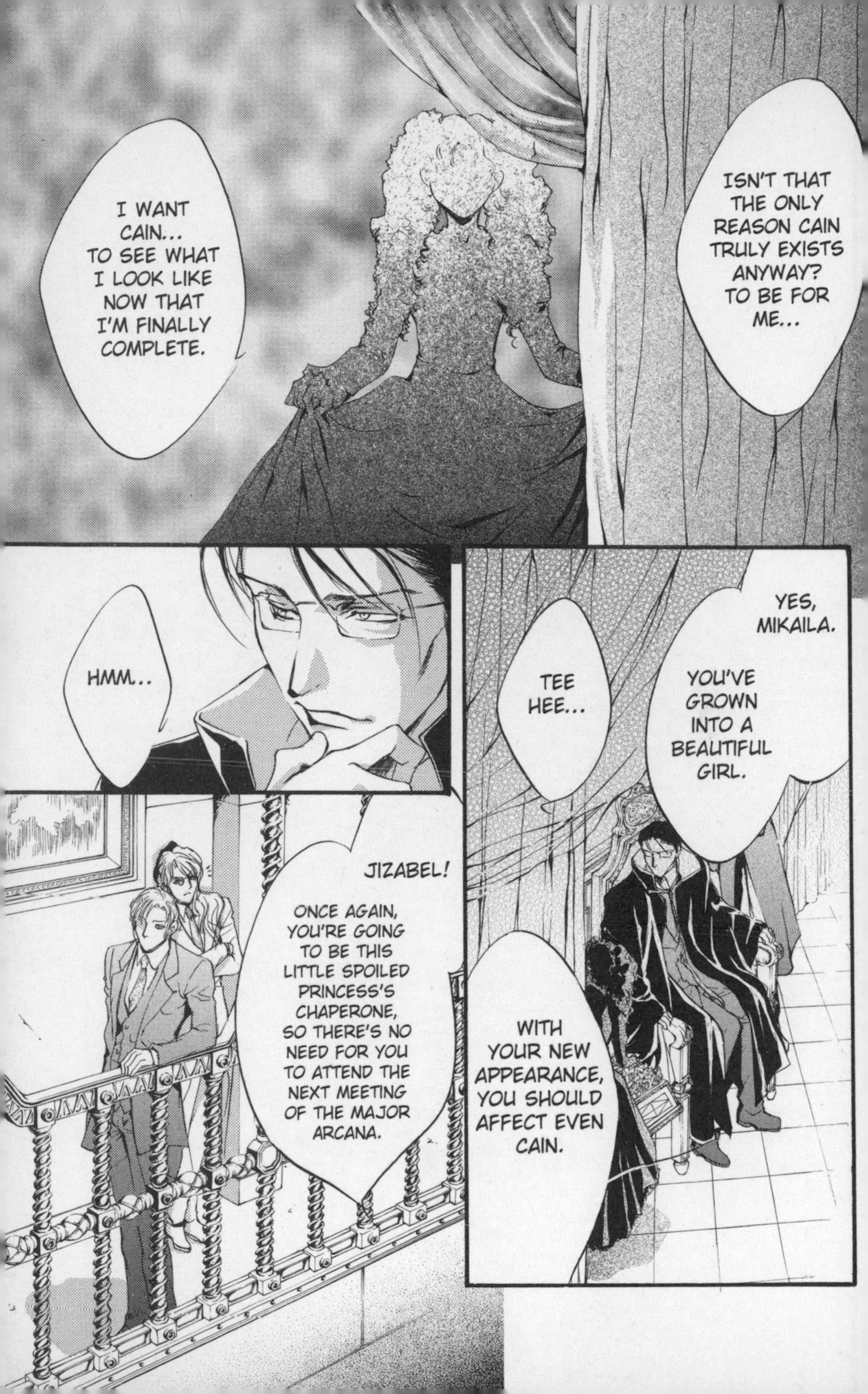
ISN'T THAT THE ONLY REASON CAIN TRULY EXISTS ANYWAY? TO BE FOR ME...
I WANT CAIN... TO SEE WHAT I LOOK LIKE NOW THAT I'M FINALLY COMPLETE.
YES, MIKAILA.
YOU'VE GROWN INTO A BEAUTIFUL GIRL.
TEE HEE...
WITH YOUR NEW APPEARANCE, YOU SHOULD AFFECT EVEN CAIN.
HMM...
JIZABEL!
ONCE AGAIN, YOU'RE GOING TO BE THIS LITTLE SPOILED PRINCESS'S CHAPERONE, SO THERE'S NO NEED FOR YOU TO ATTEND THE NEXT MEETING OF THE MAJOR ARCANA.

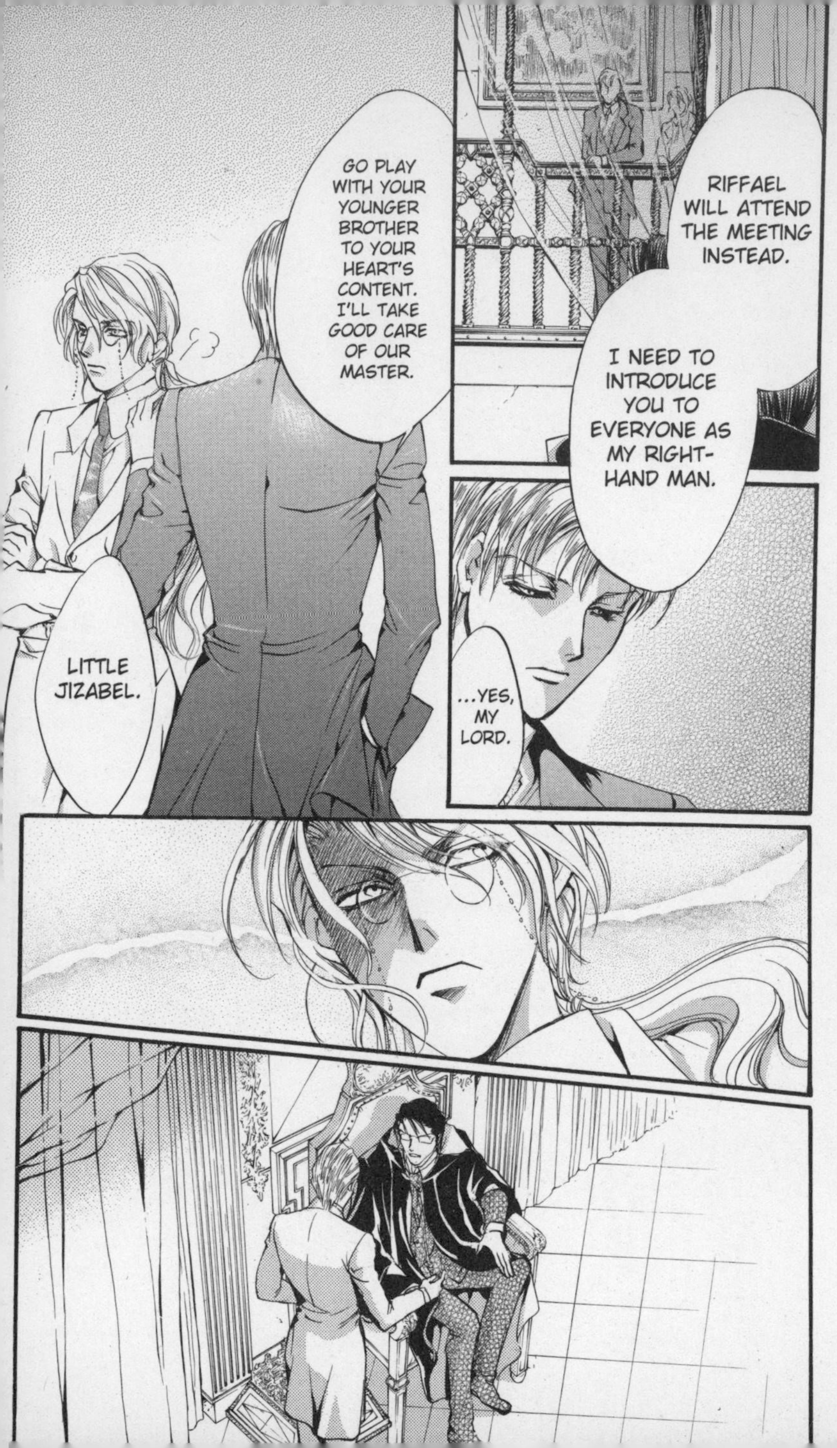
RIFFAEL WILL ATTEND THE MEETING INSTEAD.
I NEED TO INTRODUCE YOU TO EVERYONE AS MY RIGHT-HAND MAN.
...YES, MY LORD.
GO PLAY WITH YOUR YOUNGER BROTHER TO YOUR HEART'S CONTENT. I'LL TAKE GOOD CARE OF OUR MASTER.
LITTLE JIZABEL.

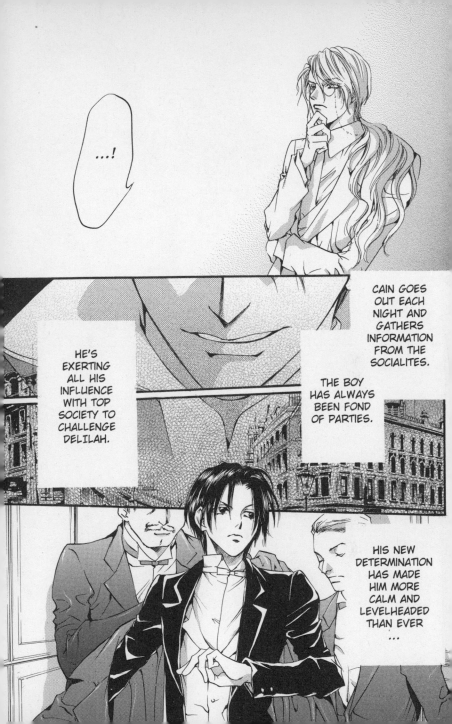

....!

CAIN GOES
OUT EACH
NIGHT AND
GATHERS
INFORMATION
FROM THE
SOCIALITES.

THE BOY
HAS ALWAYS
BEEN FOND
OF PARTIES.

HE'S
EXERTING
ALL HIS
INFLUENCE
WITH TOP
SOCIETY TO
CHALLENGE
DELILAH.

HIS NEW
DETERMINATION
HAS MADE
HIM MORE
CALM AND
LEVELHEADED
THAN EVER
...

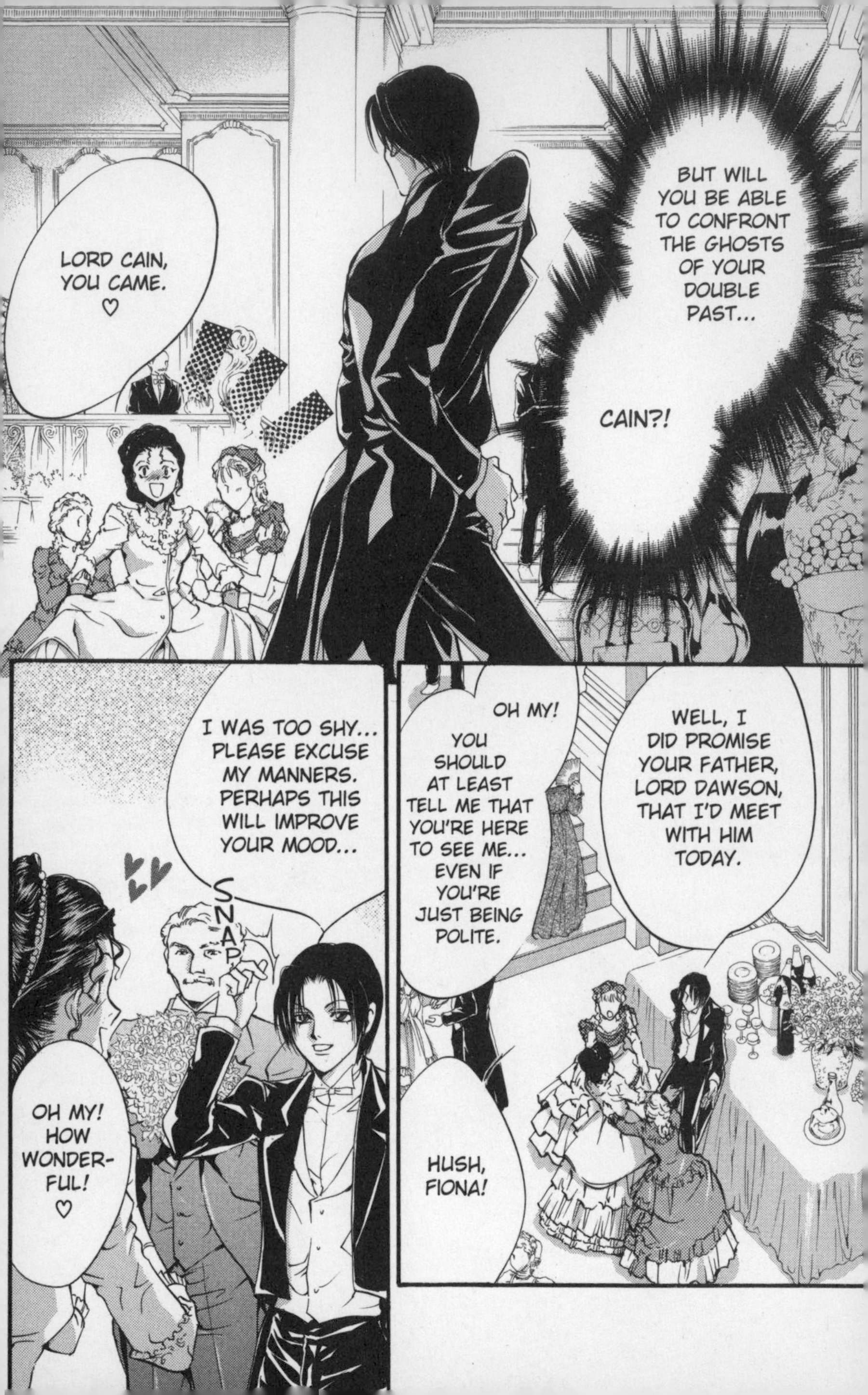
BUT WILL YOU BE ABLE TO CONFRONT THE GHOSTS OF YOUR DOUBLE PAST...
CAIN?!
LORD CAIN, YOU CAME. ♡
WELL, I DID PROMISE YOUR FATHER, LORD DAWSON, THAT I'D MEET WITH HIM TODAY.
OH MY!
YOU SHOULD AT LEAST TELL ME THAT YOU'RE HERE TO SEE ME... EVEN IF YOU'RE JUST BEING POLITE.
HUSH, FIONA!
I WAS TOO SHY... PLEASE EXCUSE MY MANNERS. PERHAPS THIS WILL IMPROVE YOUR MOOD...
SNAP
OH MY! HOW WONDER-FUL! ♡

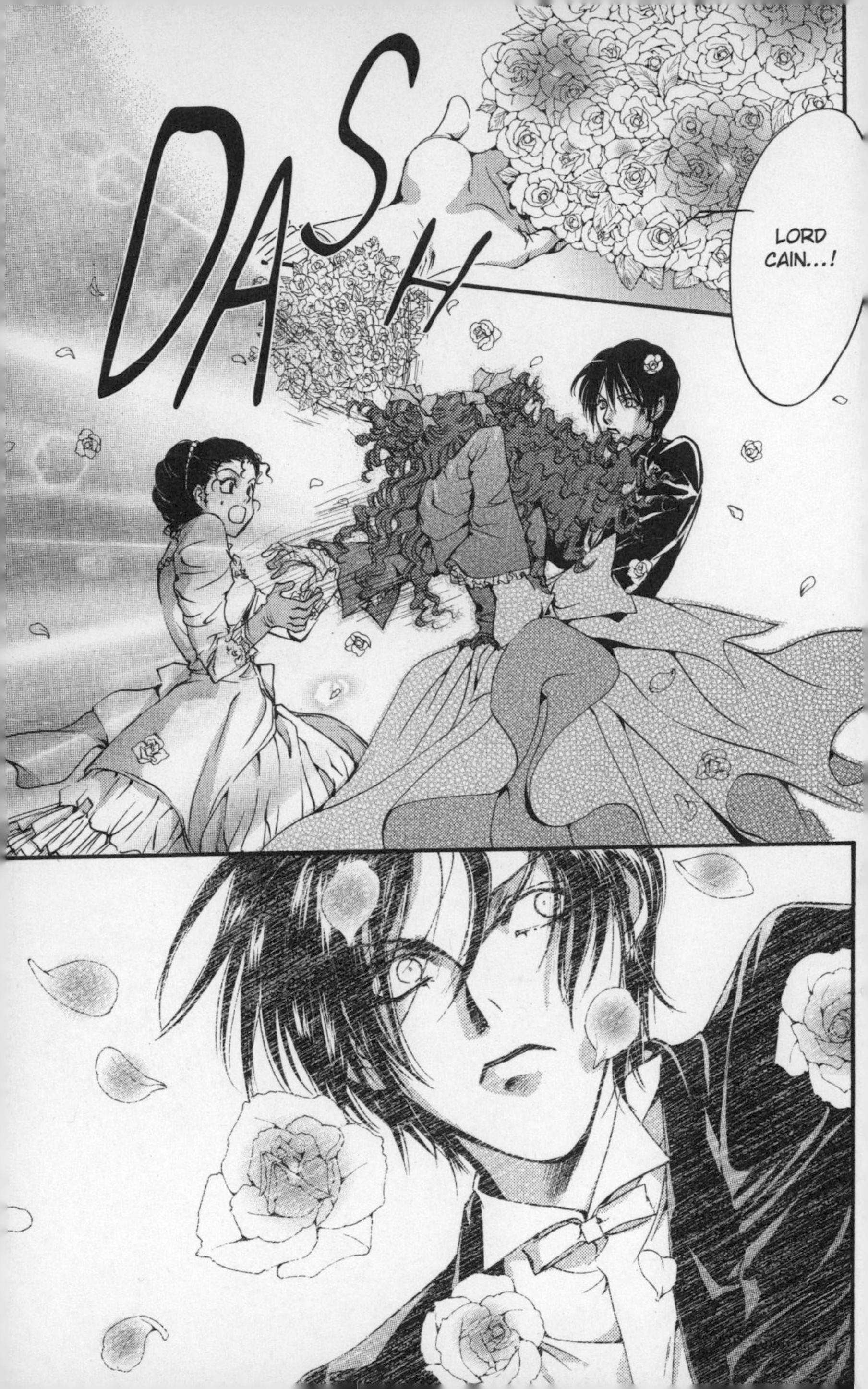
LORD CAIN...!
DASH

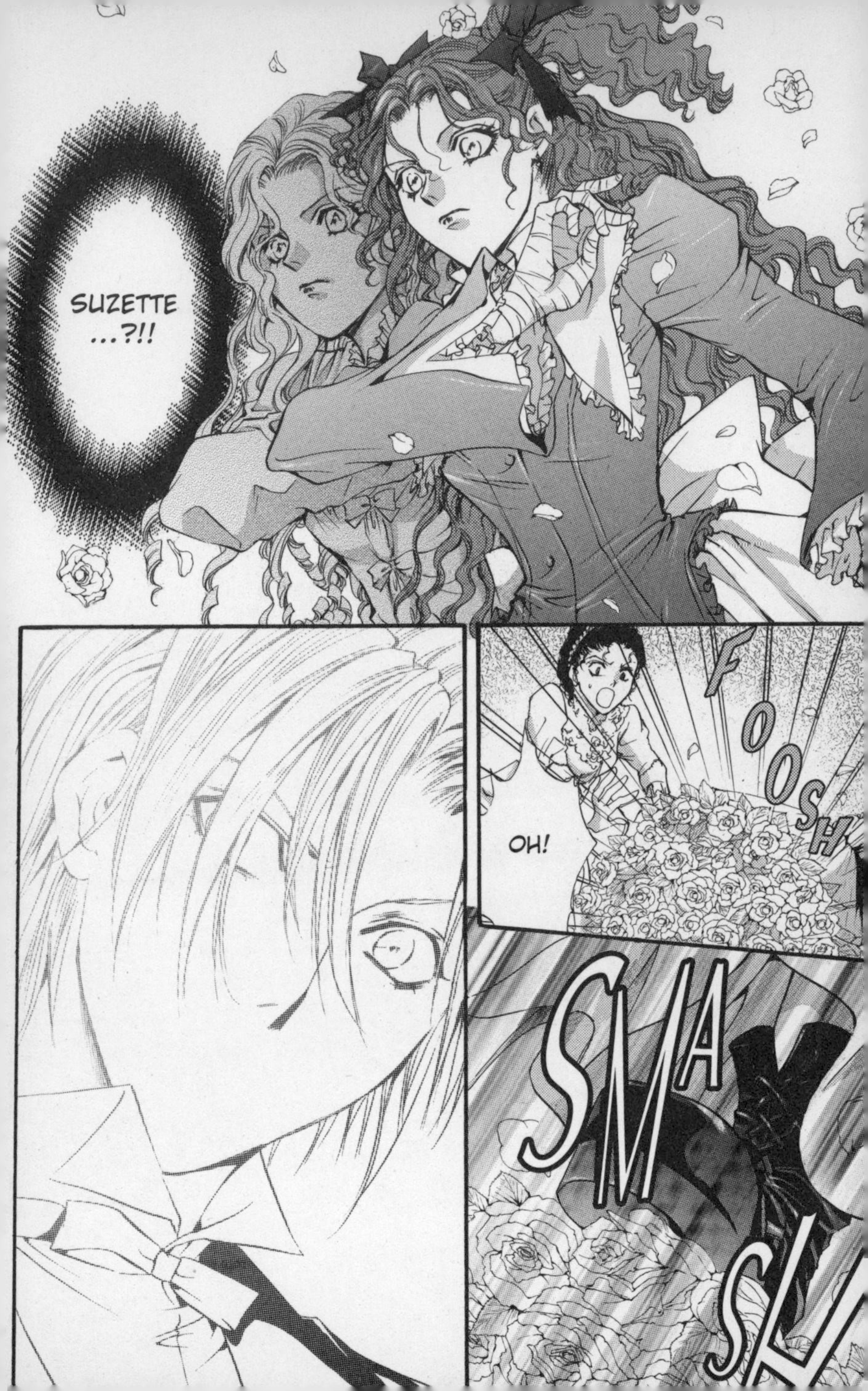
SUZETTE ...?!!
FOOSH
OH!
SMA
SH

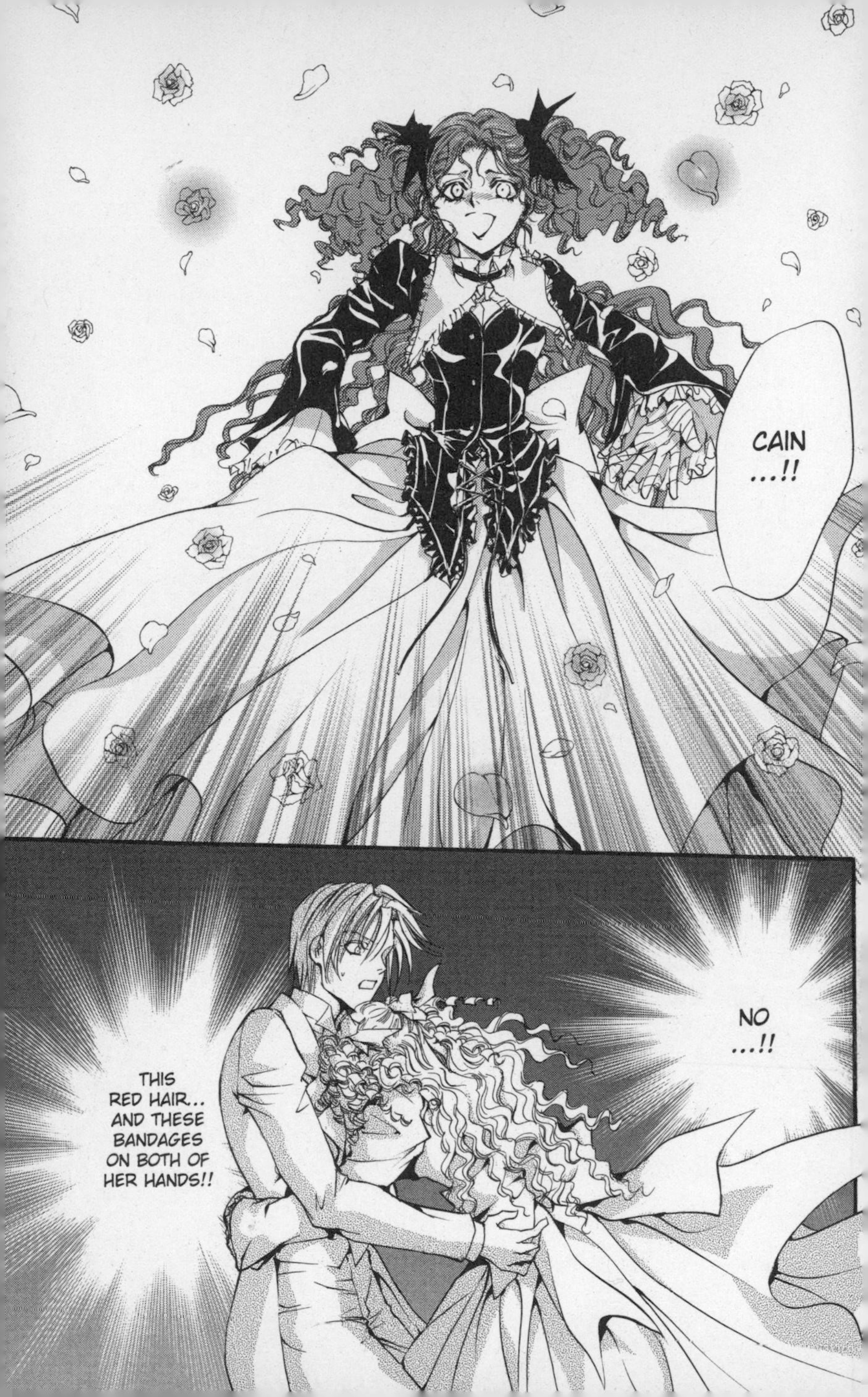
CAIN ...!!
NO ...!!
THIS RED HAIR... AND THESE BANDAGES ON BOTH OF HER HANDS!!

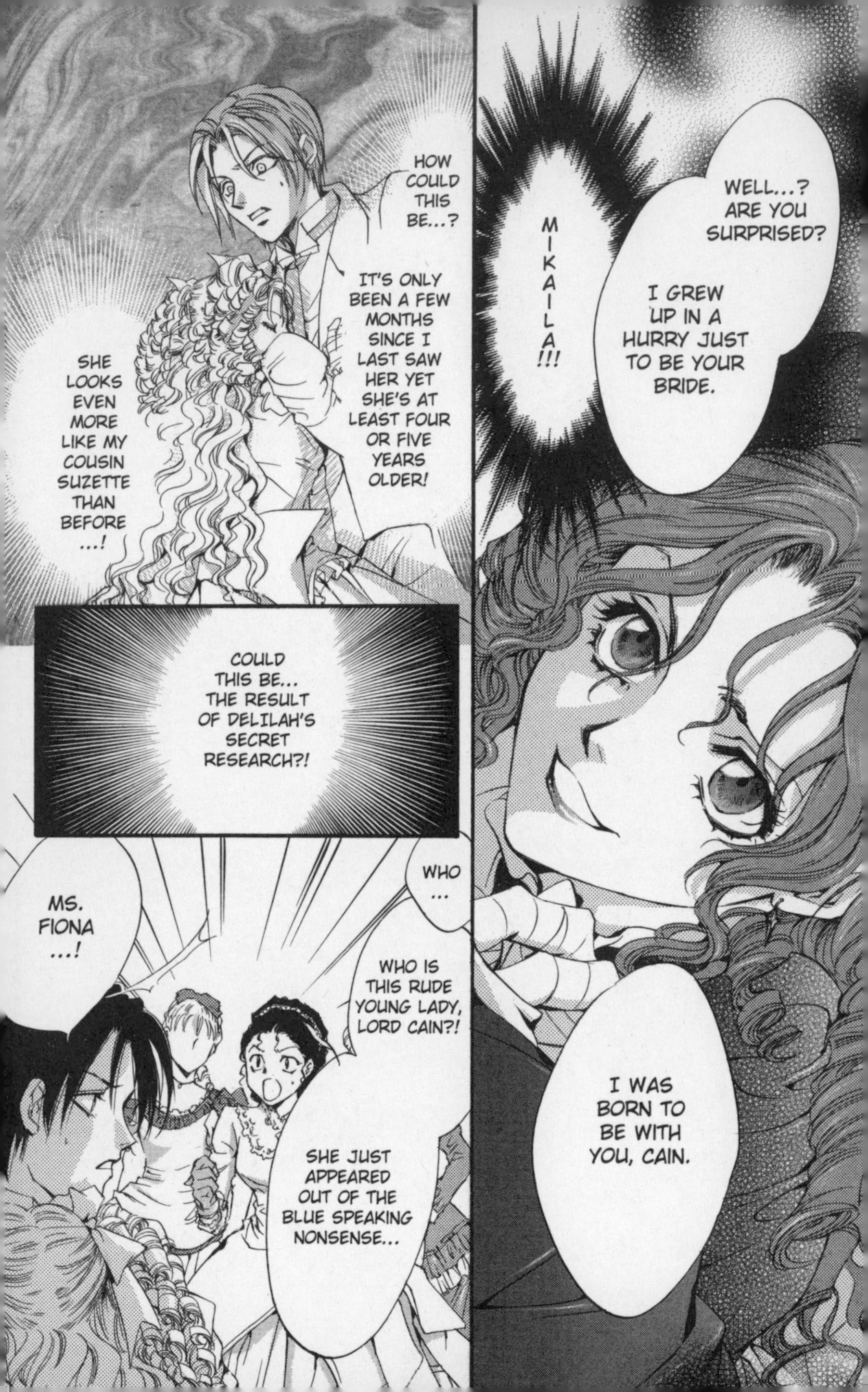
WELL...? ARE YOU SURPRISED?
I GREW UP IN A HURRY JUST TO BE YOUR BRIDE.
MIKAILA!!!
I WAS BORN TO BE WITH YOU, CAIN.
HOW COULD THIS BE...?
IT'S ONLY BEEN A FEW MONTHS SINCE I LAST SAW HER YET SHE'S AT LEAST FOUR OR FIVE YEARS OLDER!
SHE LOOKS EVEN MORE LIKE MY COUSIN SUZETTE THAN BEFORE ...!
COULD THIS BE... THE RESULT OF DELILAH'S SECRET RESEARCH?!
WHO ...
WHO IS THIS RUDE YOUNG LADY, LORD CAIN?!
SHE JUST APPEARED OUT OF THE BLUE SPEAKING NONSENSE...
MS. FIONA ...!

Hello, it's a new volume!! The story is really moving along now and honestly, this feels like the final leg of the race. Really. The name Oedipus that was used in the title comes from the root word of the Oedipus complex and is also the name of a character from a Greek myth. Oedipus loved his mother and hated his father. Tragically, he kills his father according to prophecy and then marries his own mother. In the end he rips out his eyes and dies... What a scary story... Mikaila also makes another appearance. I love Mikaila because she's so pretty but the actual work is very labor-intensive. For example, thinking up ideas and drawing her... Especially her curly hair...

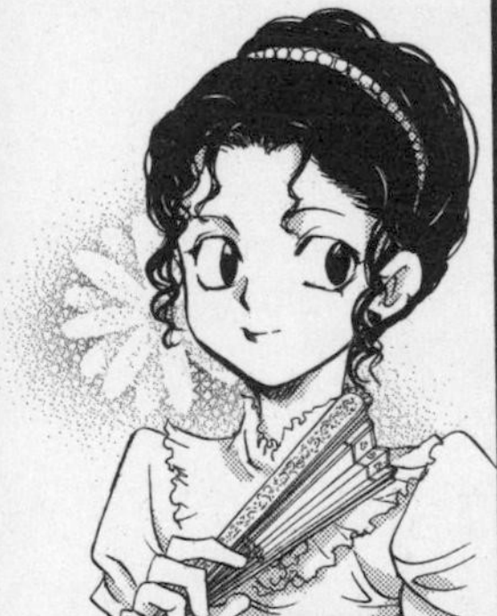

Ms. Fiona.

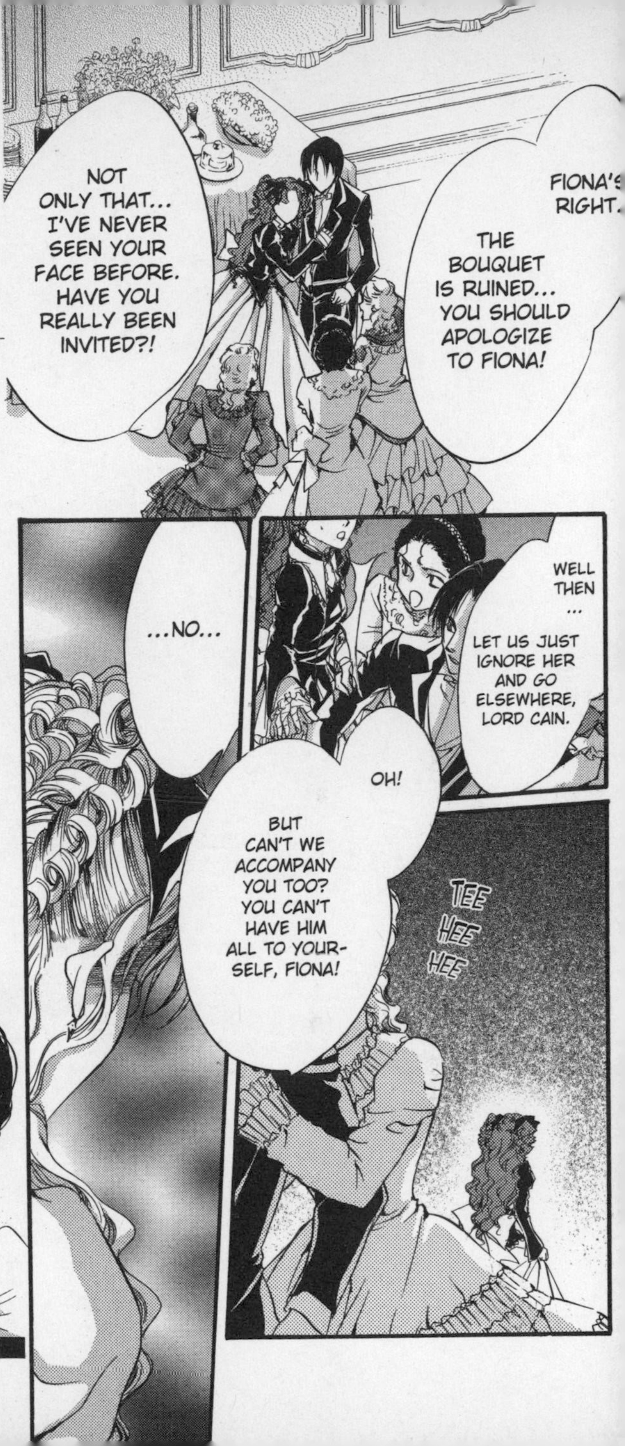
FIONA'S RIGHT.
THE BOUQUET IS RUINED... YOU SHOULD APOLOGIZE TO FIONA!
NOT ONLY THAT... I'VE NEVER SEEN YOUR FACE BEFORE. HAVE YOU REALLY BEEN INVITED?!
WELL THEN ...
LET US JUST IGNORE HER AND GO ELSEWHERE, LORD CAIN.
OH!
BUT CAN'T WE ACCOMPANY YOU TOO? YOU CAN'T HAVE HIM ALL TO YOURSELF, FIONA!
TEE HEE HEE
...NO...

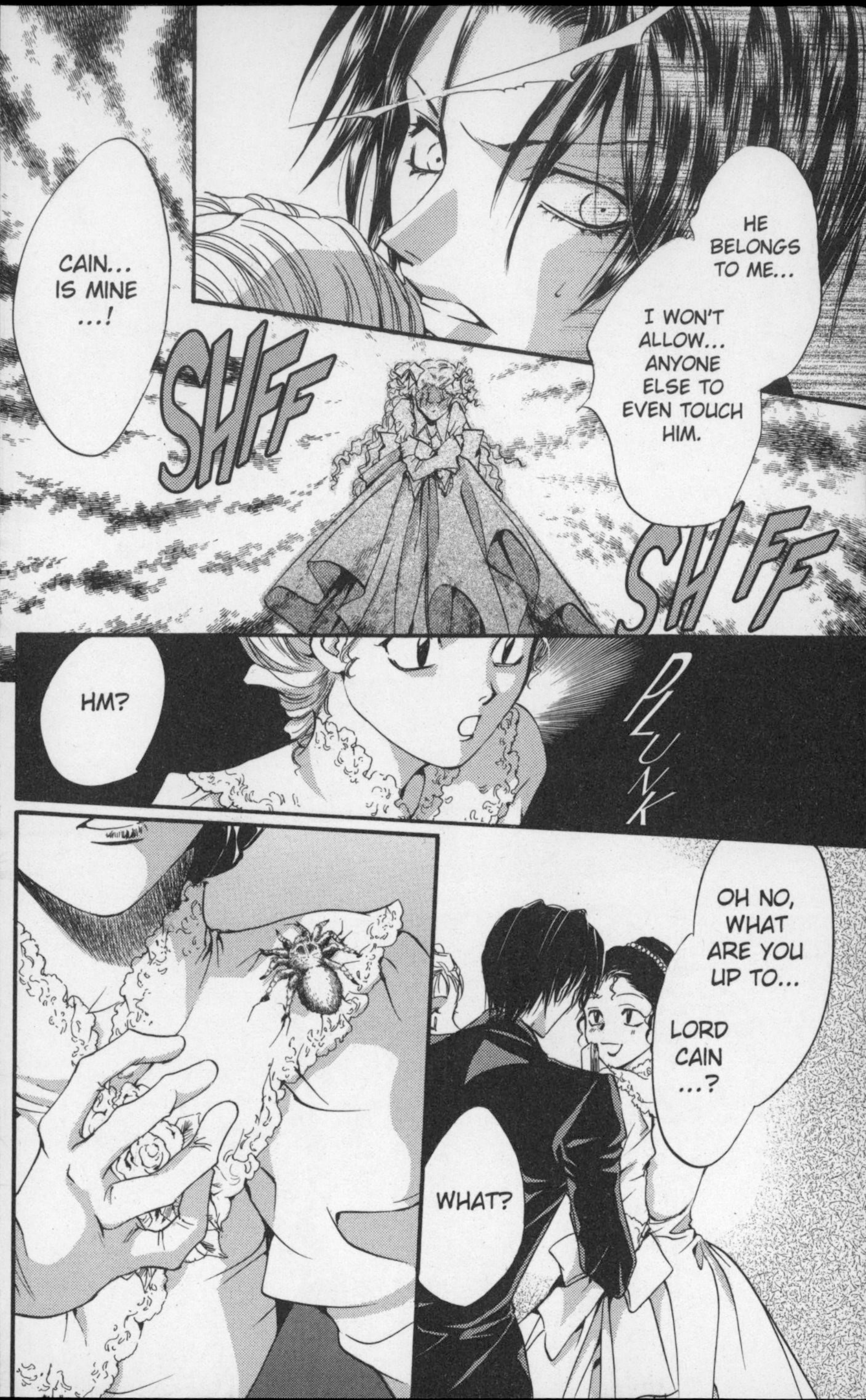
HE BELONGS TO ME...
I WON'T ALLOW... ANYONE ELSE TO EVEN TOUCH HIM.
SHIFF
CAIN... IS MINE ...!
SHIFF
PLUNK
HM?
OH NO, WHAT ARE YOU UP TO...
LORD CAIN ...?
WHAT?

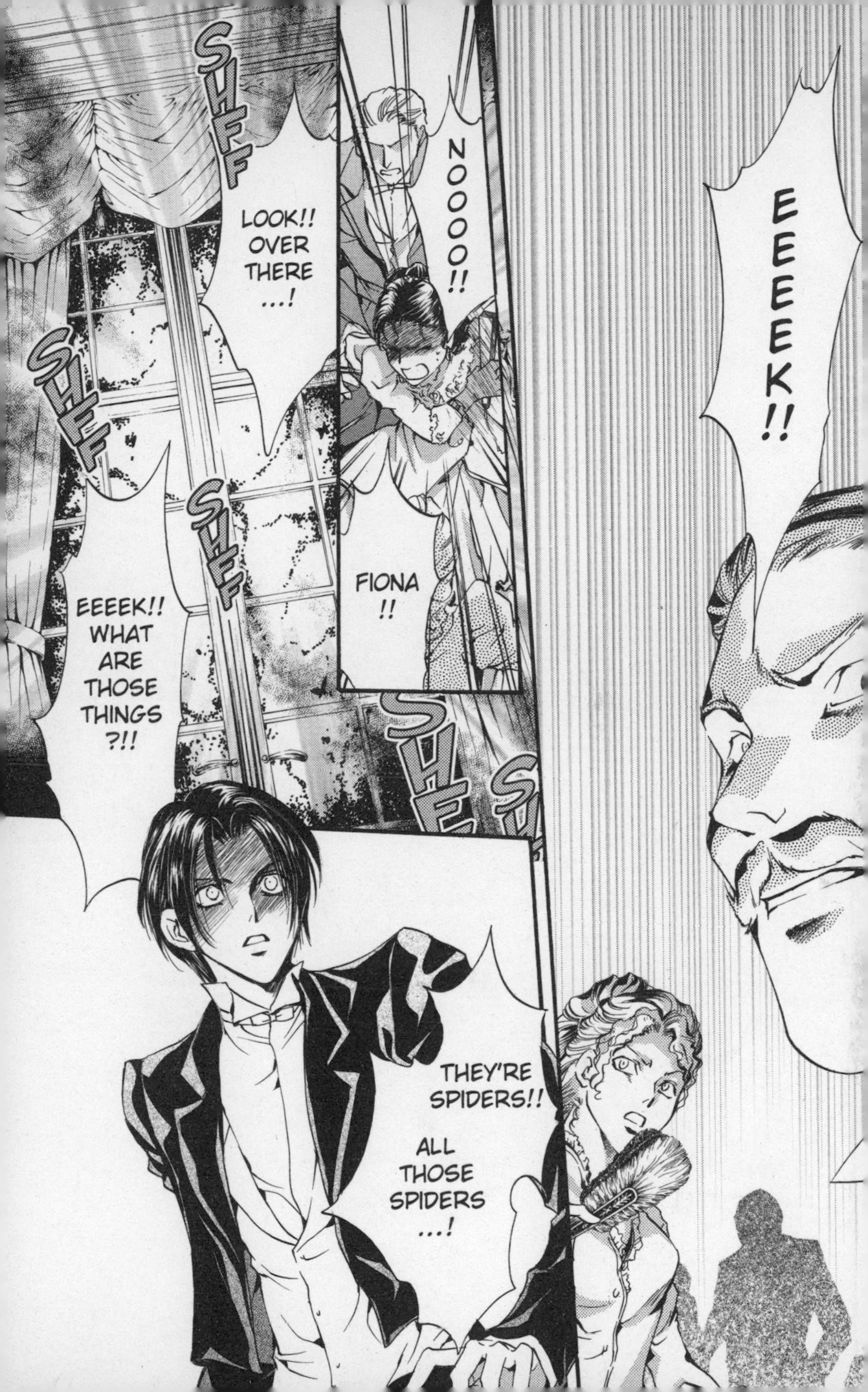
EEEEK!!
NOOOOO!!
FIONA!!
SHFF
LOOK!! OVER THERE ...!
SHFF
SHFF
EEEEK!! WHAT ARE THOSE THINGS?!!
SHFF
THEY'RE SPIDERS!!
ALL THOSE SPIDERS ...!

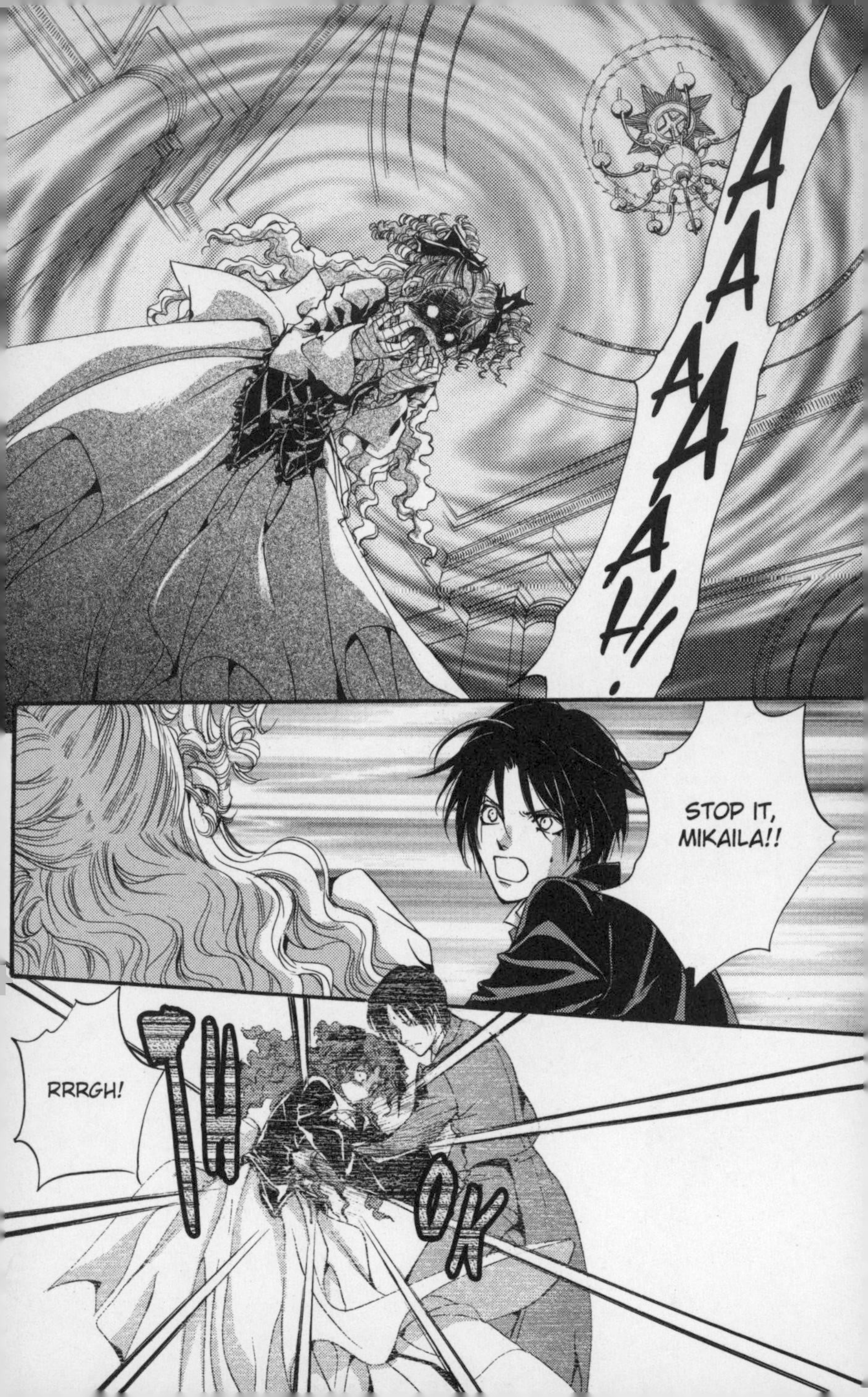
AAAAAAH!!
STOP IT, MIKAILA!!
THOK
RRRGH!

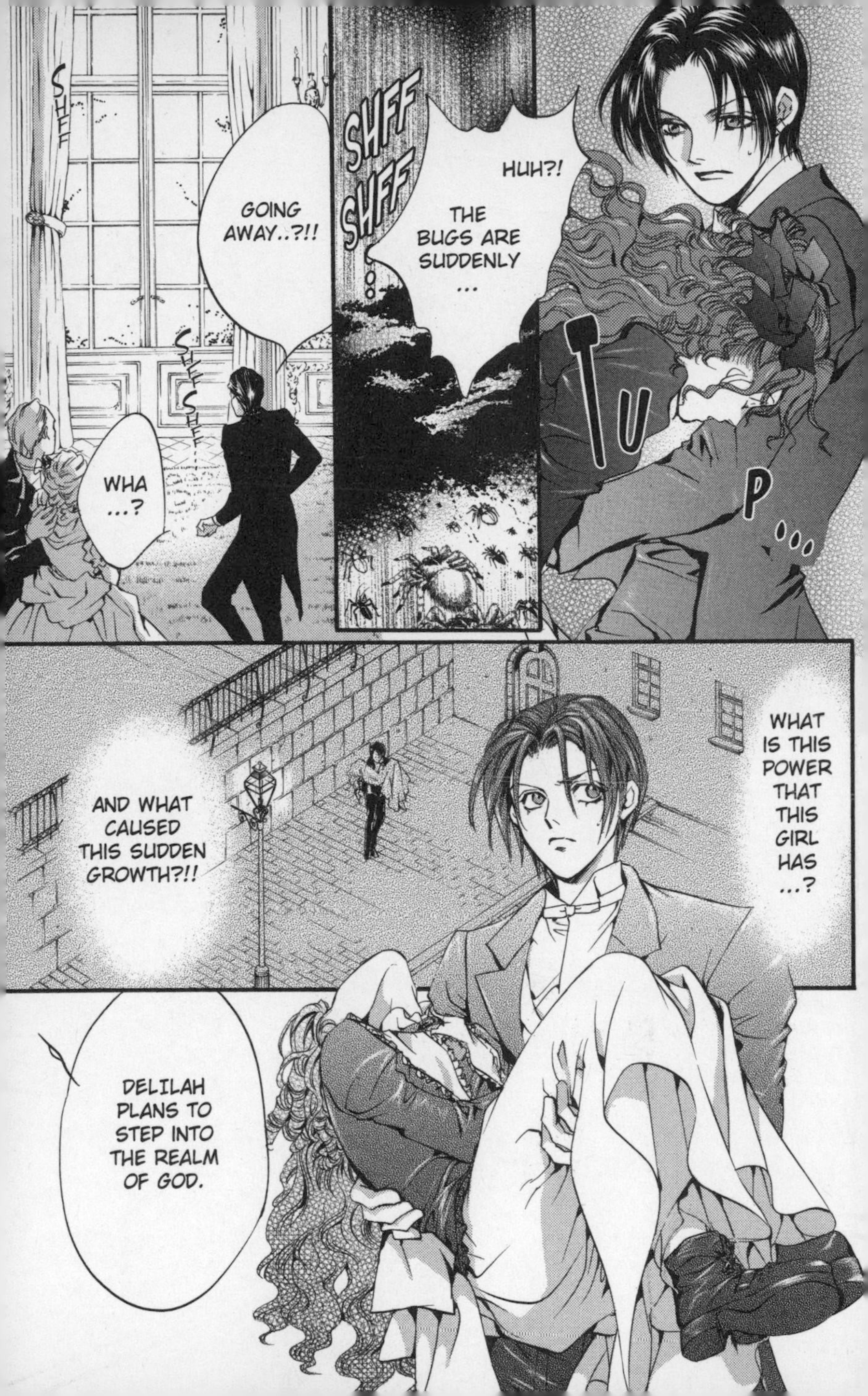

TUP...
SHFF SHFF
HUH?!
THE BUGS ARE SUDDENLY ...
GOING AWAY..?!!
SHFF
SHFF SHFF
WHA ...?
WHAT IS THIS POWER THAT THIS GIRL HAS ...?
AND WHAT CAUSED THIS SUDDEN GROWTH?!!
DELILAH PLANS TO STEP INTO THE REALM OF GOD.

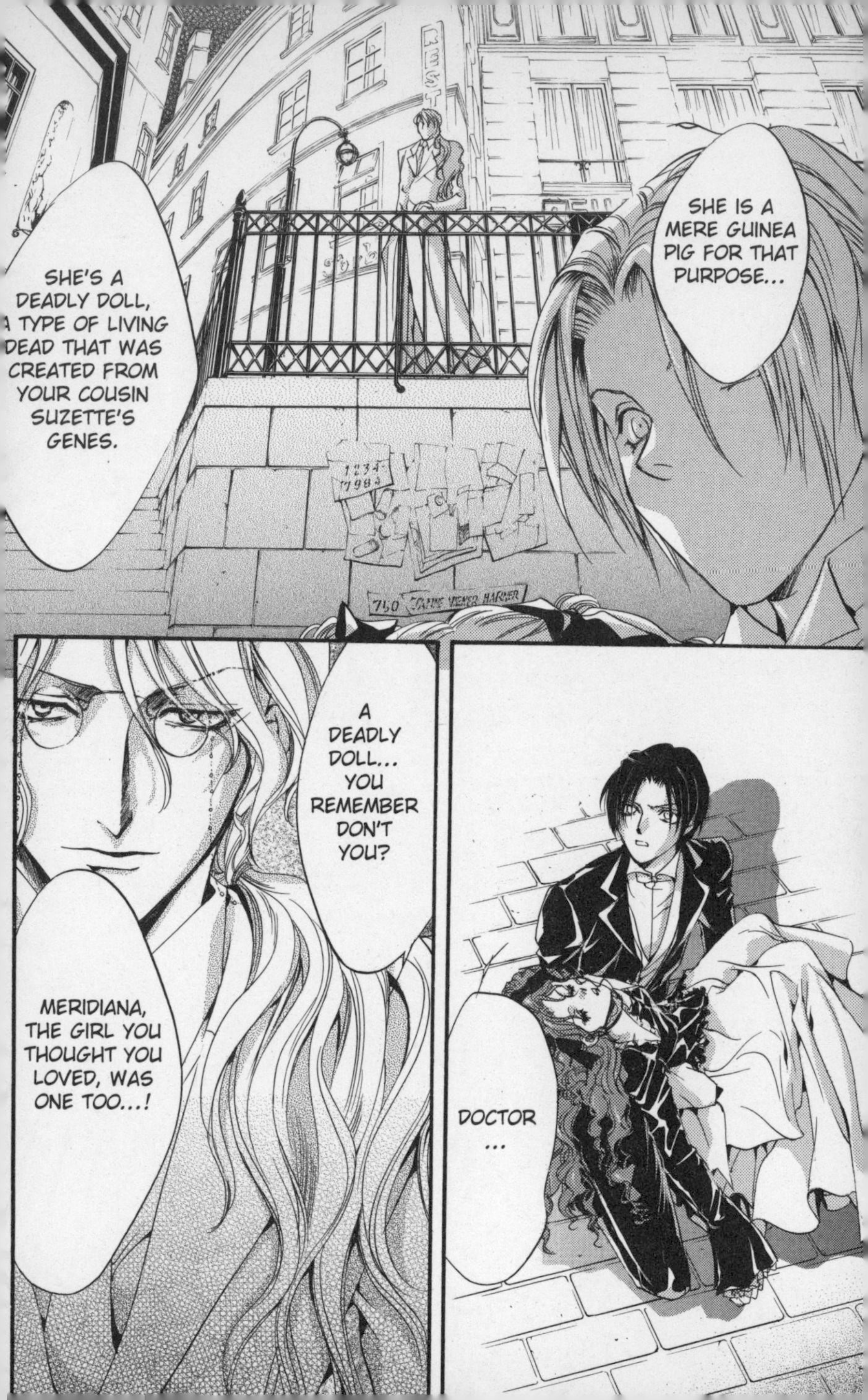
SHE IS A MERE GUINEA PIG FOR THAT PURPOSE...
SHE'S A DEADLY DOLL, A TYPE OF LIVING DEAD THAT WAS CREATED FROM YOUR COUSIN SUZETTE'S GENES.
DOCTOR ...
A DEADLY DOLL... YOU REMEMBER DON'T YOU?
MERIDIANA, THE GIRL YOU THOUGHT YOU LOVED, WAS ONE TOO...!

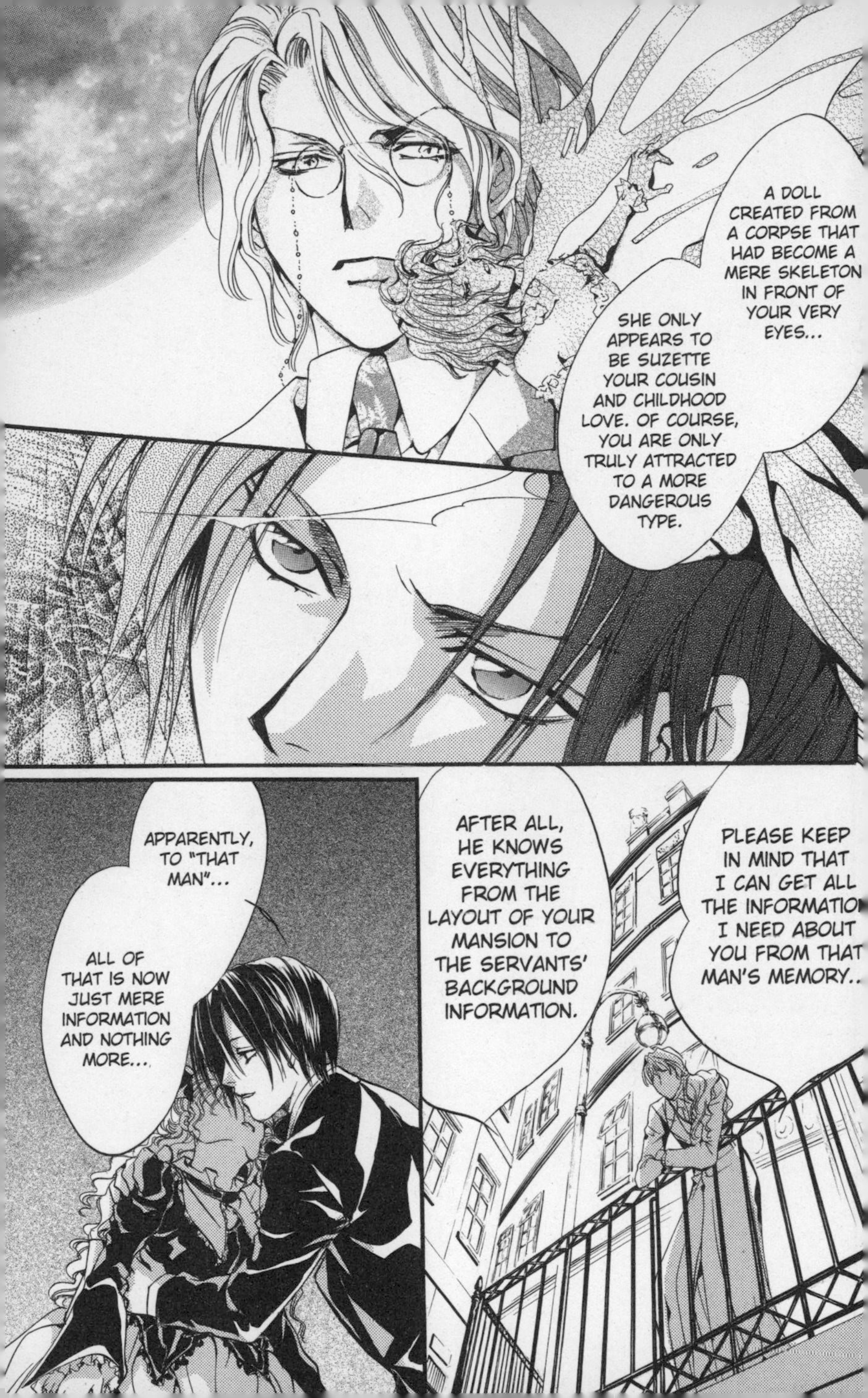

A DOLL CREATED FROM A CORPSE THAT HAD BECOME A MERE SKELETON IN FRONT OF YOUR VERY EYES...
SHE ONLY APPEARS TO BE SUZETTE YOUR COUSIN AND CHILDHOOD LOVE. OF COURSE, YOU ARE ONLY TRULY ATTRACTED TO A MORE DANGEROUS TYPE.
PLEASE KEEP IN MIND THAT I CAN GET ALL THE INFORMATIO I NEED ABOUT YOU FROM THAT MAN'S MEMORY...
AFTER ALL, HE KNOWS EVERYTHING FROM THE LAYOUT OF YOUR MANSION TO THE SERVANTS' BACKGROUND INFORMATION.
APPARENTLY, TO "THAT MAN"...
ALL OF THAT IS NOW JUST MERE INFORMATION AND NOTHING MORE...

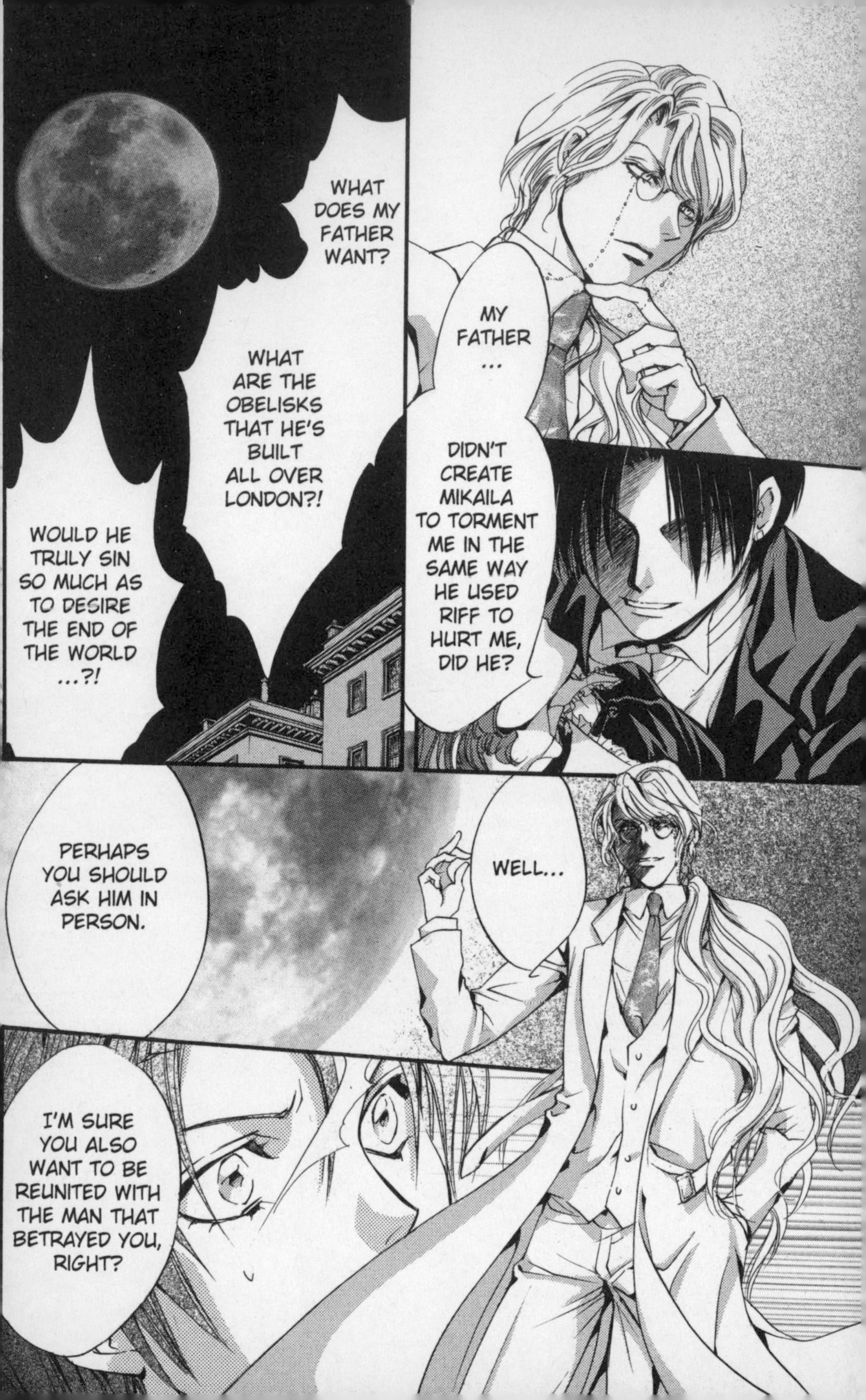
MY FATHER ...
DIDN'T CREATE MIKAILA TO TORMENT ME IN THE SAME WAY HE USED RIFF TO HURT ME, DID HE?
WHAT DOES MY FATHER WANT?
WHAT ARE THE OBELISKS THAT HE'S BUILT ALL OVER LONDON?!
WOULD HE TRULY SIN SO MUCH AS TO DESIRE THE END OF THE WORLD ...?!
WELL...
PERHAPS YOU SHOULD ASK HIM IN PERSON.
I'M SURE YOU ALSO WANT TO BE REUNITED WITH THE MAN THAT BETRAYED YOU, RIGHT?

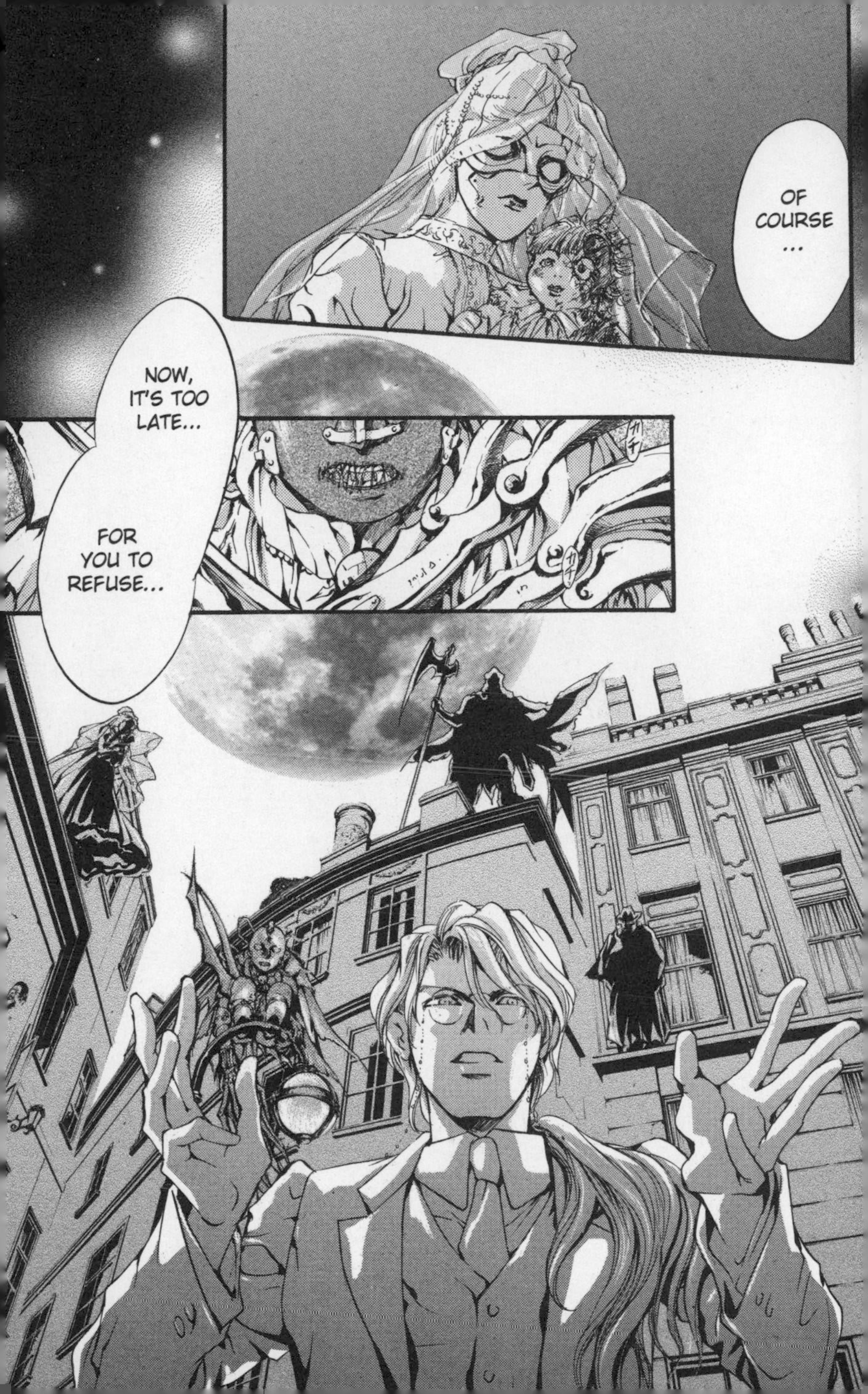
OF COURSE ...
NOW, IT'S TOO LATE...
カチ
カチ
FOR YOU TO REFUSE...

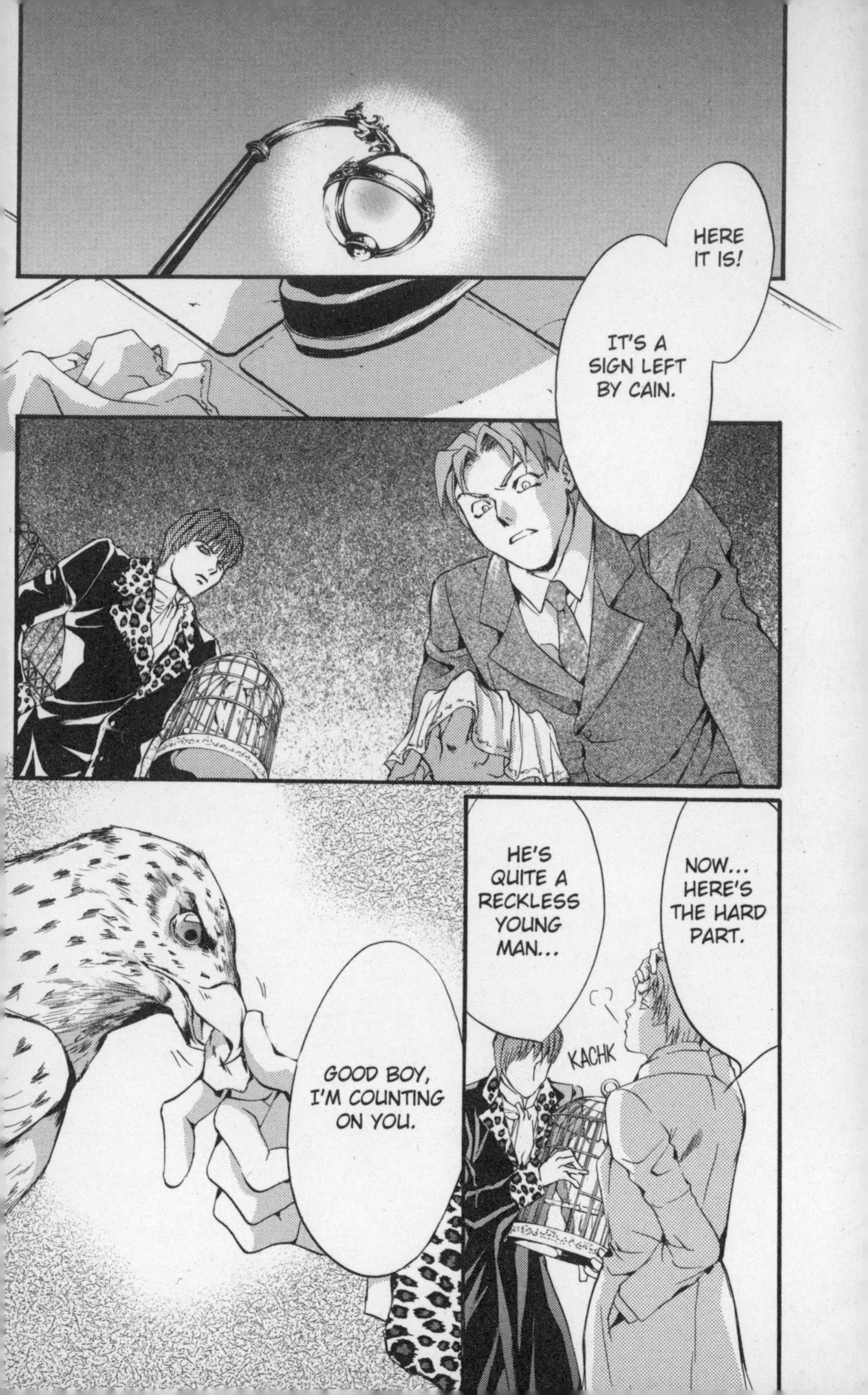
HERE IT IS!
IT'S A SIGN LEFT BY CAIN.
NOW... HERE'S THE HARD PART.
HE'S QUITE A RECKLESS YOUNG MAN...
KACHK
GOOD BOY, I'M COUNTING ON YOU.

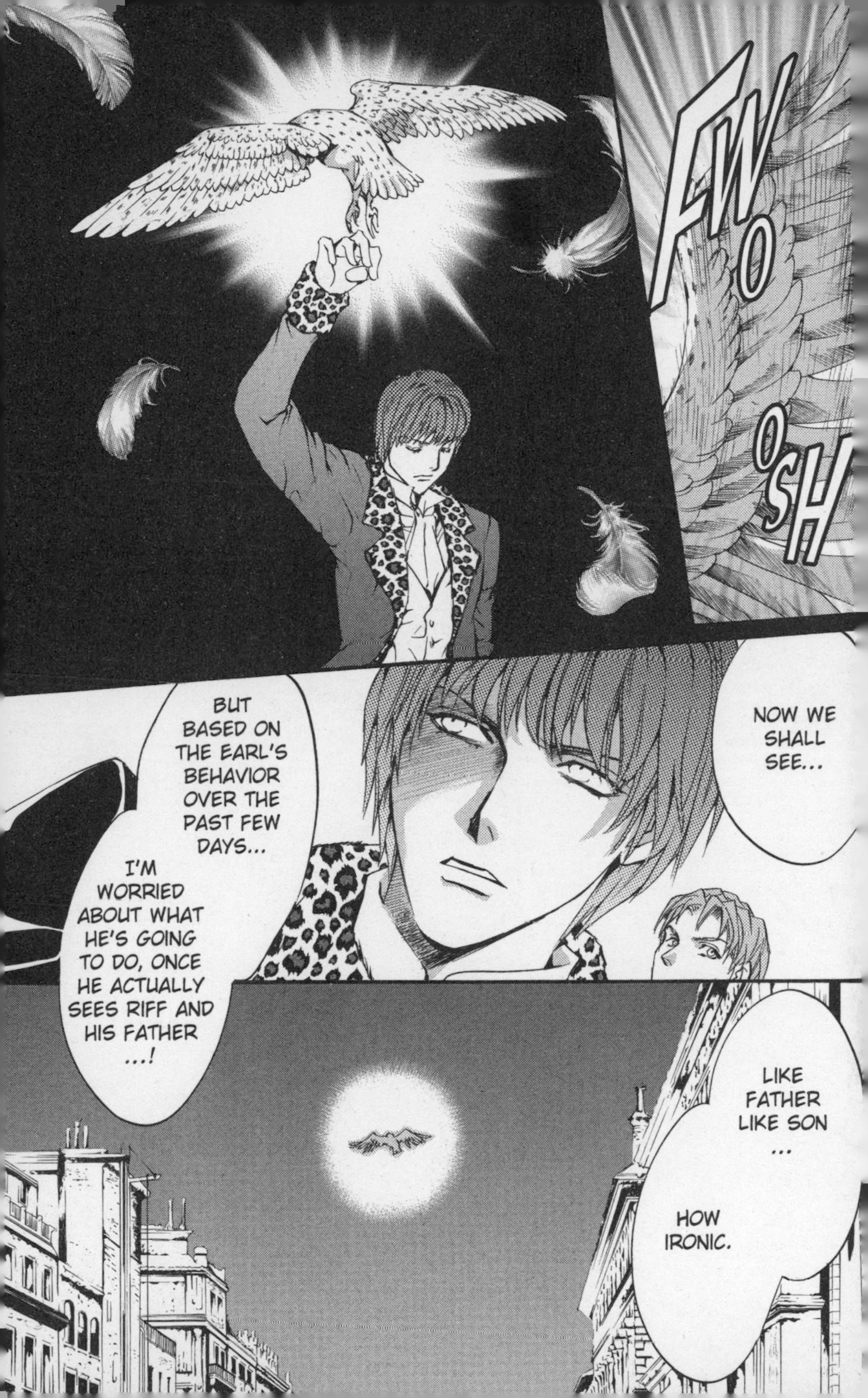
FWOOSH
NOW WE SHALL SEE...
BUT BASED ON THE EARL'S BEHAVIOR OVER THE PAST FEW DAYS...
I'M WORRIED ABOUT WHAT HE'S GOING TO DO, ONCE HE ACTUALLY SEES RIFF AND HIS FATHER ...!
LIKE FATHER LIKE SON ...
HOW IRONIC.

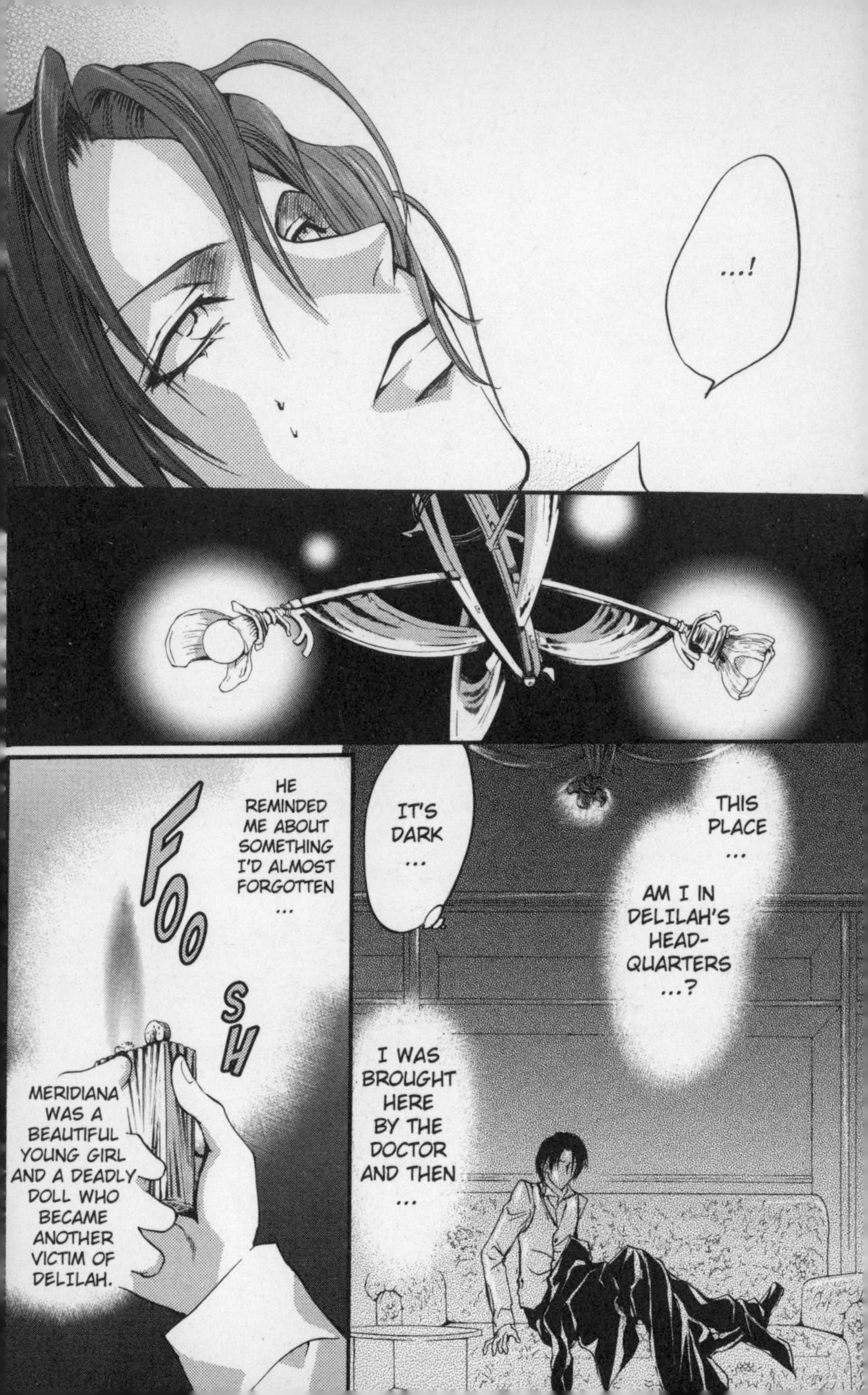
...!
THIS PLACE ...
AM I IN DELILAH'S HEAD-QUARTERS ...?
IT'S DARK ...
I WAS BROUGHT HERE BY THE DOCTOR AND THEN ...
HE REMINDED ME ABOUT SOMETHING I'D ALMOST FORGOTTEN ...
FOOSH
MERIDIANA WAS A BEAUTIFUL YOUNG GIRL AND A DEADLY DOLL WHO BECAME ANOTHER VICTIM OF DELILAH.

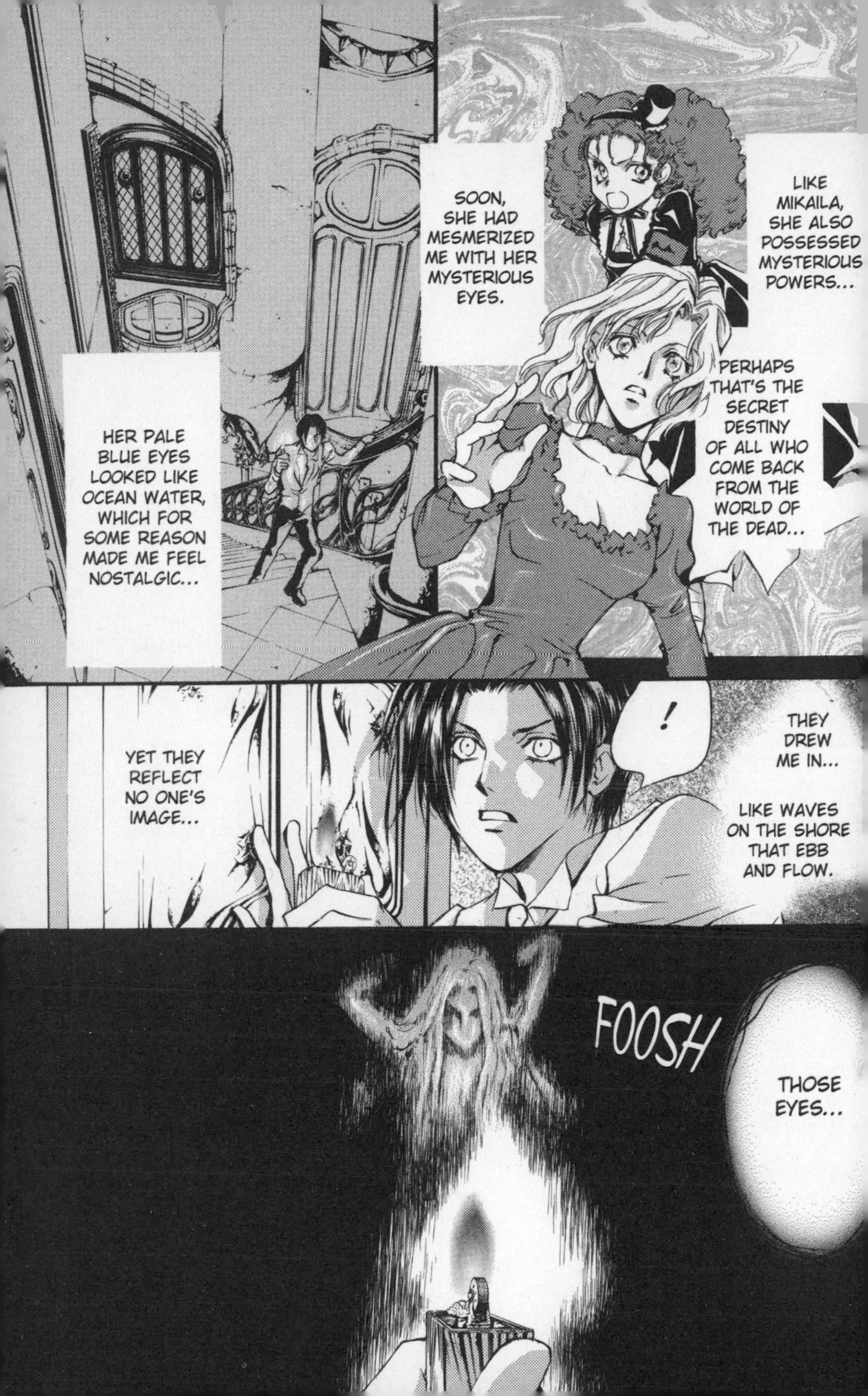
LIKE MIKAILA, SHE ALSO POSSESSED MYSTERIOUS POWERS...
SOON, SHE HAD MESMERIZED ME WITH HER MYSTERIOUS EYES.
PERHAPS THAT'S THE SECRET DESTINY OF ALL WHO COME BACK FROM THE WORLD OF THE DEAD...
HER PALE BLUE EYES LOOKED LIKE OCEAN WATER, WHICH FOR SOME REASON MADE ME FEEL NOSTALGIC...
THEY DREW ME IN...
LIKE WAVES ON THE SHORE THAT EBB AND FLOW.
!
YET THEY REFLECT NO ONE'S IMAGE...
FOOSH
THOSE EYES...

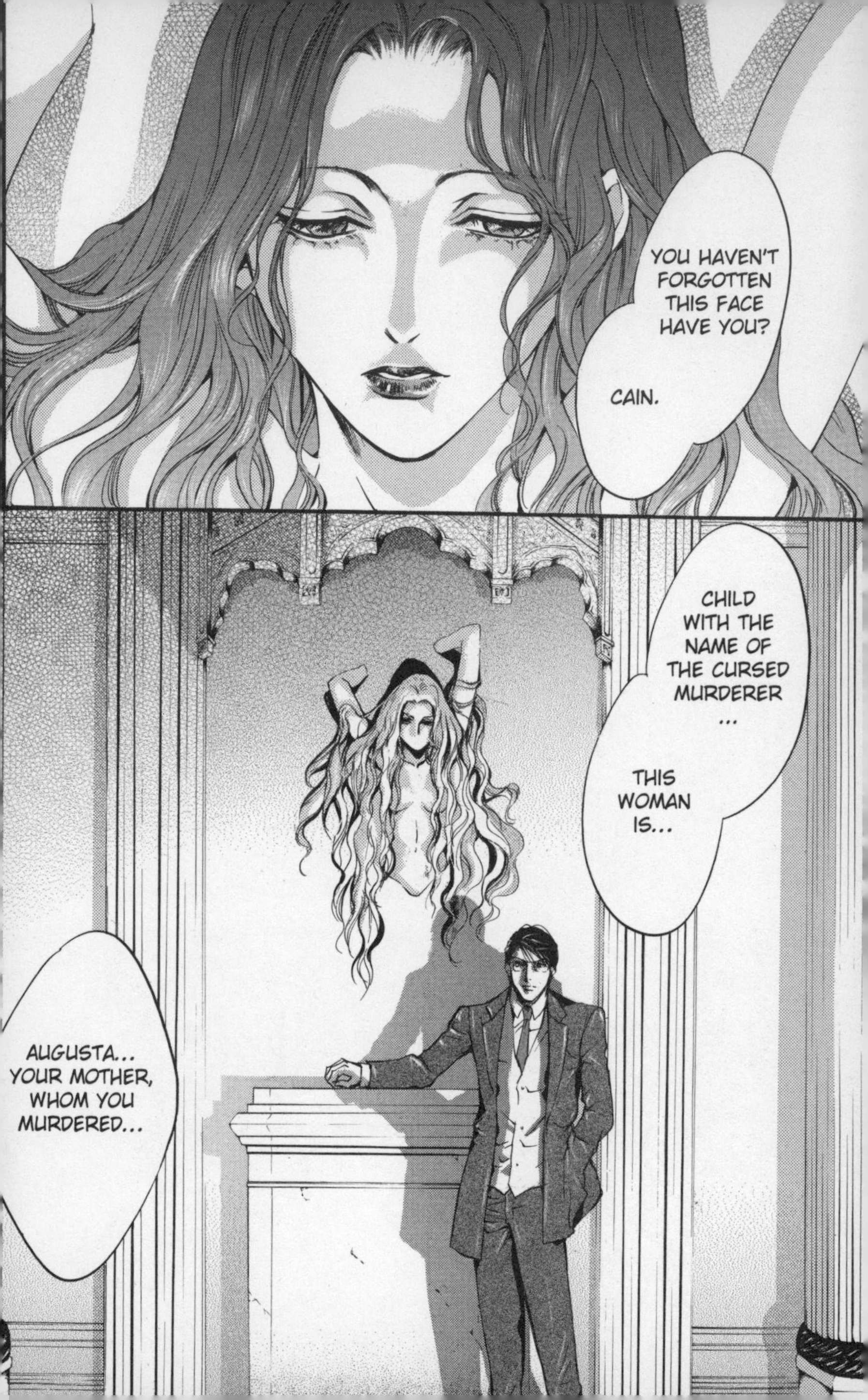
YOU HAVEN'T FORGOTTEN THIS FACE HAVE YOU?
CAIN.
CHILD WITH THE NAME OF THE CURSED MURDERER ...
THIS WOMAN IS...
AUGUSTA... YOUR MOTHER, WHOM YOU MURDERED...

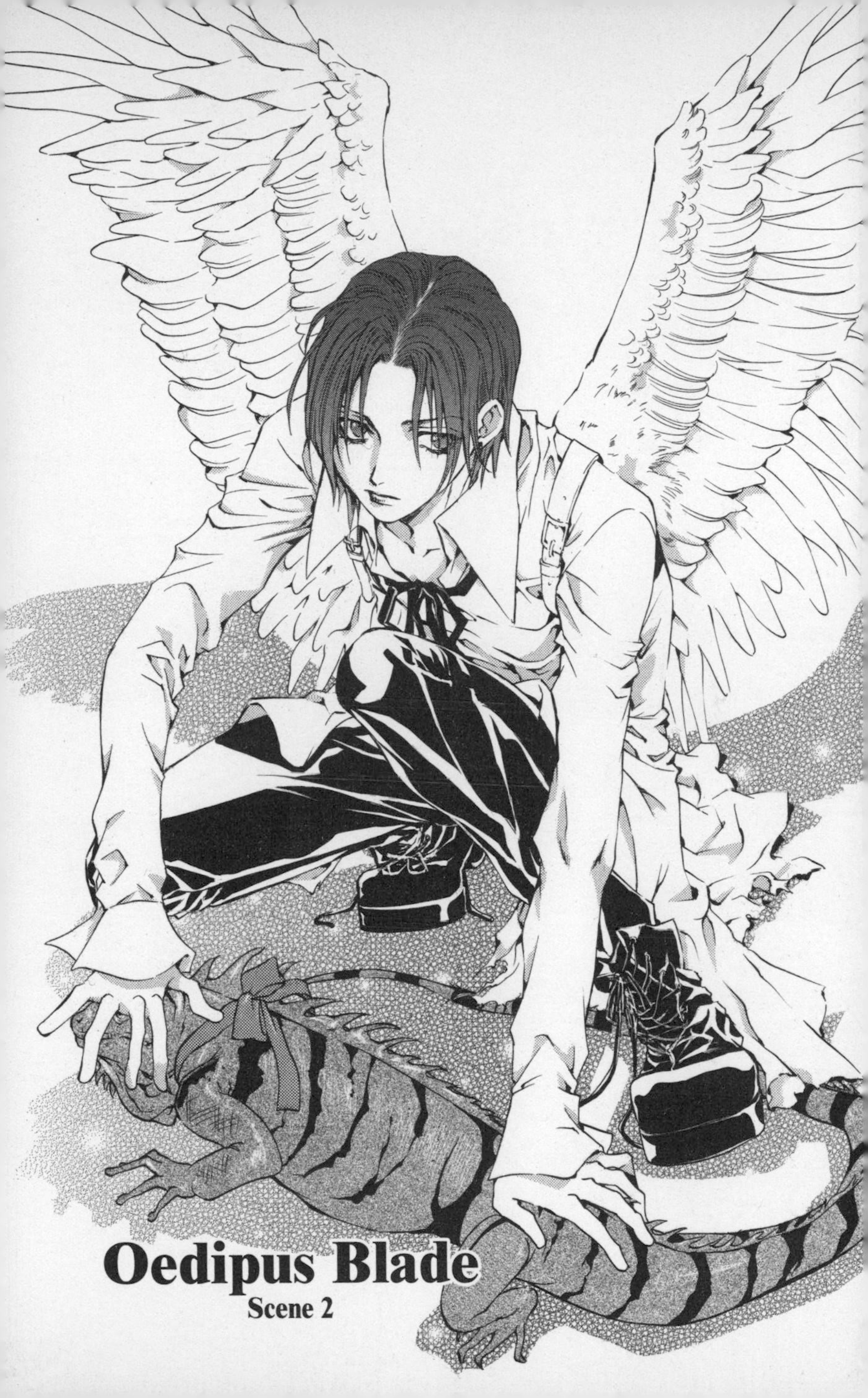

Oedipus Blade

Scene 2

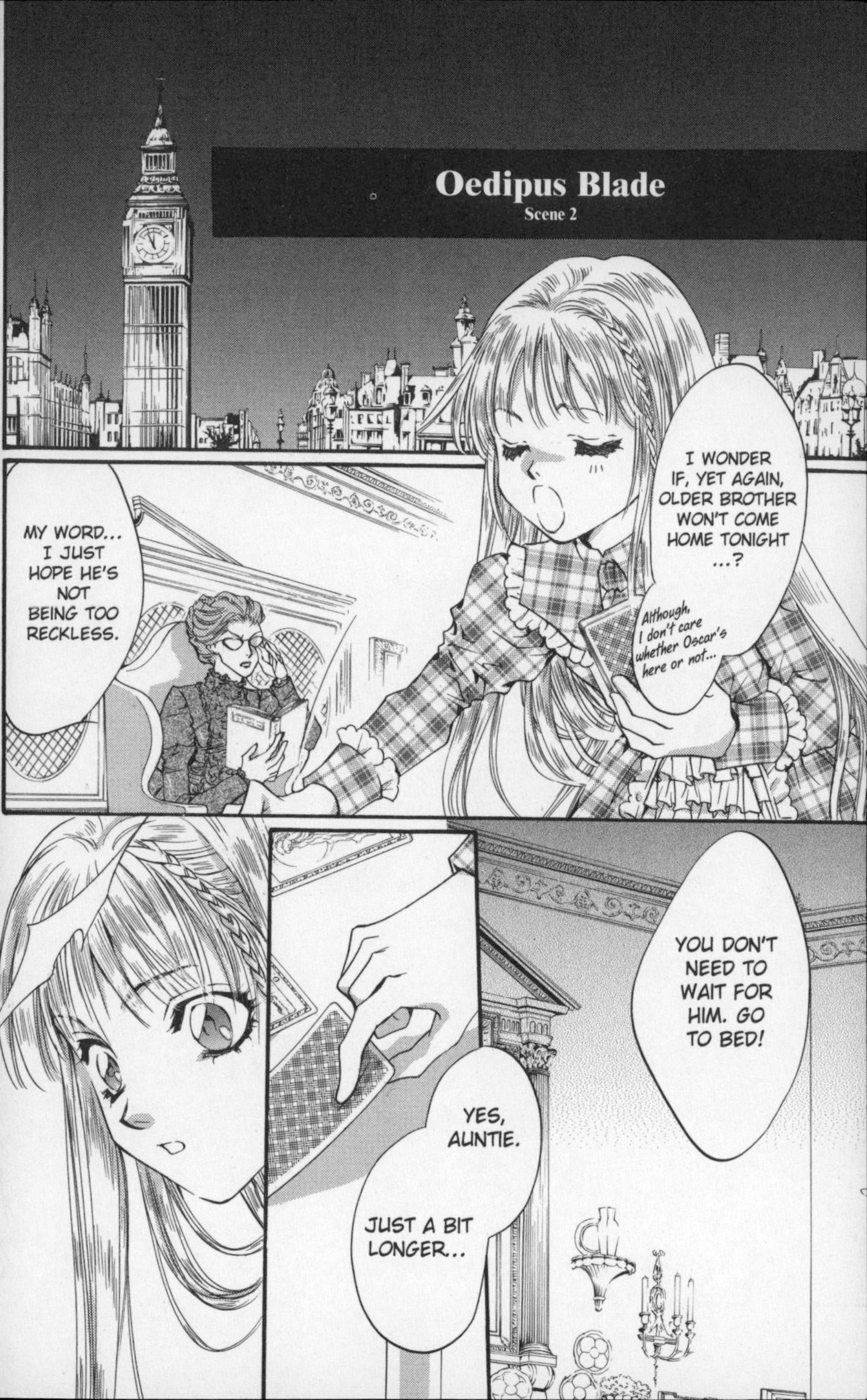
Oedipus Blade
Scene 2
I WONDER IF, YET AGAIN, OLDER BROTHER WON'T COME HOME TONIGHT ...?
Although, I don't care whether Oscar's here or not...
MY WORD... I JUST HOPE HE'S NOT BEING TOO RECKLESS.
YOU DON'T NEED TO WAIT FOR HIM. GO TO BED!
YES, AUNTIE.
JUST A BIT LONGER...

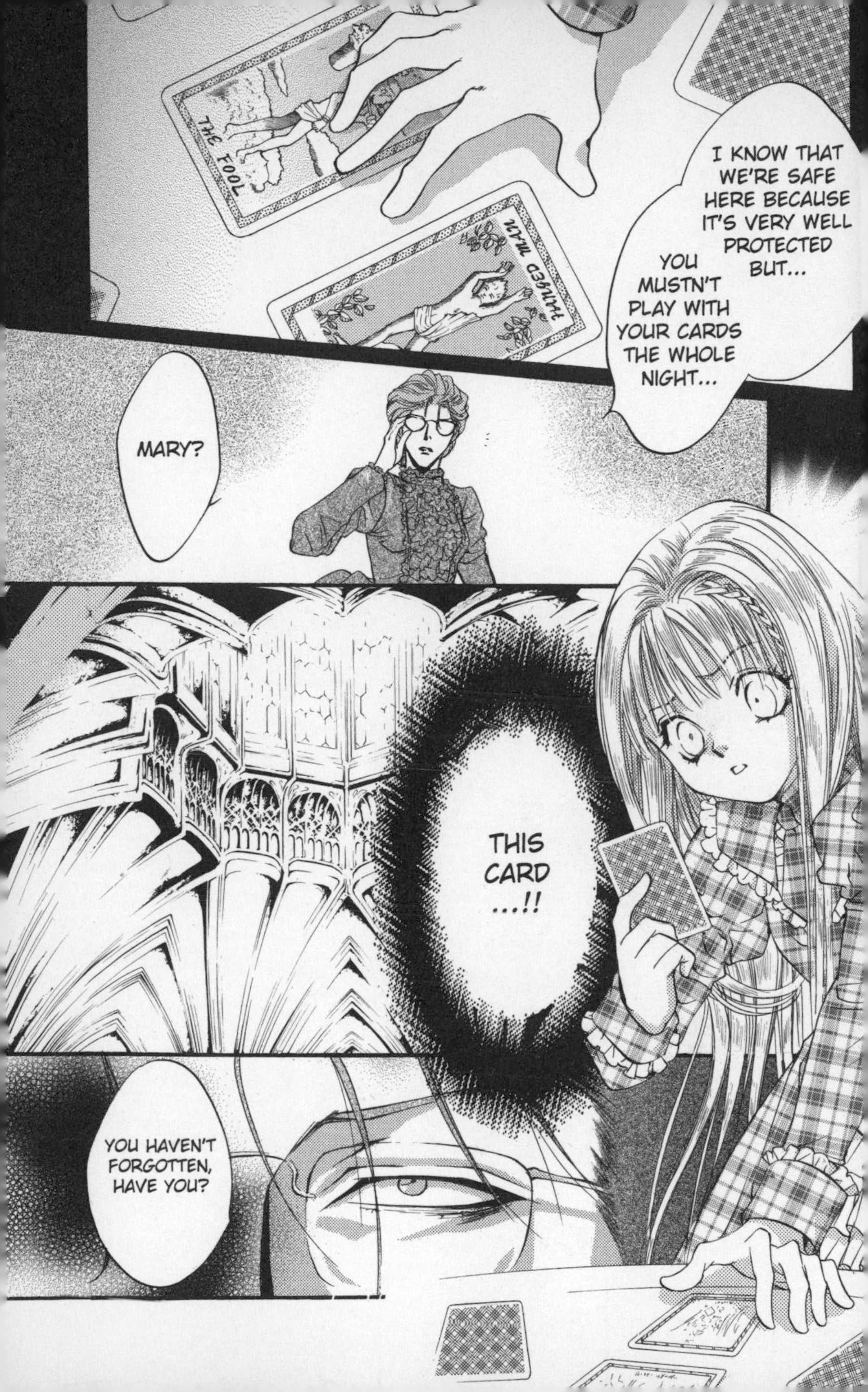
I KNOW THAT WE'RE SAFE HERE BECAUSE IT'S VERY WELL PROTECTED BUT...
YOU MUSTN'T PLAY WITH YOUR CARDS THE WHOLE NIGHT...
THE FOOL
HANGED MAN
MARY?
THIS CARD ...!!
YOU HAVEN'T FORGOTTEN, HAVE YOU?

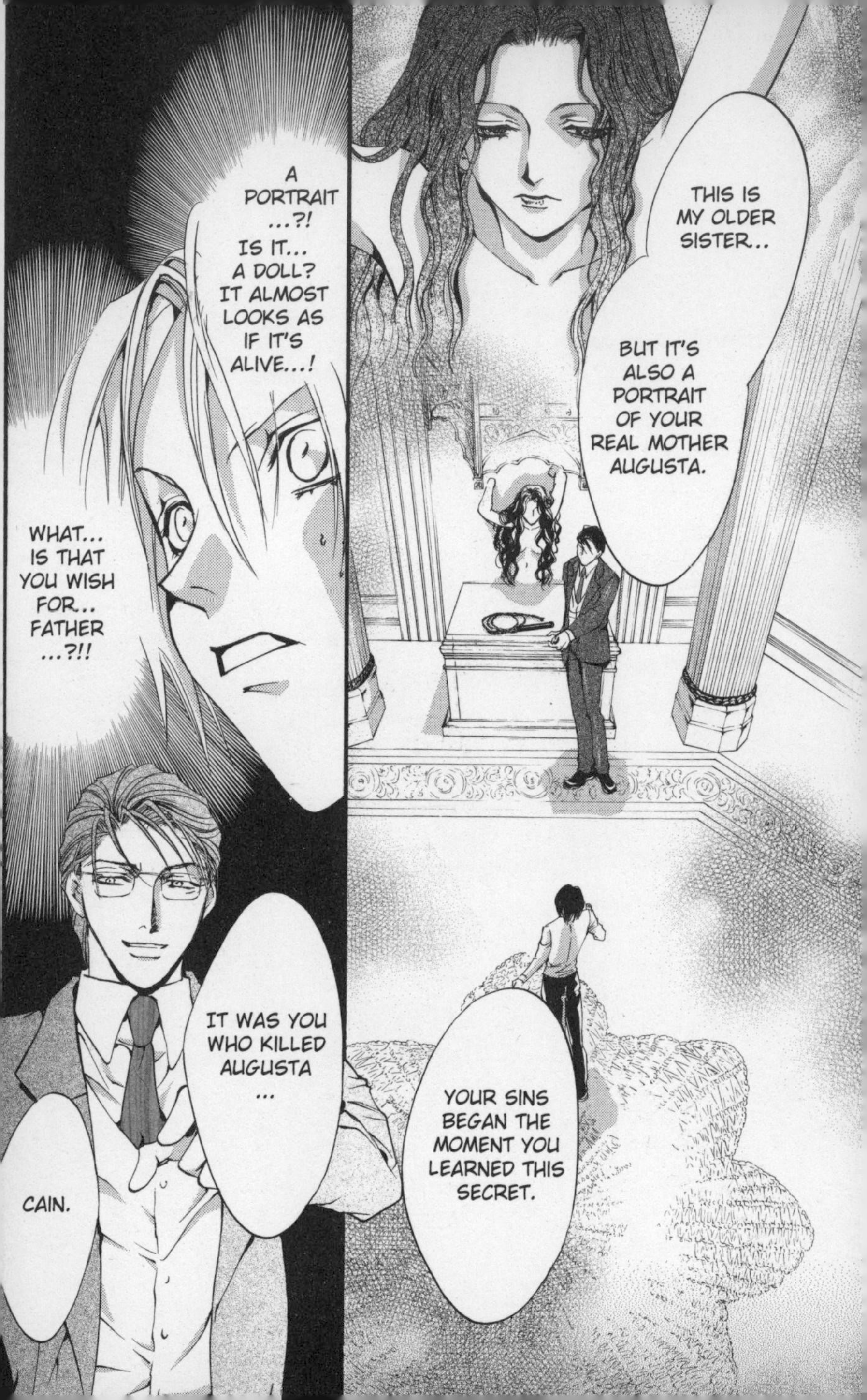
THIS IS MY OLDER SISTER..
BUT IT'S ALSO A PORTRAIT OF YOUR REAL MOTHER AUGUSTA.
A PORTRAIT ...?! IS IT... A DOLL? IT ALMOST LOOKS AS IF IT'S ALIVE...!
WHAT... IS THAT YOU WISH FOR.. FATHER ...?!!
YOUR SINS BEGAN THE MOMENT YOU LEARNED THIS SECRET.
IT WAS YOU WHO KILLED AUGUSTA ...
CAIN.

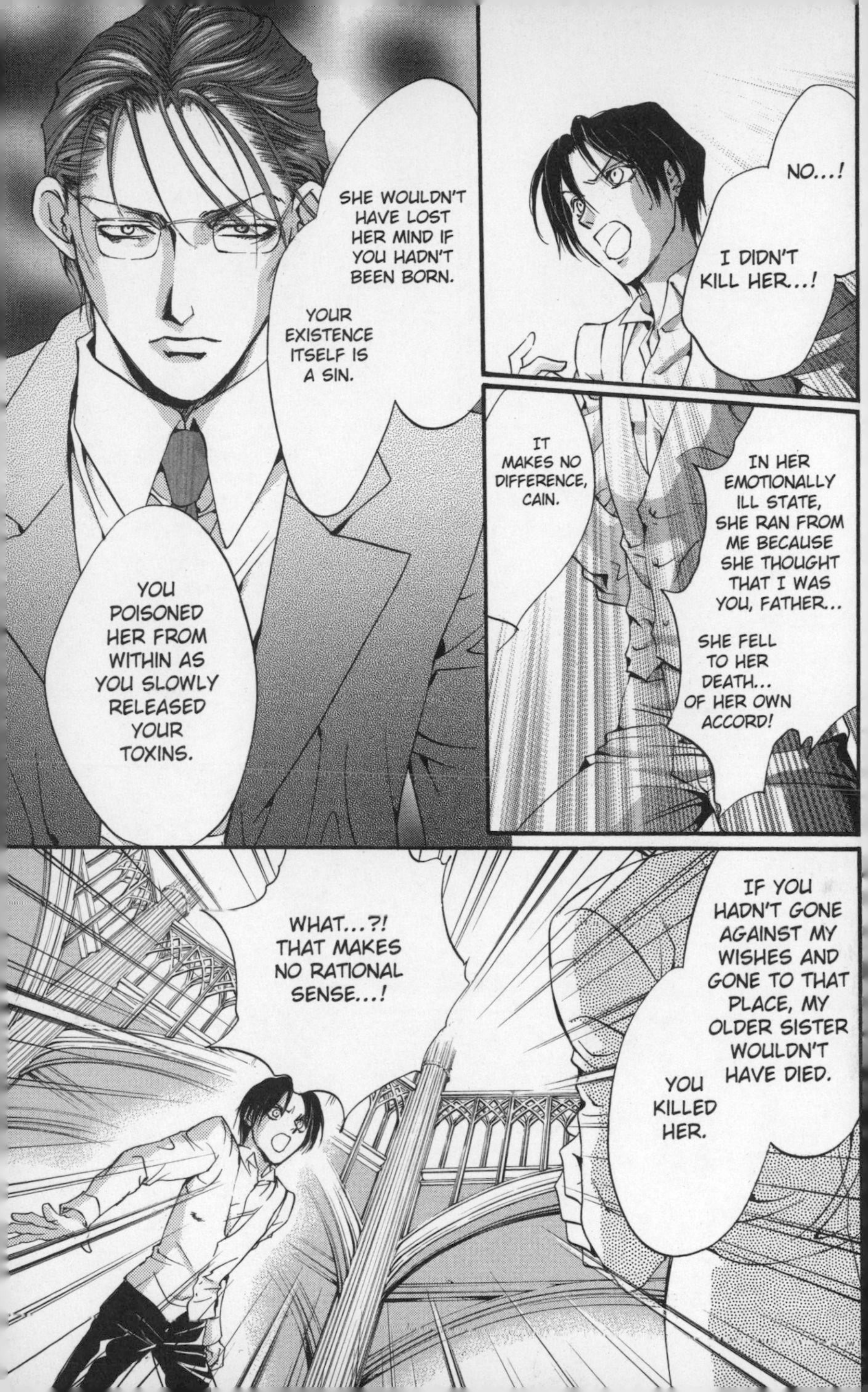
NO...!
I DIDN'T KILL HER...!
IN HER EMOTIONALLY ILL STATE, SHE RAN FROM ME BECAUSE SHE THOUGHT THAT I WAS YOU, FATHER...
SHE FELL TO HER DEATH... OF HER OWN ACCORD!
IT MAKES NO DIFFERENCE, CAIN.
SHE WOULDN'T HAVE LOST HER MIND IF YOU HADN'T BEEN BORN.
YOUR EXISTENCE ITSELF IS A SIN.
YOU POISONED HER FROM WITHIN AS YOU SLOWLY RELEASED YOUR TOXINS.
IF YOU HADN'T GONE AGAINST MY WISHES AND GONE TO THAT PLACE, MY OLDER SISTER WOULDN'T HAVE DIED.
YOU KILLED HER.
WHAT...?! THAT MAKES NO RATIONAL SENSE...!

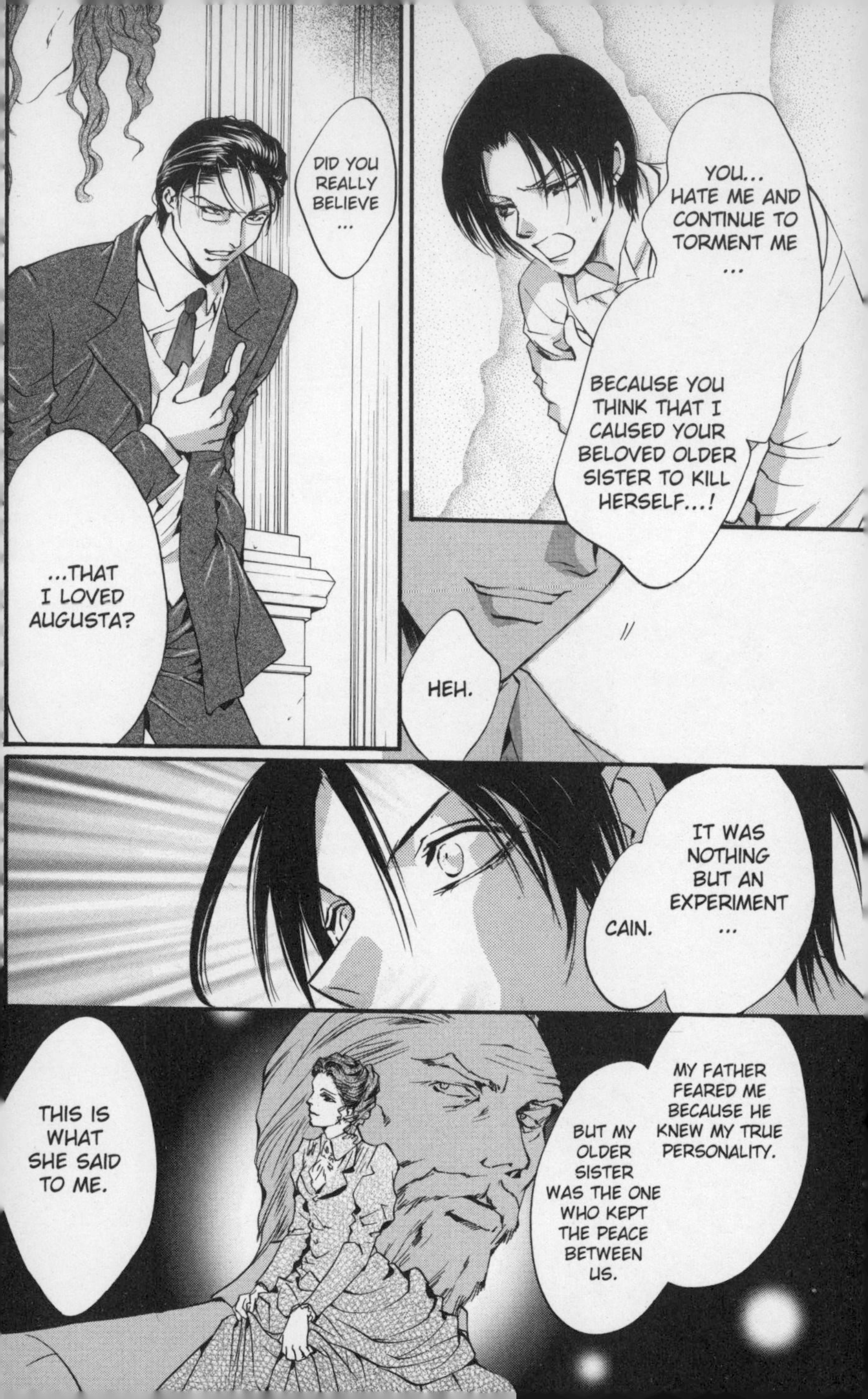
YOU... HATE ME AND CONTINUE TO TORMENT ME ...
BECAUSE YOU THINK THAT I CAUSED YOUR BELOVED OLDER SISTER TO KILL HERSELF...!
HEH.
DID YOU REALLY BELIEVE ...
...THAT I LOVED AUGUSTA?
IT WAS NOTHING BUT AN EXPERIMENT ...
CAIN.
MY FATHER FEARED ME BECAUSE HE KNEW MY TRUE PERSONALITY.
BUT MY OLDER SISTER WAS THE ONE WHO KEPT THE PEACE BETWEEN US.
THIS IS WHAT SHE SAID TO ME.

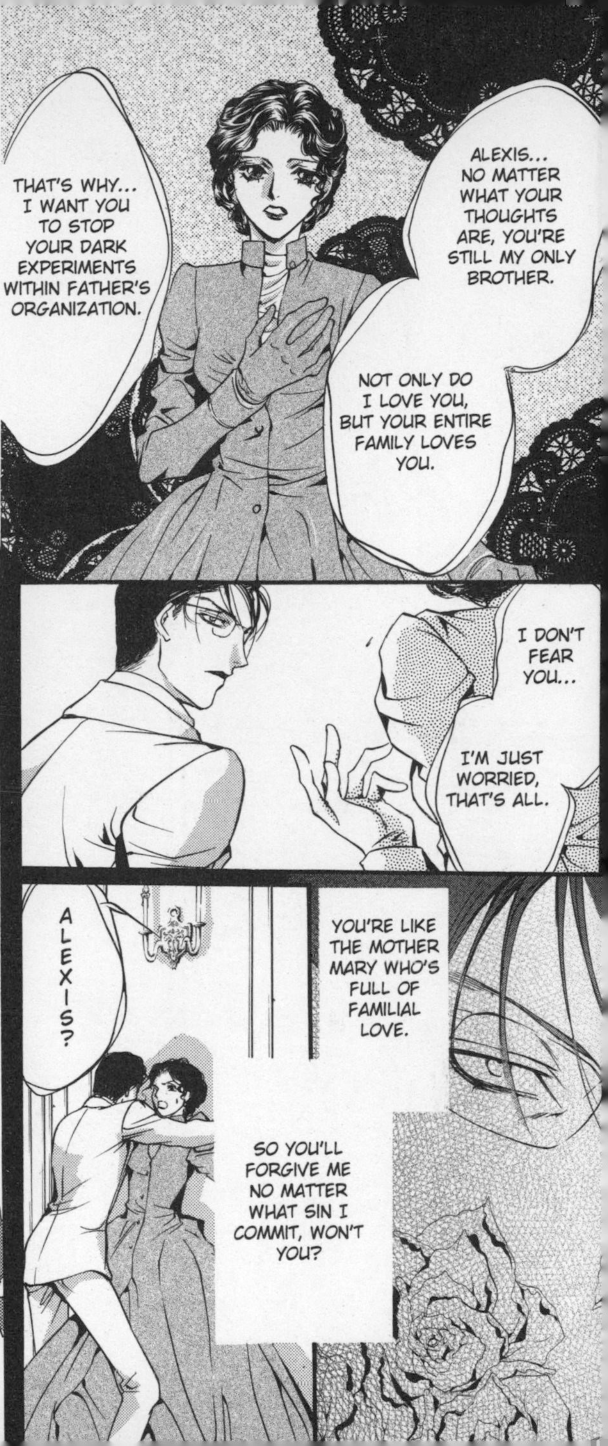
ALEXIS... NO MATTER WHAT YOUR THOUGHTS ARE, YOU'RE STILL MY ONLY BROTHER.
NOT ONLY DO I LOVE YOU, BUT YOUR ENTIRE FAMILY LOVES YOU.
THAT'S WHY... I WANT YOU TO STOP YOUR DARK EXPERIMENTS WITHIN FATHER'S ORGANIZATION.
I DON'T FEAR YOU...
I'M JUST WORRIED, THAT'S ALL.
YOU'RE LIKE THE MOTHER MARY WHO'S FULL OF FAMILIAL LOVE.
SO YOU'LL FORGIVE ME NO MATTER WHAT SIN I COMMIT, WON'T YOU?
ALEXIS?

Katina is a relative of Cain's stepmother Lenora who acts as a governess for Mary. Although she's not Cain's blood relation, I've always thought that people like her and Uncle Neil who tell you bluntly what they think are the ones who really care about you... At the same time I understand why someone would consider them annoying. But I think it's important to tell friends and loved ones if you don't agree with what they're doing because it's for their own good. It's not always easy for me to take criticism but I do appreciate it. Why did I start talking about this all of a sudden?

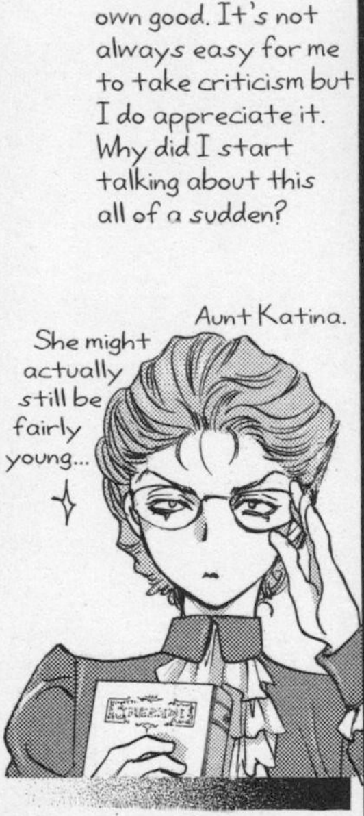
Aunt Katina.
She might actually still be fairly young...

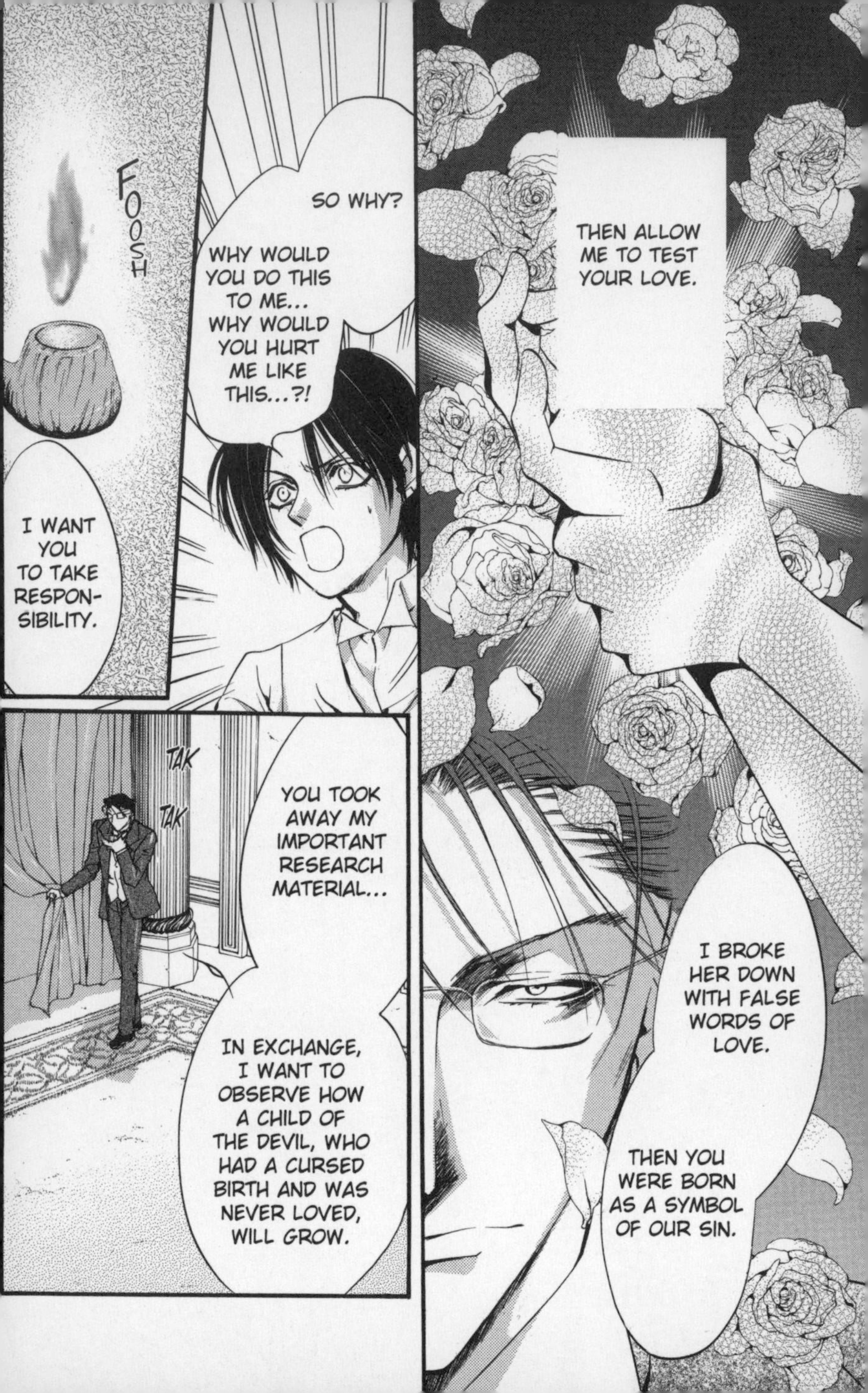
THEN ALLOW ME TO TEST YOUR LOVE.
I BROKE HER DOWN WITH FALSE WORDS OF LOVE.
THEN YOU WERE BORN AS A SYMBOL OF OUR SIN.
SO WHY?
WHY WOULD YOU DO THIS TO ME... WHY WOULD YOU HURT ME LIKE THIS...?!
FOOSH
I WANT YOU TO TAKE RESPON-SIBILITY.
YOU TOOK AWAY MY IMPORTANT RESEARCH MATERIAL...
TAK
TAK
IN EXCHANGE, I WANT TO OBSERVE HOW A CHILD OF THE DEVIL, WHO HAD A CURSED BIRTH AND WAS NEVER LOVED, WILL GROW.

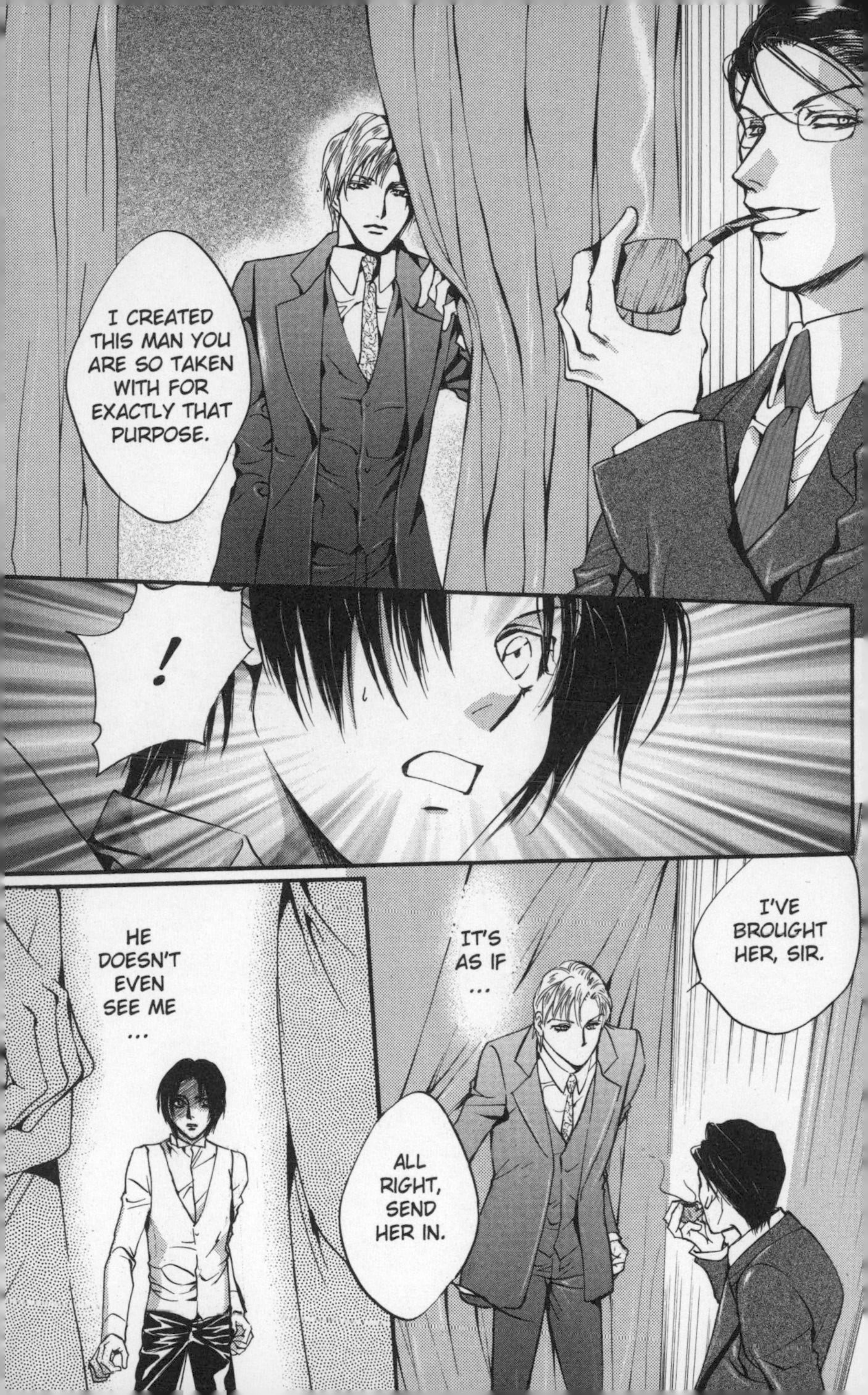
I CREATED THIS MAN YOU ARE SO TAKEN WITH FOR EXACTLY THAT PURPOSE.
!
I'VE BROUGHT HER, SIR.
IT'S AS IF ...
ALL RIGHT, SEND HER IN.
HE DOESN'T EVEN SEE ME ...

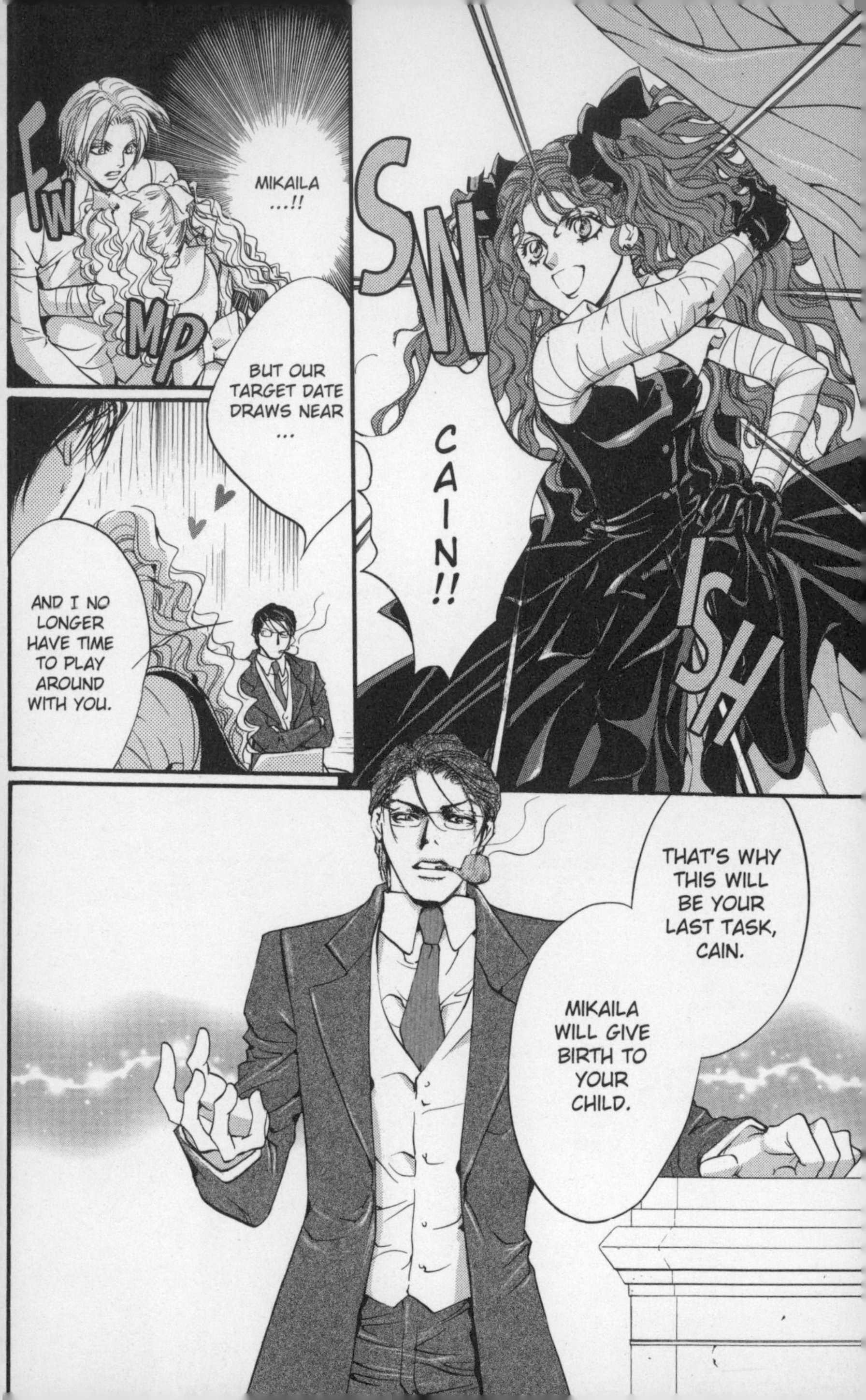
SW
CAIN!!
ISH
FW
MP
MIKAILA ...!!
BUT OUR TARGET DATE DRAWS NEAR ...
AND I NO LONGER HAVE TIME TO PLAY AROUND WITH YOU.
THAT'S WHY THIS WILL BE YOUR LAST TASK, CAIN.
MIKAILA WILL GIVE BIRTH TO YOUR CHILD.

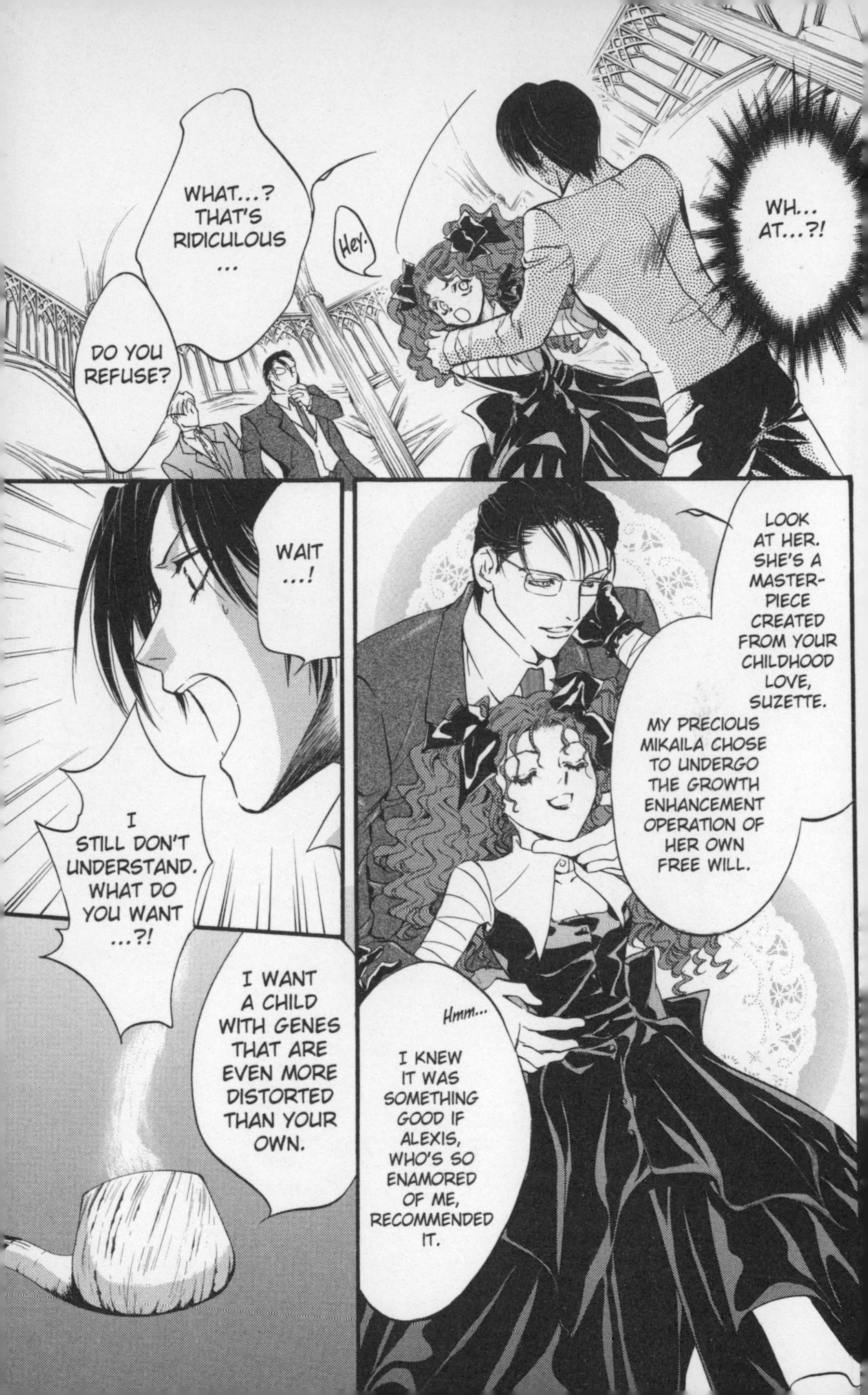
WH... AT...?!
Hey.
WHAT...? THAT'S RIDICULOUS ...
DO YOU REFUSE?
LOOK AT HER. SHE'S A MASTER-PIECE CREATED FROM YOUR CHILDHOOD LOVE, SUZETTE.
MY PRECIOUS MIKAILA CHOSE TO UNDERGO THE GROWTH ENHANCEMENT OPERATION OF HER OWN FREE WILL.
Hmm...
I KNEW IT WAS SOMETHING GOOD IF ALEXIS, WHO'S SO ENAMORED OF ME, RECOMMENDED IT.
WAIT ...!
I STILL DON'T UNDERSTAND. WHAT DO YOU WANT ...?!
I WANT A CHILD WITH GENES THAT ARE EVEN MORE DISTORTED THAN YOUR OWN.

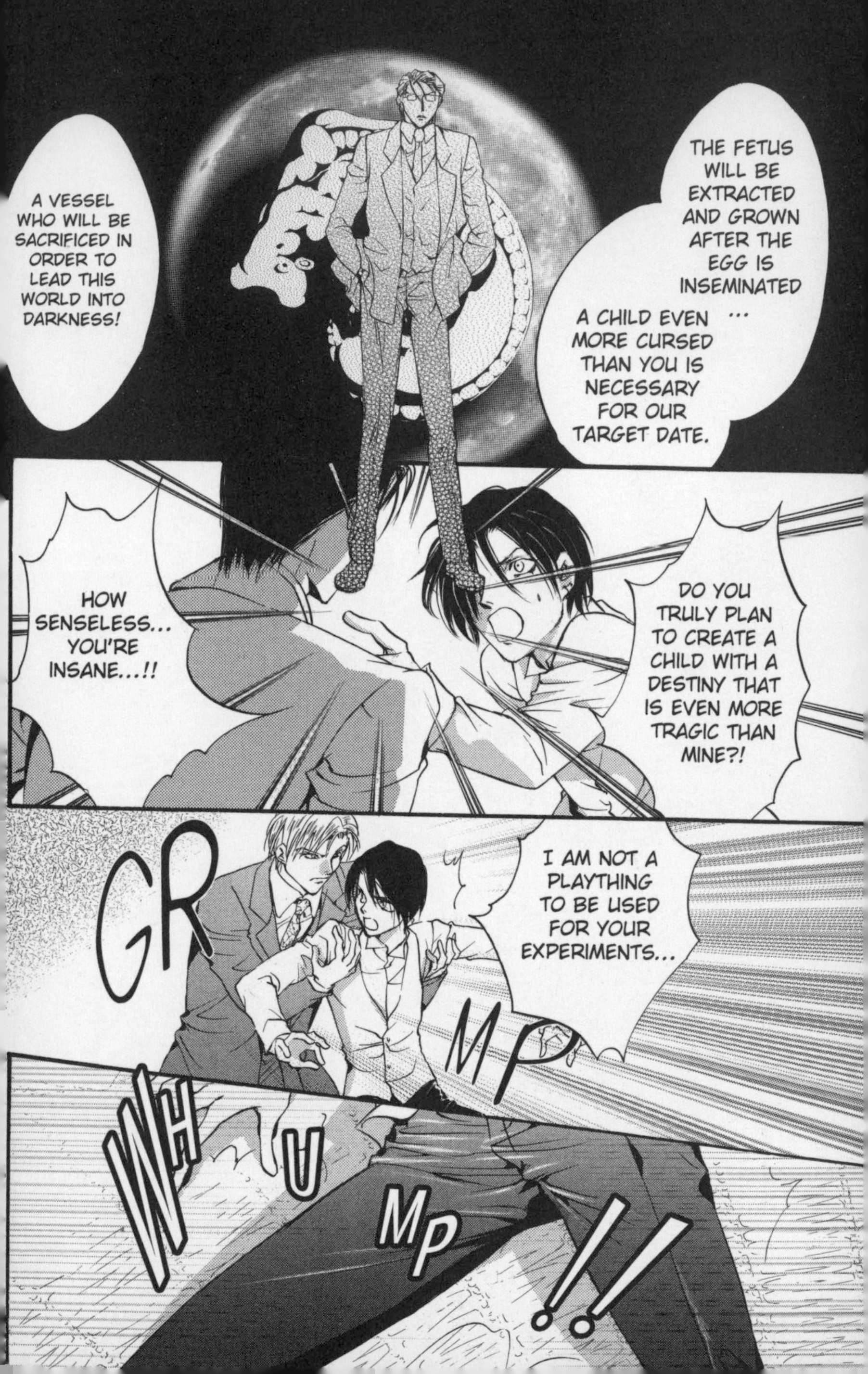
THE FETUS WILL BE EXTRACTED AND GROWN AFTER THE EGG IS INSEMINATED ...
A CHILD EVEN MORE CURSED THAN YOU IS NECESSARY FOR OUR TARGET DATE.
A VESSEL WHO WILL BE SACRIFICED IN ORDER TO LEAD THIS WORLD INTO DARKNESS!
DO YOU TRULY PLAN TO CREATE A CHILD WITH A DESTINY THAT IS EVEN MORE TRAGIC THAN MINE?!
HOW SENSELESS... YOU'RE INSANE...!!
I AM NOT A PLAYTHING TO BE USED FOR YOUR EXPERIMENTS...
GRMP
WHUMP!!

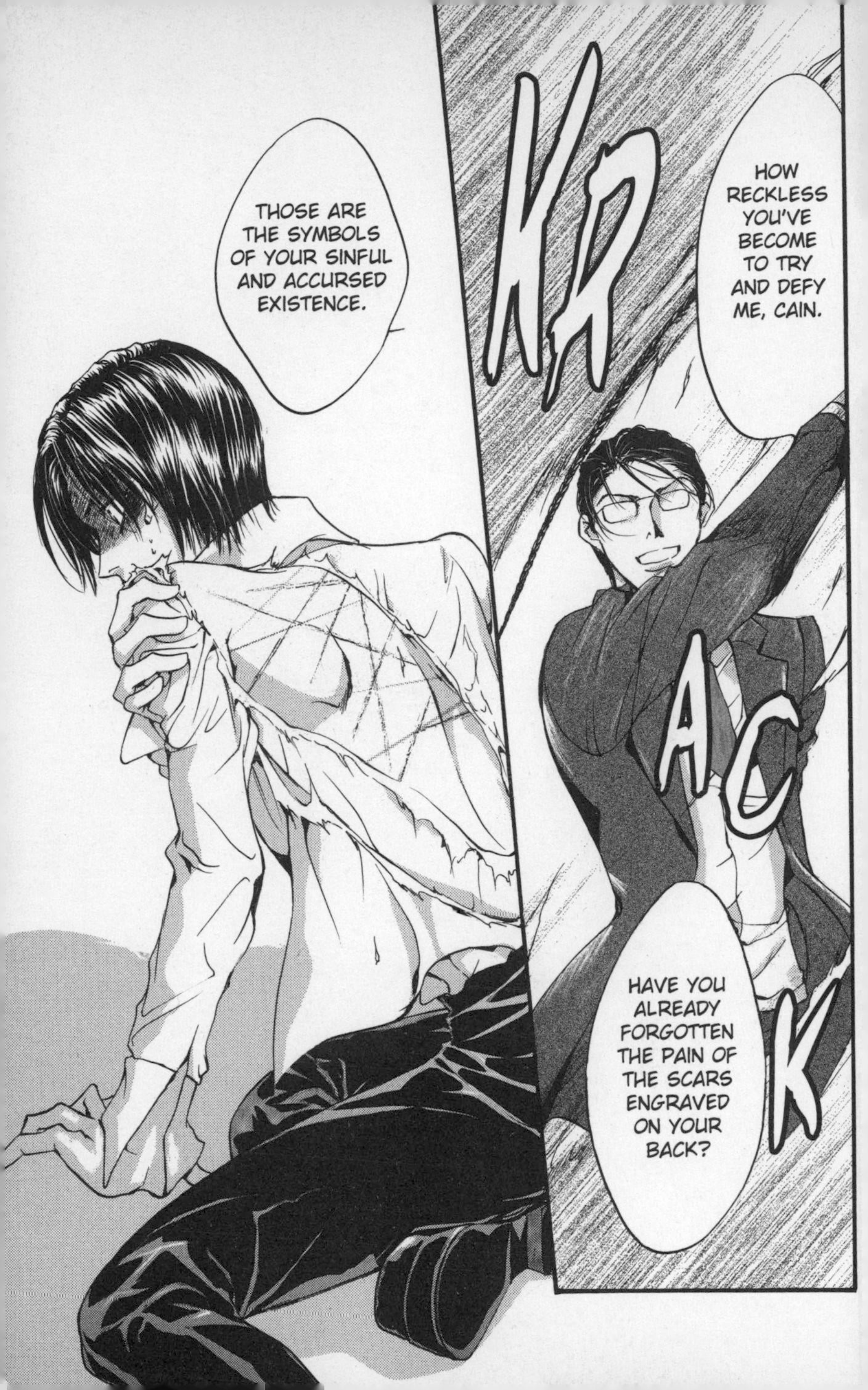
KRACK
HOW RECKLESS YOU'VE BECOME TO TRY AND DEFY ME, CAIN.
HAVE YOU ALREADY FORGOTTEN THE PAIN OF THE SCARS ENGRAVED ON YOUR BACK?
THOSE ARE THE SYMBOLS OF YOUR SINFUL AND ACCURSED EXISTENCE.

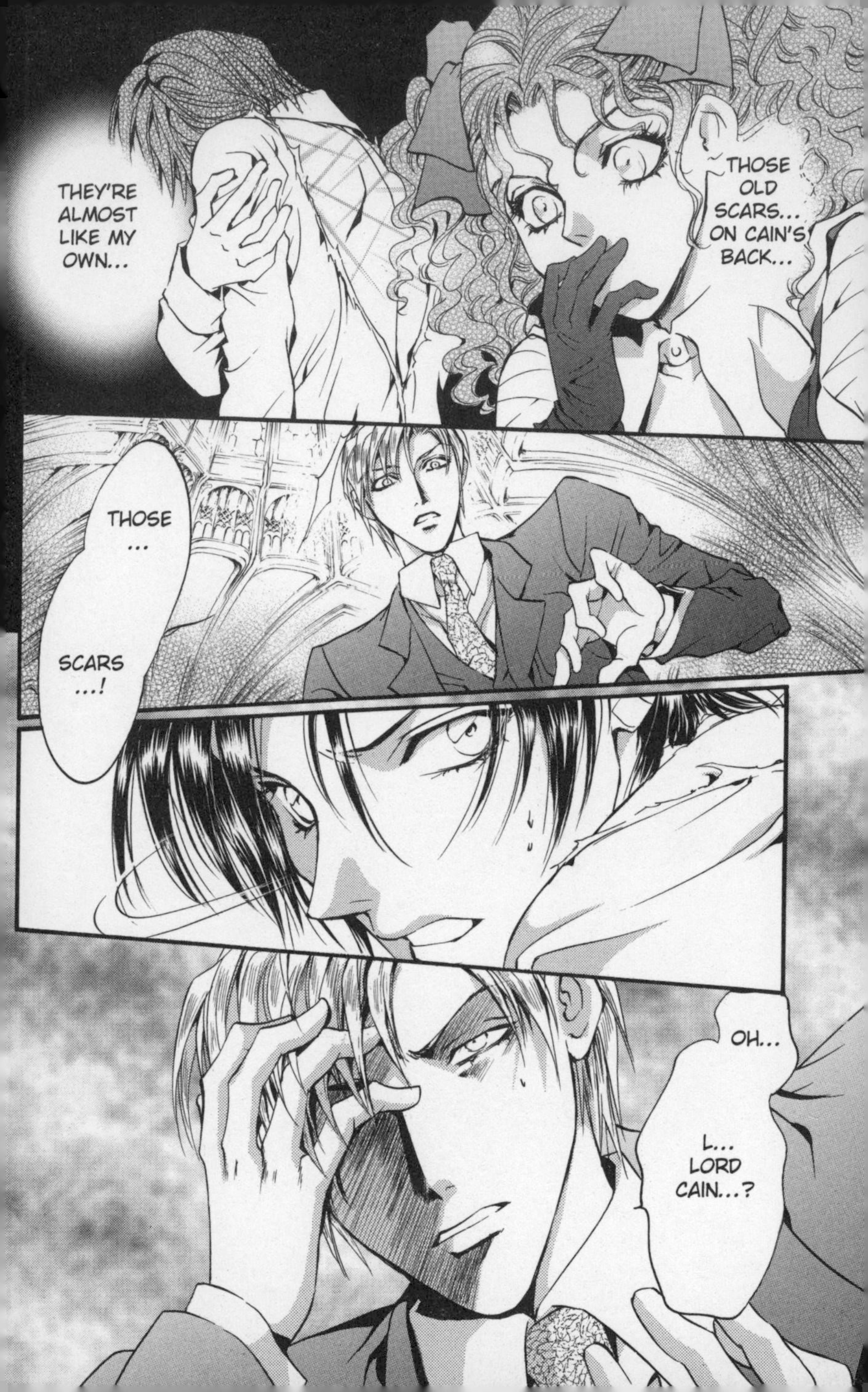
THOSE OLD SCARS... ON CAIN'S BACK...
THEY'RE ALMOST LIKE MY OWN...
THOSE ... SCARS ...!
OH...
L... LORD CAIN...?

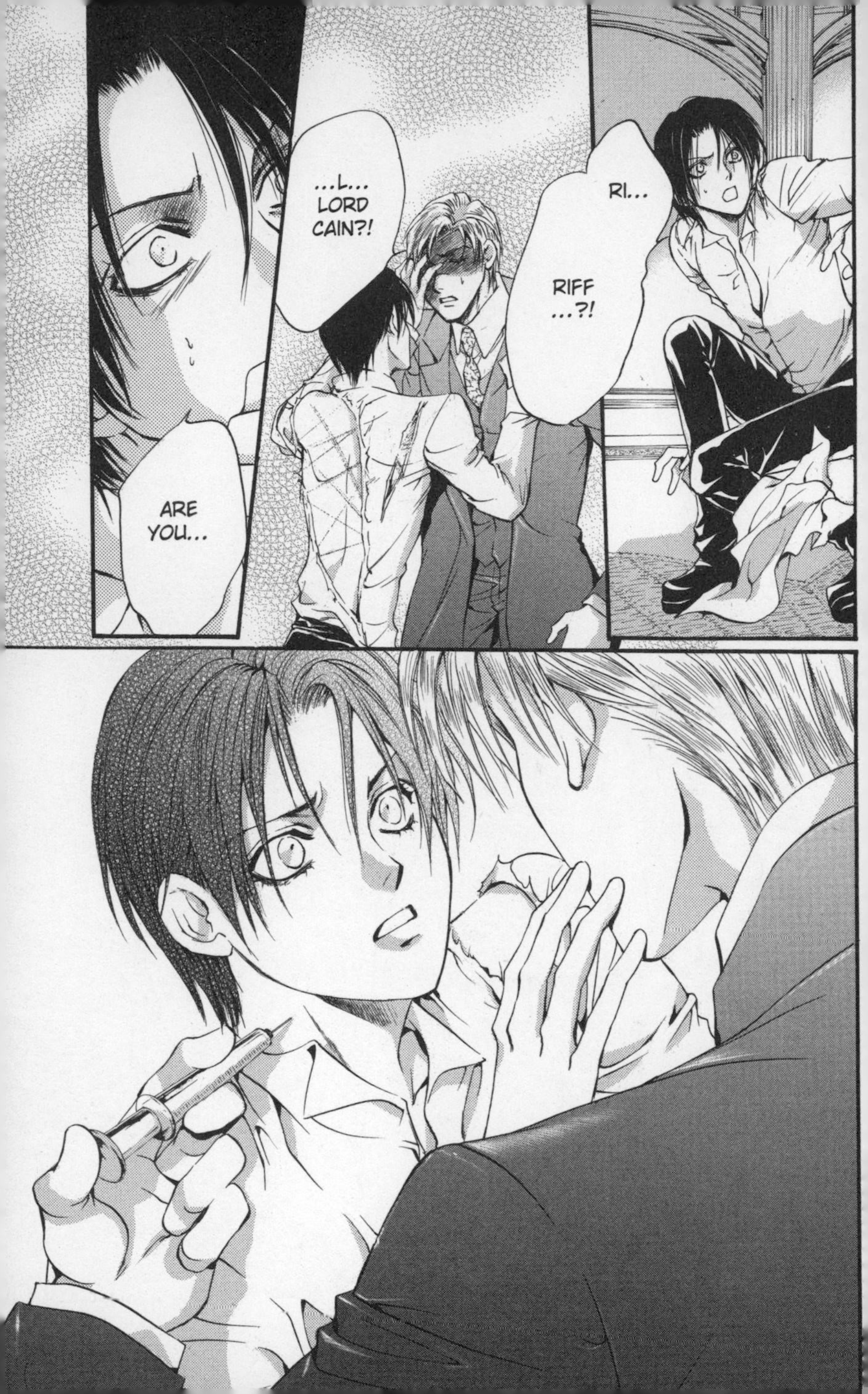
RI...
RIFF ...?!
...L... LORD CAIN?!
ARE YOU...

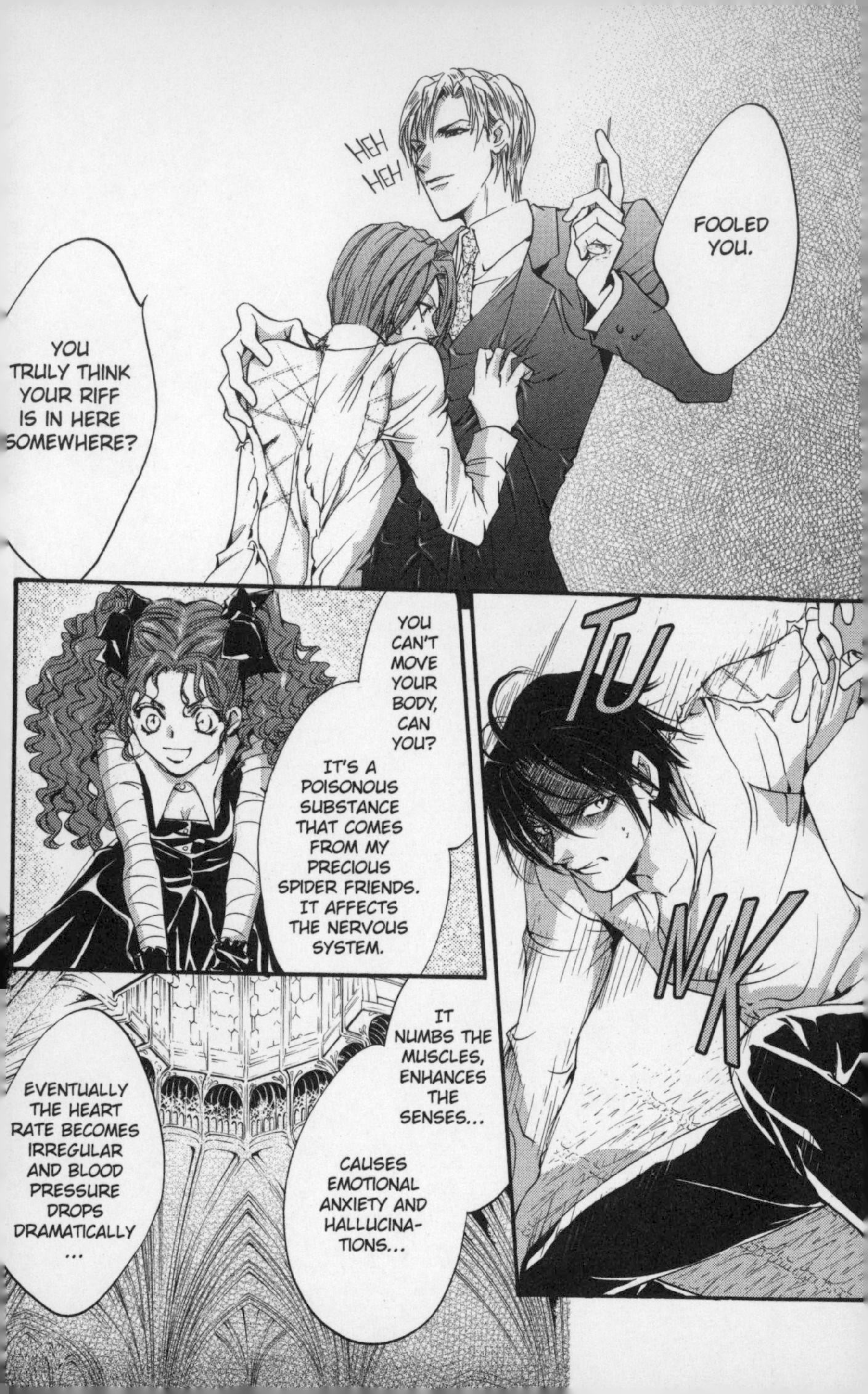
HEH HEH
FOOLED YOU.
YOU TRULY THINK YOUR RIFF IS IN HERE SOMEWHERE?
TUNK
YOU CAN'T MOVE YOUR BODY, CAN YOU?
IT'S A POISONOUS SUBSTANCE THAT COMES FROM MY PRECIOUS SPIDER FRIENDS. IT AFFECTS THE NERVOUS SYSTEM.
IT NUMBS THE MUSCLES, ENHANCES THE SENSES...
CAUSES EMOTIONAL ANXIETY AND HALLUCINA-TIONS...
EVENTUALLY THE HEART RATE BECOMES IRREGULAR AND BLOOD PRESSURE DROPS DRAMATICALLY ...

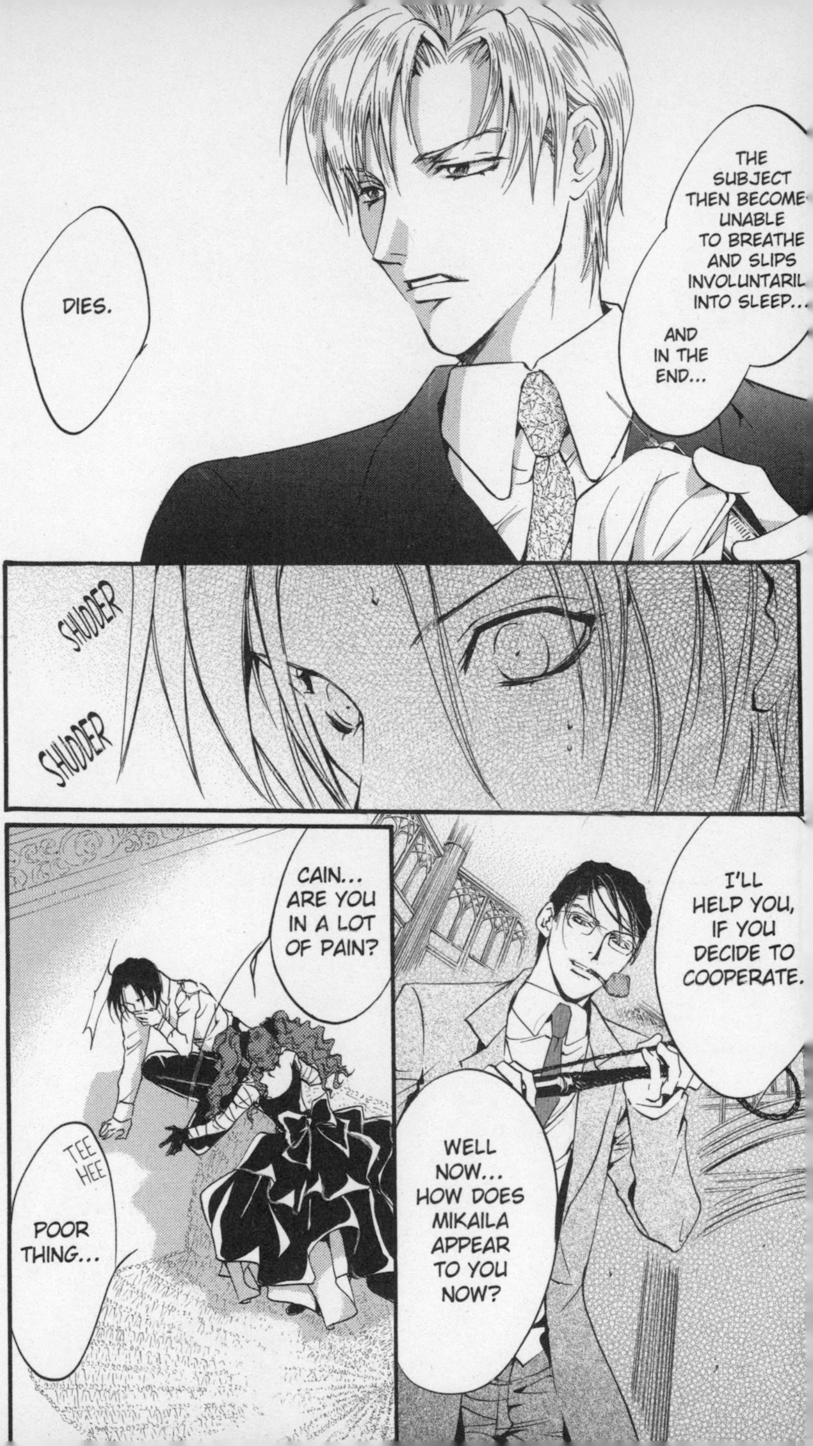
THE SUBJECT THEN BECOME UNABLE TO BREATHE AND SLIPS INVOLUNTARIL INTO SLEEP...
AND IN THE END...
DIES.
SHUDDER
SHUDDER
I'LL HELP YOU, IF YOU DECIDE TO COOPERATE..
WELL NOW... HOW DOES MIKAILA APPEAR TO YOU NOW?
CAIN... ARE YOU IN A LOT OF PAIN?
TEE HEE
POOR THING...

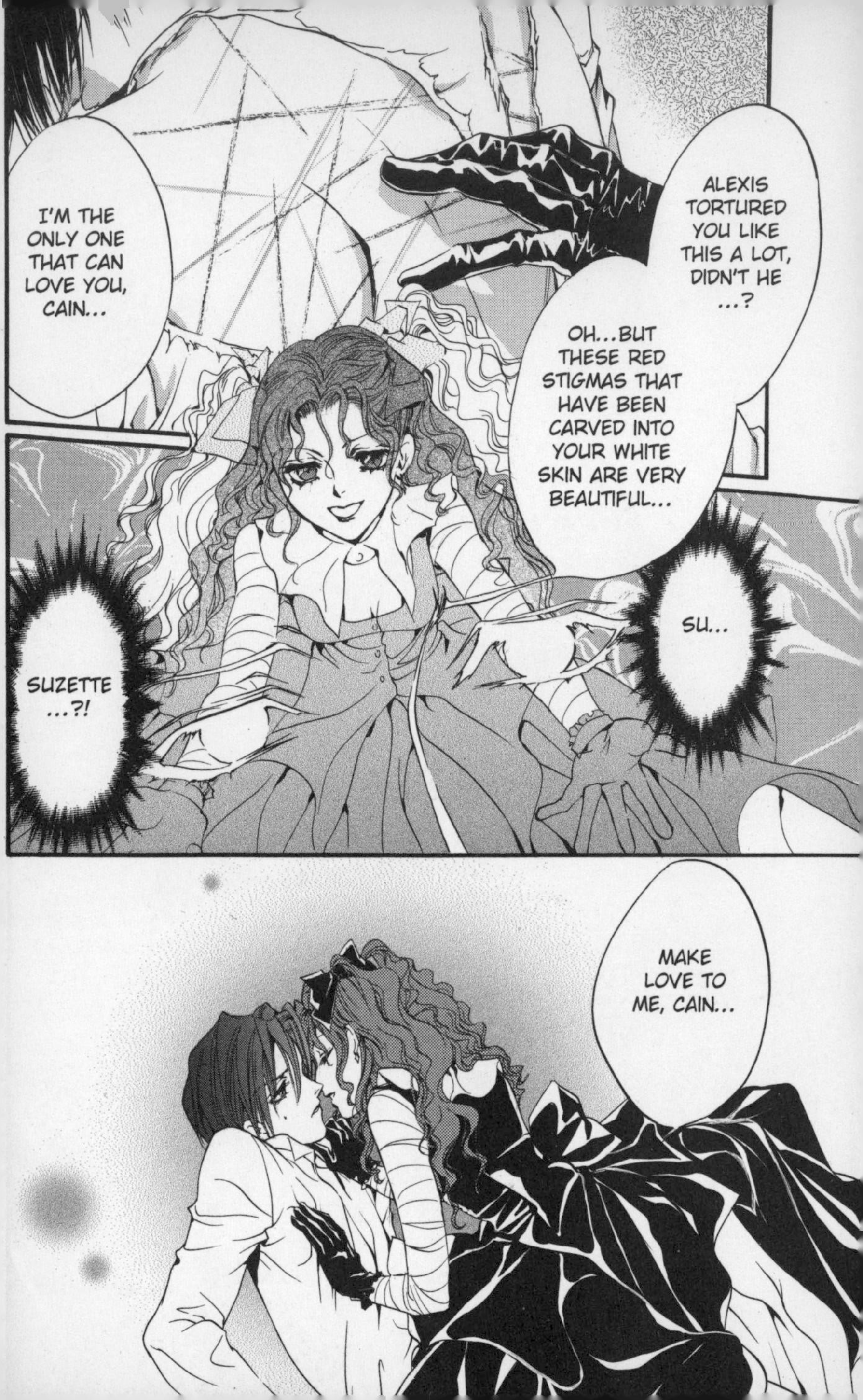
ALEXIS TORTURED YOU LIKE THIS A LOT, DIDN'T HE ...?
OH...BUT THESE RED STIGMAS THAT HAVE BEEN CARVED INTO YOUR WHITE SKIN ARE VERY BEAUTIFUL...
I'M THE ONLY ONE THAT CAN LOVE YOU, CAIN...
SU...
SUZETTE ...?!
MAKE LOVE TO ME, CAIN...

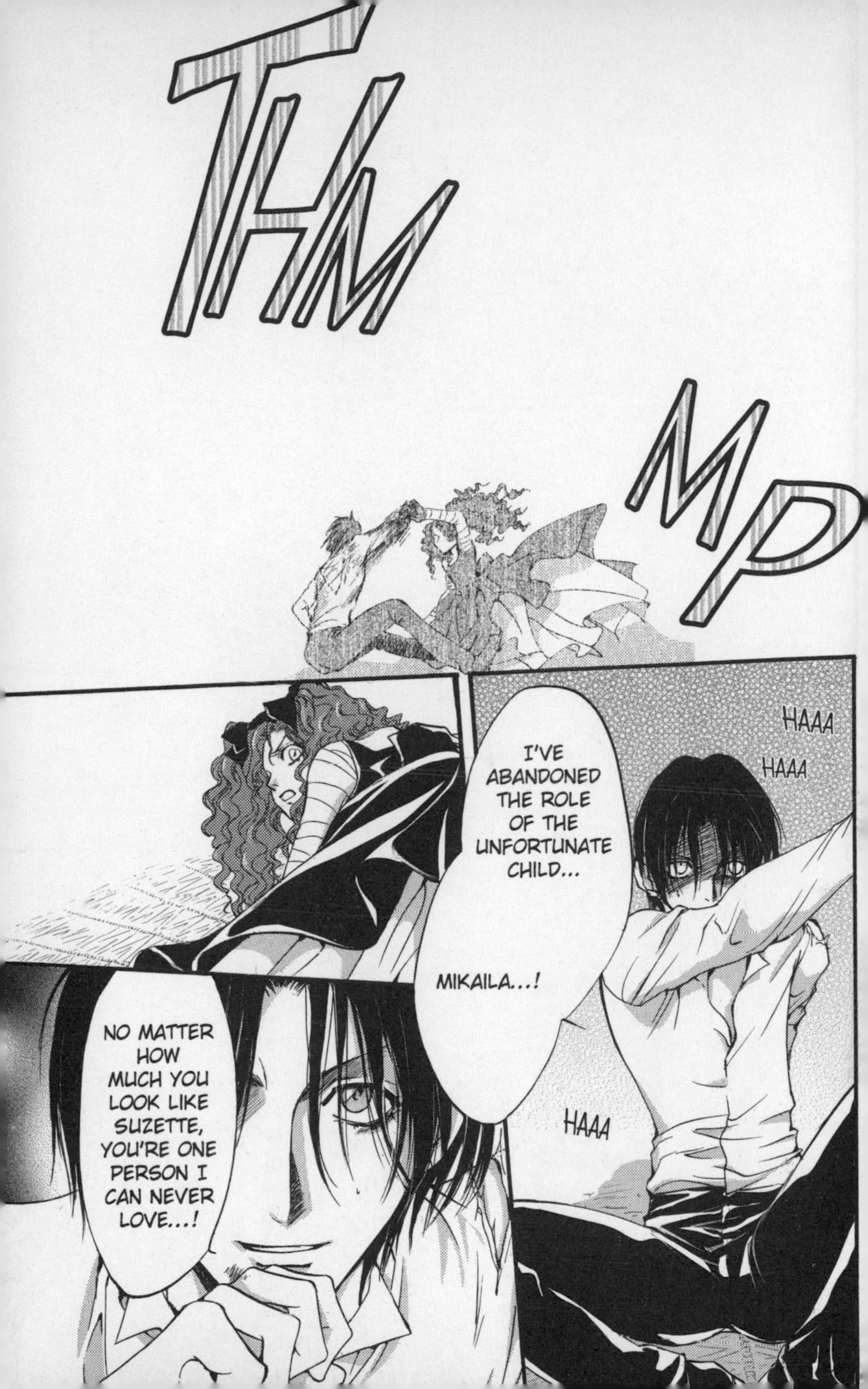
THUMP
HAAA
HAAA
I'VE ABANDONED THE ROLE OF THE UNFORTUNATE CHILD...
MIKAILA...!
HAAA
NO MATTER HOW MUCH YOU LOOK LIKE SUZETTE, YOU'RE ONE PERSON I CAN NEVER LOVE...!

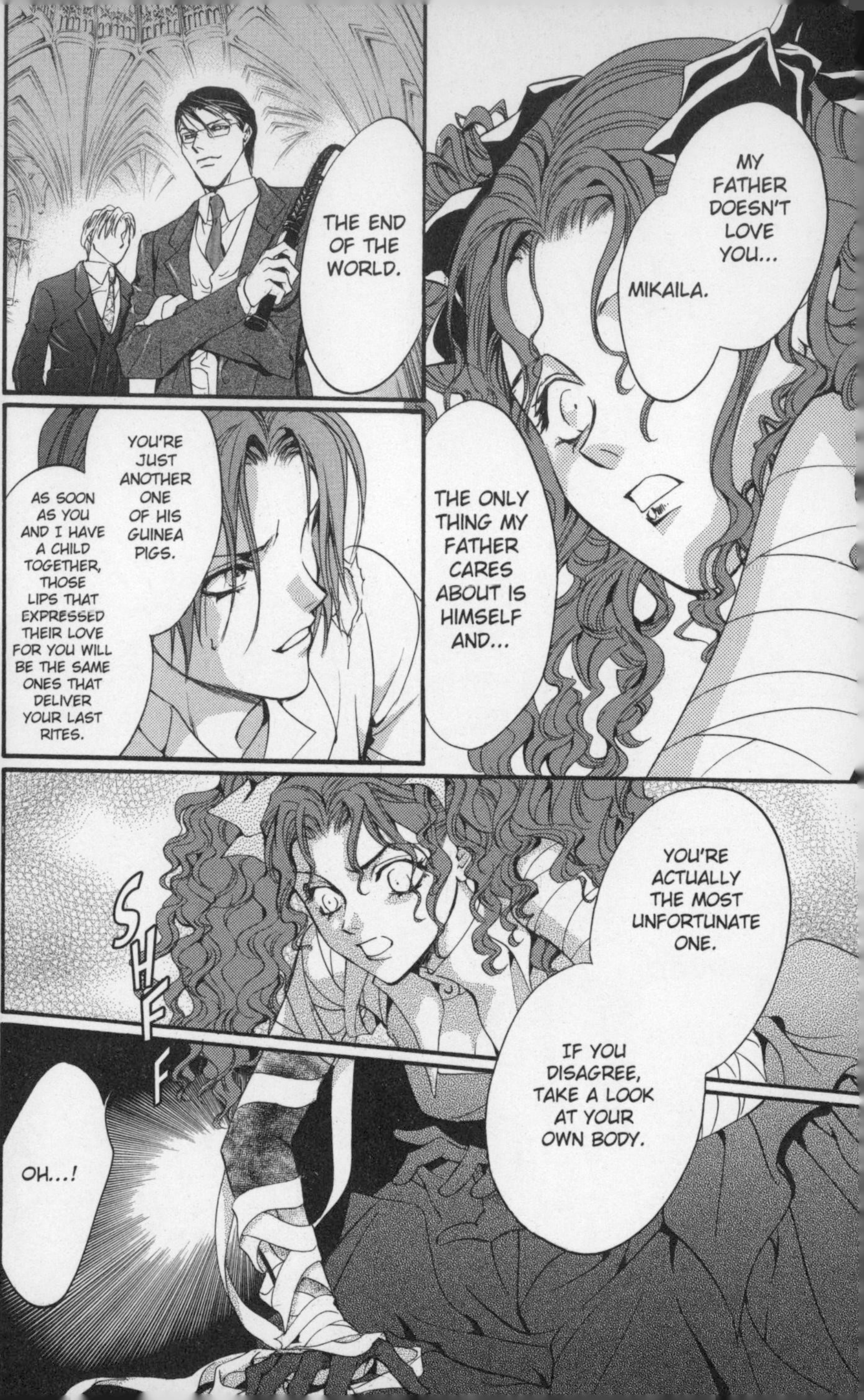
MY FATHER DOESN'T LOVE YOU...
MIKAILA.
THE ONLY THING MY FATHER CARES ABOUT IS HIMSELF AND...
THE END OF THE WORLD.
YOU'RE JUST ANOTHER ONE OF HIS GUINEA PIGS.
AS SOON AS YOU AND I HAVE A CHILD TOGETHER, THOSE LIPS THAT EXPRESSED THEIR LOVE FOR YOU WILL BE THE SAME ONES THAT DELIVER YOUR LAST RITES.
YOU'RE ACTUALLY THE MOST UNFORTUNATE ONE.
SHFF
IF YOU DISAGREE, TAKE A LOOK AT YOUR OWN BODY.
OH...!

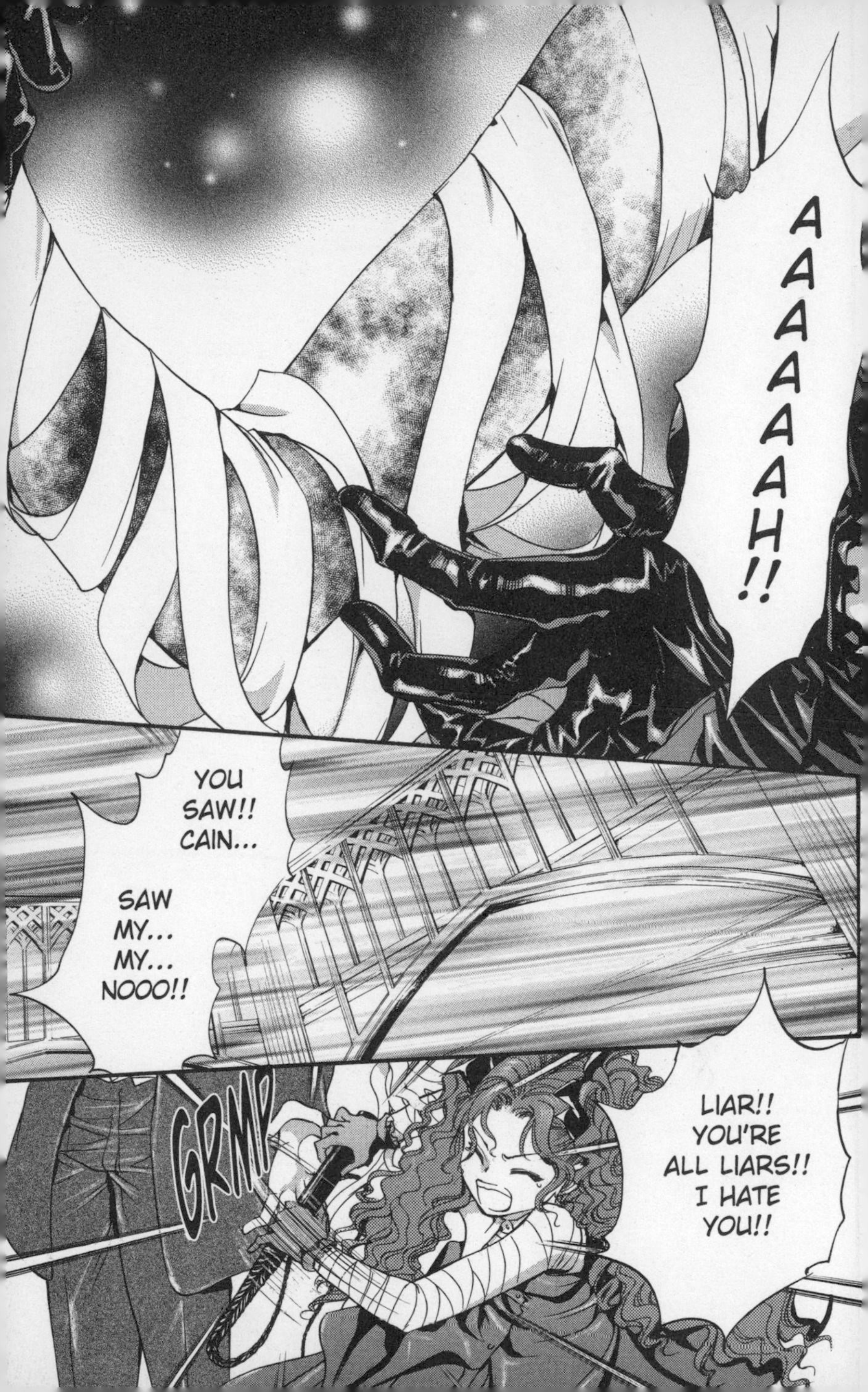
AAAAAAAH!!
YOU SAW!! CAIN...
SAW MY... MY... NOOO!!
LIAR!! YOU'RE ALL LIARS!! I HATE YOU!!
GRMP

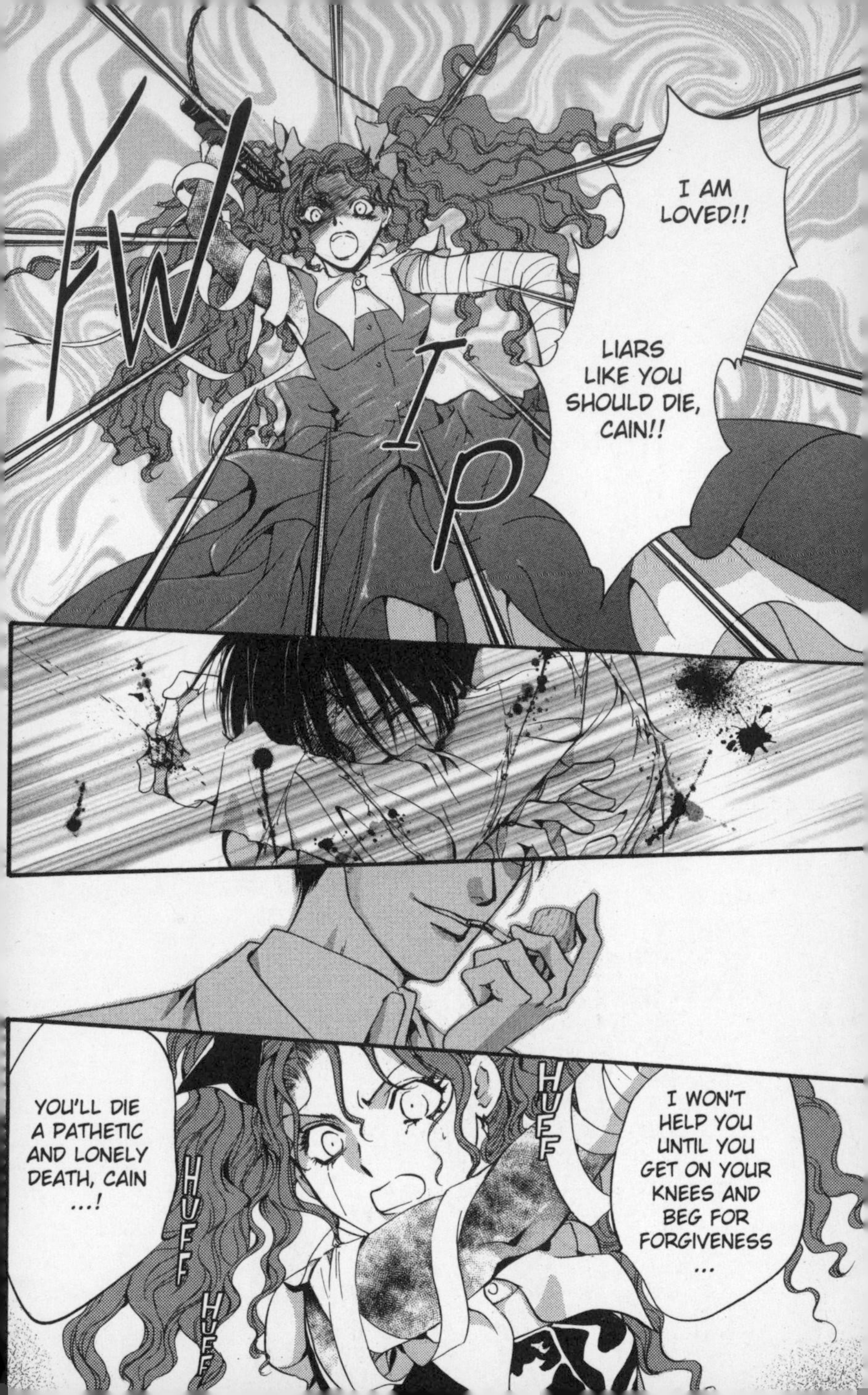
I AM LOVED!!
LIARS LIKE YOU SHOULD DIE, CAIN!!
FWIP
HUFF
I WON'T HELP YOU UNTIL YOU GET ON YOUR KNEES AND BEG FOR FORGIVENESS ...
YOU'LL DIE A PATHETIC AND LONELY DEATH, CAIN ...!
HUFF
HUFF

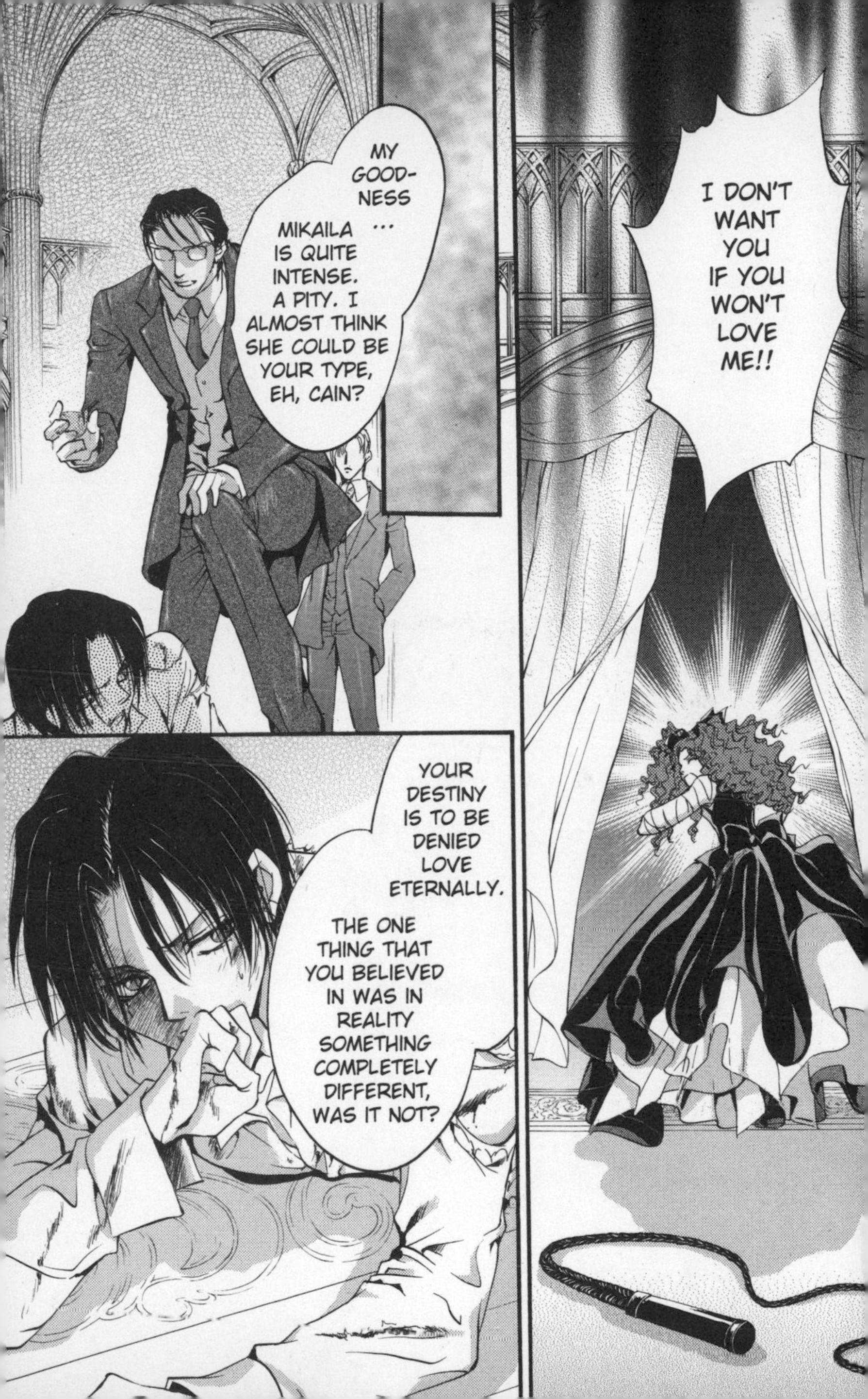
I DON'T WANT YOU IF YOU WON'T LOVE ME!!
MY GOODNESS ... MIKAILA IS QUITE INTENSE.
A PITY. I ALMOST THINK SHE COULD BE YOUR TYPE, EH, CAIN?
YOUR DESTINY IS TO BE DENIED LOVE ETERNALLY.
THE ONE THING THAT YOU BELIEVED IN WAS IN REALITY SOMETHING COMPLETELY DIFFERENT, WAS IT NOT?

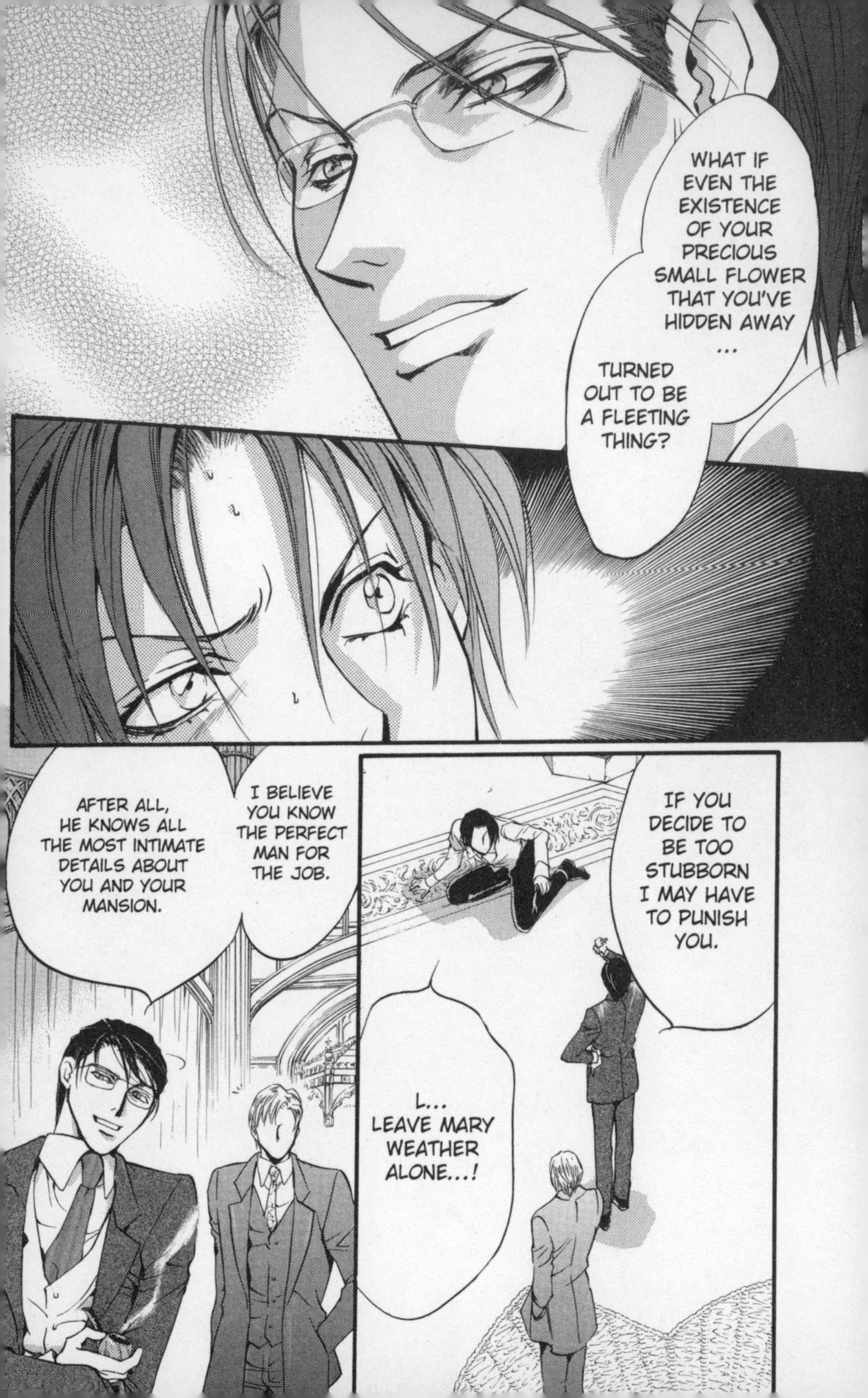
WHAT IF EVEN THE EXISTENCE OF YOUR PRECIOUS SMALL FLOWER THAT YOU'VE HIDDEN AWAY ...
TURNED OUT TO BE A FLEETING THING?
IF YOU DECIDE TO BE TOO STUBBORN I MAY HAVE TO PUNISH YOU.
L... LEAVE MARY WEATHER ALONE...!
I BELIEVE YOU KNOW THE PERFECT MAN FOR THE JOB.
AFTER ALL, HE KNOWS ALL THE MOST INTIMATE DETAILS ABOUT YOU AND YOUR MANSION.

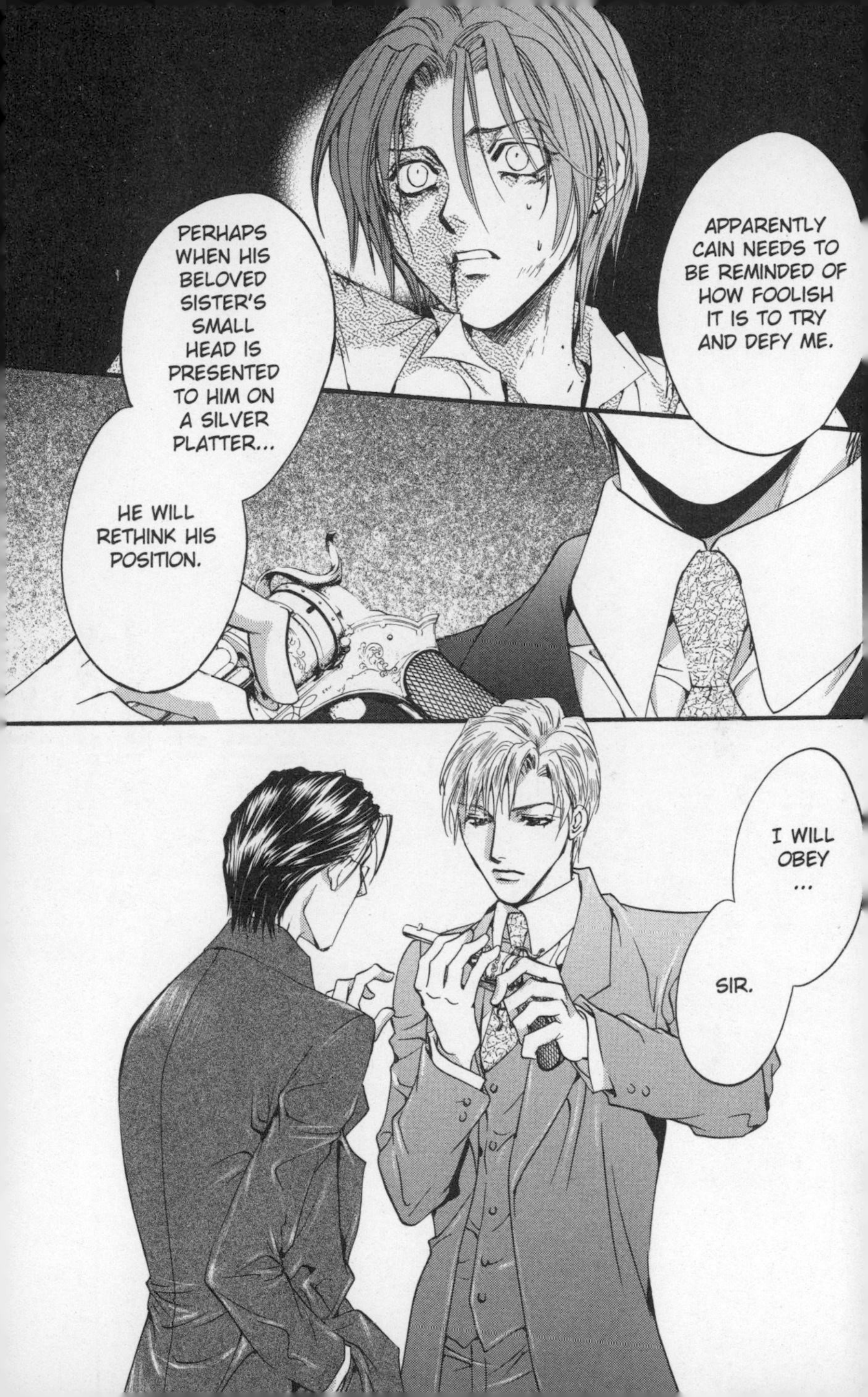
APPARENTLY CAIN NEEDS TO BE REMINDED OF HOW FOOLISH IT IS TO TRY AND DEFY ME.
PERHAPS WHEN HIS BELOVED SISTER'S SMALL HEAD IS PRESENTED TO HIM ON A SILVER PLATTER...
HE WILL RETHINK HIS POSITION.
I WILL OBEY ...
SIR.

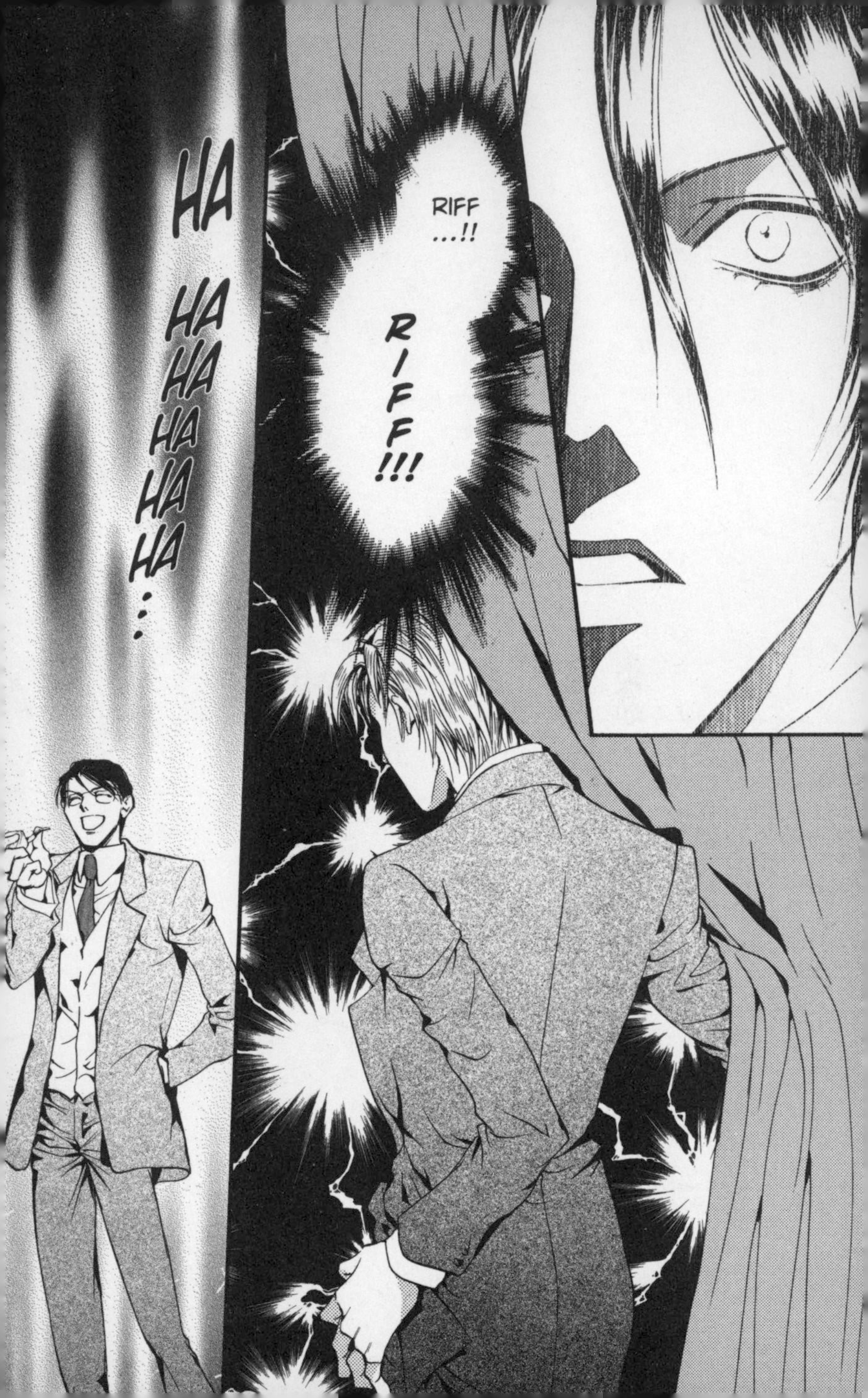
RIFF ...!!
RIFF!!!
HA HA HA HA HA HA HA...

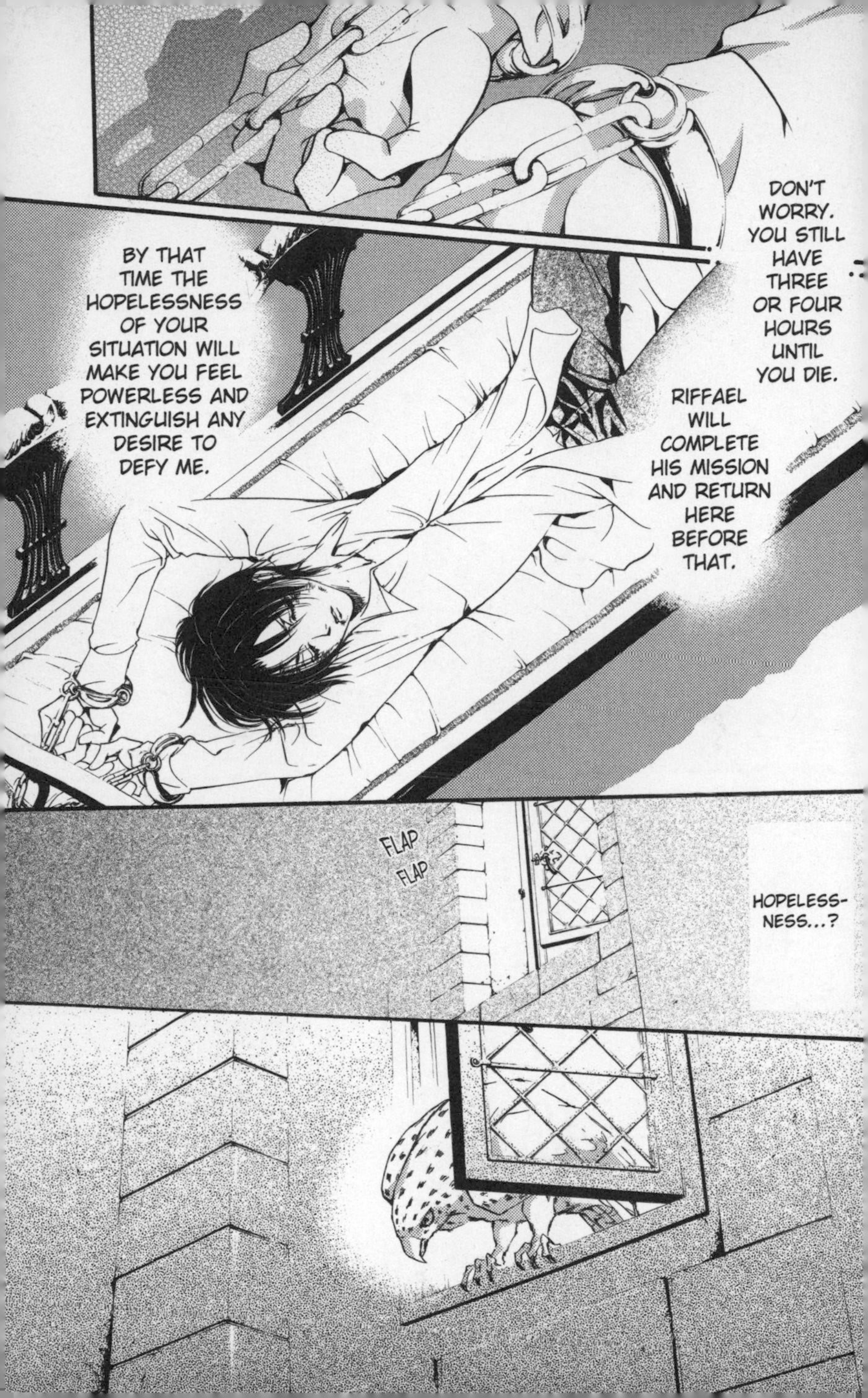
DON'T WORRY. YOU STILL HAVE THREE OR FOUR HOURS UNTIL YOU DIE.
RIFFAEL WILL COMPLETE HIS MISSION AND RETURN HERE BEFORE THAT.
BY THAT TIME THE HOPELESSNESS OF YOUR SITUATION WILL MAKE YOU FEEL POWERLESS AND EXTINGUISH ANY DESIRE TO DEFY ME.
HOPELESS-NESS...?
FLAP FLAP

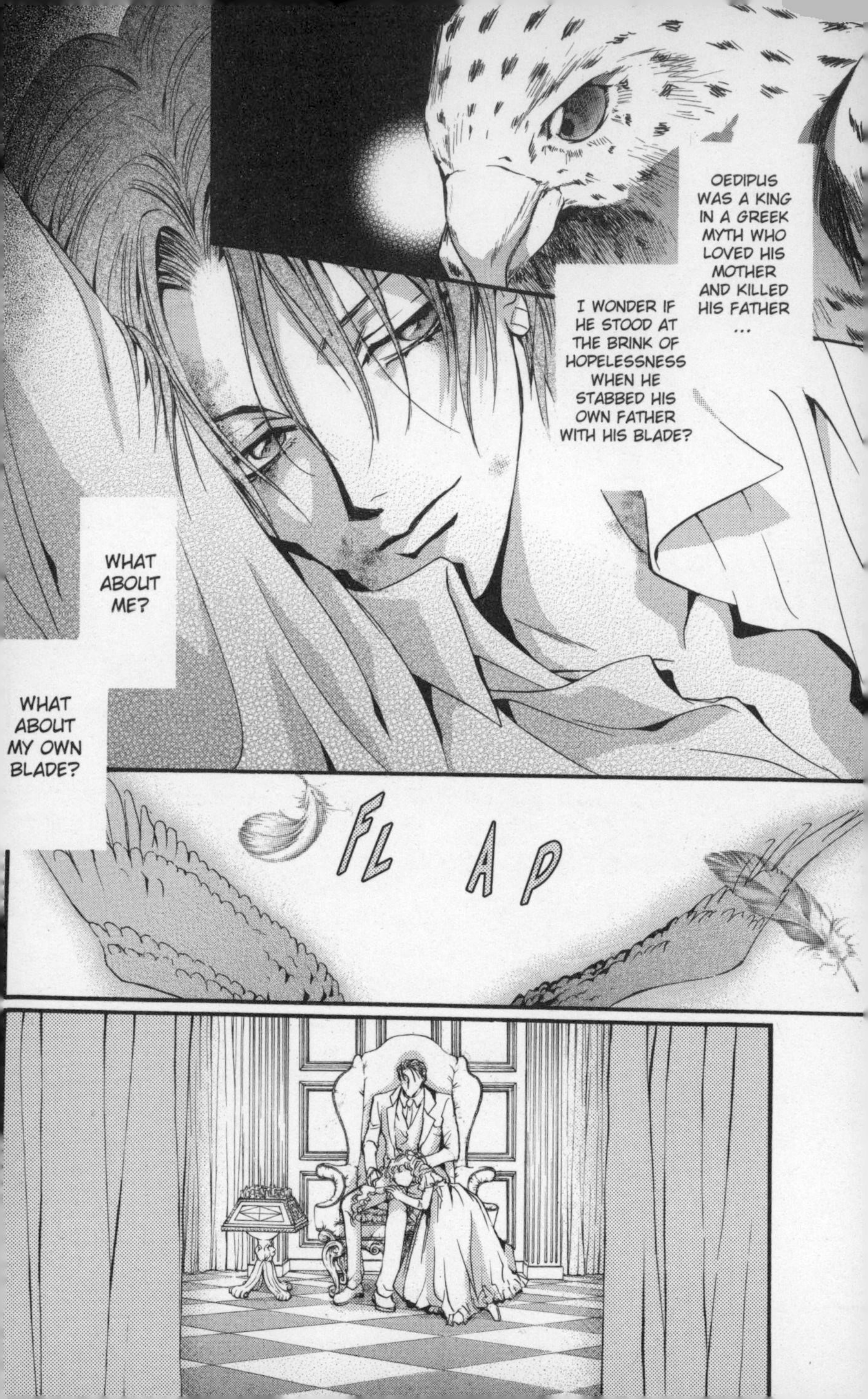
OEDIPUS WAS A KING IN A GREEK MYTH WHO LOVED HIS MOTHER AND KILLED HIS FATHER ...
I WONDER IF HE STOOD AT THE BRINK OF HOPELESSNESS WHEN HE STABBED HIS OWN FATHER WITH HIS BLADE?
WHAT ABOUT ME?
WHAT ABOUT MY OWN BLADE?
FLAP

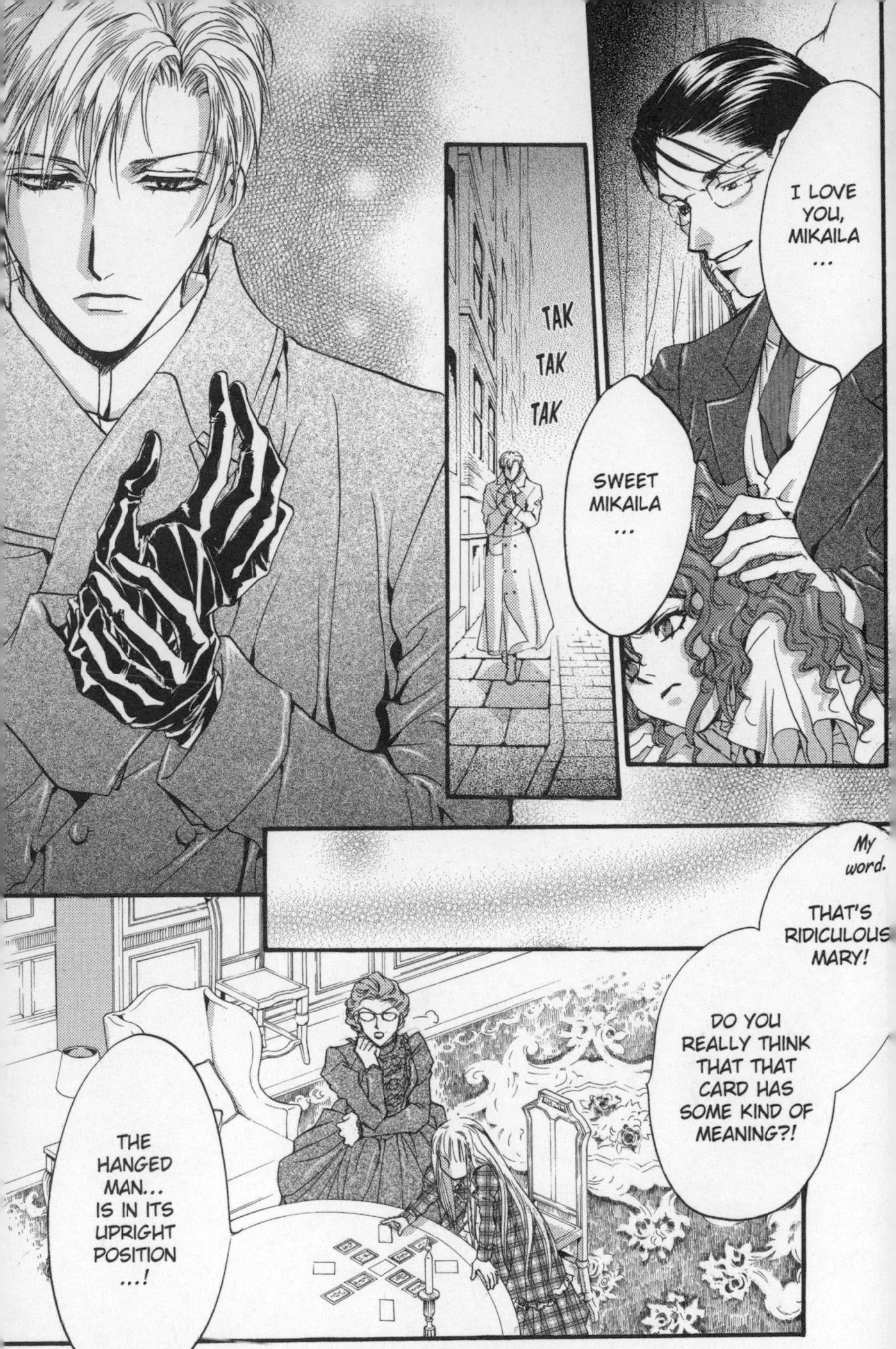
I LOVE YOU, MIKAILA ...
SWEET MIKAILA ...
TAK
TAK
TAK
My word.
THAT'S RIDICULOUS MARY!
DO YOU REALLY THINK THAT THAT CARD HAS SOME KIND OF MEANING?!
THE HANGED MAN... IS IN ITS UPRIGHT POSITION ...!

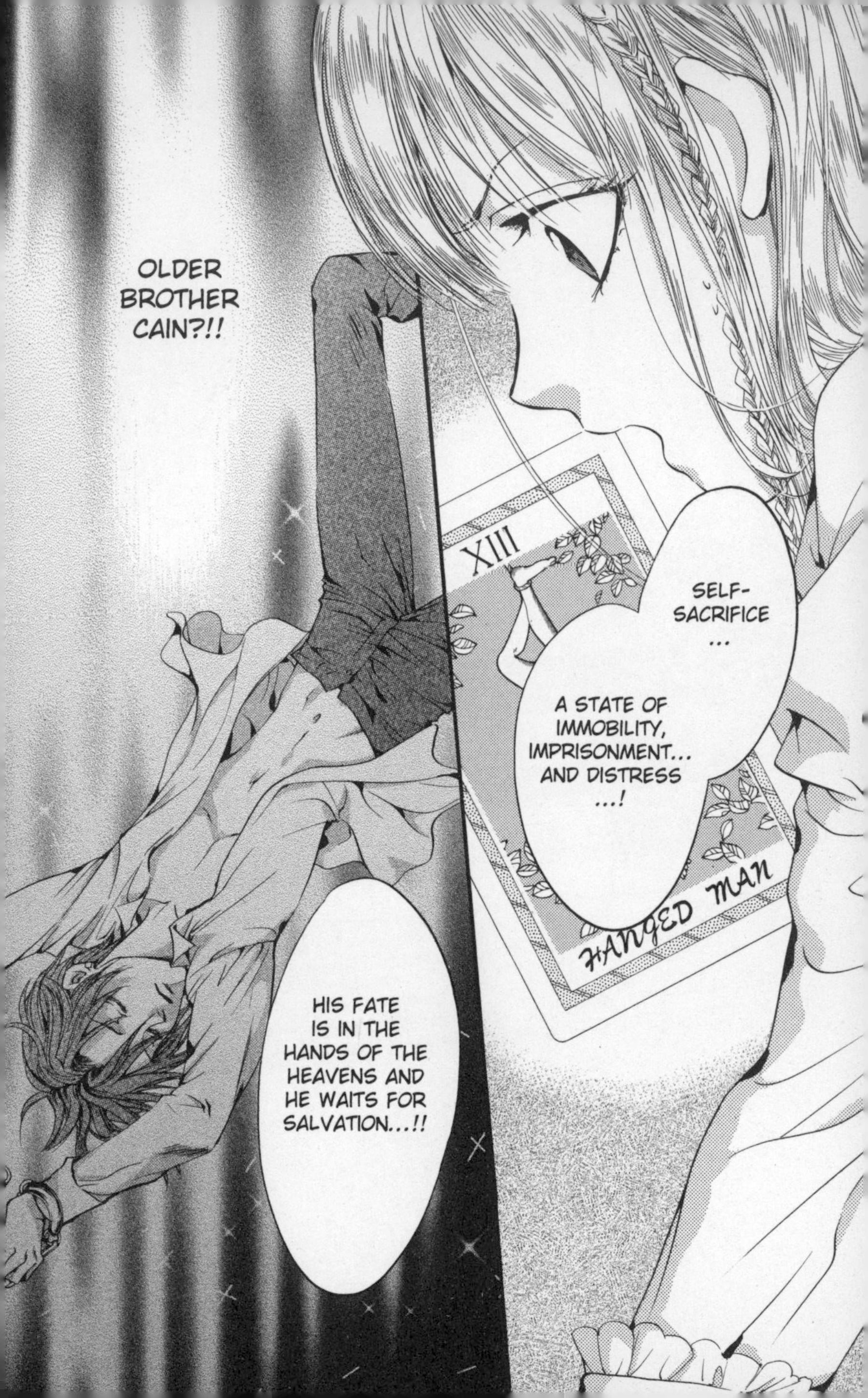
XIII
SELF-SACRIFICE ...
A STATE OF IMMOBILITY, IMPRISONMENT... AND DISTRESS ...!
HANGED MAN
OLDER BROTHER CAIN?!!
HIS FATE IS IN THE HANDS OF THE HEAVENS AND HE WAITS FOR SALVATION...!!

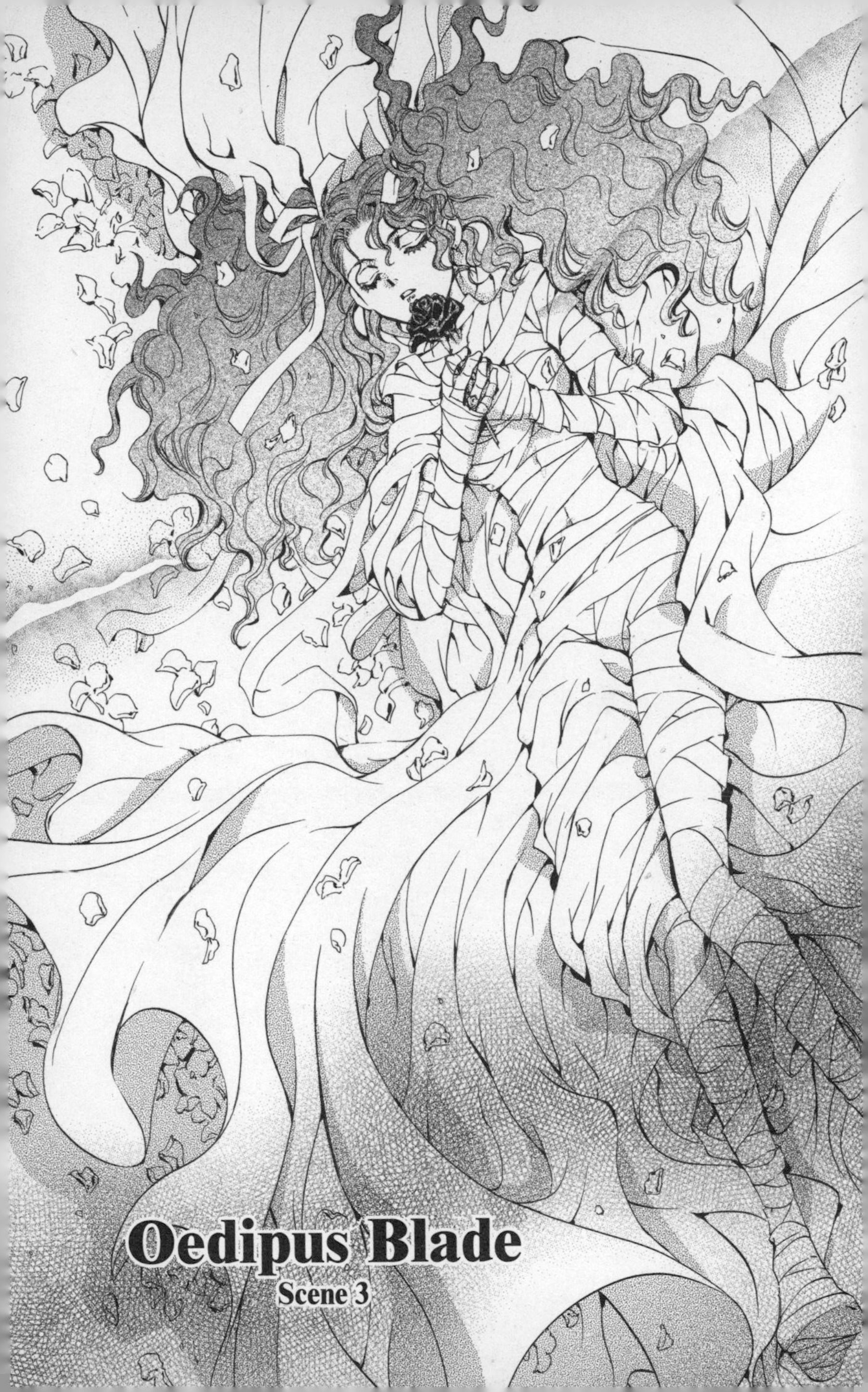
Oedipus Blade
Scene 3

Oedipus Blade

Scene 3

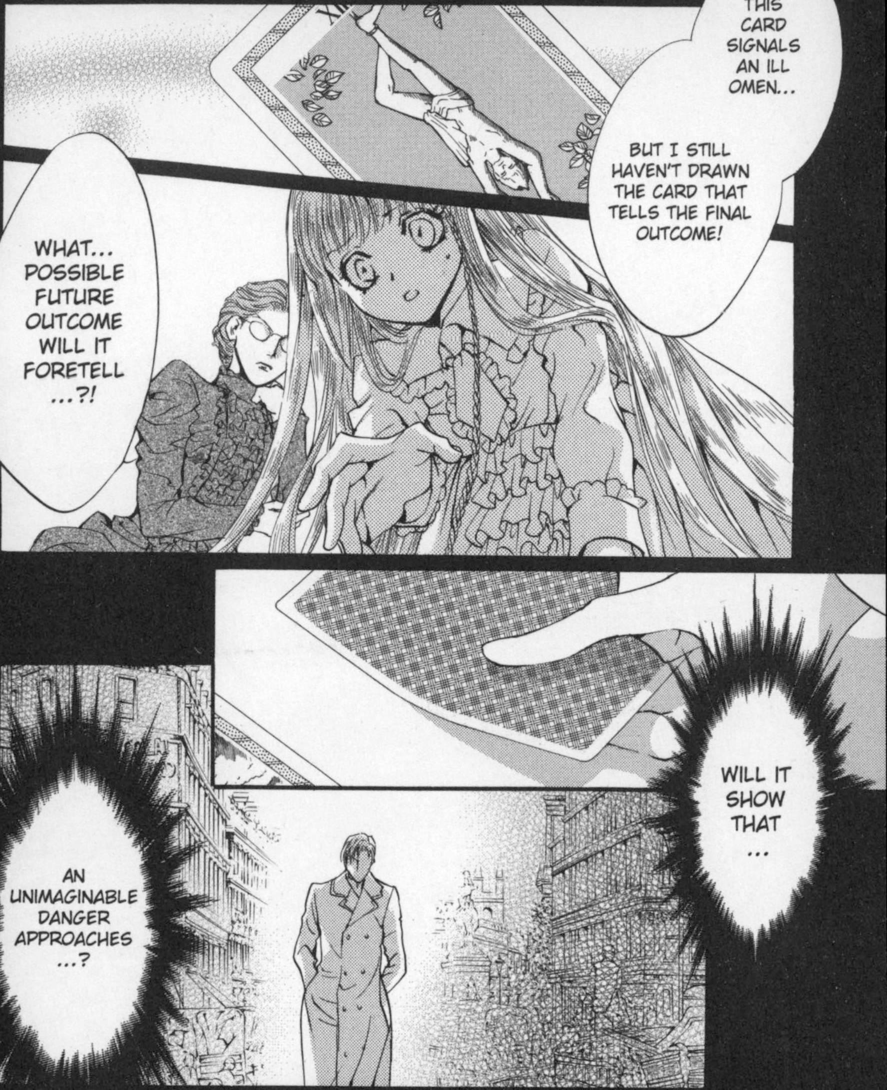
THIS CARD SIGNALS AN ILL OMEN...
BUT I STILL HAVEN'T DRAWN THE CARD THAT TELLS THE FINAL OUTCOME!
WHAT... POSSIBLE FUTURE OUTCOME WILL IT FORETELL ...?!
WILL IT SHOW THAT ...
AN UNIMAGINABLE DANGER APPROACHES ...?

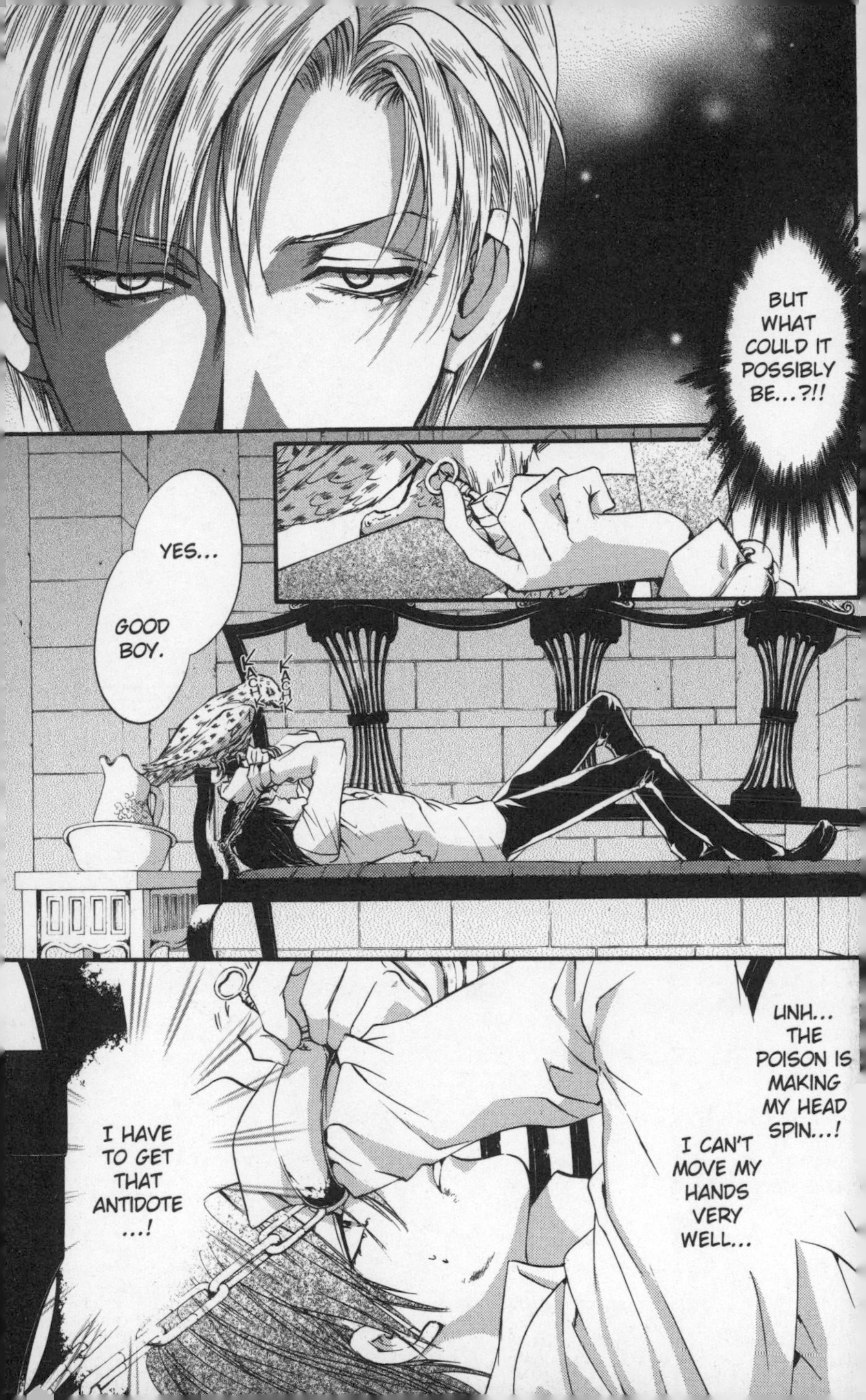
BUT WHAT COULD IT POSSIBLY BE...?!!
YES...
GOOD BOY.
KACHK
KACHK
UNH... THE POISON IS MAKING MY HEAD SPIN...!
I CAN'T MOVE MY HANDS VERY WELL...
I HAVE TO GET THAT ANTIDOTE ...!

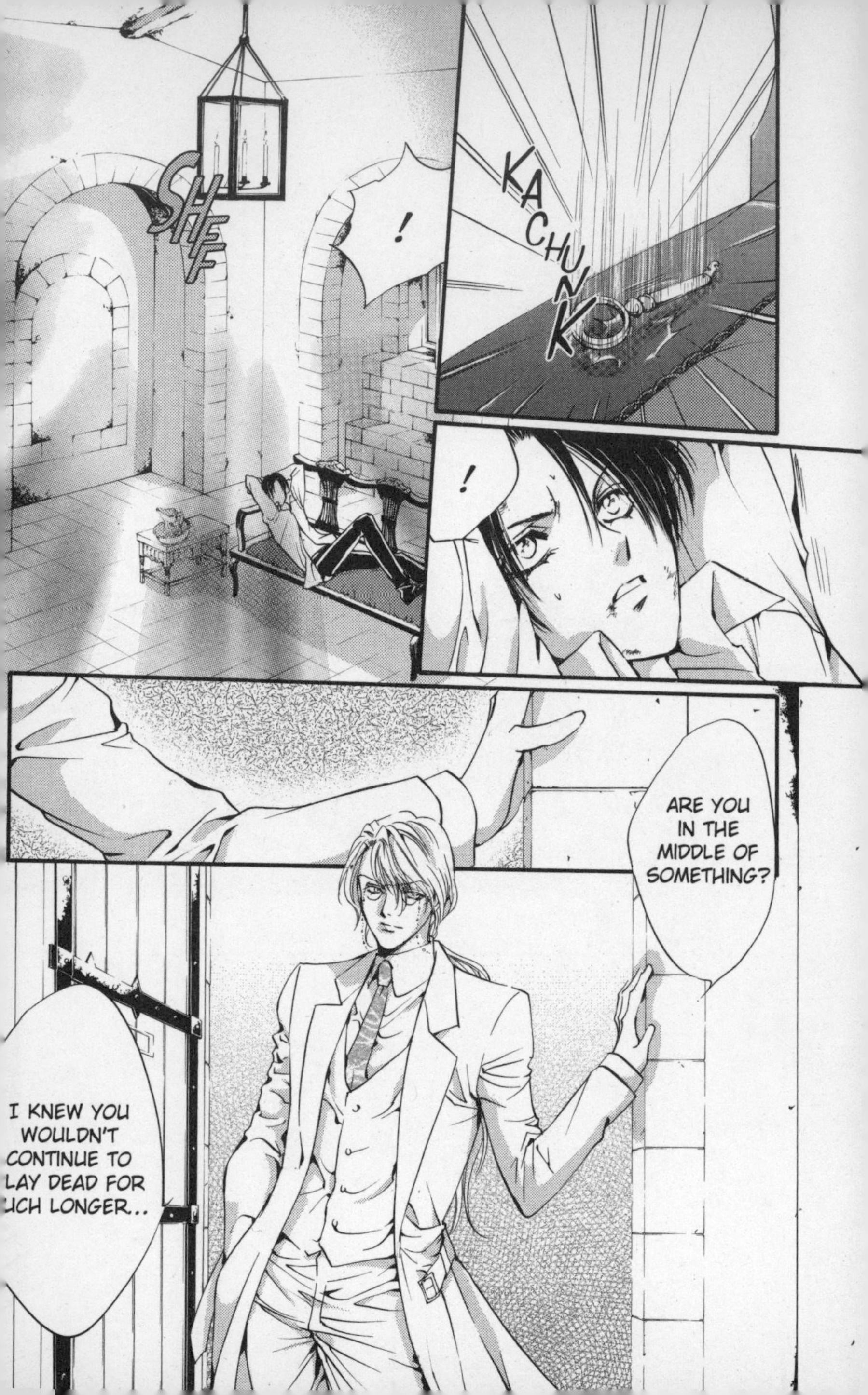
KACHUNK
!
SHFF
!
ARE YOU IN THE MIDDLE OF SOMETHING?
I KNEW YOU WOULDN'T CONTINUE TO LAY DEAD FOR UCH LONGER...

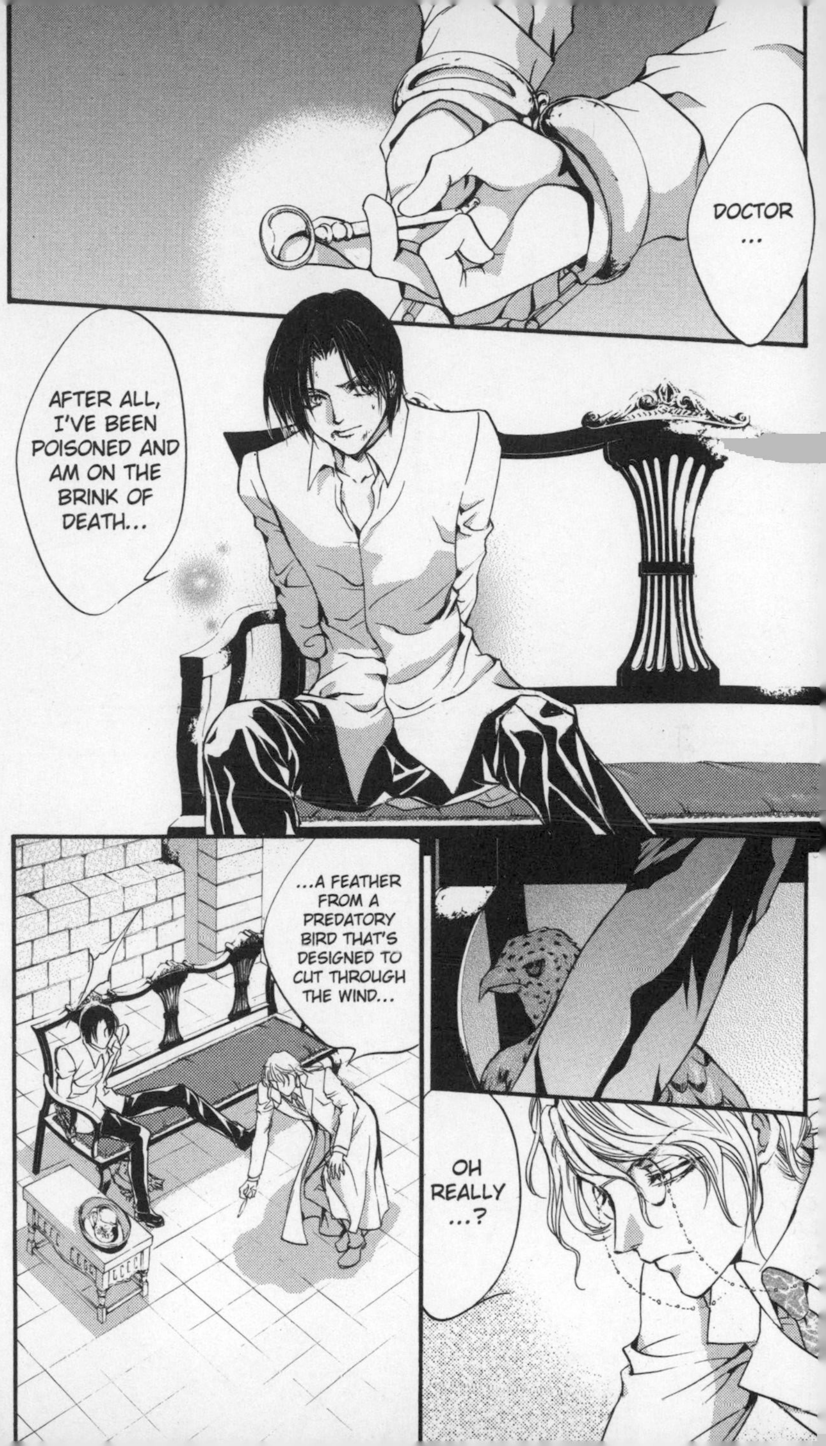
DOCTOR ...
AFTER ALL, I'VE BEEN POISONED AND AM ON THE BRINK OF DEATH...
...A FEATHER FROM A PREDATORY BIRD THAT'S DESIGNED TO CUT THROUGH THE WIND...
OH REALLY ...?

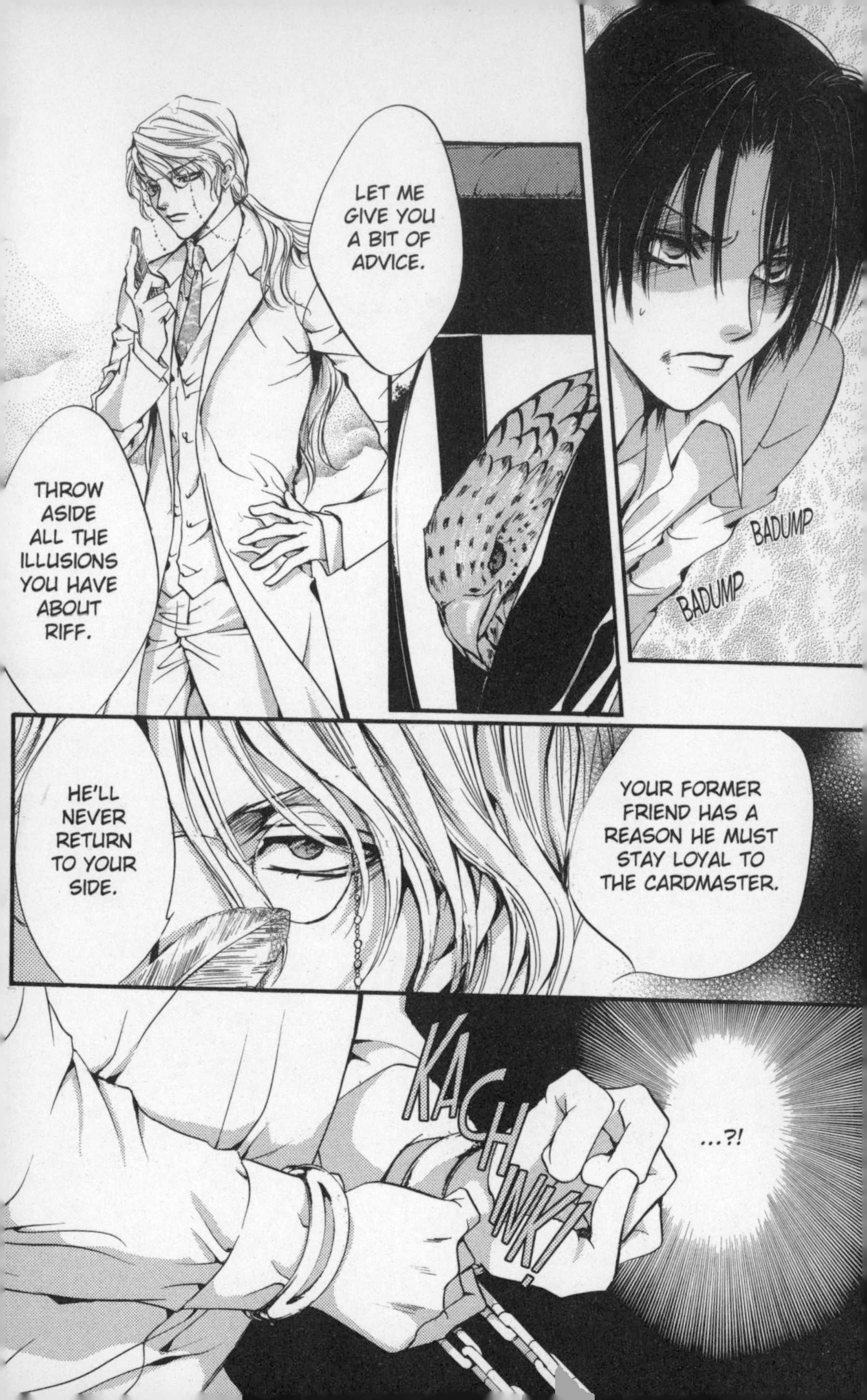
BADUMP
BADUMP
LET ME GIVE YOU A BIT OF ADVICE.
THROW ASIDE ALL THE ILLUSIONS YOU HAVE ABOUT RIFF.
YOUR FORMER FRIEND HAS A REASON HE MUST STAY LOYAL TO THE CARDMASTER.
HE'LL NEVER RETURN TO YOUR SIDE.
KACHINK!
...?!

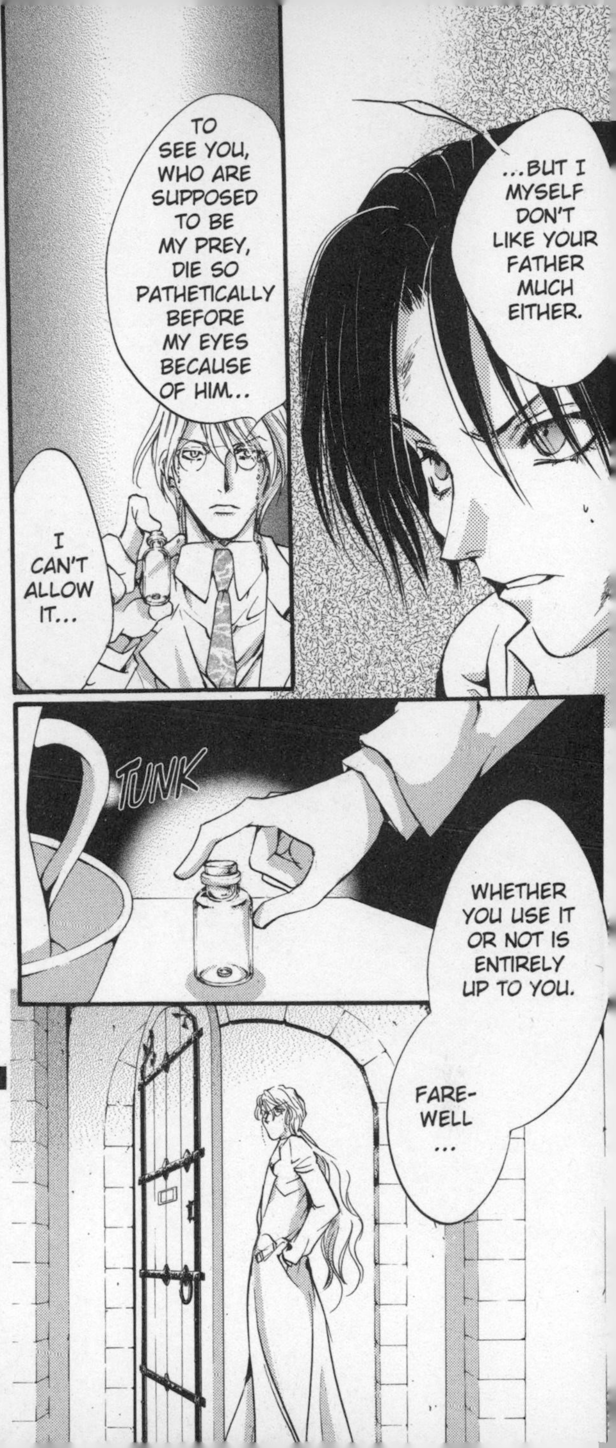
...BUT I MYSELF DON'T LIKE YOUR FATHER MUCH EITHER.
TO SEE YOU, WHO ARE SUPPOSED TO BE MY PREY, DIE SO PATHETICALLY BEFORE MY EYES BECAUSE OF HIM...
I CAN'T ALLOW IT...
TUNK
WHETHER YOU USE IT OR NOT IS ENTIRELY UP TO YOU.
FARE-WELL ...

This has nothing to do with the story, but I haven't repaired my broken computer for a year now... So not being able to do research on the Internet has been a problem. Not to mention getting hints for video games... (I haven't played my Playstation for a long time now. But I did play "Mother" on the Advanced...) But now I really want to do something about that... ♡ The diagrams below are different types of feathers.

The reference material was in hiragana so I don't know if my kanji is correct...

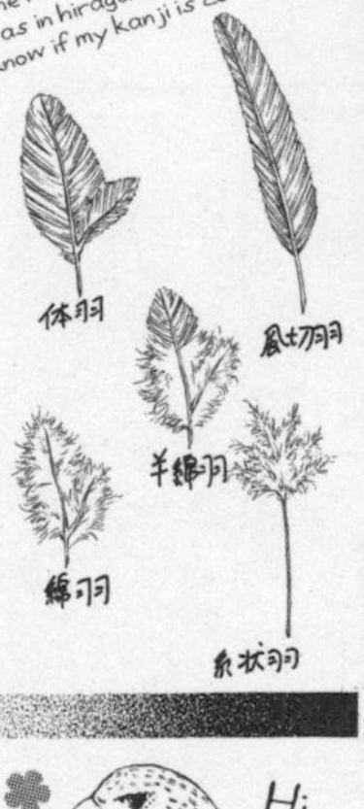
体羽
風切羽
羊綿羽
綿羽
糸状羽

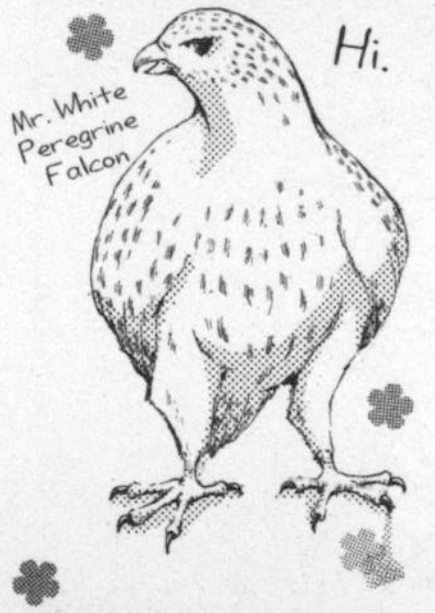
Hi.
Mr. White Peregrine Falcon

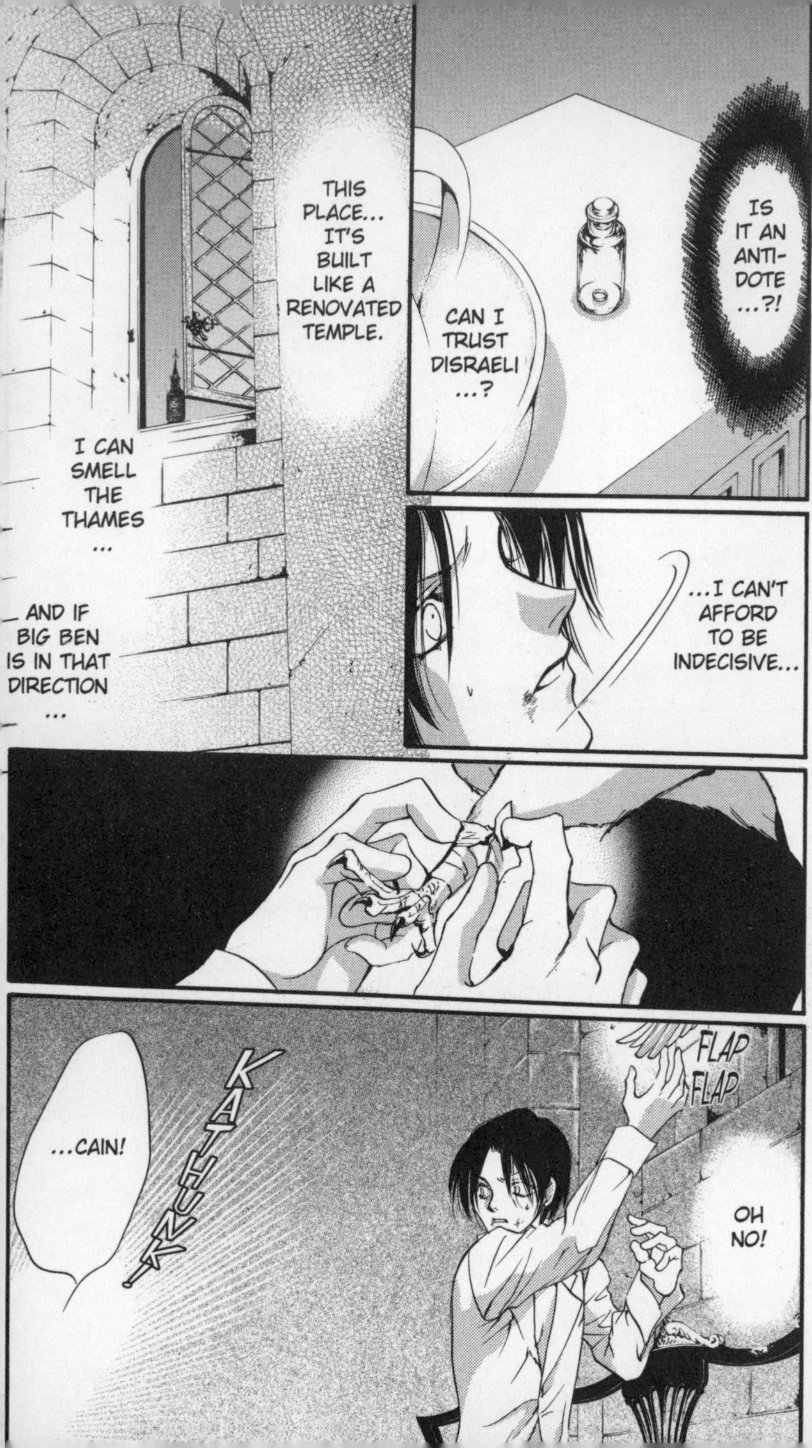

IS IT AN ANTI-DOTE ...?!
CAN I TRUST DISRAELI ...?
...I CAN'T AFFORD TO BE INDECISIVE...
THIS PLACE... IT'S BUILT LIKE A RENOVATED TEMPLE.
I CAN SMELL THE THAMES ...
AND IF BIG BEN IS IN THAT DIRECTION ...
FLAP FLAP
OH NO!
KATHUNK
...CAIN!

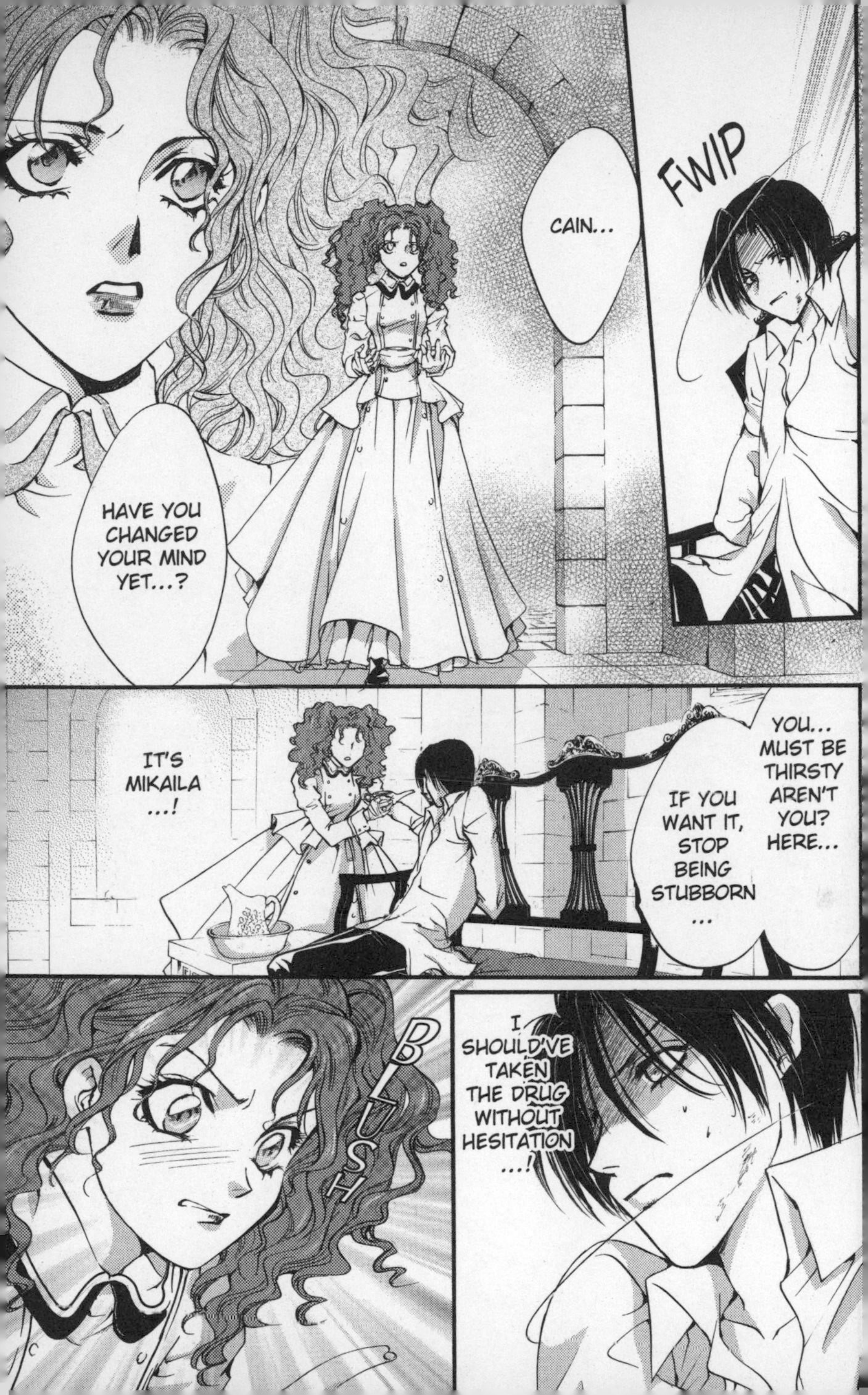
FWIP
CAIN...
HAVE YOU CHANGED YOUR MIND YET...?
YOU... MUST BE THIRSTY AREN'T YOU? HERE...
IF YOU WANT IT, STOP BEING STUBBORN...
IT'S MIKAILA...!
I SHOULD'VE TAKEN THE DRUG WITHOUT HESITATION...!
BLUSH

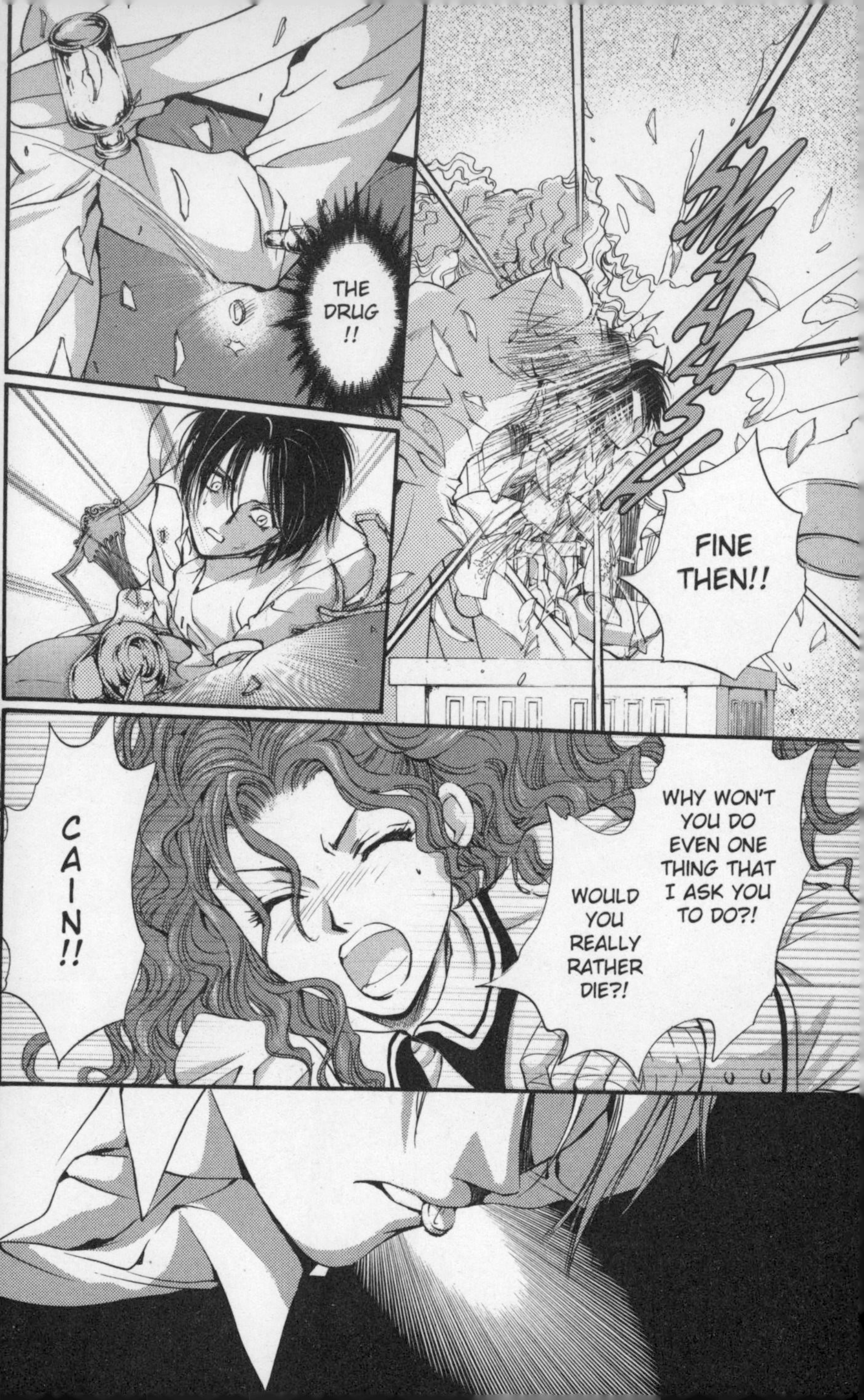
SMAAASH
FINE THEN!!
THE DRUG!!
WHY WON'T YOU DO EVEN ONE THING THAT I ASK YOU TO DO?!
WOULD YOU REALLY RATHER DIE?!
CAIN!!

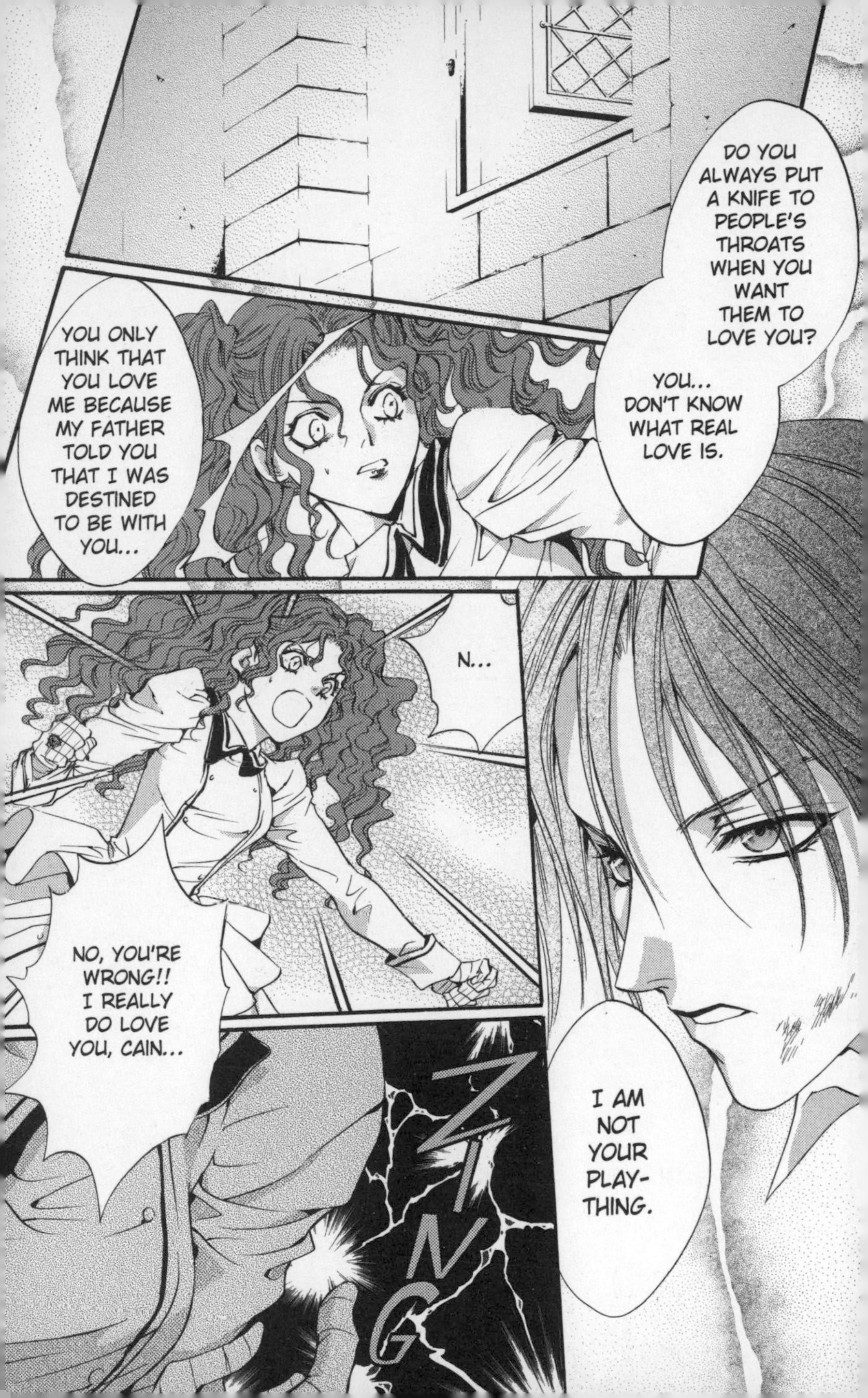
DO YOU ALWAYS PUT A KNIFE TO PEOPLE'S THROATS WHEN YOU WANT THEM TO LOVE YOU?
YOU... DON'T KNOW WHAT REAL LOVE IS.
YOU ONLY THINK THAT YOU LOVE ME BECAUSE MY FATHER TOLD YOU THAT I WAS DESTINED TO BE WITH YOU...
I AM NOT YOUR PLAY-THING.
N...
NO, YOU'RE WRONG!! I REALLY DO LOVE YOU, CAIN...
ZZING

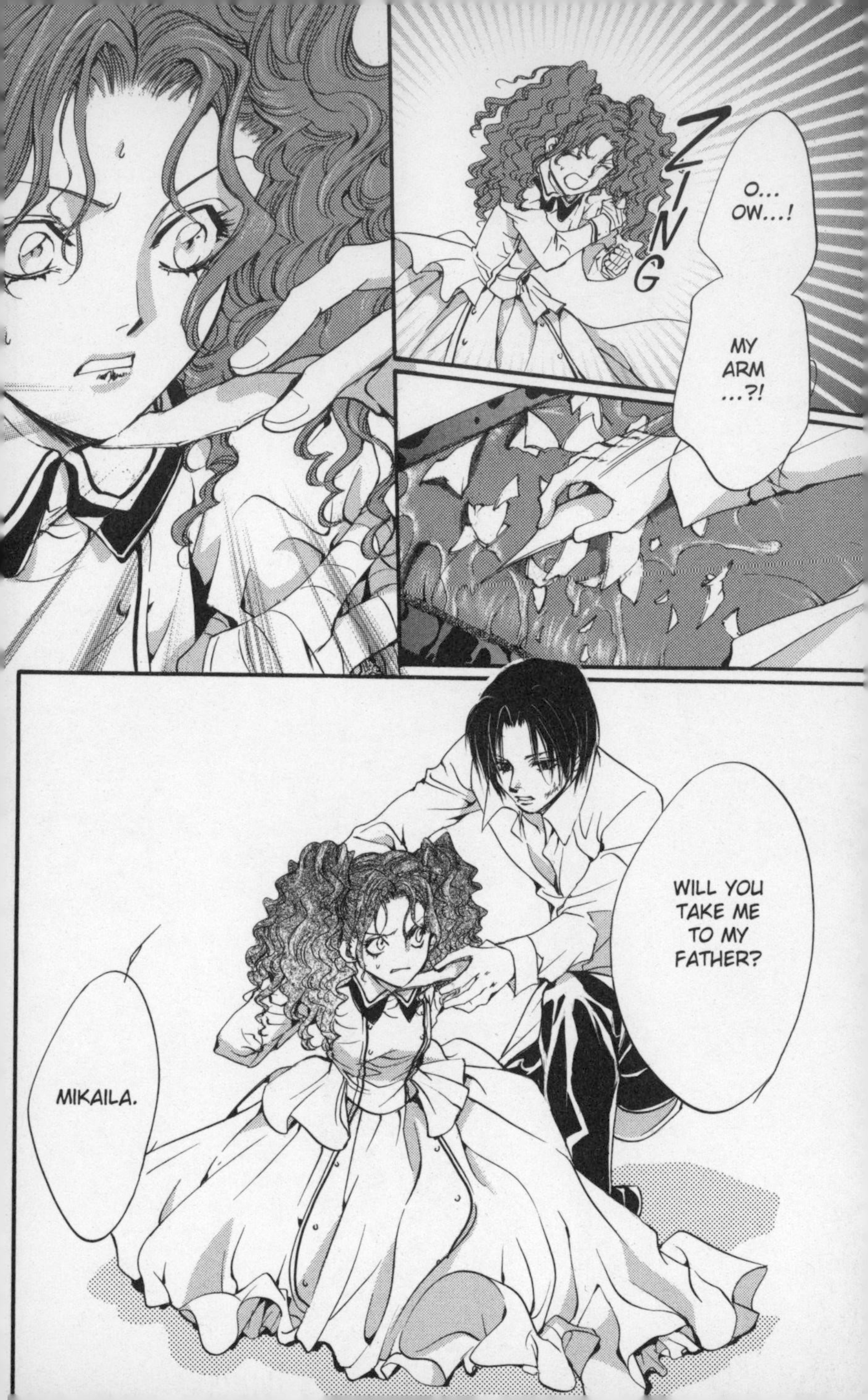
ZING
O... OW...!
MY ARM ...?!
WILL YOU TAKE ME TO MY FATHER?
MIKAILA.

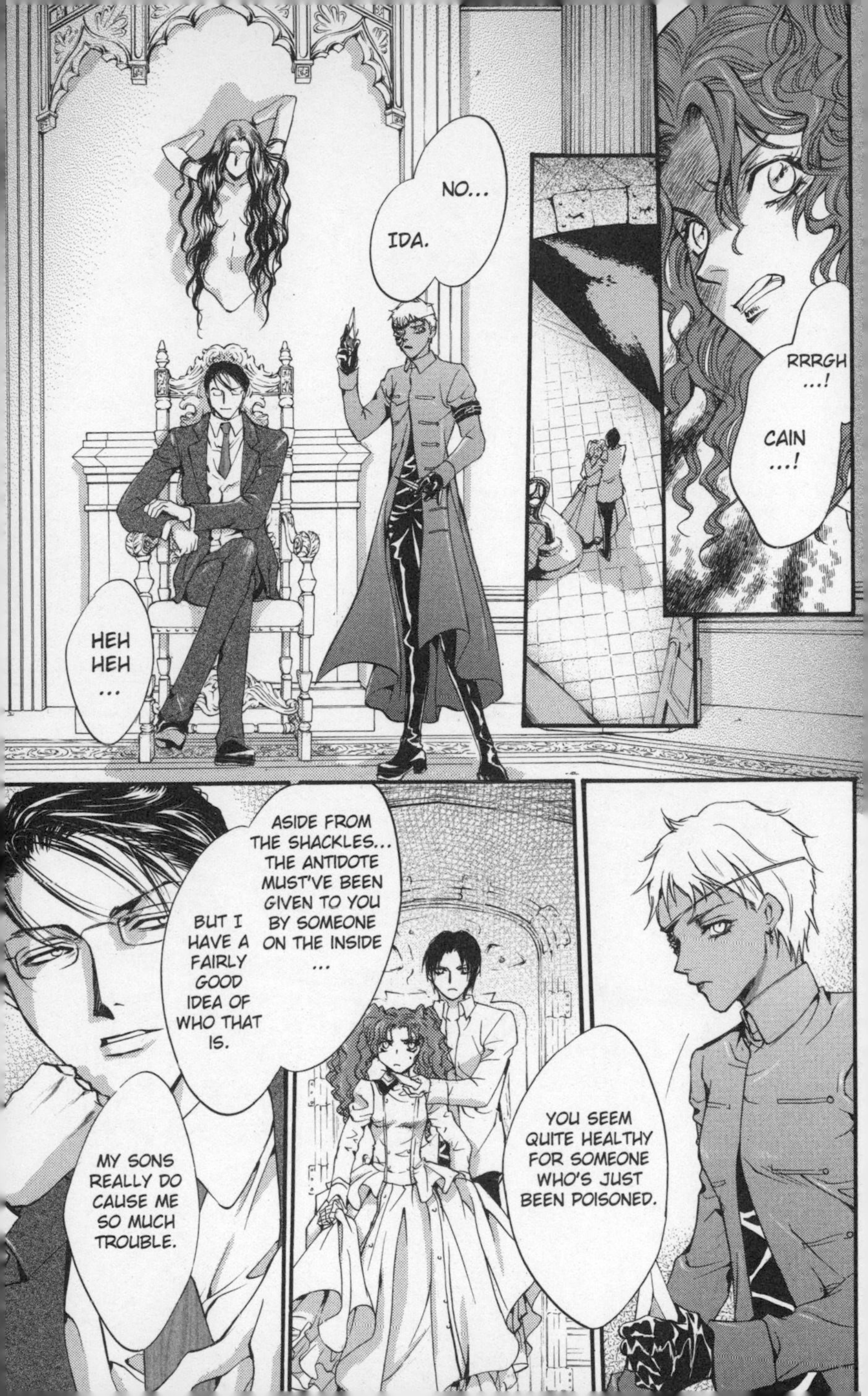
RRRGH ...!
CAIN ...!
NO...
IDA.
HEH HEH ...
YOU SEEM QUITE HEALTHY FOR SOMEONE WHO'S JUST BEEN POISONED.
ASIDE FROM THE SHACKLES... THE ANTIDOTE MUST'VE BEEN GIVEN TO YOU BY SOMEONE ON THE INSIDE ...
BUT I HAVE A FAIRLY GOOD IDEA OF WHO THAT IS.
MY SONS REALLY DO CAUSE ME SO MUCH TROUBLE.

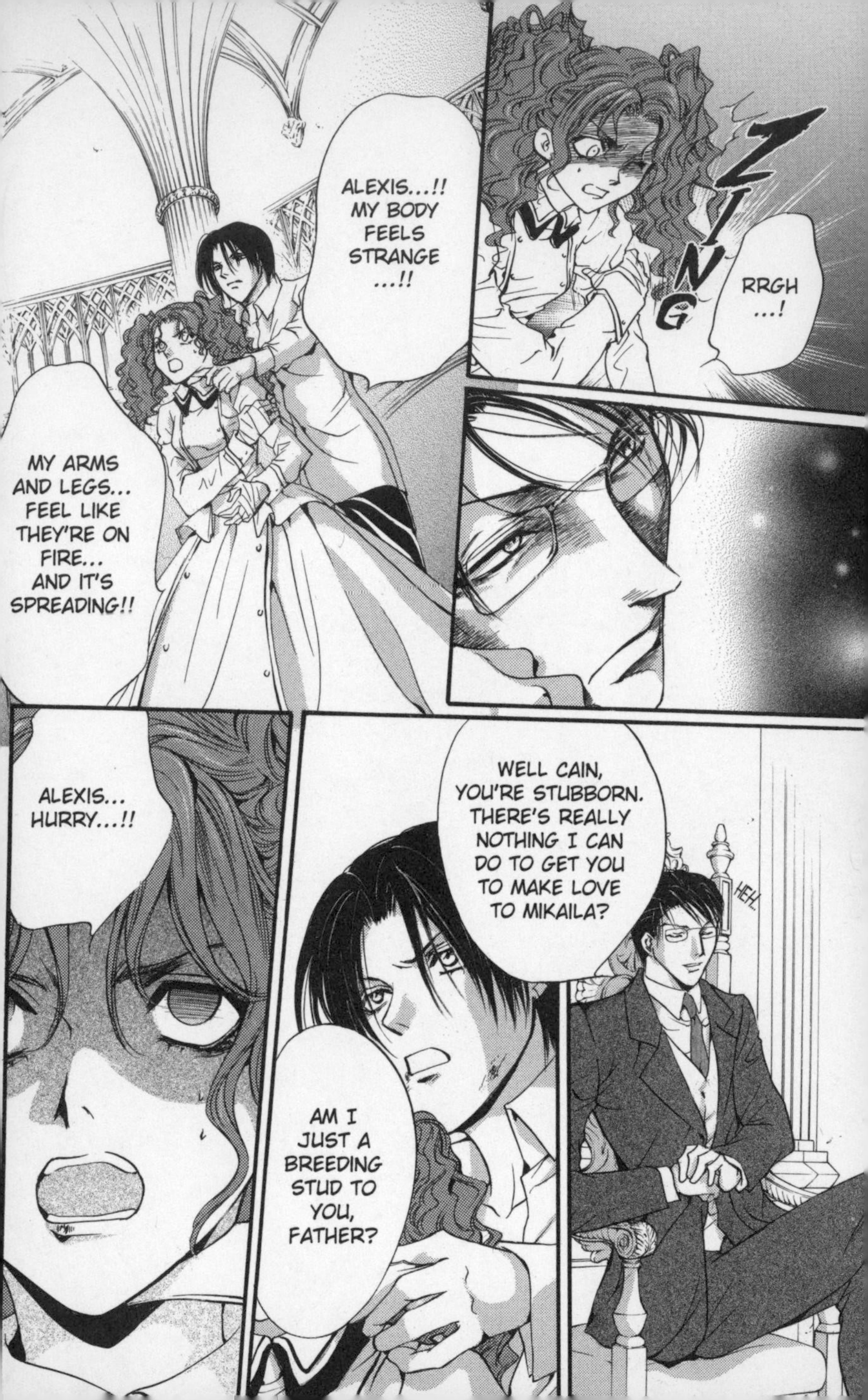
RRGH ...!
ZING
ALEXIS...!! MY BODY FEELS STRANGE ...!!
MY ARMS AND LEGS... FEEL LIKE THEY'RE ON FIRE... AND IT'S SPREADING!!
WELL CAIN, YOU'RE STUBBORN. THERE'S REALLY NOTHING I CAN DO TO GET YOU TO MAKE LOVE TO MIKAILA?
HEH.
AM I JUST A BREEDING STUD TO YOU, FATHER?
ALEXIS... HURRY...!!

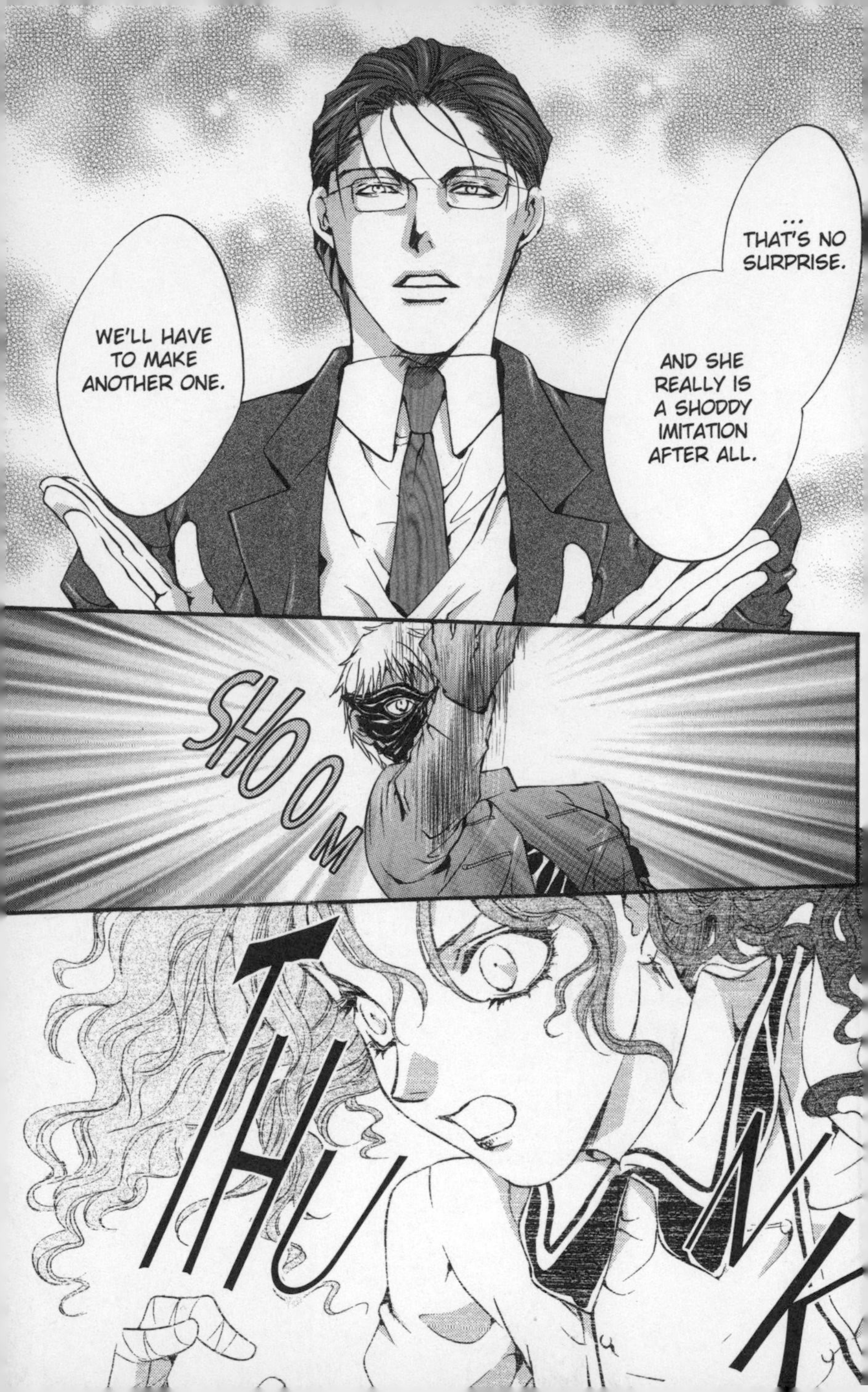
... THAT'S NO SURPRISE.
AND SHE REALLY IS A SHODDY IMITATION AFTER ALL.
WE'LL HAVE TO MAKE ANOTHER ONE.
SHOOM
THUNK

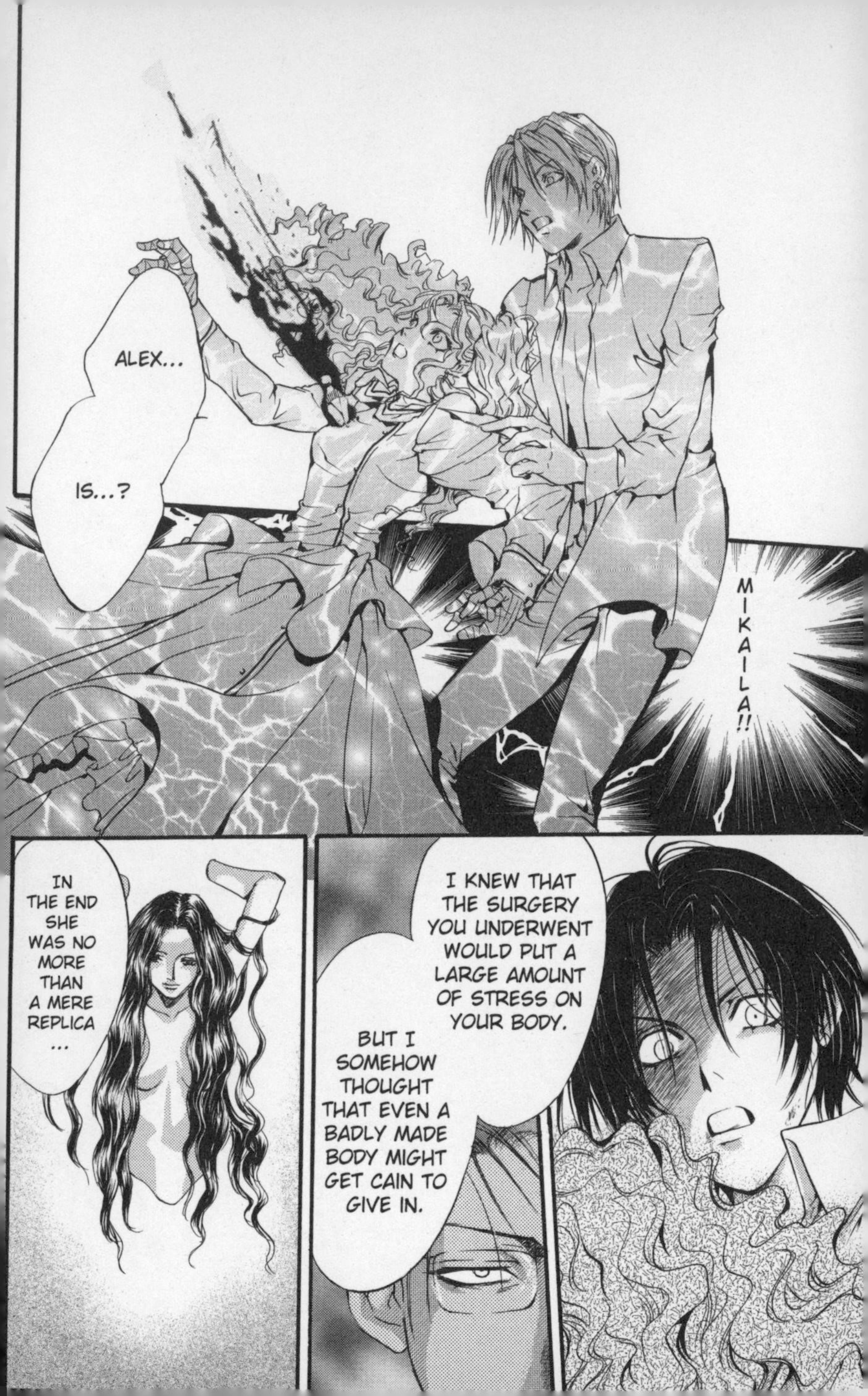
MIKAILA!!
ALEX... IS...?
I KNEW THAT THE SURGERY YOU UNDERWENT WOULD PUT A LARGE AMOUNT OF STRESS ON YOUR BODY.
BUT I SOMEHOW THOUGHT THAT EVEN A BADLY MADE BODY MIGHT GET CAIN TO GIVE IN.
IN THE END SHE WAS NO MORE THAN A MERE REPLICA ...

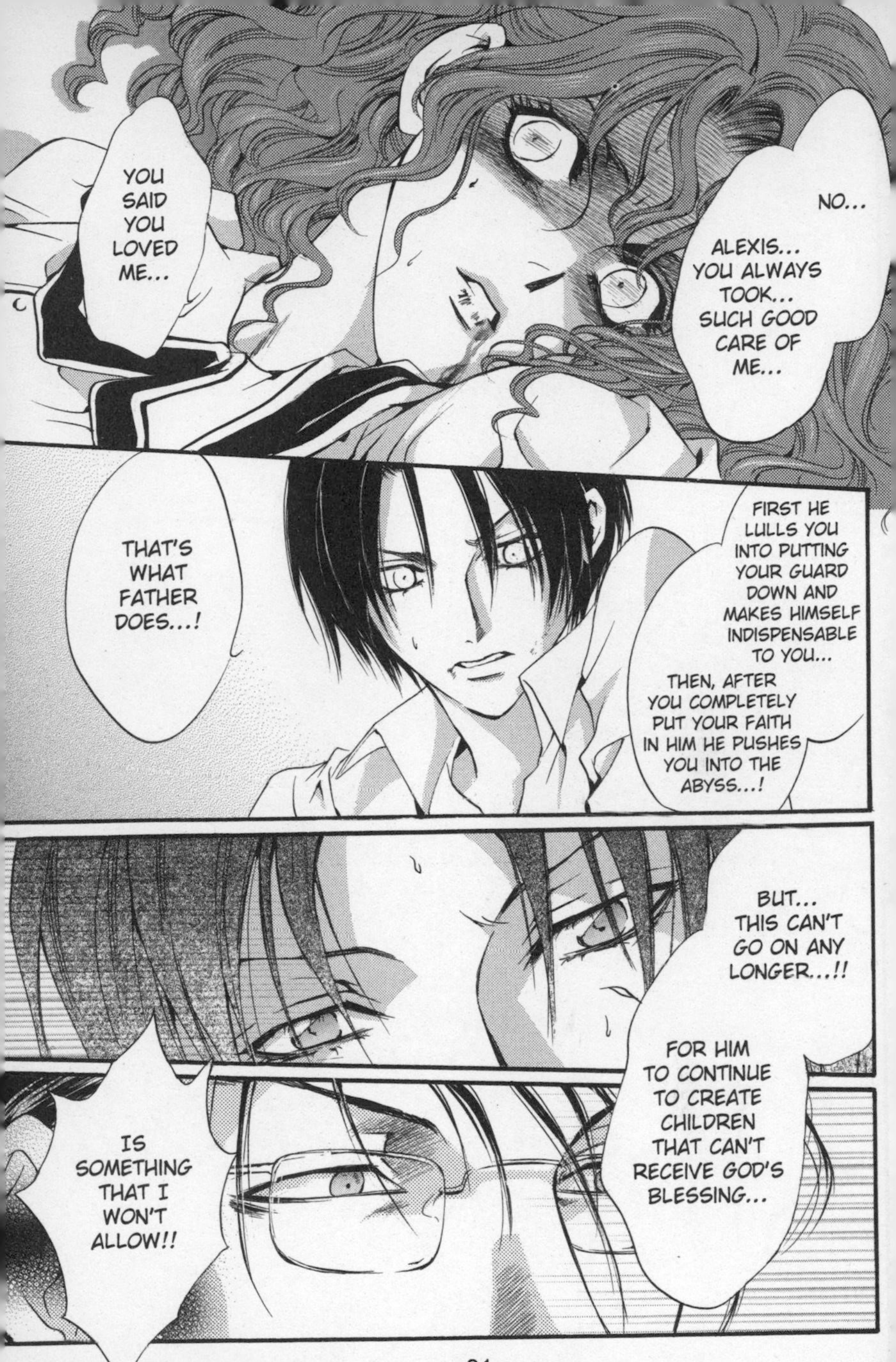
NO...
ALEXIS... YOU ALWAYS TOOK... SUCH GOOD CARE OF ME...
YOU SAID YOU LOVED ME...
FIRST HE LULLS YOU INTO PUTTING YOUR GUARD DOWN AND MAKES HIMSELF INDISPENSABLE TO YOU...
THEN, AFTER YOU COMPLETELY PUT YOUR FAITH IN HIM HE PUSHES YOU INTO THE ABYSS...!
THAT'S WHAT FATHER DOES...!
BUT... THIS CAN'T GO ON ANY LONGER...!!
FOR HIM TO CONTINUE TO CREATE CHILDREN THAT CAN'T RECEIVE GOD'S BLESSING...
IS SOMETHING THAT I WON'T ALLOW!!

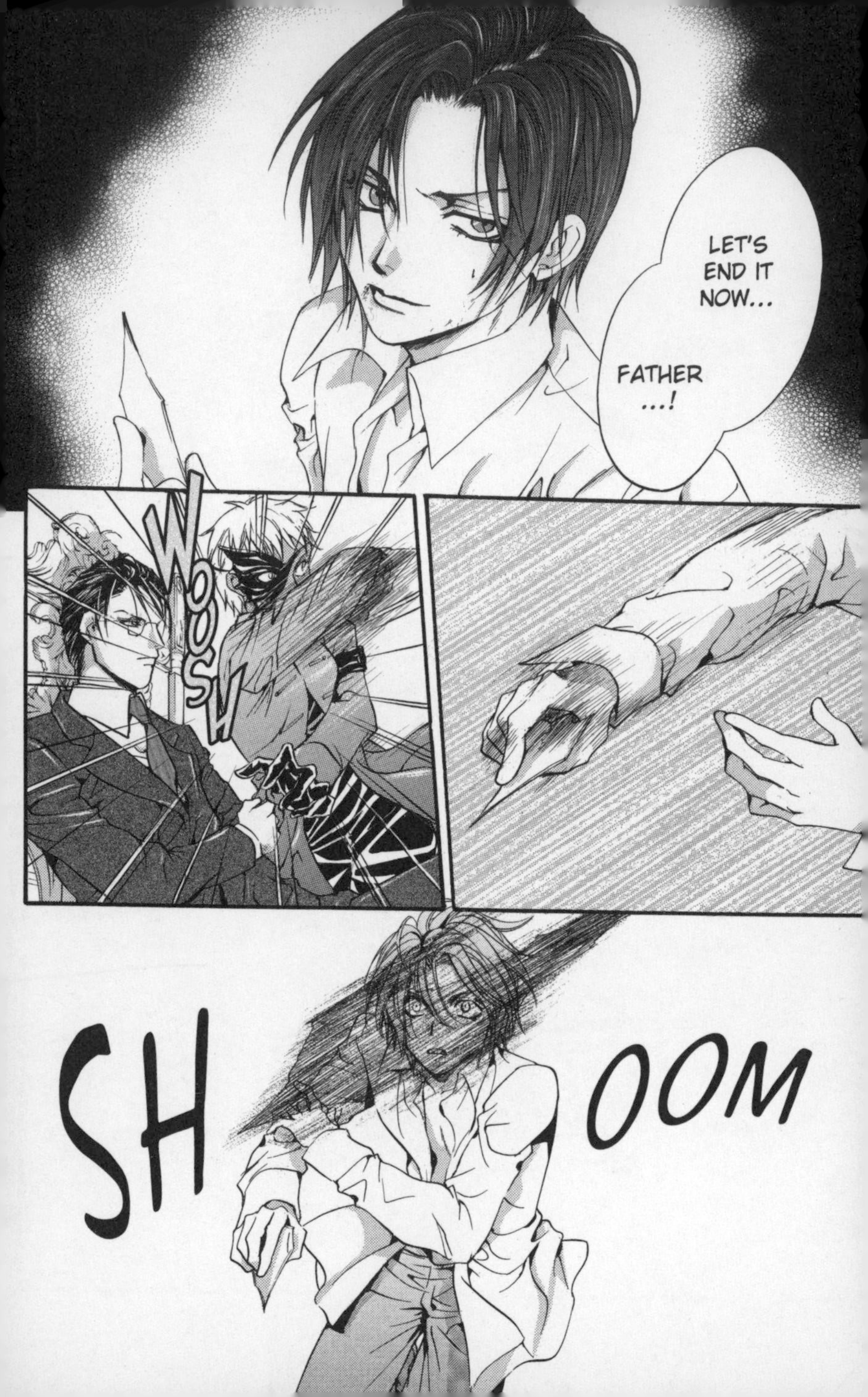
LET'S END IT NOW...
FATHER ...!
WOOSH
SH OOM

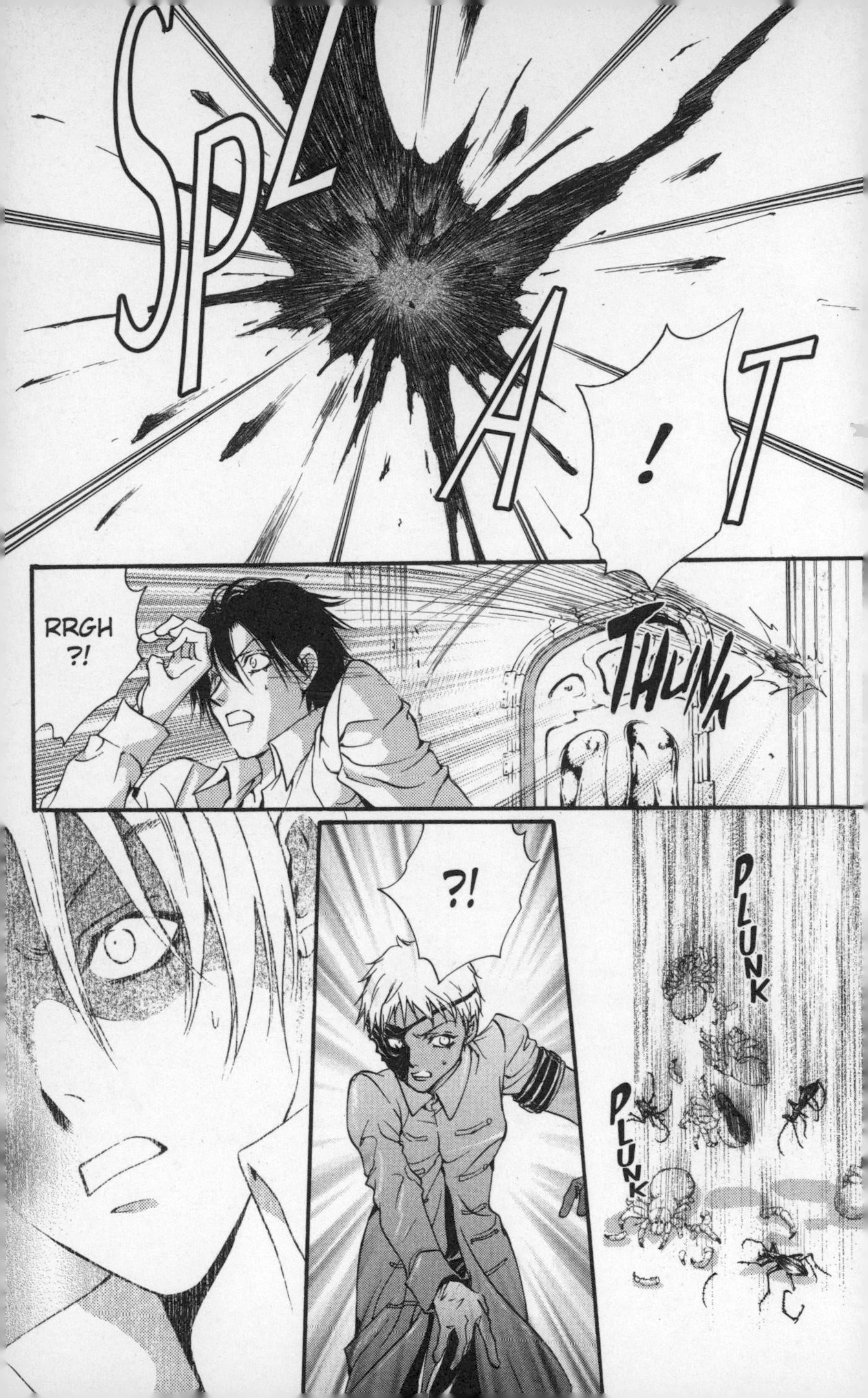
SPLAT
!
THUNK
RRGH ?!
PLUNK
PLUNK
?!

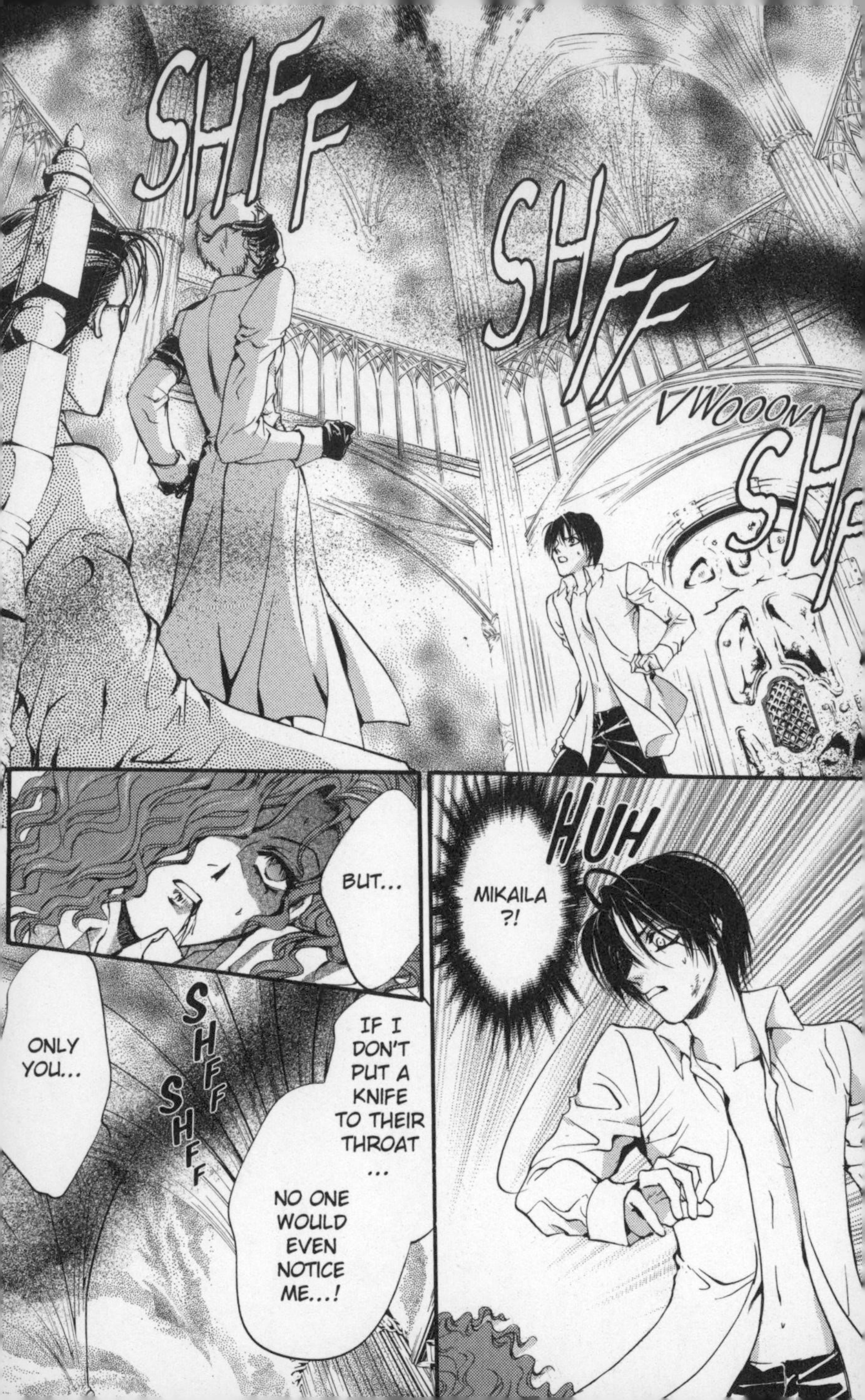
SHF
VWOOON
SHFF
SHFF
HUH
MIKAILA ?!
BUT...
IF I DON'T PUT A KNIFE TO THEIR THROAT ...
NO ONE WOULD EVEN NOTICE ME...!
SHFF
SHFF
ONLY YOU...

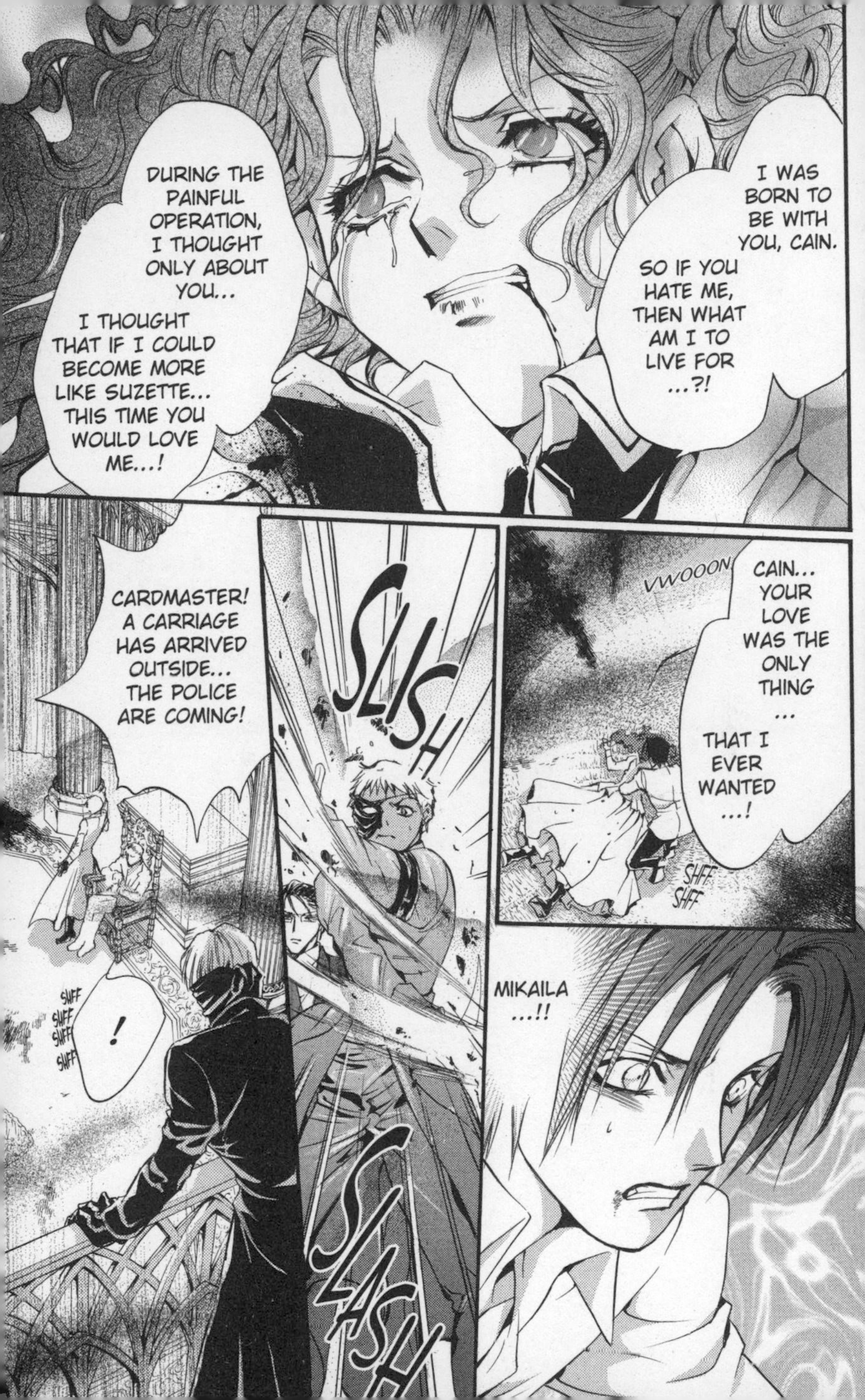
I WAS BORN TO BE WITH YOU, CAIN.
SO IF YOU HATE ME, THEN WHAT AM I TO LIVE FOR ...?!
DURING THE PAINFUL OPERATION, I THOUGHT ONLY ABOUT YOU...
I THOUGHT THAT IF I COULD BECOME MORE LIKE SUZETTE... THIS TIME YOU WOULD LOVE ME...!
VWOOON
CAIN... YOUR LOVE WAS THE ONLY THING ...
THAT I EVER WANTED ...!
SHFF SHFF
MIKAILA ...!!
SLISH
SLASH
CARDMASTER! A CARRIAGE HAS ARRIVED OUTSIDE... THE POLICE ARE COMING!
SHFF SHFF SHFF SHFF
!

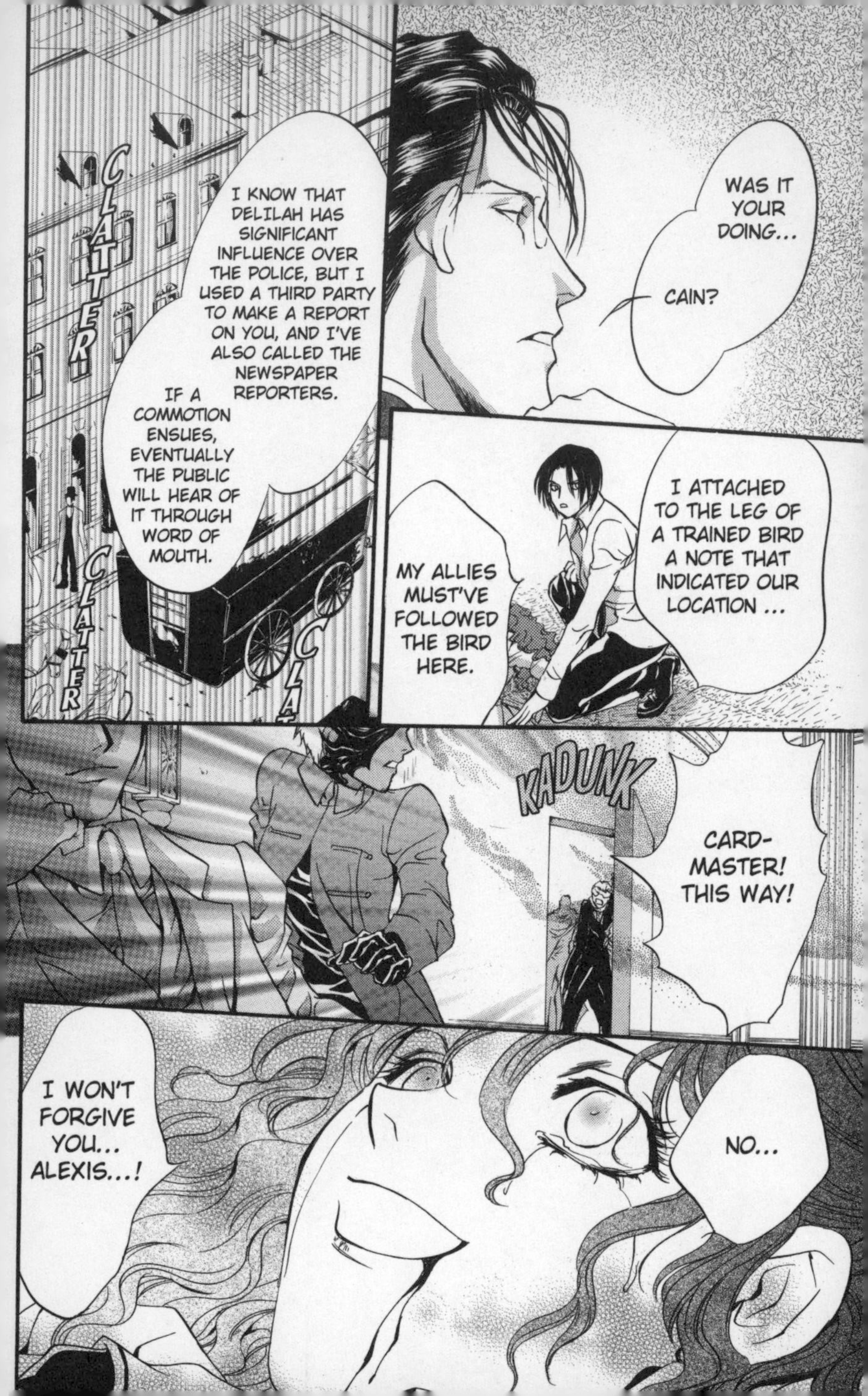
WAS IT YOUR DOING...
CAIN?
I ATTACHED TO THE LEG OF A TRAINED BIRD A NOTE THAT INDICATED OUR LOCATION ...
MY ALLIES MUST'VE FOLLOWED THE BIRD HERE.
CLATTER
I KNOW THAT DELILAH HAS SIGNIFICANT INFLUENCE OVER THE POLICE, BUT I USED A THIRD PARTY TO MAKE A REPORT ON YOU, AND I'VE ALSO CALLED THE NEWSPAPER REPORTERS.
IF A COMMOTION ENSUES, EVENTUALLY THE PUBLIC WILL HEAR OF IT THROUGH WORD OF MOUTH.
CLATTER
CLAT
KADUNK
CARD-MASTER! THIS WAY!
NO...
I WON'T FORGIVE YOU... ALEXIS...!

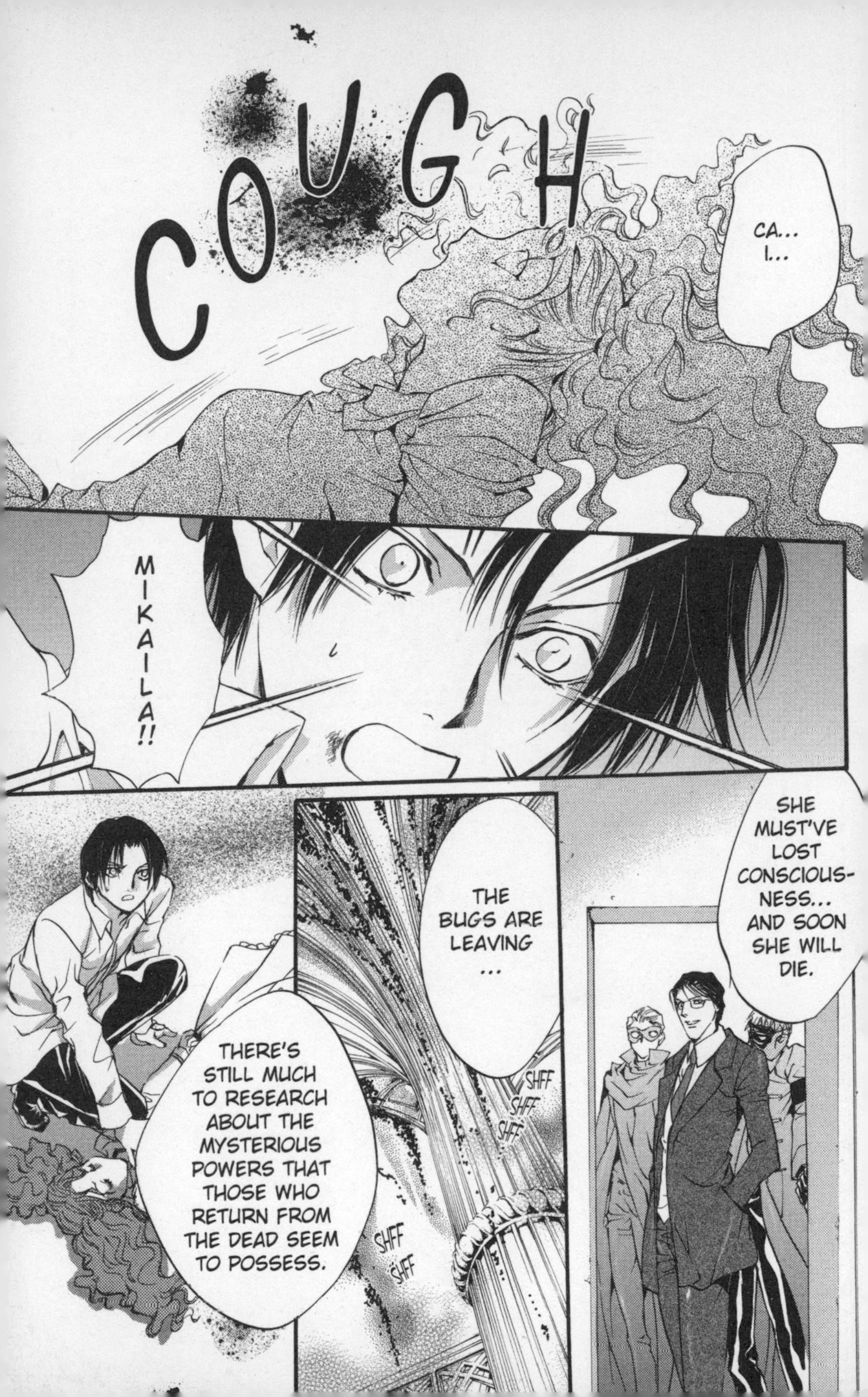
CA... I...
COUGH
MIKAILA!!
SHE MUST'VE LOST CONSCIOUS-NESS... AND SOON SHE WILL DIE.
THE BUGS ARE LEAVING ...
SHFF SHFF SHFF
THERE'S STILL MUCH TO RESEARCH ABOUT THE MYSTERIOUS POWERS THAT THOSE WHO RETURN FROM THE DEAD SEEM TO POSSESS.
SHFF SHFF

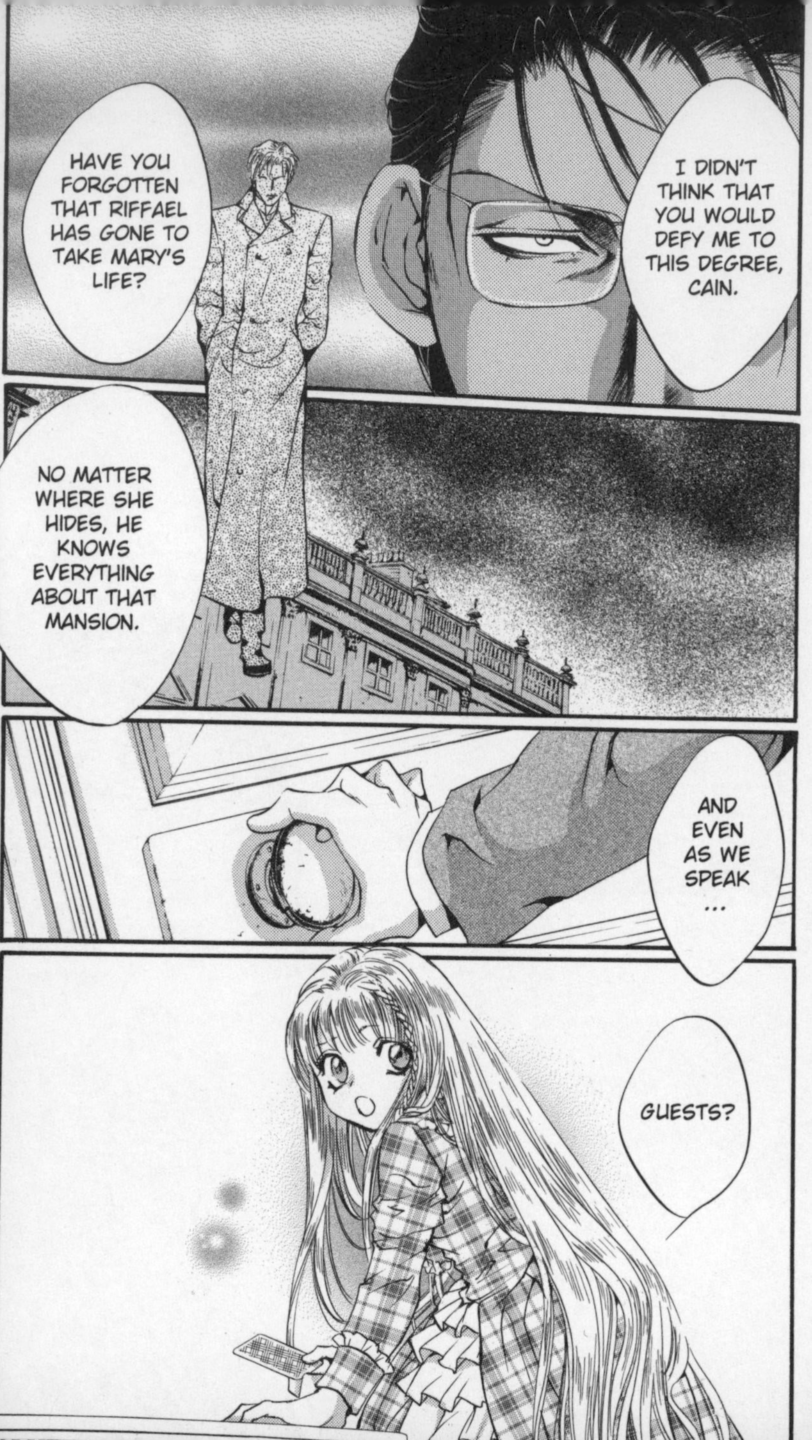
I DIDN'T THINK THAT YOU WOULD DEFY ME TO THIS DEGREE, CAIN.
HAVE YOU FORGOTTEN THAT RIFFAEL HAS GONE TO TAKE MARY'S LIFE?
NO MATTER WHERE SHE HIDES, HE KNOWS EVERYTHING ABOUT THAT MANSION.
AND EVEN AS WE SPEAK ...
GUESTS?

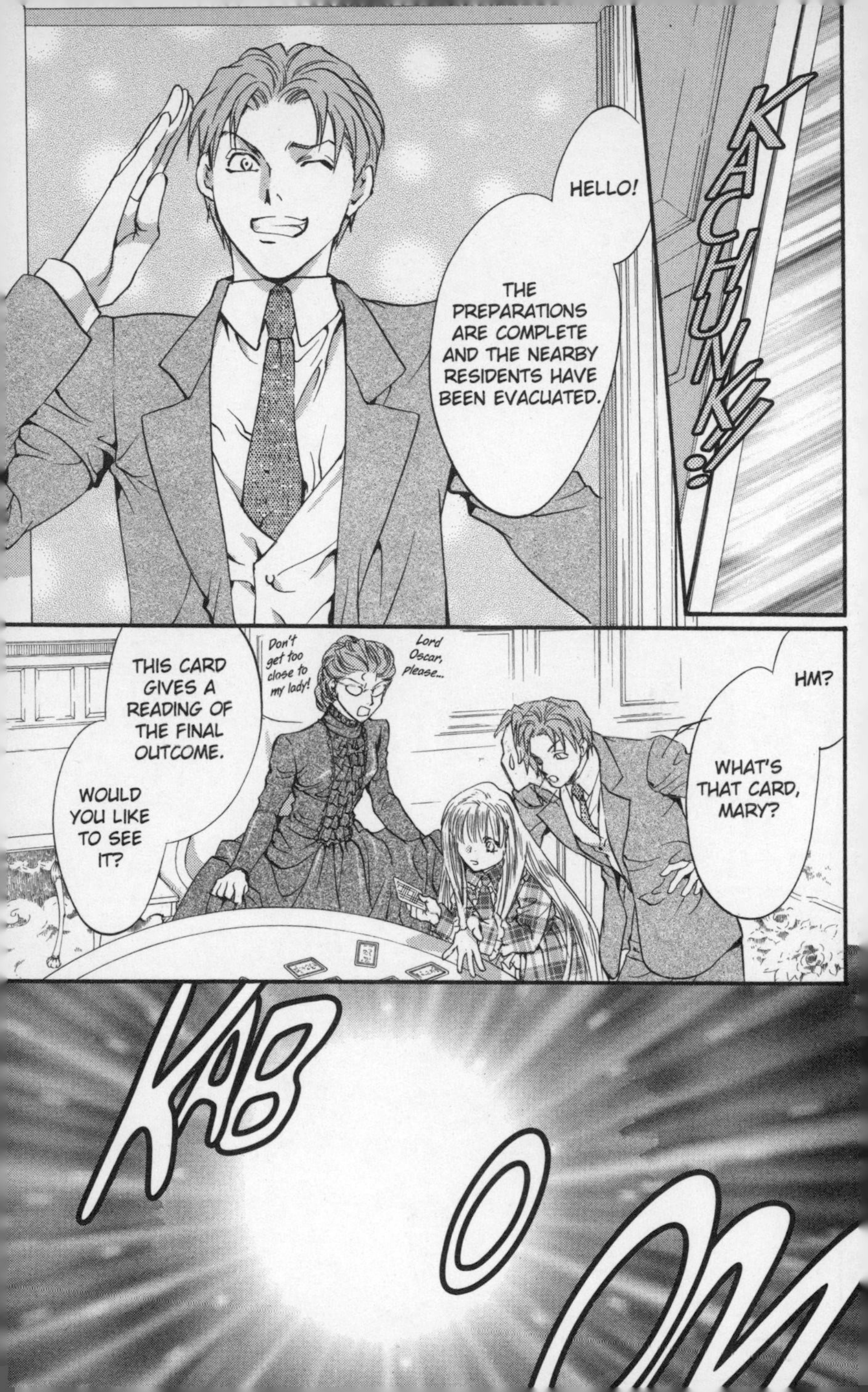
KACHUNK!!
HELLO!
THE PREPARATIONS ARE COMPLETE AND THE NEARBY RESIDENTS HAVE BEEN EVACUATED.
HM?
WHAT'S THAT CARD, MARY?
Lord Oscar, please...
Don't get too close to my lady!
THIS CARD GIVES A READING OF THE FINAL OUTCOME.
WOULD YOU LIKE TO SEE IT?
KABOOM

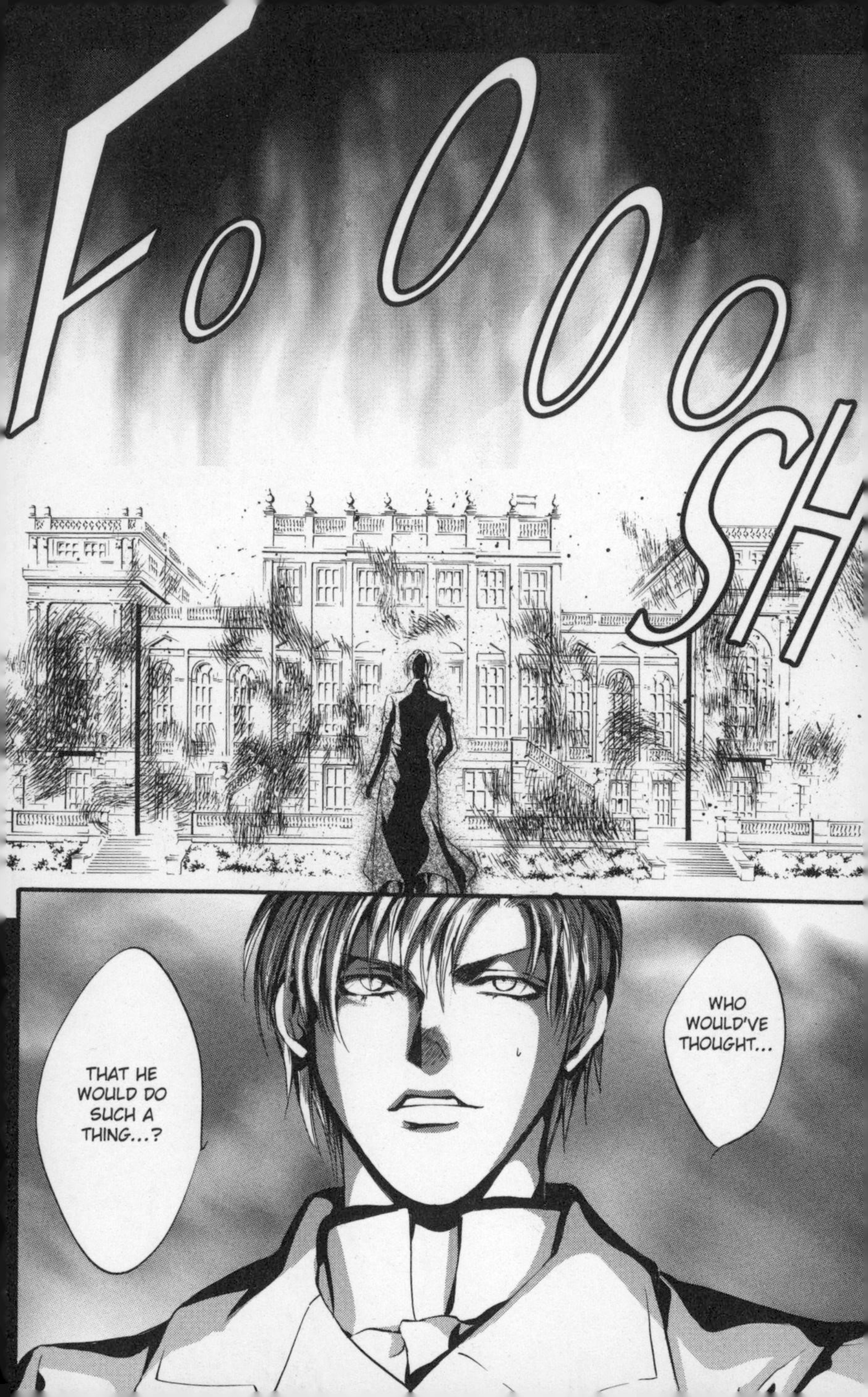
FOOOOSH
WHO WOULD'VE THOUGHT...
THAT HE WOULD DO SUCH A THING...?

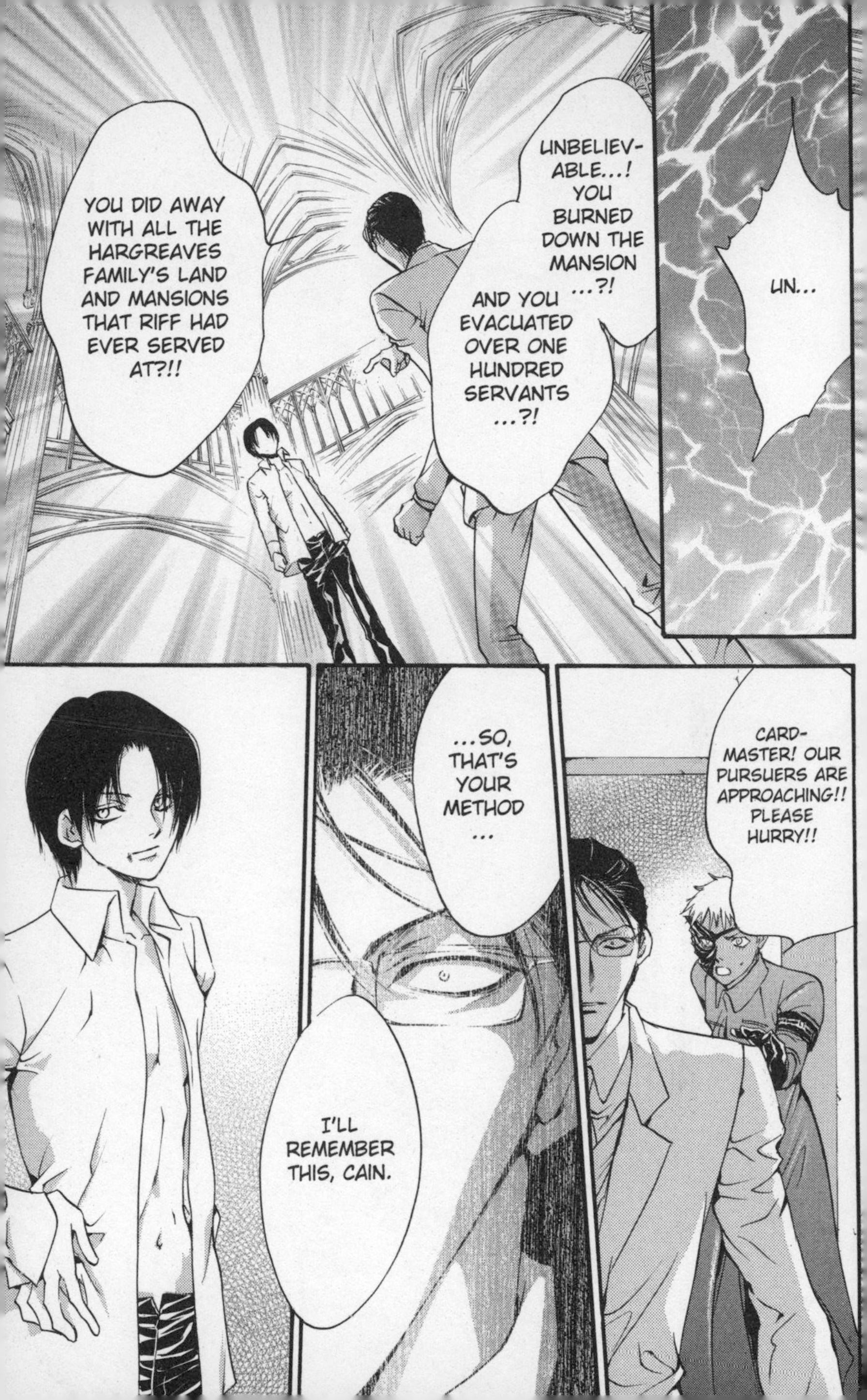
UN...
UNBELIEVABLE...! YOU BURNED DOWN THE MANSION ...?!
AND YOU EVACUATED OVER ONE HUNDRED SERVANTS ...?!
YOU DID AWAY WITH ALL THE HARGREAVES FAMILY'S LAND AND MANSIONS THAT RIFF HAD EVER SERVED AT?!!
CARD-MASTER! OUR PURSUERS ARE APPROACHING!! PLEASE HURRY!!
...SO, THAT'S YOUR METHOD ...
I'LL REMEMBER THIS, CAIN.

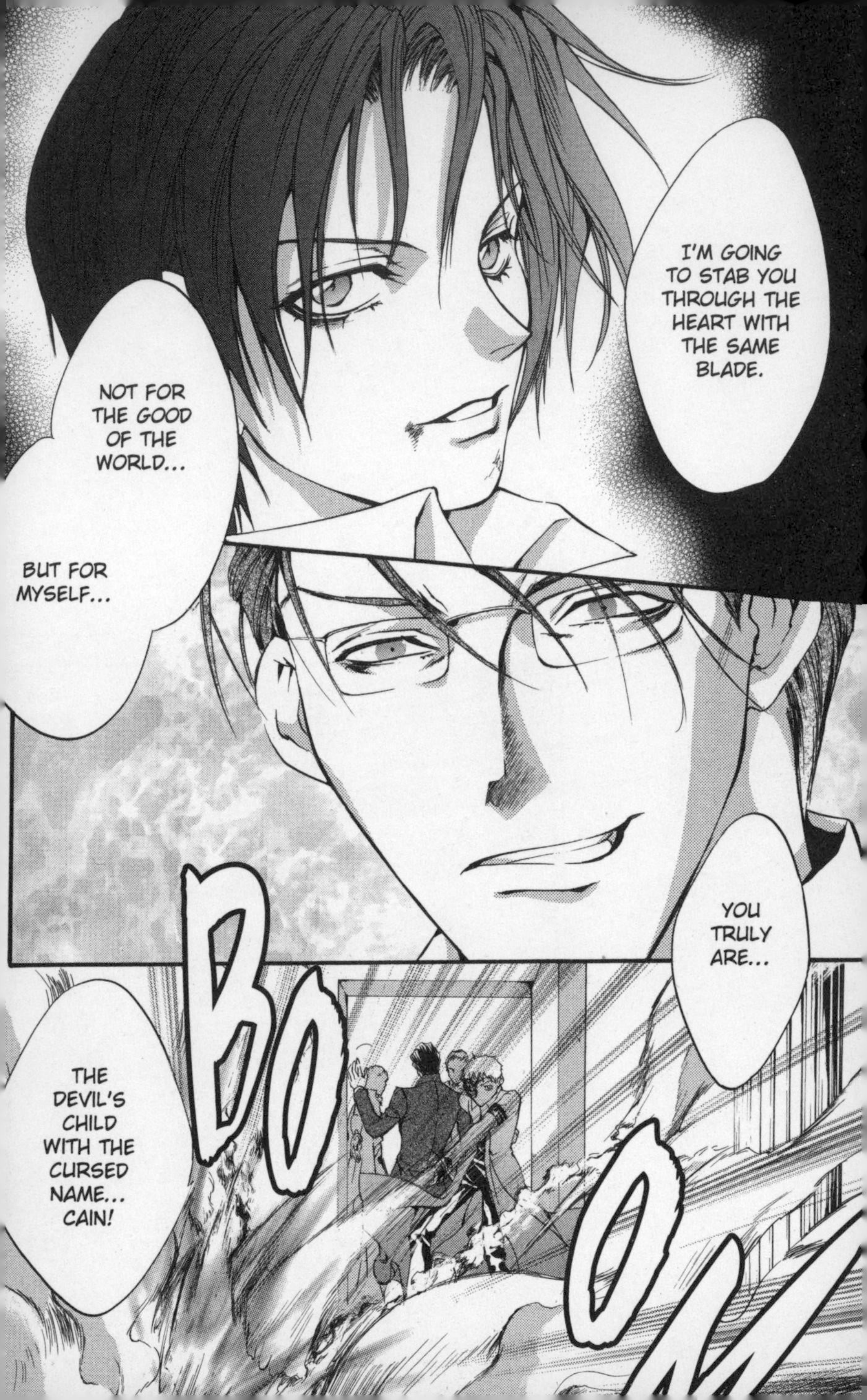
I'M GOING TO STAB YOU THROUGH THE HEART WITH THE SAME BLADE.
NOT FOR THE GOOD OF THE WORLD...
BUT FOR MYSELF...
YOU TRULY ARE...
THE DEVIL'S CHILD WITH THE CURSED NAME... CAIN!
BOOM

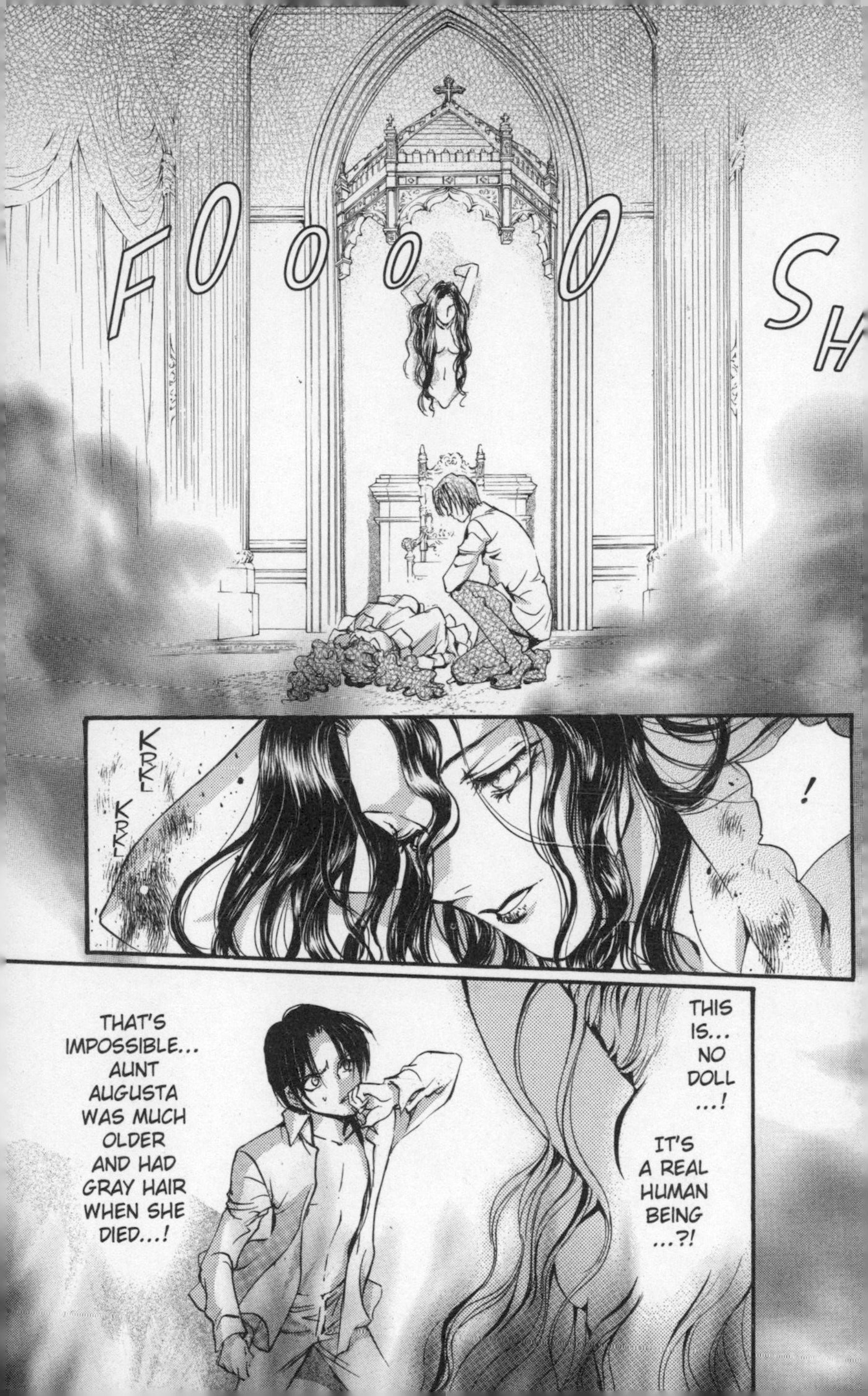
FOOOOOSH
KRKL KRKL
!
THIS IS... NO DOLL...!
IT'S A REAL HUMAN BEING...?!
THAT'S IMPOSSIBLE... AUNT AUGUSTA WAS MUCH OLDER AND HAD GRAY HAIR WHEN SHE DIED...!

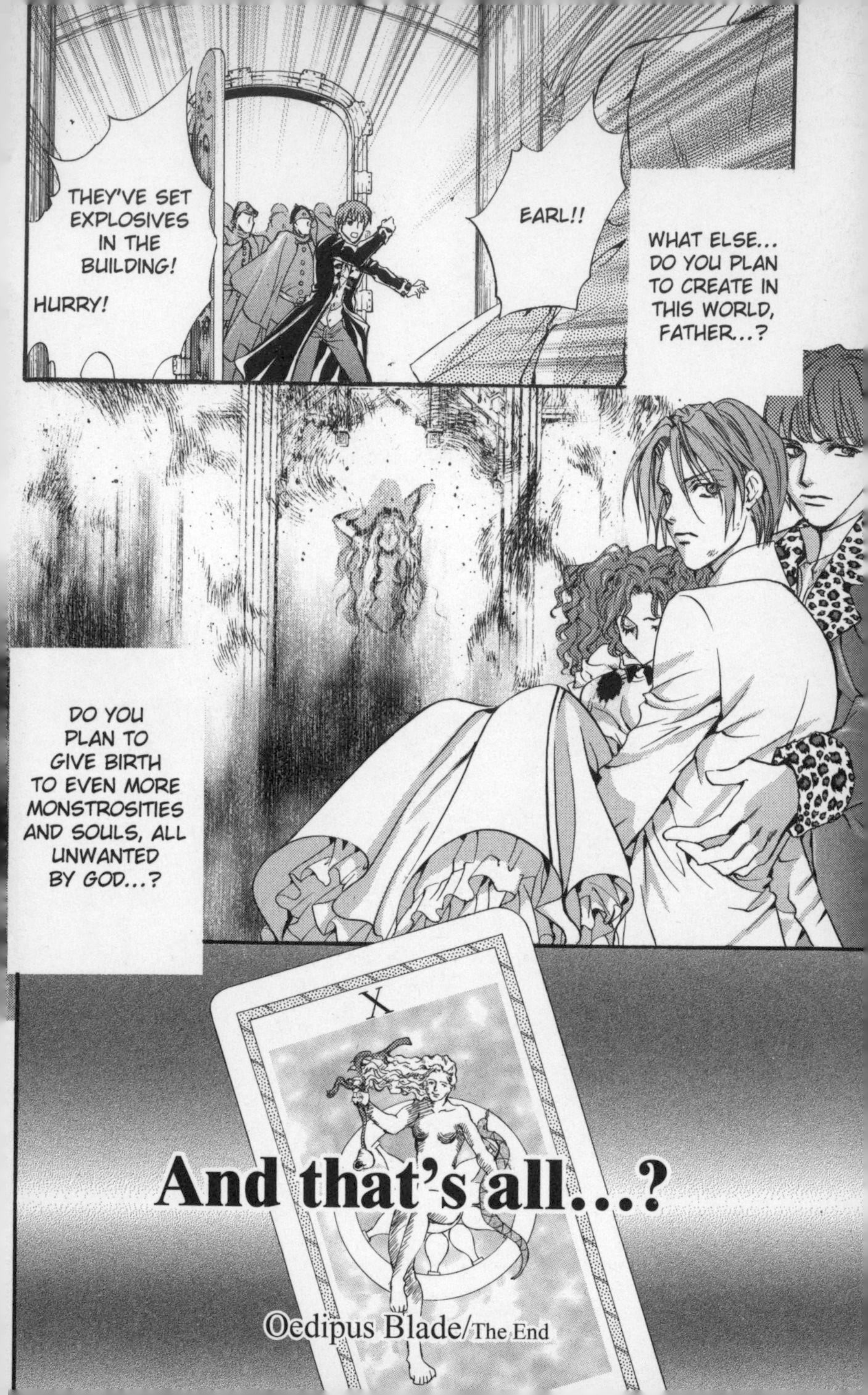
EARL!!
THEY'VE SET EXPLOSIVES IN THE BUILDING!
HURRY!
WHAT ELSE... DO YOU PLAN TO CREATE IN THIS WORLD, FATHER...?
DO YOU PLAN TO GIVE BIRTH TO EVEN MORE MONSTROSITIES AND SOULS, ALL UNWANTED BY GOD...?
X
And that's all...?
Oedipus Blade/The End

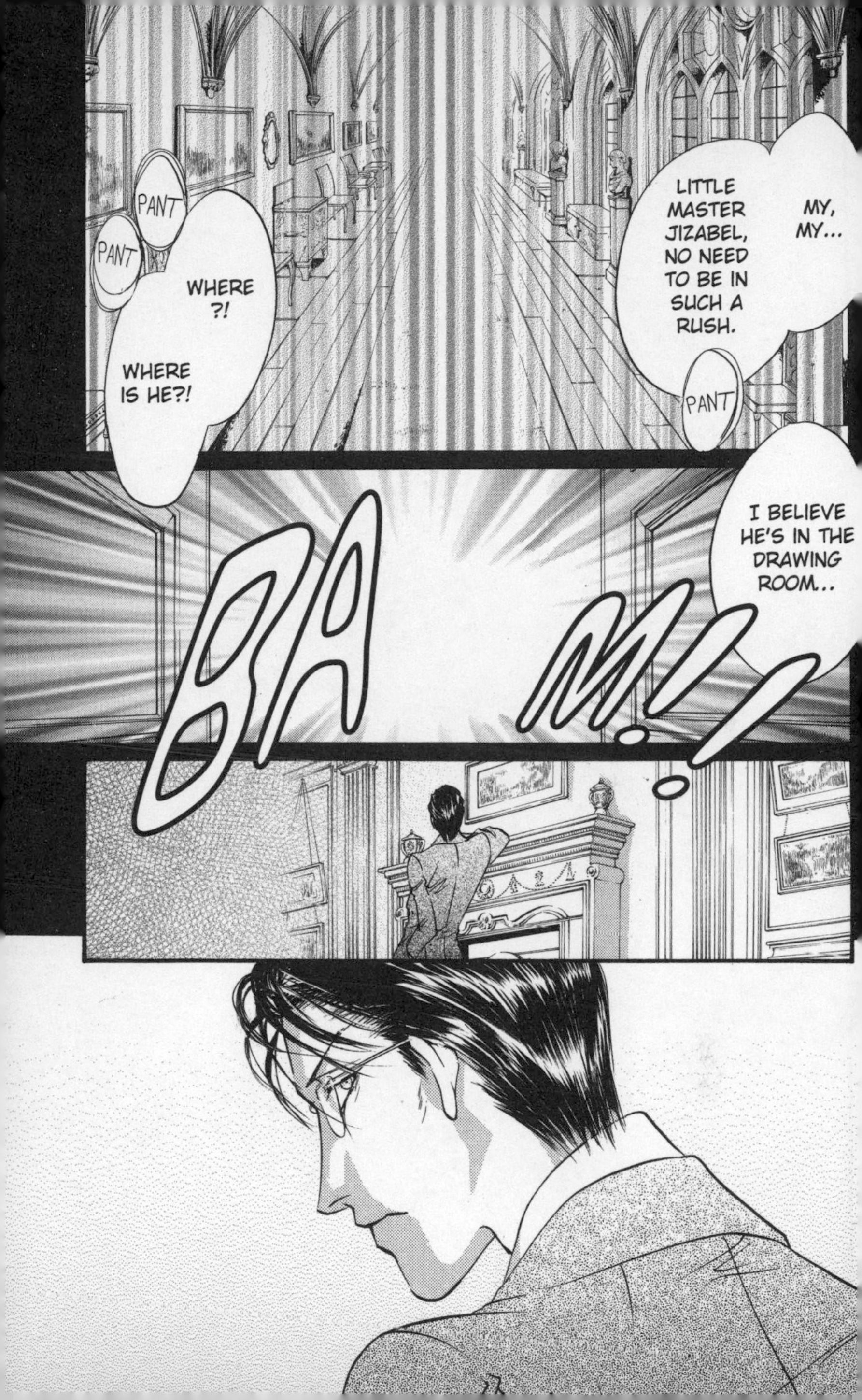
MY, MY...
LITTLE MASTER JIZABEL, NO NEED TO BE IN SUCH A RUSH.
PANT
PANT
PANT
WHERE ?!
WHERE IS HE?!
I BELIEVE HE'S IN THE DRAWING ROOM...
BAM!!

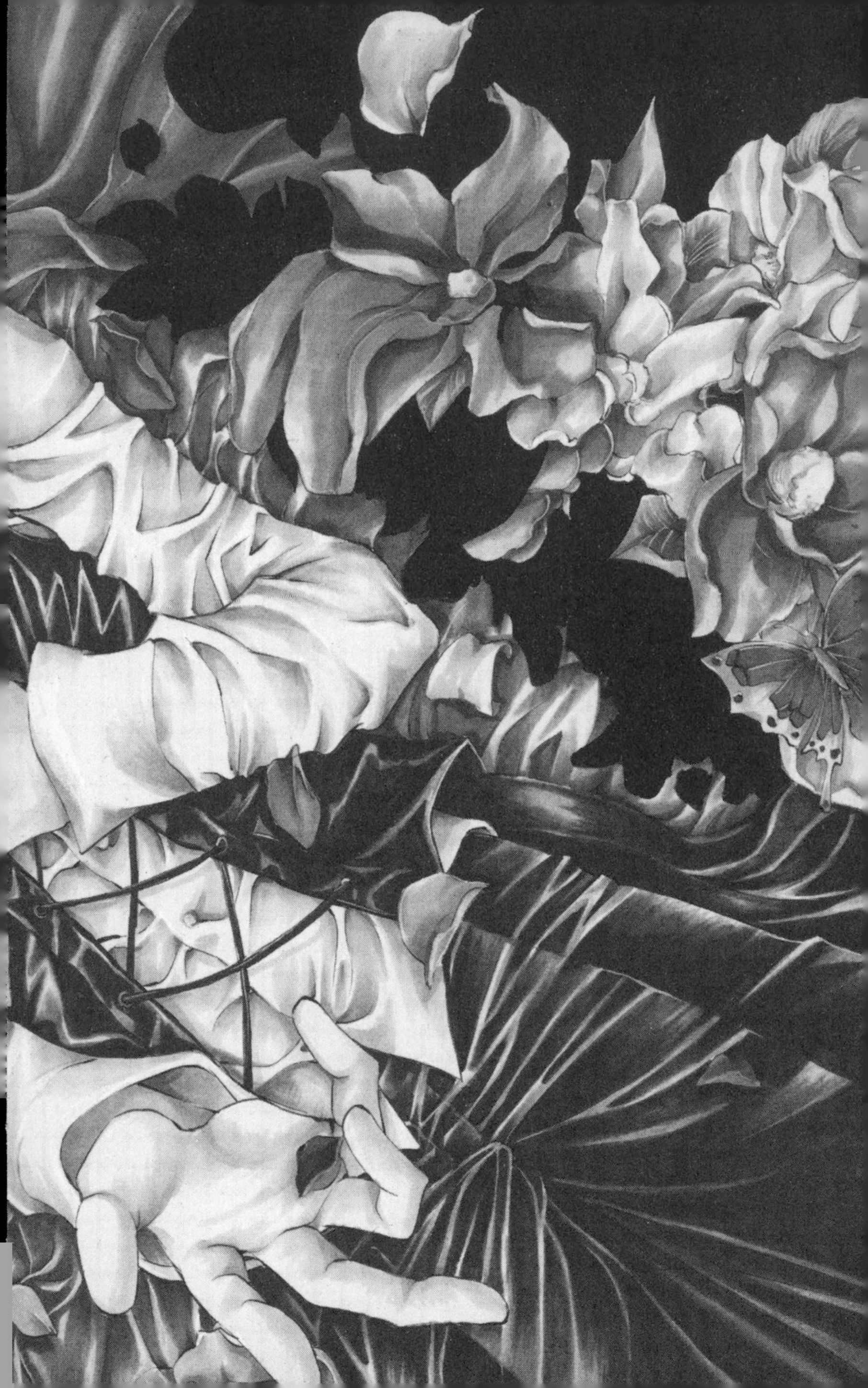

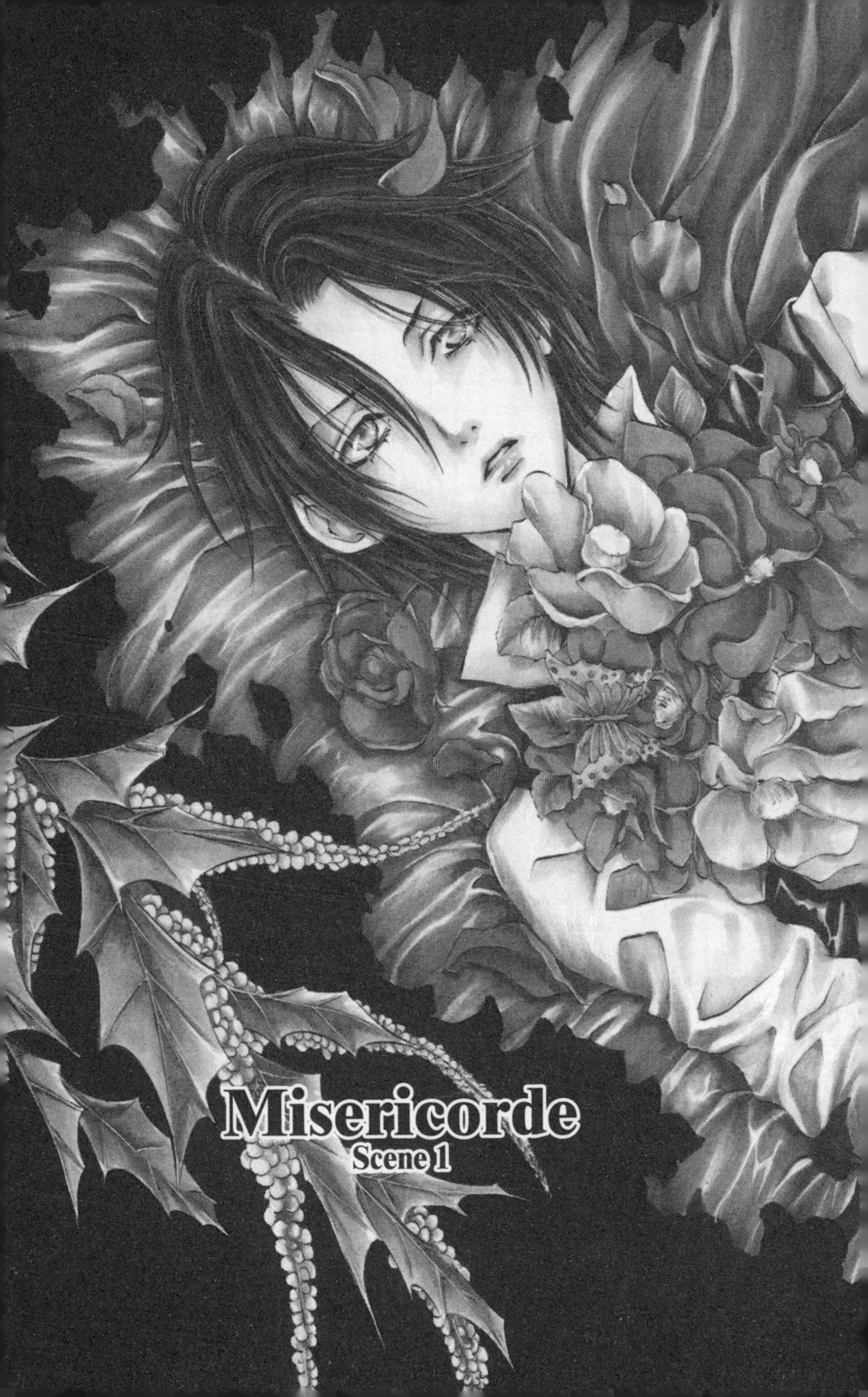
Misericorde
Scene 1

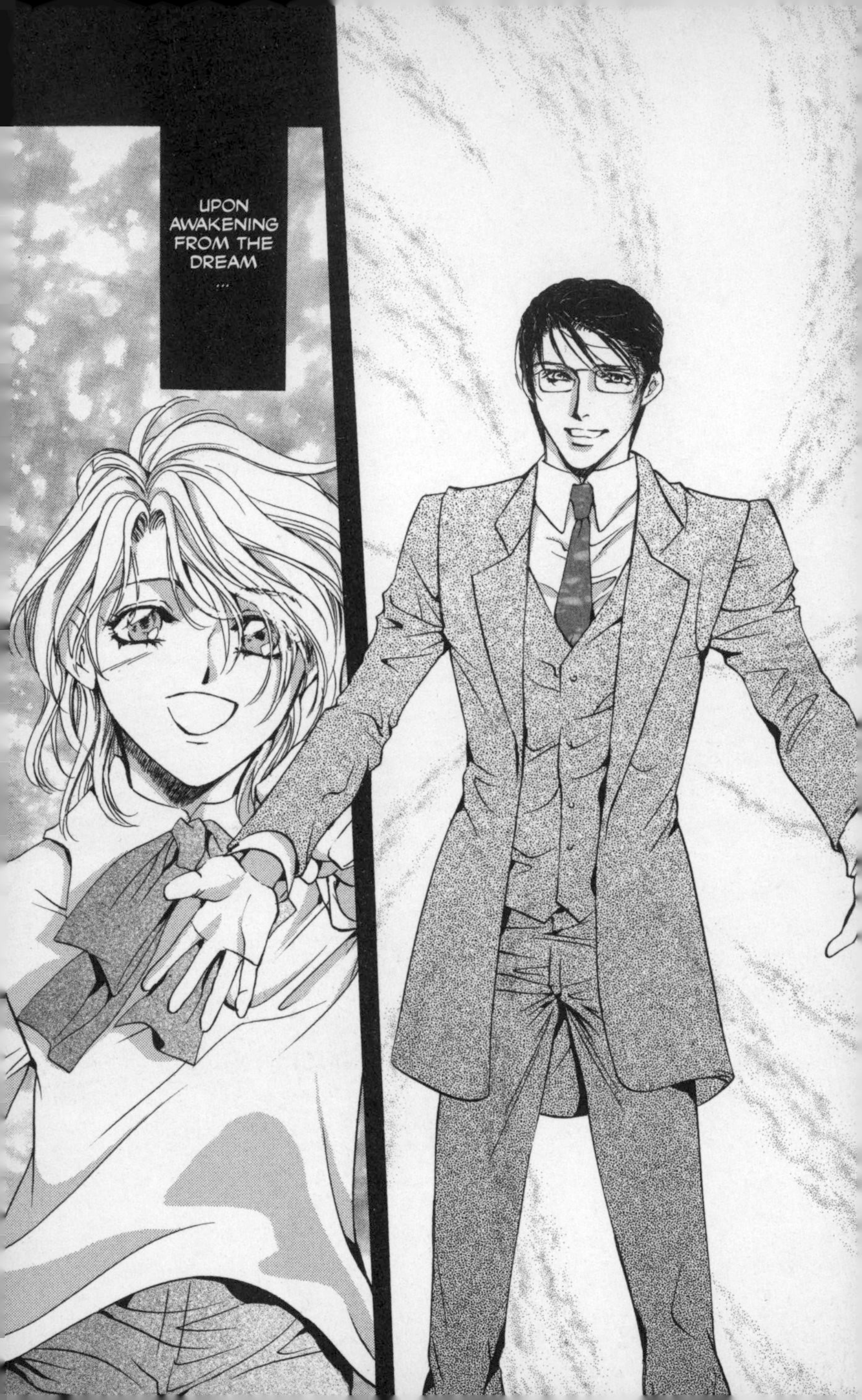
UPON AWAKENING FROM THE DREAM ...

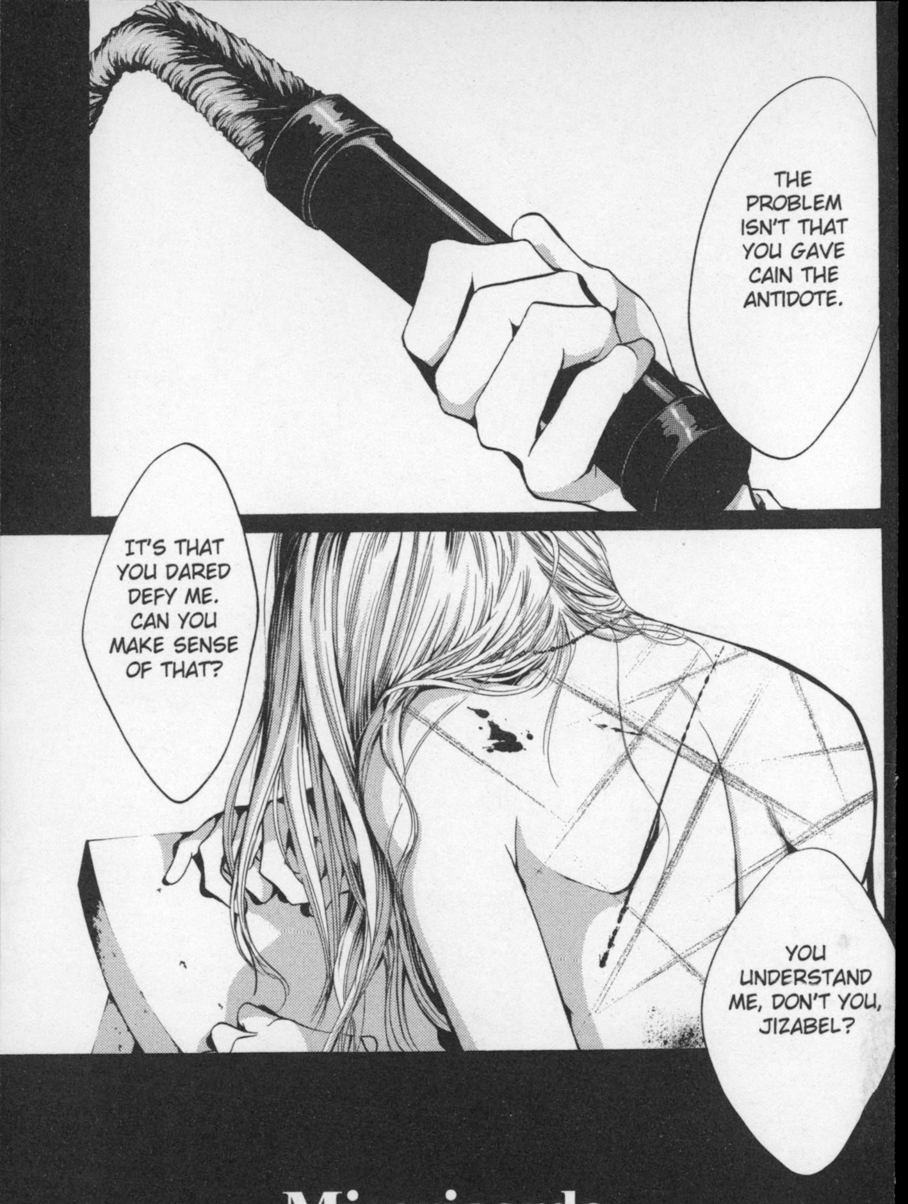
THE PROBLEM ISN'T THAT YOU GAVE CAIN THE ANTIDOTE.
IT'S THAT YOU DARED DEFY ME. CAN YOU MAKE SENSE OF THAT?
YOU UNDERSTAND ME, DON'T YOU, JIZABEL?

Misericorde

Scene 1

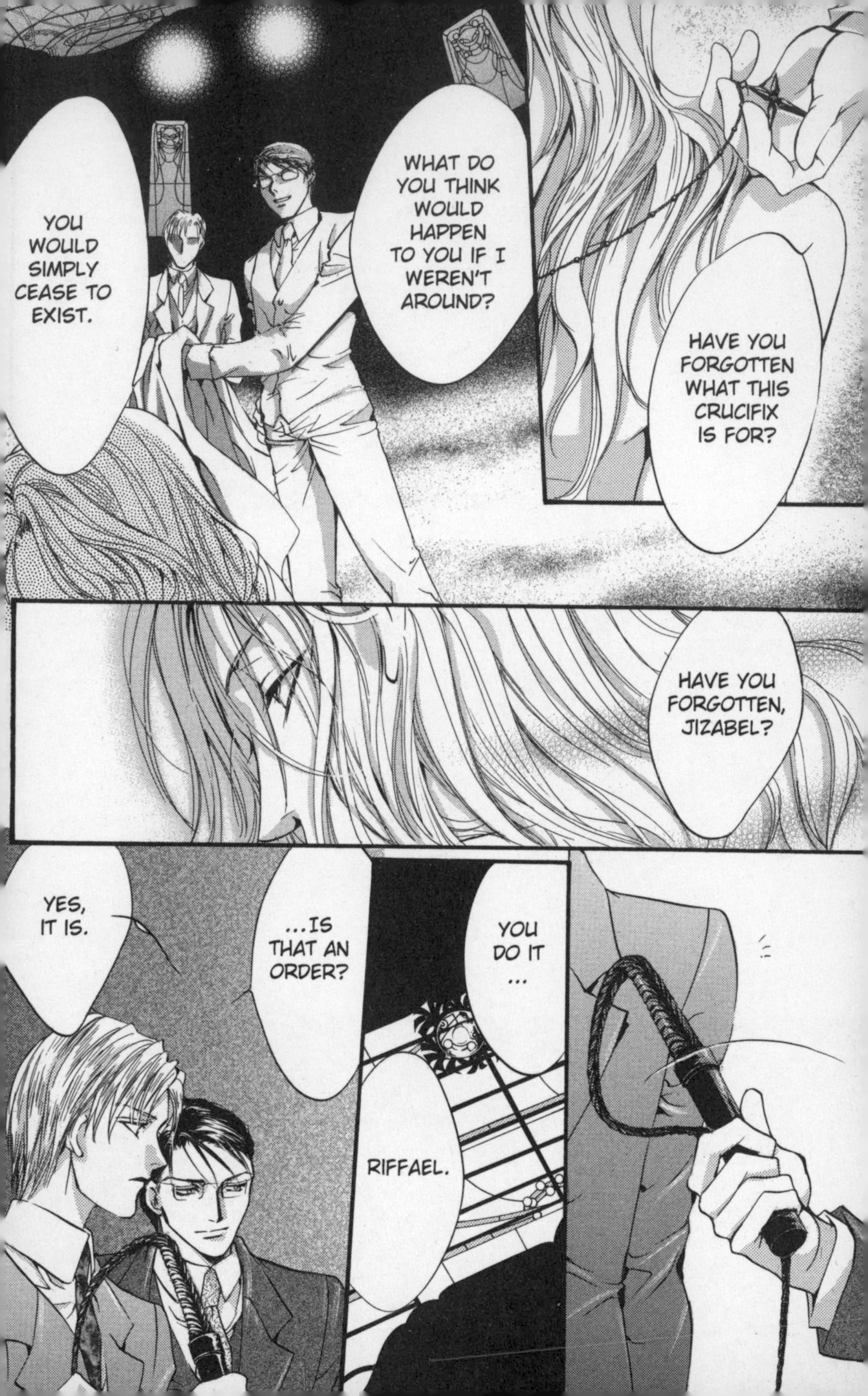
HAVE YOU FORGOTTEN WHAT THIS CRUCIFIX IS FOR?
WHAT DO YOU THINK WOULD HAPPEN TO YOU IF I WEREN'T AROUND?
YOU WOULD SIMPLY CEASE TO EXIST.
HAVE YOU FORGOTTEN, JIZABEL?
YOU DO IT ...
RIFFAEL.
...IS THAT AN ORDER?
YES, IT IS.

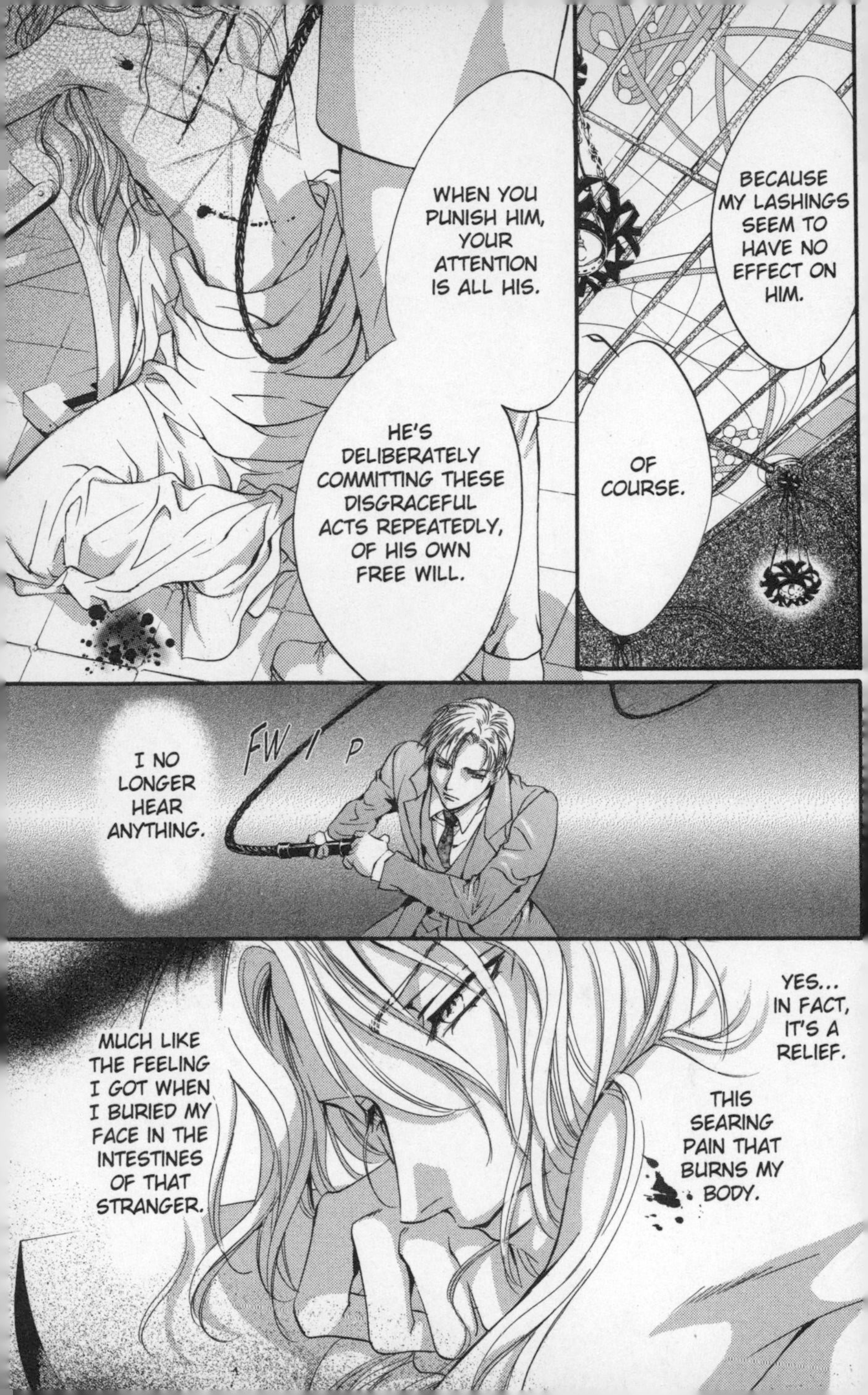

BECAUSE MY LASHINGS SEEM TO HAVE NO EFFECT ON HIM.
OF COURSE.
WHEN YOU PUNISH HIM, YOUR ATTENTION IS ALL HIS.
HE'S DELIBERATELY COMMITTING THESE DISGRACEFUL ACTS REPEATEDLY, OF HIS OWN FREE WILL.
FWIP
I NO LONGER HEAR ANYTHING.
YES... IN FACT, IT'S A RELIEF.
THIS SEARING PAIN THAT BURNS MY BODY.
MUCH LIKE THE FEELING I GOT WHEN I BURIED MY FACE IN THE INTESTINES OF THAT STRANGER.

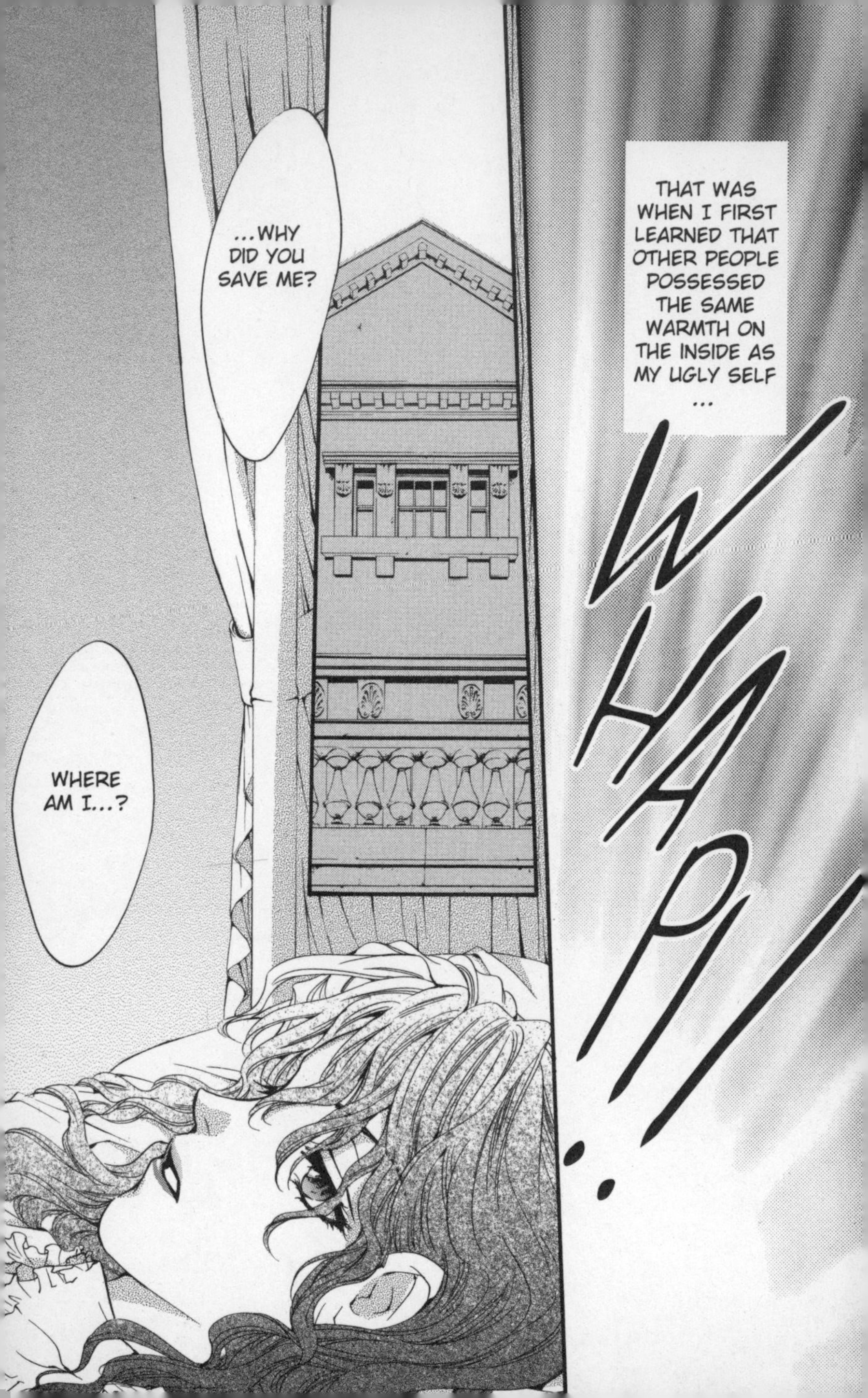
THAT WAS WHEN I FIRST LEARNED THAT OTHER PEOPLE POSSESSED THE SAME WARMTH ON THE INSIDE AS MY UGLY SELF ...
WHAP!!
...WHY DID YOU SAVE ME?
WHERE AM I...?

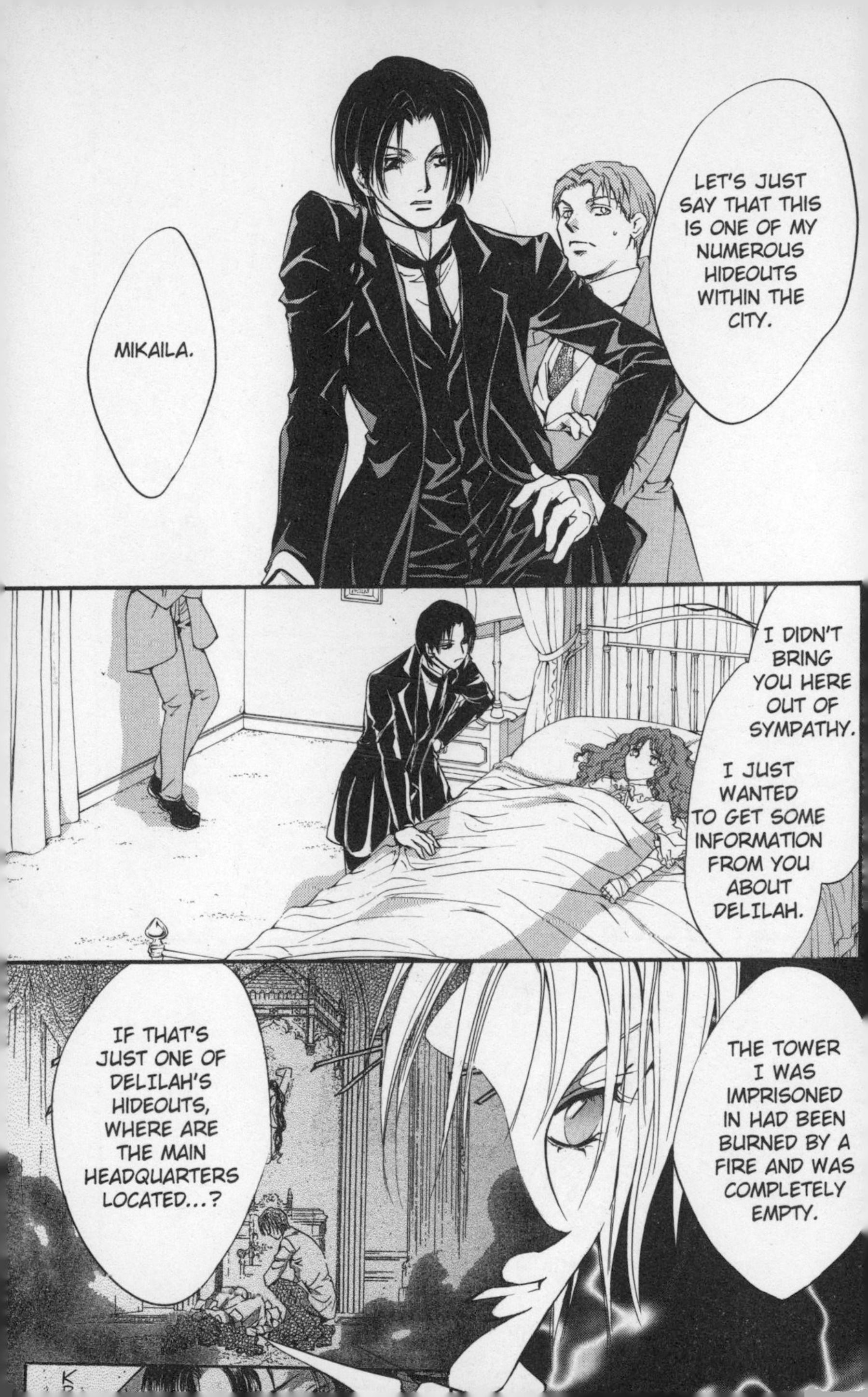
LET'S JUST SAY THAT THIS IS ONE OF MY NUMEROUS HIDEOUTS WITHIN THE CITY.
MIKAILA.
I DIDN'T BRING YOU HERE OUT OF SYMPATHY.
I JUST WANTED TO GET SOME INFORMATION FROM YOU ABOUT DELILAH.
THE TOWER I WAS IMPRISONED IN HAD BEEN BURNED BY A FIRE AND WAS COMPLETELY EMPTY.
IF THAT'S JUST ONE OF DELILAH'S HIDEOUTS, WHERE ARE THE MAIN HEADQUARTERS LOCATED...?

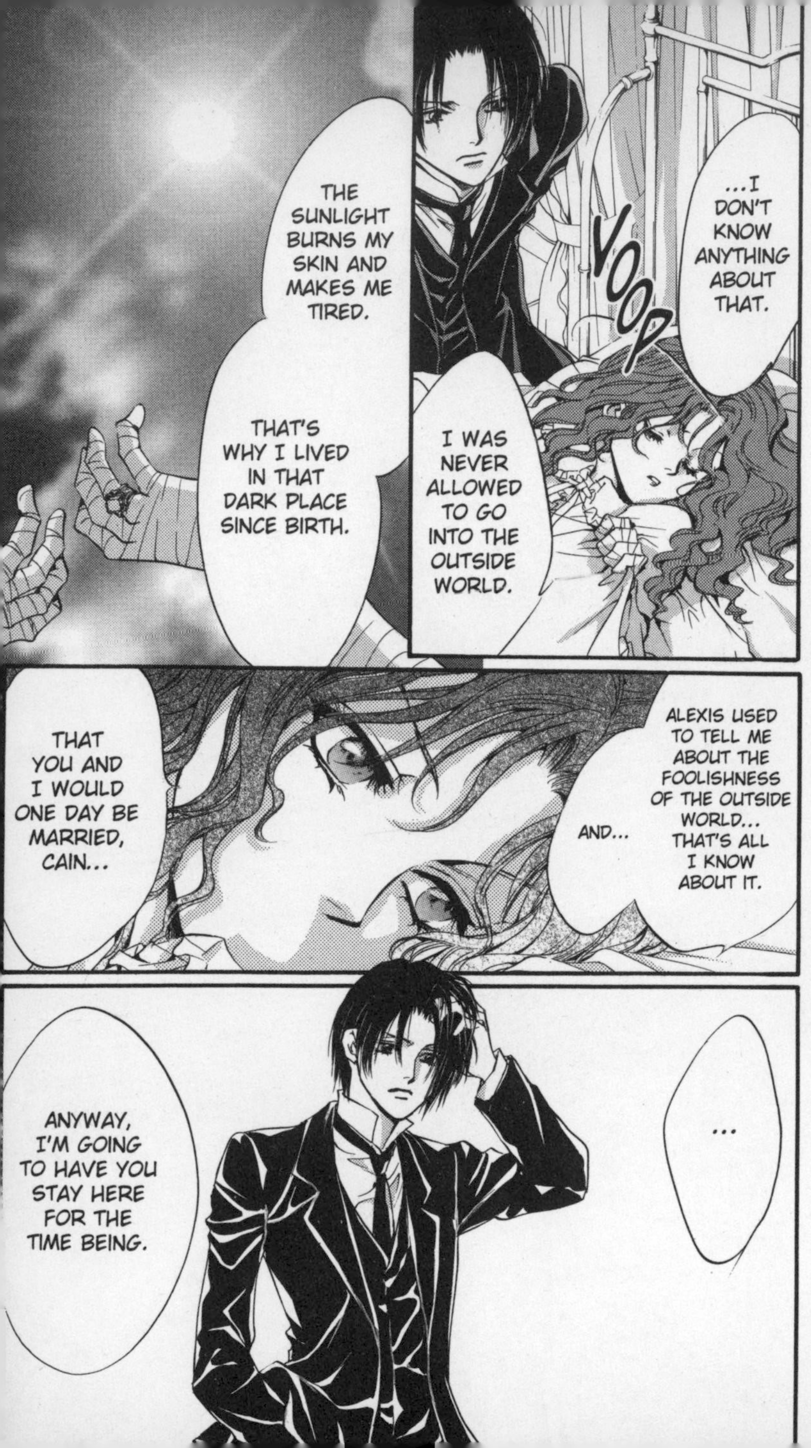
...I DON'T KNOW ANYTHING ABOUT THAT.
VOOP
I WAS NEVER ALLOWED TO GO INTO THE OUTSIDE WORLD.
THE SUNLIGHT BURNS MY SKIN AND MAKES ME TIRED.
THAT'S WHY I LIVED IN THAT DARK PLACE SINCE BIRTH.
ALEXIS USED TO TELL ME ABOUT THE FOOLISHNESS OF THE OUTSIDE WORLD... THAT'S ALL I KNOW ABOUT IT.
AND...
THAT YOU AND I WOULD ONE DAY BE MARRIED, CAIN...
...
ANYWAY, I'M GOING TO HAVE YOU STAY HERE FOR THE TIME BEING.

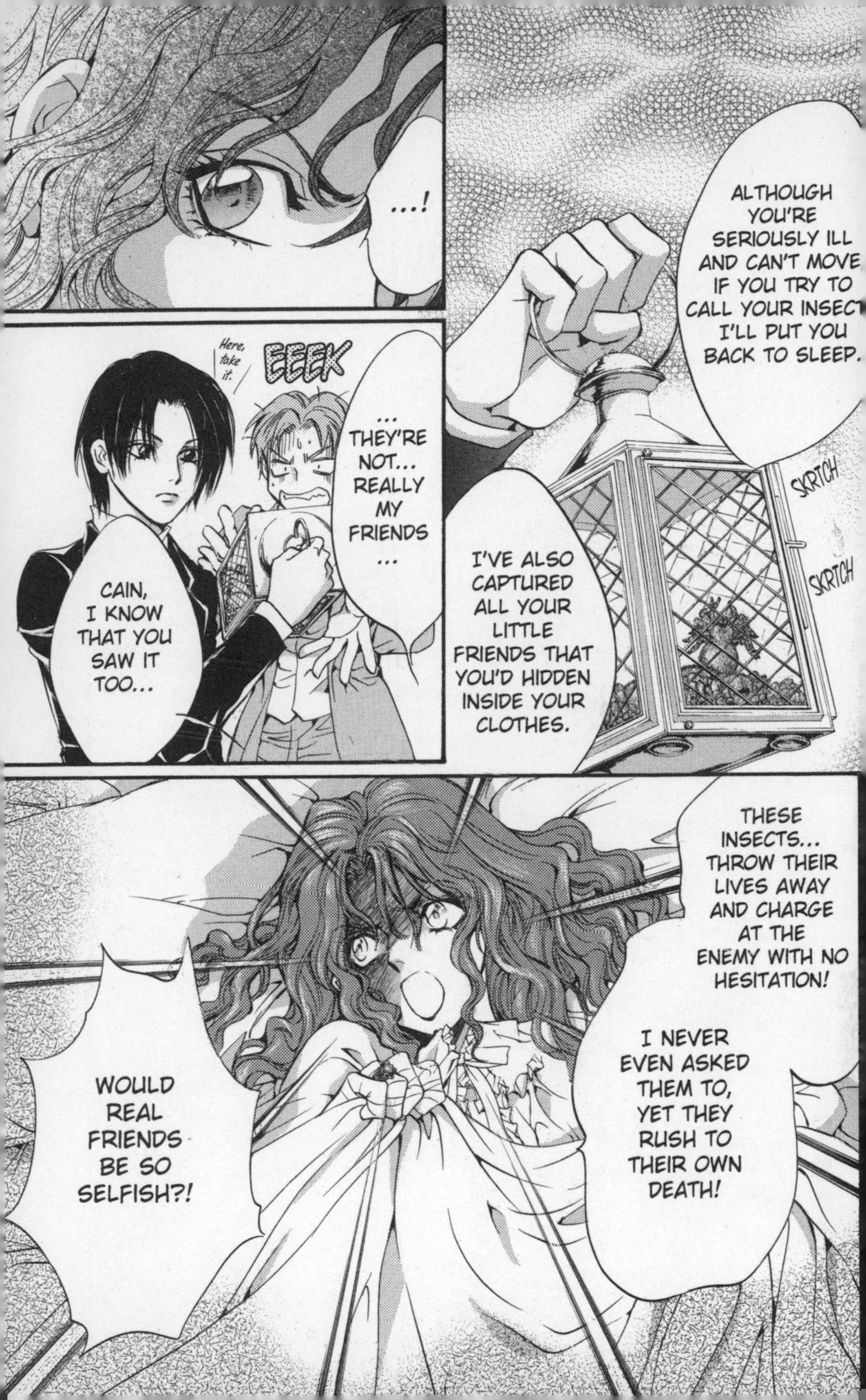
ALTHOUGH YOU'RE SERIOUSLY ILL AND CAN'T MOVE IF YOU TRY TO CALL YOUR INSECT I'LL PUT YOU BACK TO SLEEP.
SKRTCH
SKRTCH
I'VE ALSO CAPTURED ALL YOUR LITTLE FRIENDS THAT YOU'D HIDDEN INSIDE YOUR CLOTHES.
...!
... THEY'RE NOT... REALLY MY FRIENDS ...
EEEK
Here, take it.
CAIN, I KNOW THAT YOU SAW IT TOO...
THESE INSECTS... THROW THEIR LIVES AWAY AND CHARGE AT THE ENEMY WITH NO HESITATION!
I NEVER EVEN ASKED THEM TO, YET THEY RUSH TO THEIR OWN DEATH!
WOULD REAL FRIENDS BE SO SELFISH?!

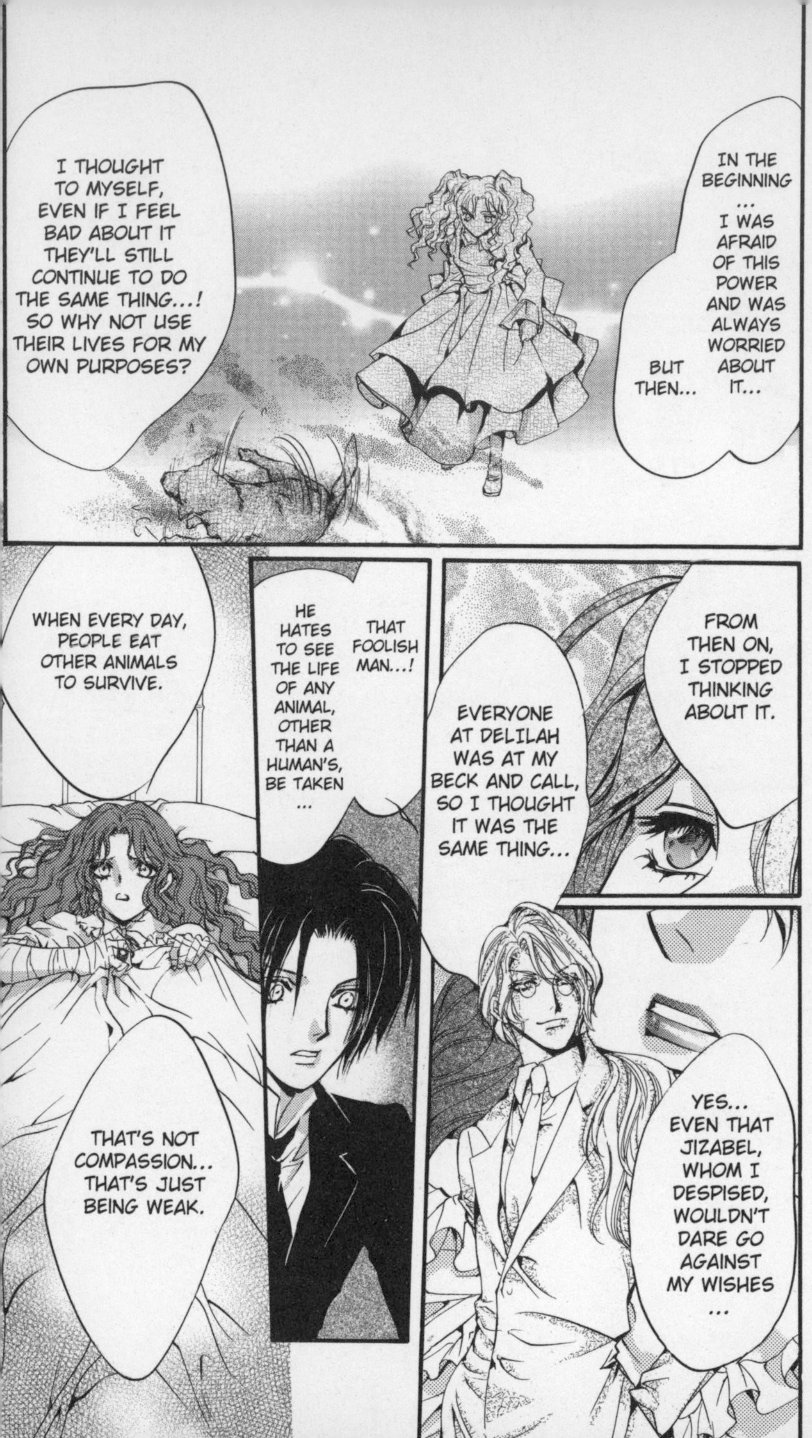
IN THE BEGINNING ... I WAS AFRAID OF THIS POWER AND WAS ALWAYS WORRIED ABOUT IT...
BUT THEN...
I THOUGHT TO MYSELF, EVEN IF I FEEL BAD ABOUT IT THEY'LL STILL CONTINUE TO DO THE SAME THING...! SO WHY NOT USE THEIR LIVES FOR MY OWN PURPOSES?
FROM THEN ON, I STOPPED THINKING ABOUT IT.
EVERYONE AT DELILAH WAS AT MY BECK AND CALL, SO I THOUGHT IT WAS THE SAME THING...
YES... EVEN THAT JIZABEL, WHOM I DESPISED, WOULDN'T DARE GO AGAINST MY WISHES ...
THAT FOOLISH MAN...!
HE HATES TO SEE THE LIFE OF ANY ANIMAL, OTHER THAN A HUMAN'S, BE TAKEN ...
WHEN EVERY DAY, PEOPLE EAT OTHER ANIMALS TO SURVIVE.
THAT'S NOT COMPASSION... THAT'S JUST BEING WEAK.

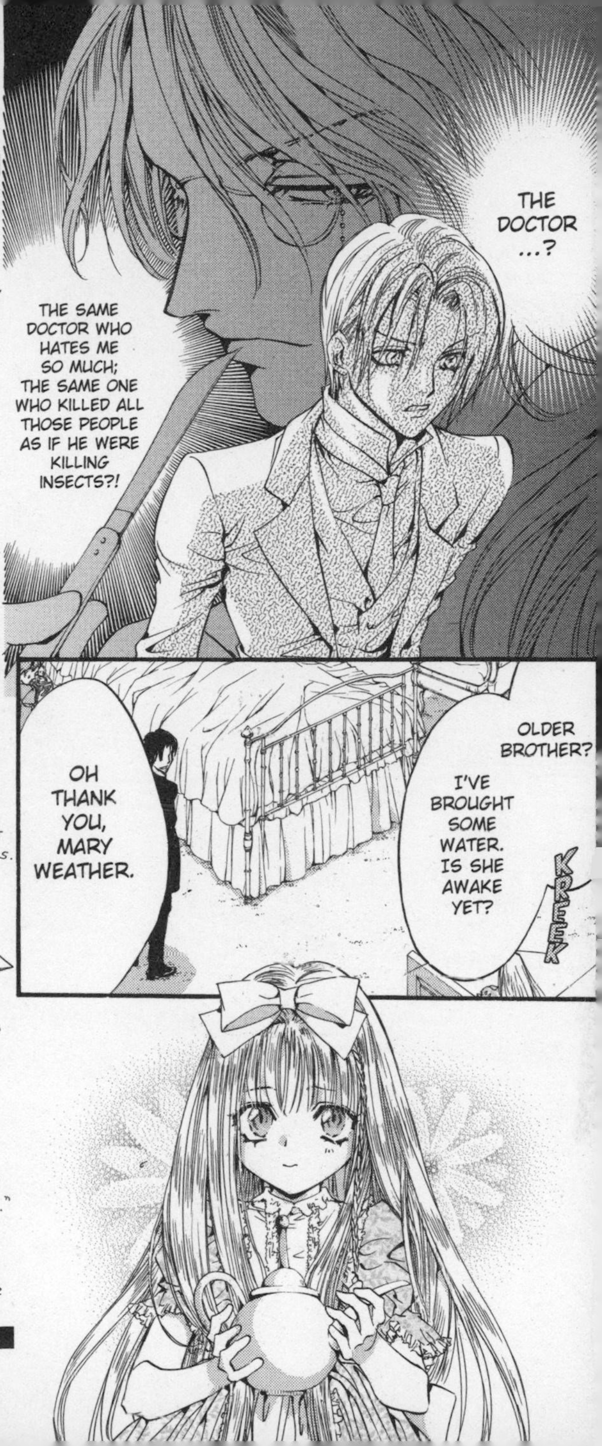
THE DOCTOR ...?
THE SAME DOCTOR WHO HATES ME SO MUCH; THE SAME ONE WHO KILLED ALL THOSE PEOPLE AS IF HE WERE KILLING INSECTS?!
OLDER BROTHER?
I'VE BROUGHT SOME WATER. IS SHE AWAKE YET?
KREEK
OH THANK YOU, MARY WEATHER.

The Misericorde is a short sword that was used in England and France during the 14th and 15th centuries... The name means, "short sword of mercy."

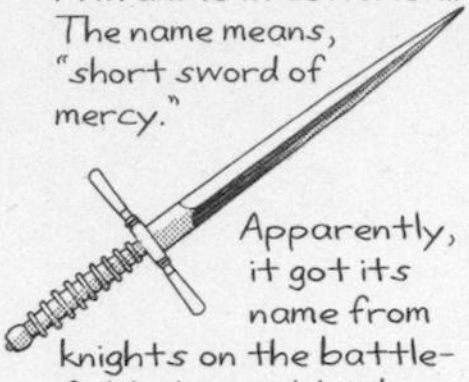

Apparently, it got its name from knights on the battlefield who would take seriously injured people out of their misery with this blade.

This one has an interesting shape because it splits into three parts.

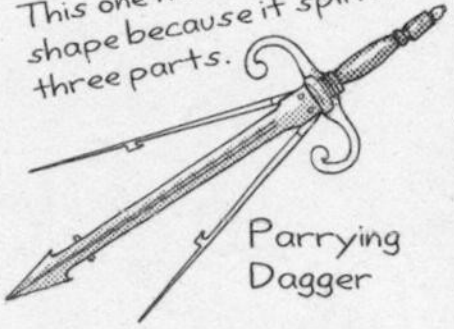

Parrying Dagger

This sword was used during duels in the 15th to 18th centuries. It's unusual because it splits into three pieces.

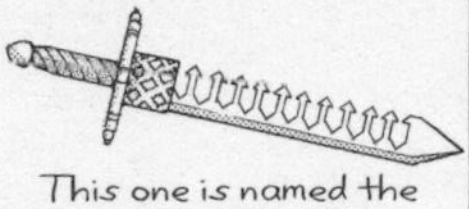

This one is named the Sword Breaker. Its shape was designed to break off the tip of the enemy's blade after blocking his attack.

This current story featuring Mikaila is based on the story of the "Mermaid Princess." Later on, I realized that the doctor who appears in this story looks exactly like uncle Neil. Not good.

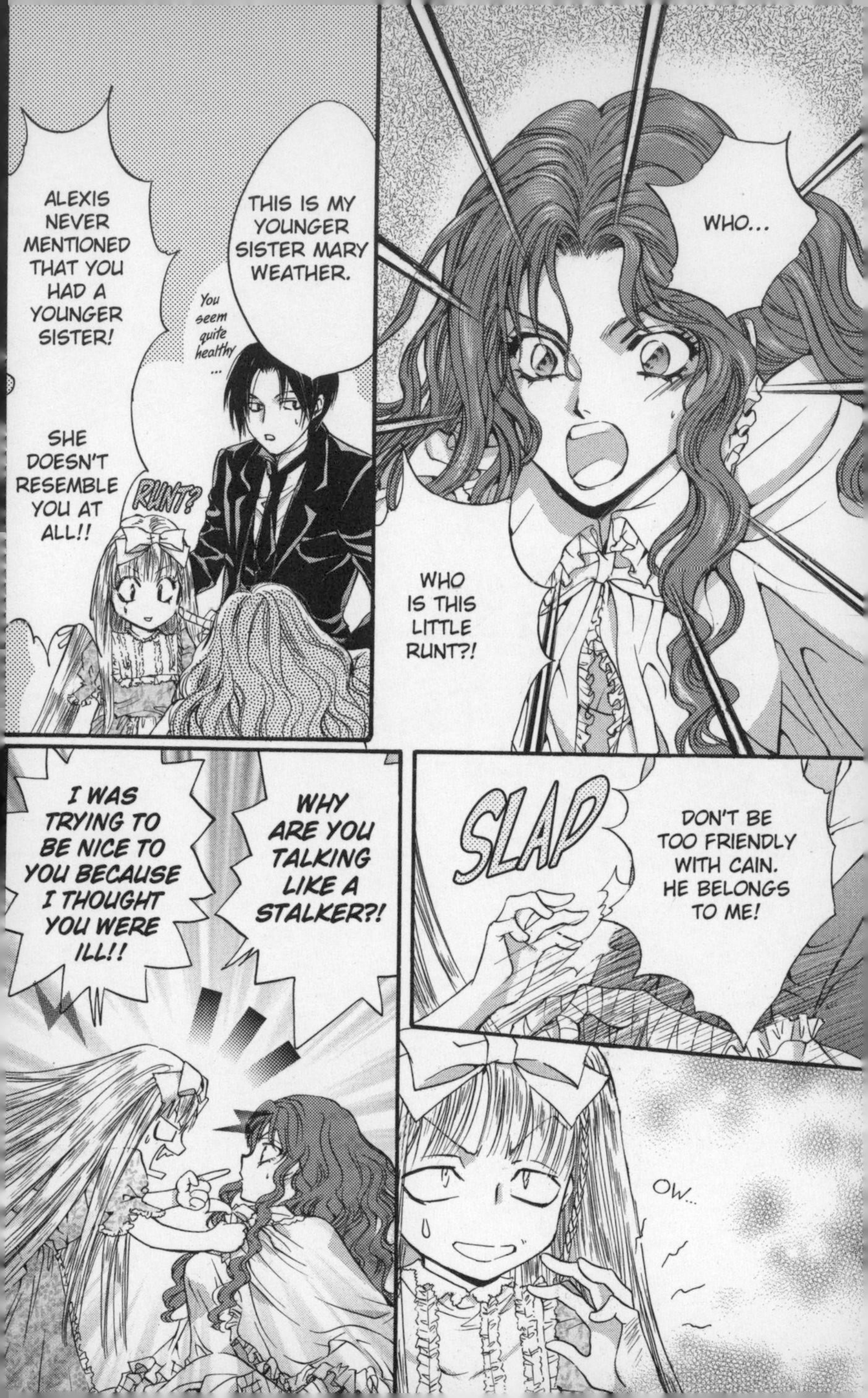
WHO...
WHO IS THIS LITTLE RUNT?!
THIS IS MY YOUNGER SISTER MARY WEATHER.
ALEXIS NEVER MENTIONED THAT YOU HAD A YOUNGER SISTER!
You seem quite healthy...
SHE DOESN'T RESEMBLE YOU AT ALL!!
RUNT?
DON'T BE TOO FRIENDLY WITH CAIN. HE BELONGS TO ME!
SLAP
OW...
WHY ARE YOU TALKING LIKE A STALKER?!
I WAS TRYING TO BE NICE TO YOU BECAUSE I THOUGHT YOU WERE ILL!!

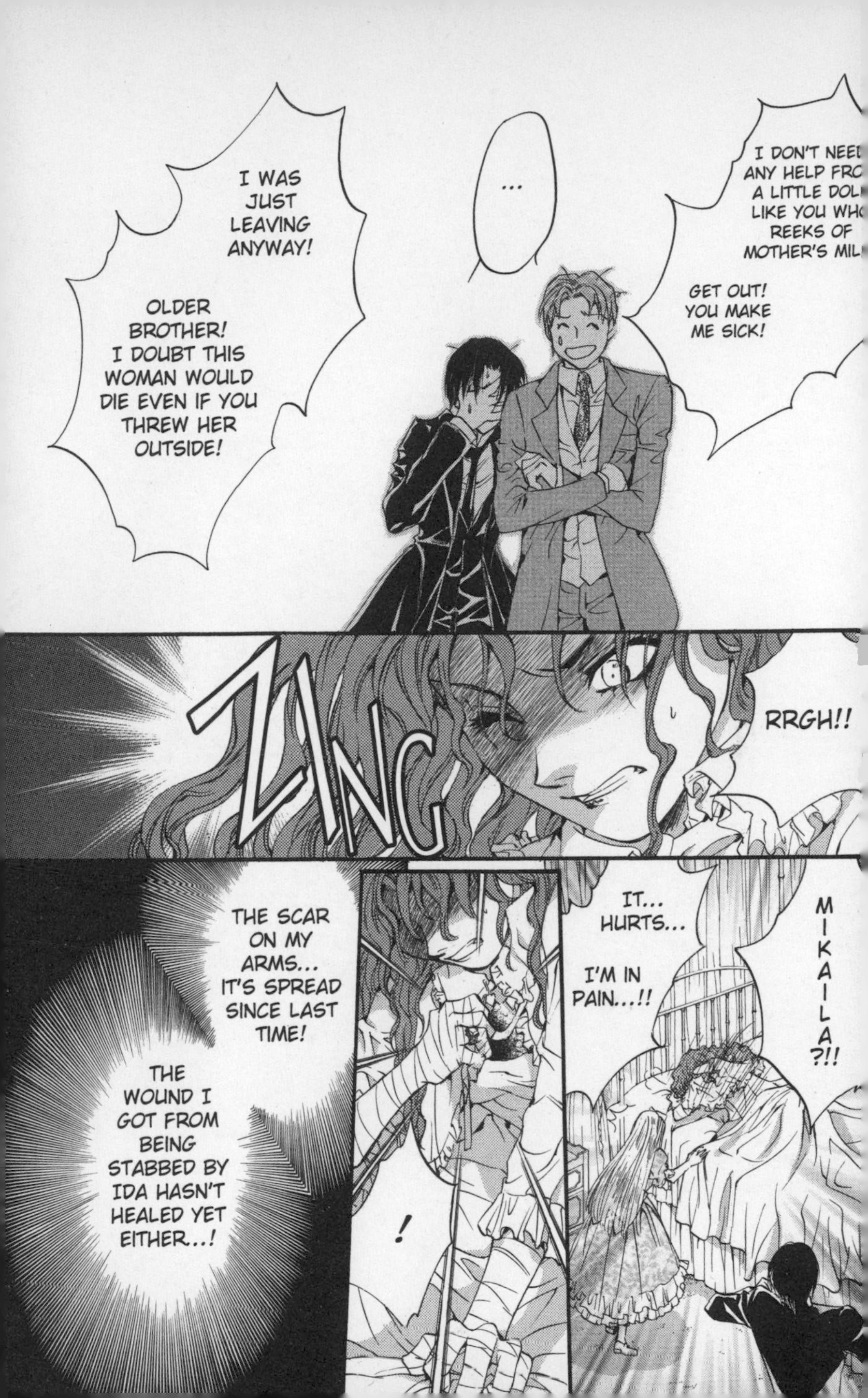
I DON'T NEE
ANY HELP FRO
A LITTLE DOL
LIKE YOU WH
REEKS OF
MOTHER'S MIL
GET OUT! YOU MAKE ME SICK!
...
I WAS JUST LEAVING ANYWAY!
OLDER BROTHER! I DOUBT THIS WOMAN WOULD DIE EVEN IF YOU THREW HER OUTSIDE!
RRGH!!
ZING
MIKAILA?!!
IT... HURTS...
I'M IN PAIN...!!
!
THE SCAR ON MY ARMS... IT'S SPREAD SINCE LAST TIME!
THE WOUND I GOT FROM BEING STABBED BY IDA HASN'T HEALED YET EITHER...!

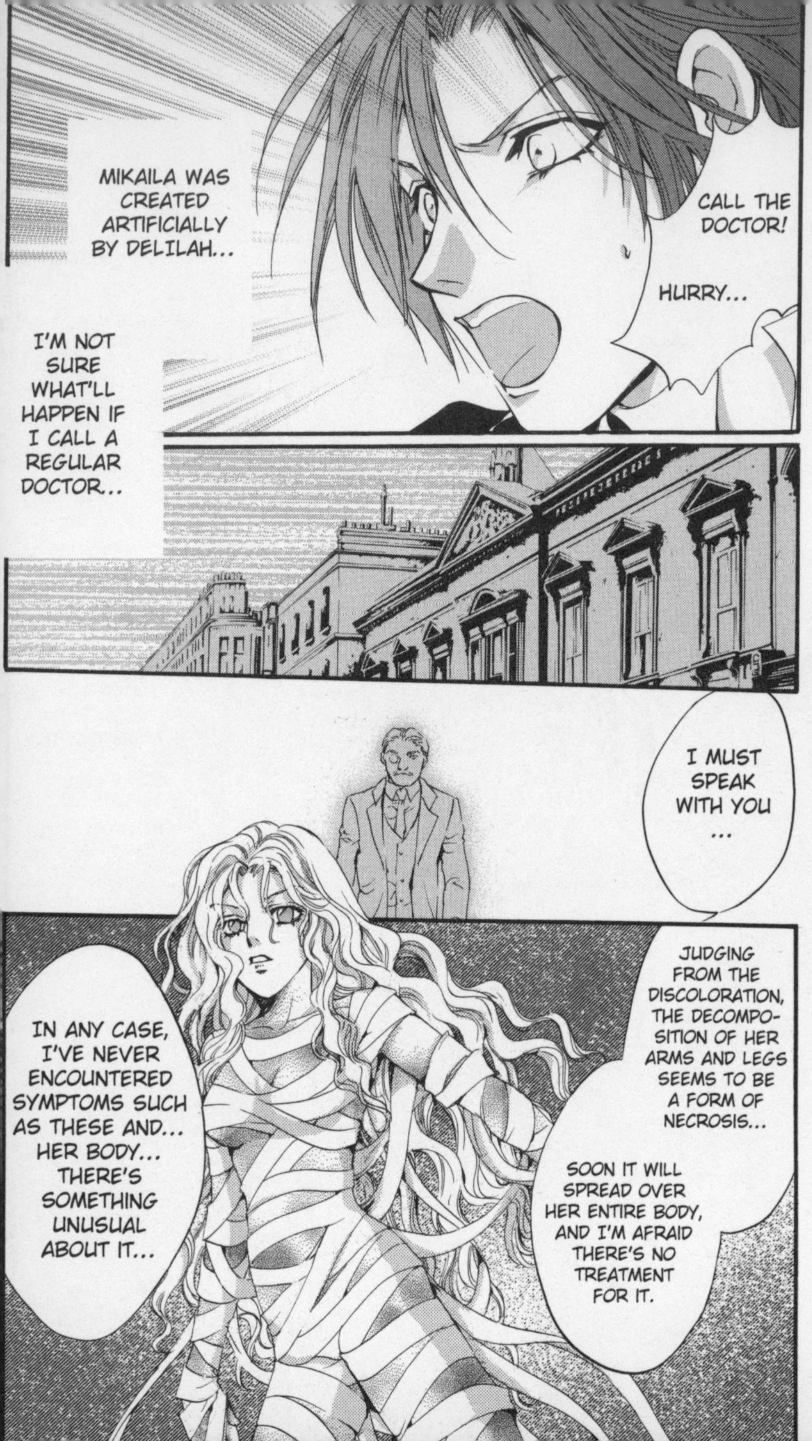
CALL THE DOCTOR!
HURRY...
MIKAILA WAS CREATED ARTIFICIALLY BY DELILAH...
I'M NOT SURE WHAT'LL HAPPEN IF I CALL A REGULAR DOCTOR...
I MUST SPEAK WITH YOU ...
JUDGING FROM THE DISCOLORATION, THE DECOMPO-SITION OF HER ARMS AND LEGS SEEMS TO BE A FORM OF NECROSIS...
SOON IT WILL SPREAD OVER HER ENTIRE BODY, AND I'M AFRAID THERE'S NO TREATMENT FOR IT.
IN ANY CASE, I'VE NEVER ENCOUNTERED SYMPTOMS SUCH AS THESE AND... HER BODY... THERE'S SOMETHING UNUSUAL ABOUT IT...

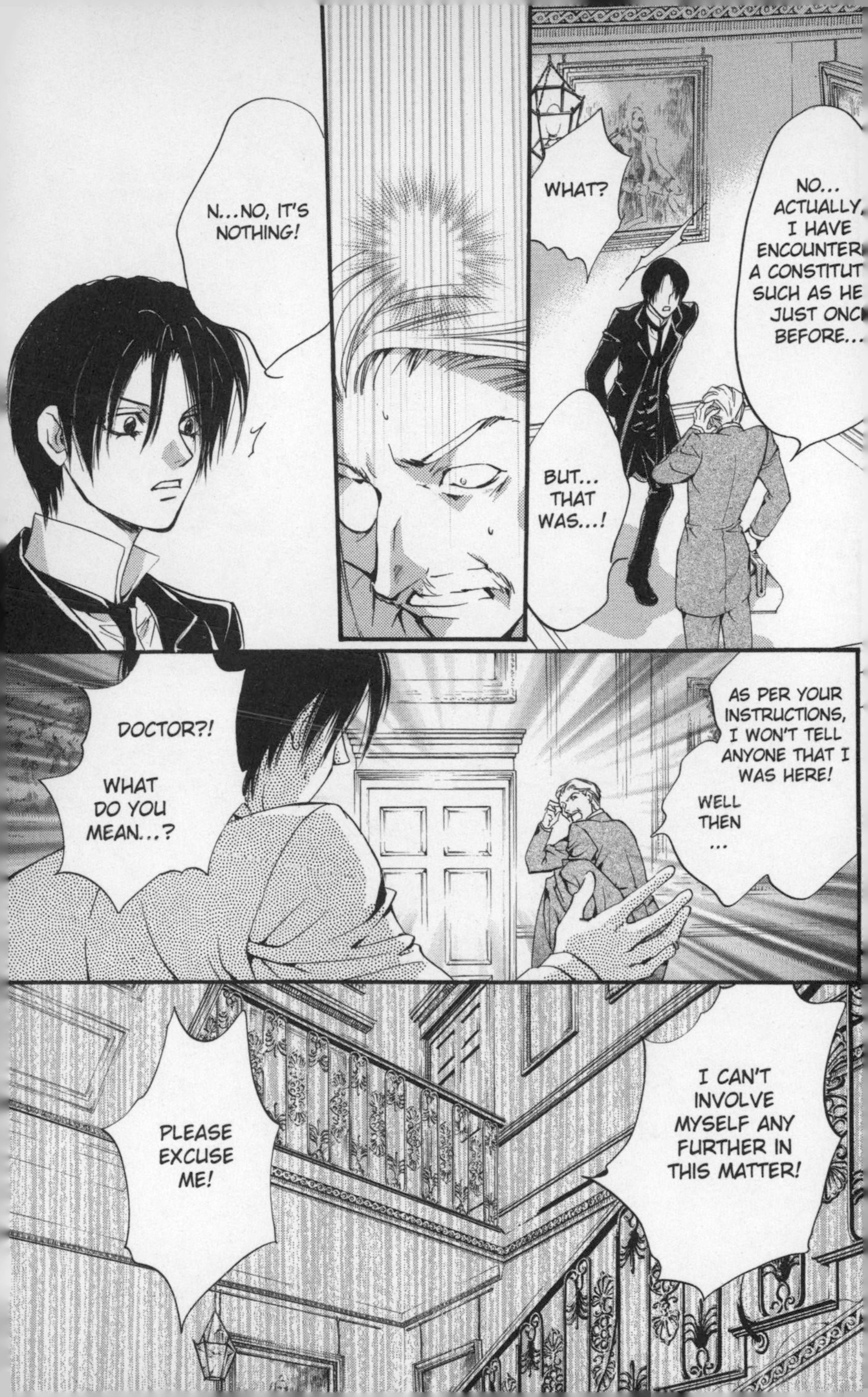
NO... ACTUALLY, I HAVE ENCOUNTER A CONSTITUT SUCH AS HE JUST ONC BEFORE...
WHAT?
BUT... THAT WAS...!
N...NO, IT'S NOTHING!
AS PER YOUR INSTRUCTIONS, I WON'T TELL ANYONE THAT I WAS HERE!
WELL THEN ...
DOCTOR?!
WHAT DO YOU MEAN...?
I CAN'T INVOLVE MYSELF ANY FURTHER IN THIS MATTER!
PLEASE EXCUSE ME!

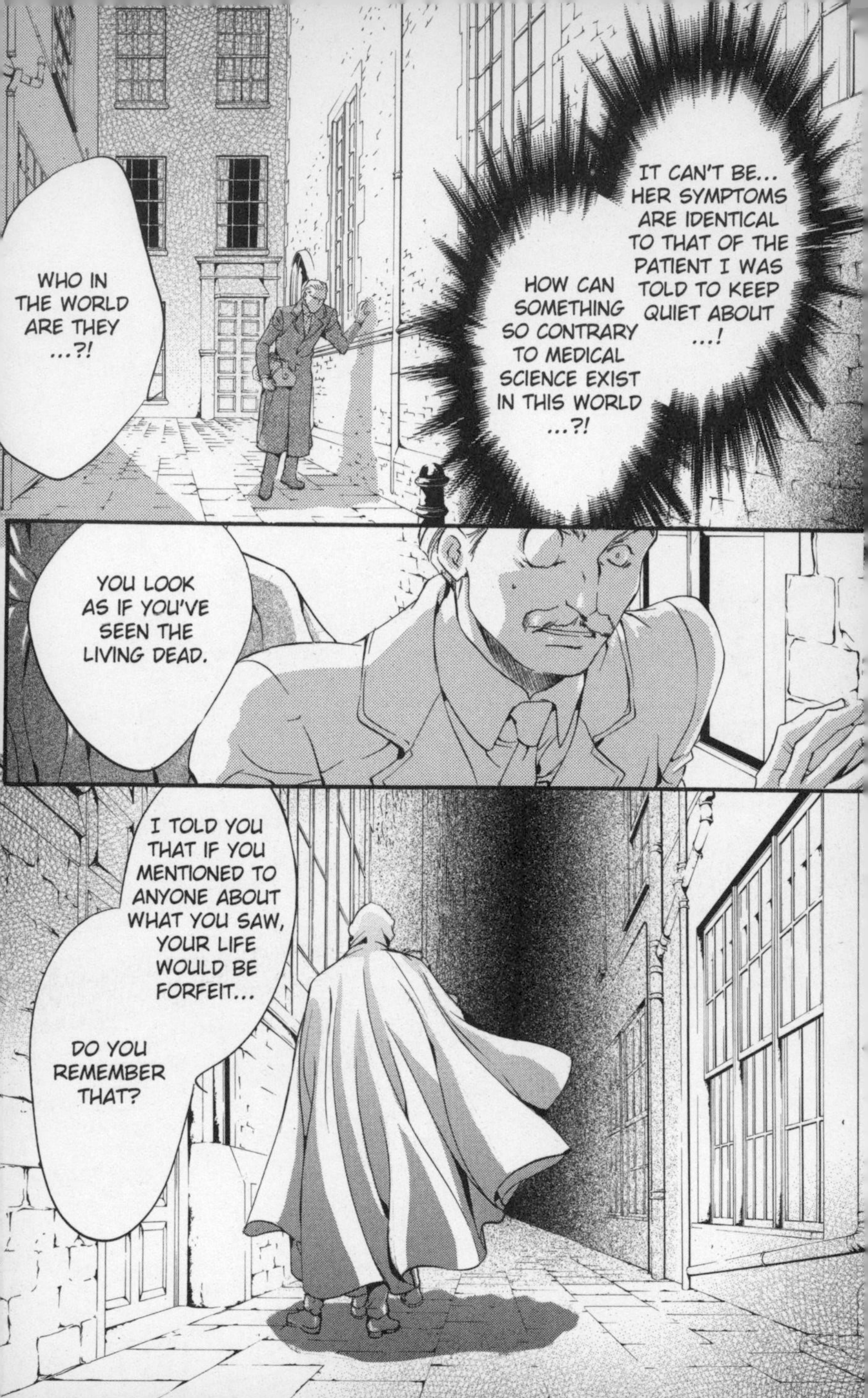
IT CAN'T BE... HER SYMPTOMS ARE IDENTICAL TO THAT OF THE PATIENT I WAS TOLD TO KEEP QUIET ABOUT ...!
HOW CAN SOMETHING SO CONTRARY TO MEDICAL SCIENCE EXIST IN THIS WORLD ...?!
WHO IN THE WORLD ARE THEY ...?!
YOU LOOK AS IF YOU'VE SEEN THE LIVING DEAD.
I TOLD YOU THAT IF YOU MENTIONED TO ANYONE ABOUT WHAT YOU SAW, YOUR LIFE WOULD BE FORFEIT...
DO YOU REMEMBER THAT?

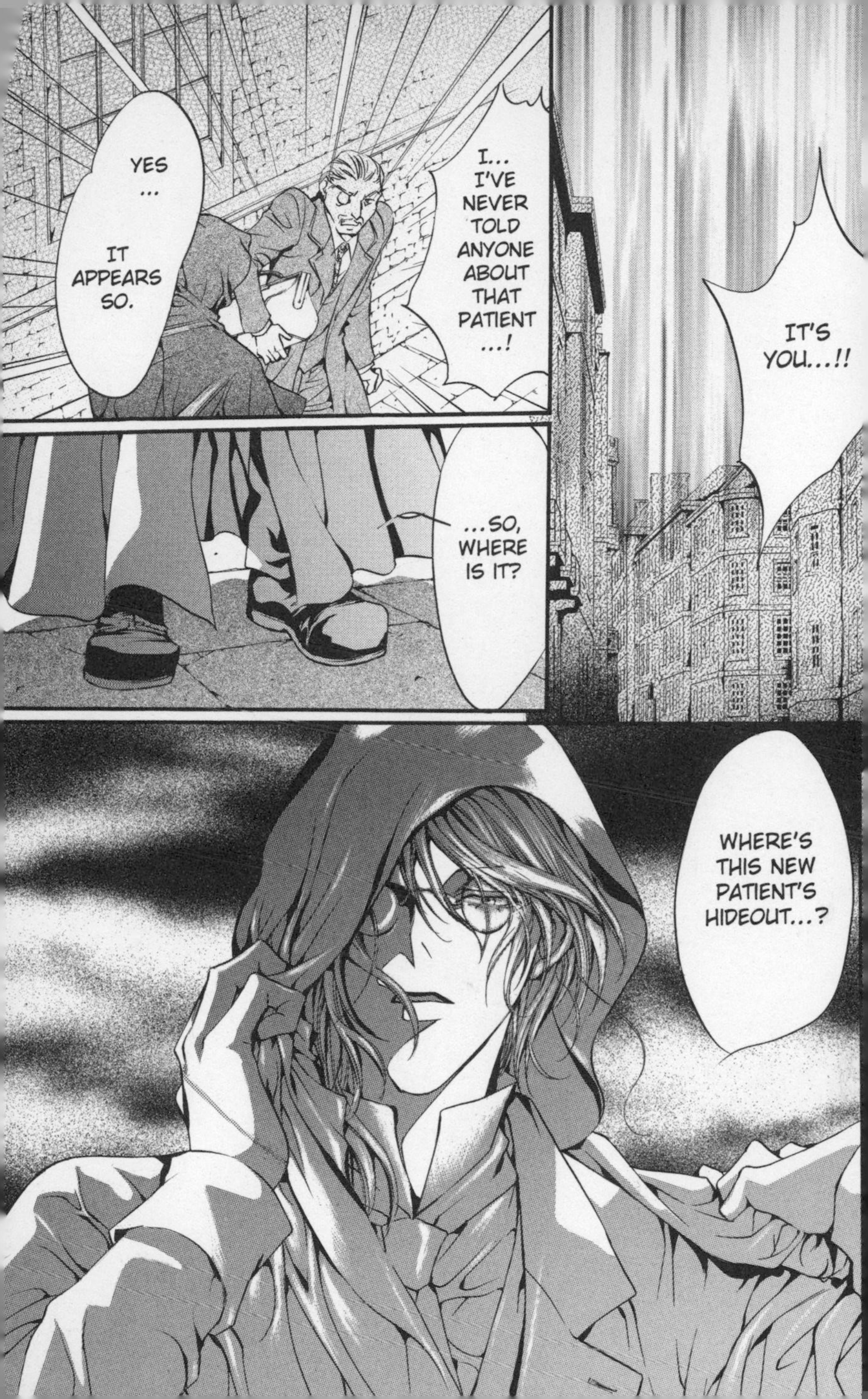
IT'S YOU...!!
I... I'VE NEVER TOLD ANYONE ABOUT THAT PATIENT ...!
YES ... IT APPEARS SO.
...SO, WHERE IS IT?
WHERE'S THIS NEW PATIENT'S HIDEOUT...?

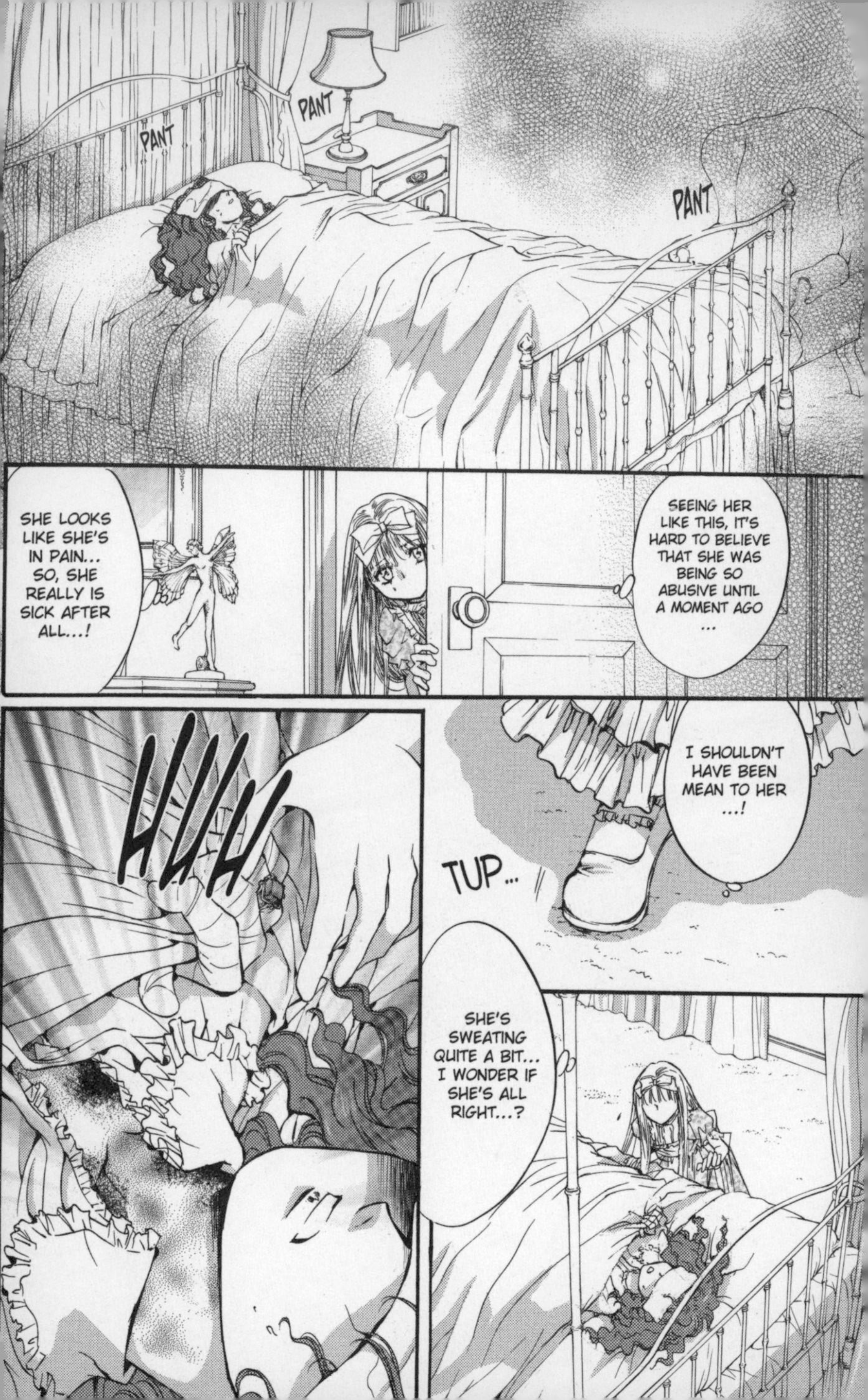
PANT
PANT
PANT
SEEING HER LIKE THIS, IT'S HARD TO BELIEVE THAT SHE WAS BEING SO ABUSIVE UNTIL A MOMENT AGO ...
SHE LOOKS LIKE SHE'S IN PAIN... SO, SHE REALLY IS SICK AFTER ALL...!
I SHOULDN'T HAVE BEEN MEAN TO HER ...!
TUP...
SHE'S SWEATING QUITE A BIT... I WONDER IF SHE'S ALL RIGHT...?
HUH

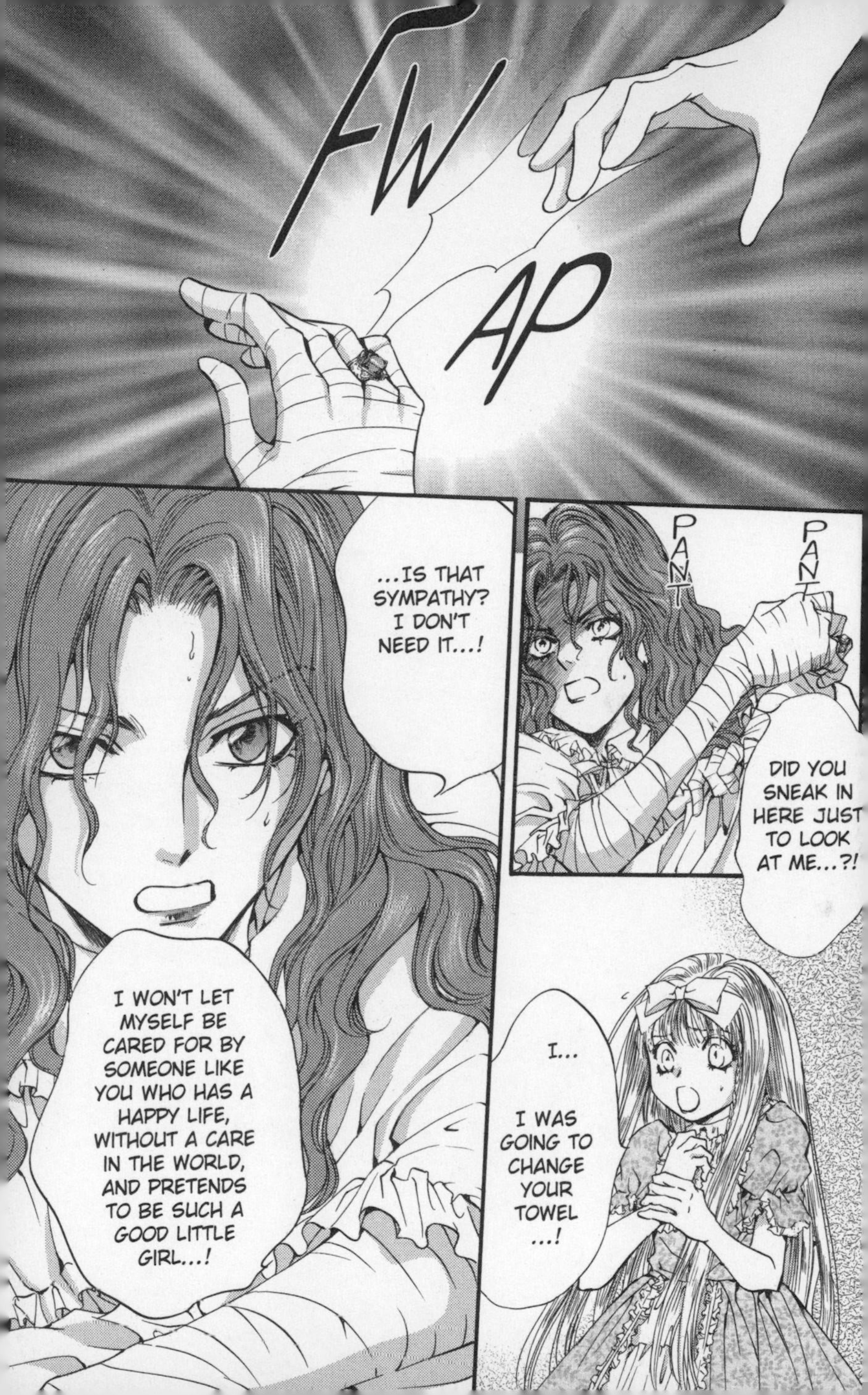
FWAP
PANT
PANT
DID YOU SNEAK IN HERE JUST TO LOOK AT ME...?!
I...
I WAS GOING TO CHANGE YOUR TOWEL ...!
...IS THAT SYMPATHY? I DON'T NEED IT...!
I WON'T LET MYSELF BE CARED FOR BY SOMEONE LIKE YOU WHO HAS A HAPPY LIFE, WITHOUT A CARE IN THE WORLD, AND PRETENDS TO BE SUCH A GOOD LITTLE GIRL...!

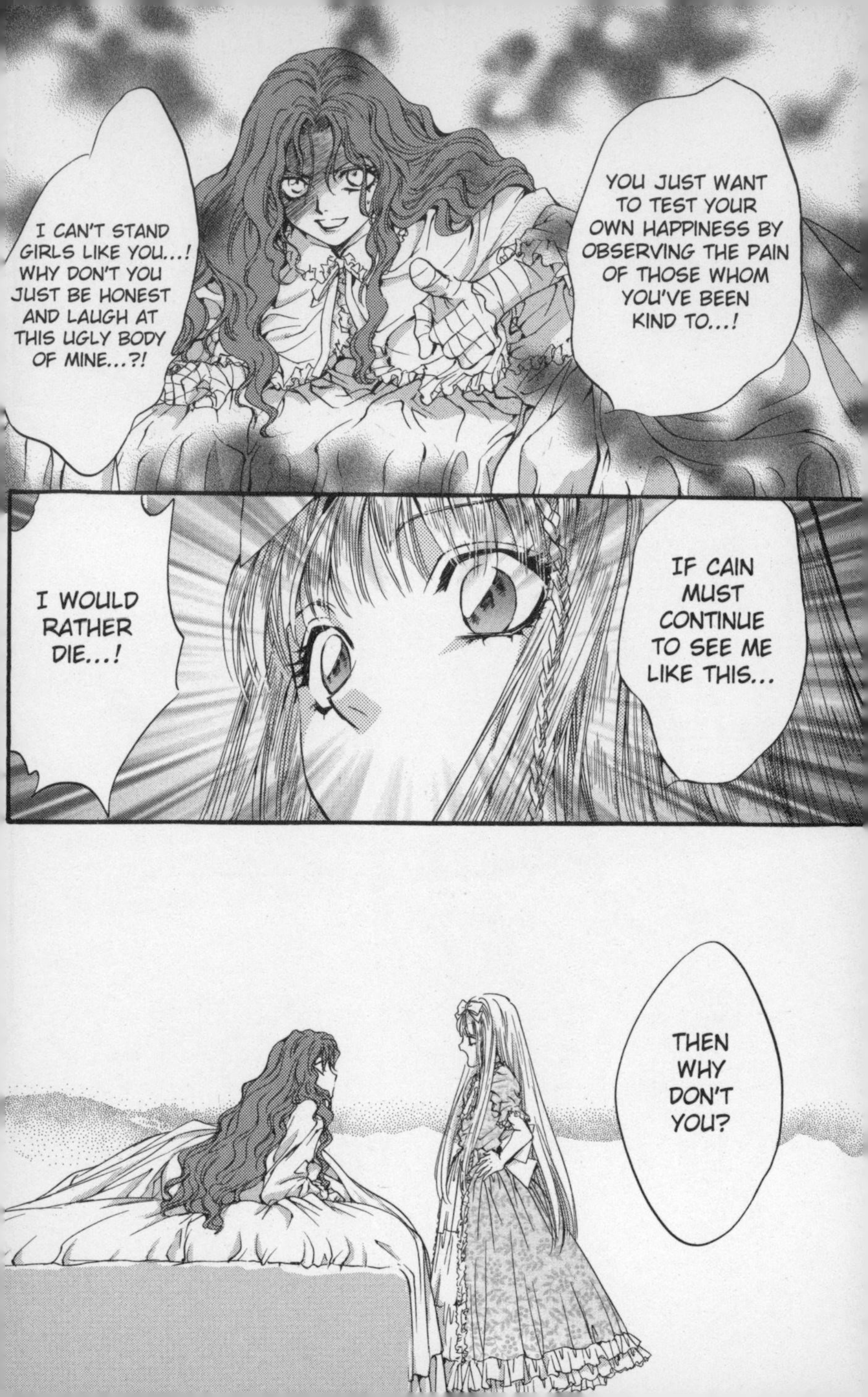
YOU JUST WANT TO TEST YOUR OWN HAPPINESS BY OBSERVING THE PAIN OF THOSE WHOM YOU'VE BEEN KIND TO...!
I CAN'T STAND GIRLS LIKE YOU...! WHY DON'T YOU JUST BE HONEST AND LAUGH AT THIS UGLY BODY OF MINE...?!
IF CAIN MUST CONTINUE TO SEE ME LIKE THIS...
I WOULD RATHER DIE...!
THEN WHY DON'T YOU?

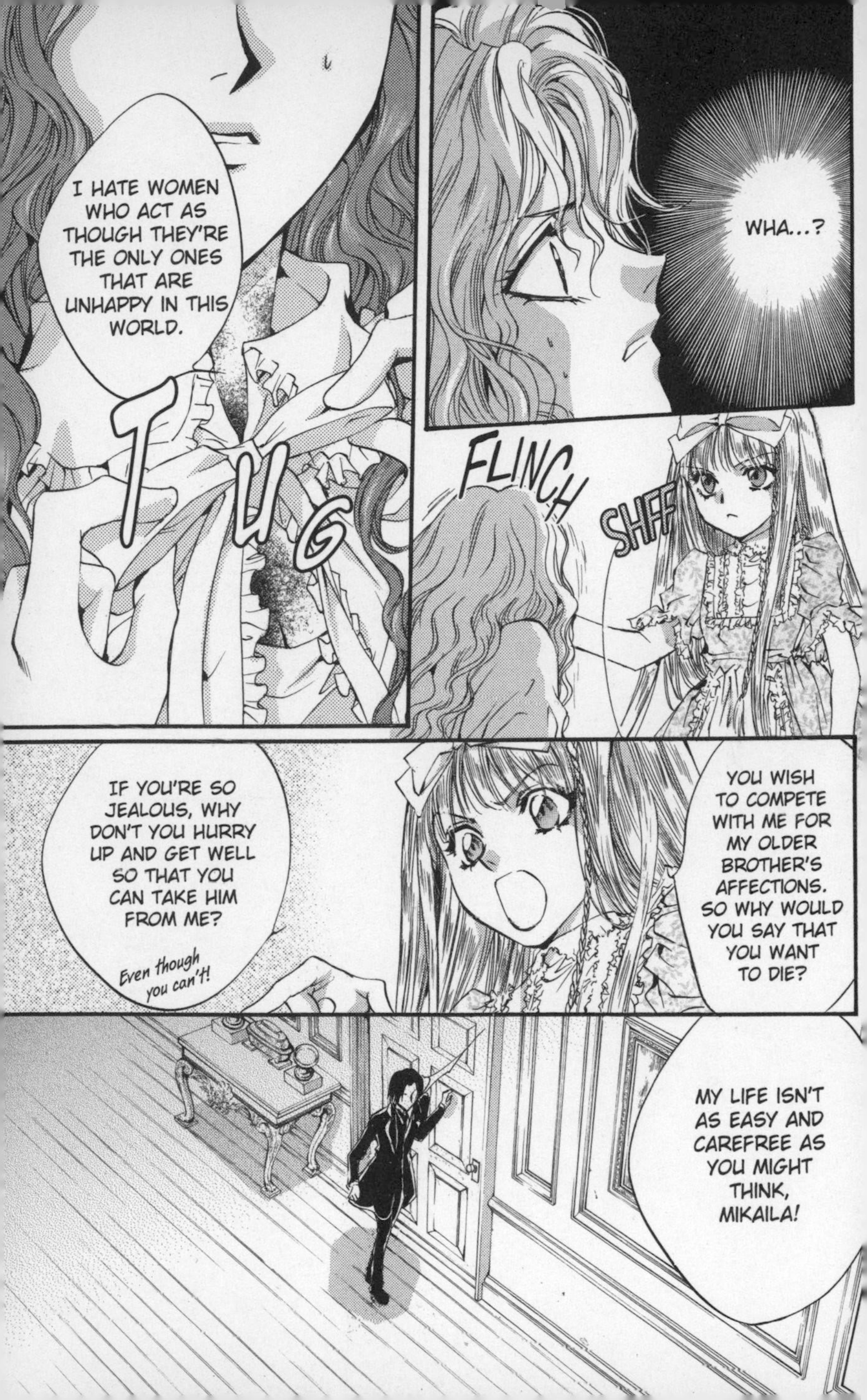
WHA...?
FLINCH
SHFF
I HATE WOMEN WHO ACT AS THOUGH THEY'RE THE ONLY ONES THAT ARE UNHAPPY IN THIS WORLD.
TUG
YOU WISH TO COMPETE WITH ME FOR MY OLDER BROTHER'S AFFECTIONS. SO WHY WOULD YOU SAY THAT YOU WANT TO DIE?
IF YOU'RE SO JEALOUS, WHY DON'T YOU HURRY UP AND GET WELL SO THAT YOU CAN TAKE HIM FROM ME?
Even though you can't!
MY LIFE ISN'T AS EASY AND CAREFREE AS YOU MIGHT THINK, MIKAILA!

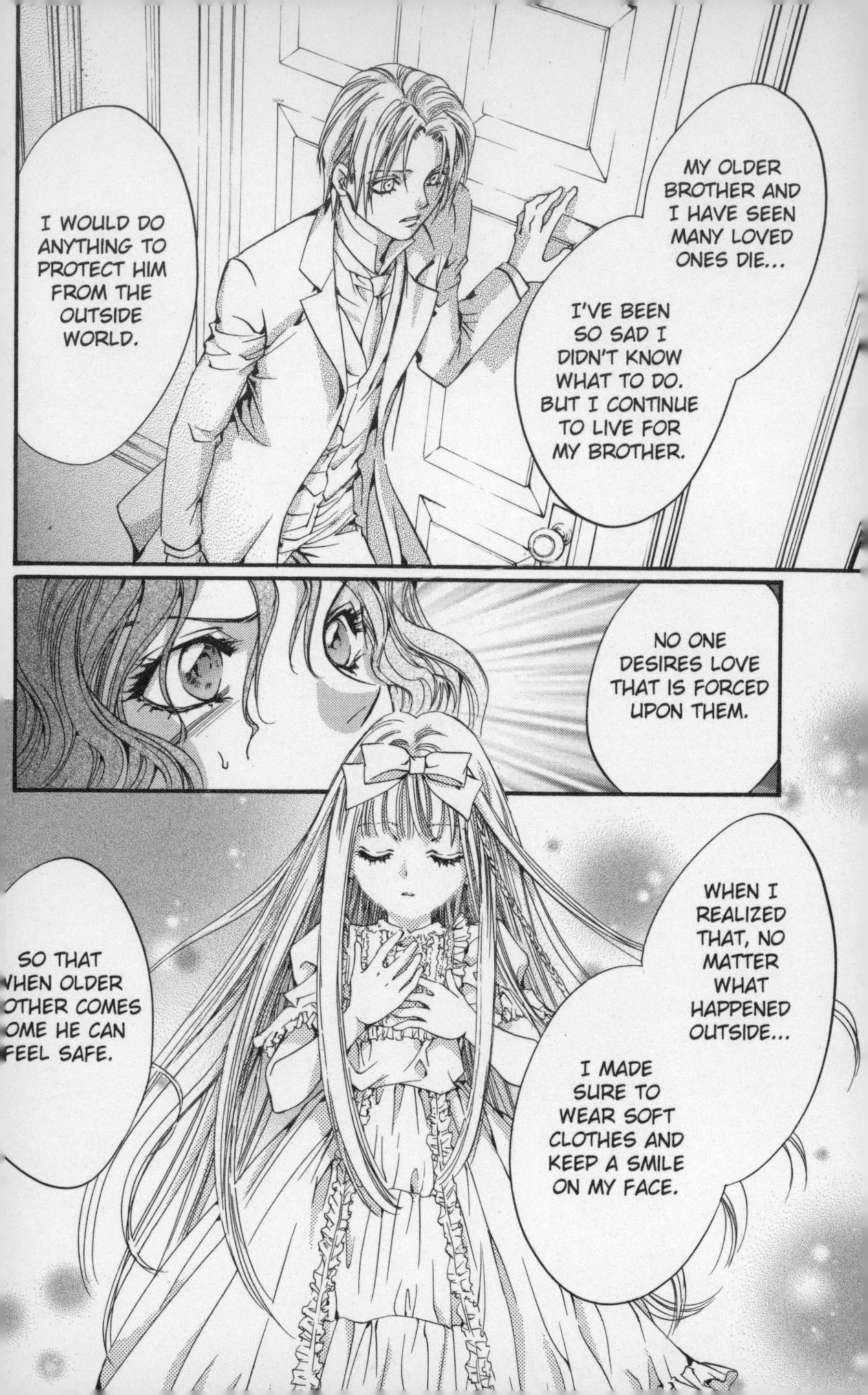
MY OLDER BROTHER AND I HAVE SEEN MANY LOVED ONES DIE...
I'VE BEEN SO SAD I DIDN'T KNOW WHAT TO DO. BUT I CONTINUE TO LIVE FOR MY BROTHER.
I WOULD DO ANYTHING TO PROTECT HIM FROM THE OUTSIDE WORLD.
NO ONE DESIRES LOVE THAT IS FORCED UPON THEM.
WHEN I REALIZED THAT, NO MATTER WHAT HAPPENED OUTSIDE...
I MADE SURE TO WEAR SOFT CLOTHES AND KEEP A SMILE ON MY FACE.
SO THAT HEN OLDER OTHER COMES OME HE CAN FEEL SAFE.

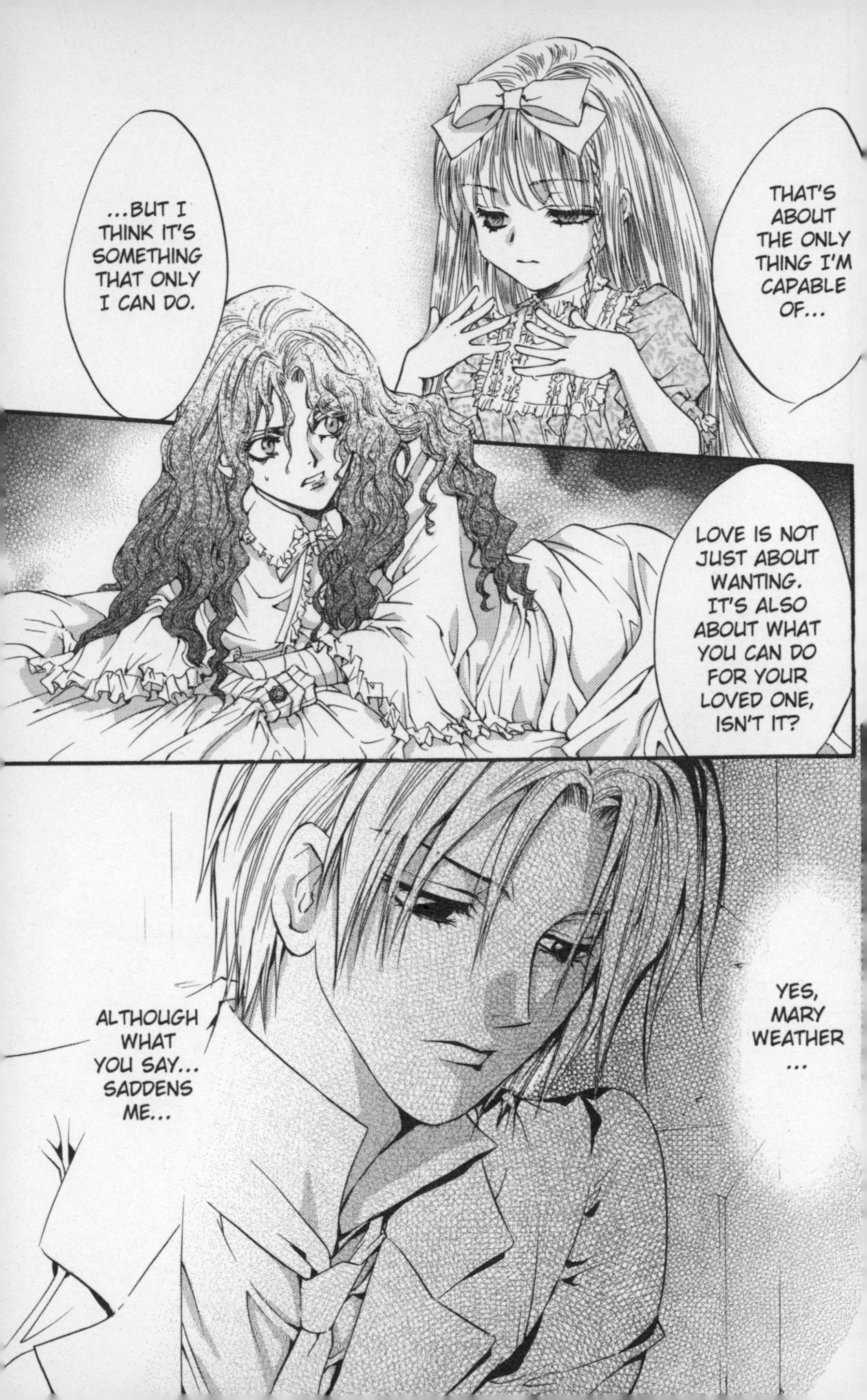
THAT'S ABOUT THE ONLY THING I'M CAPABLE OF...
...BUT I THINK IT'S SOMETHING THAT ONLY I CAN DO.
LOVE IS NOT JUST ABOUT WANTING. IT'S ALSO ABOUT WHAT YOU CAN DO FOR YOUR LOVED ONE, ISN'T IT?
YES, MARY WEATHER ...
ALTHOUGH WHAT YOU SAY... SADDENS ME...

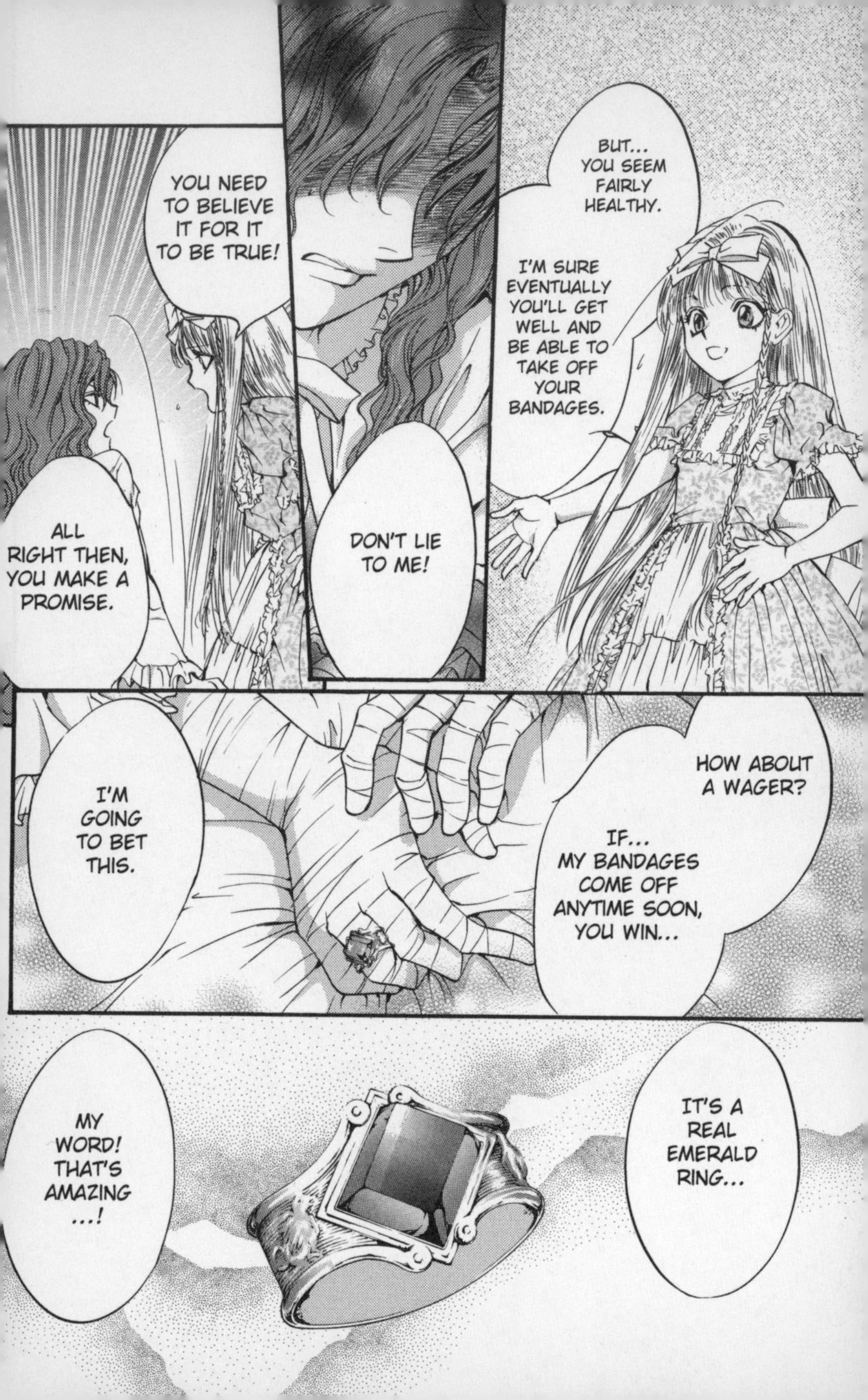
BUT... YOU SEEM FAIRLY HEALTHY.
I'M SURE EVENTUALLY YOU'LL GET WELL AND BE ABLE TO TAKE OFF YOUR BANDAGES.
DON'T LIE TO ME!
YOU NEED TO BELIEVE IT FOR IT TO BE TRUE!
ALL RIGHT THEN, YOU MAKE A PROMISE.
HOW ABOUT A WAGER?
IF... MY BANDAGES COME OFF ANYTIME SOON, YOU WIN...
I'M GOING TO BET THIS.
IT'S A REAL EMERALD RING...
MY WORD! THAT'S AMAZING ...!

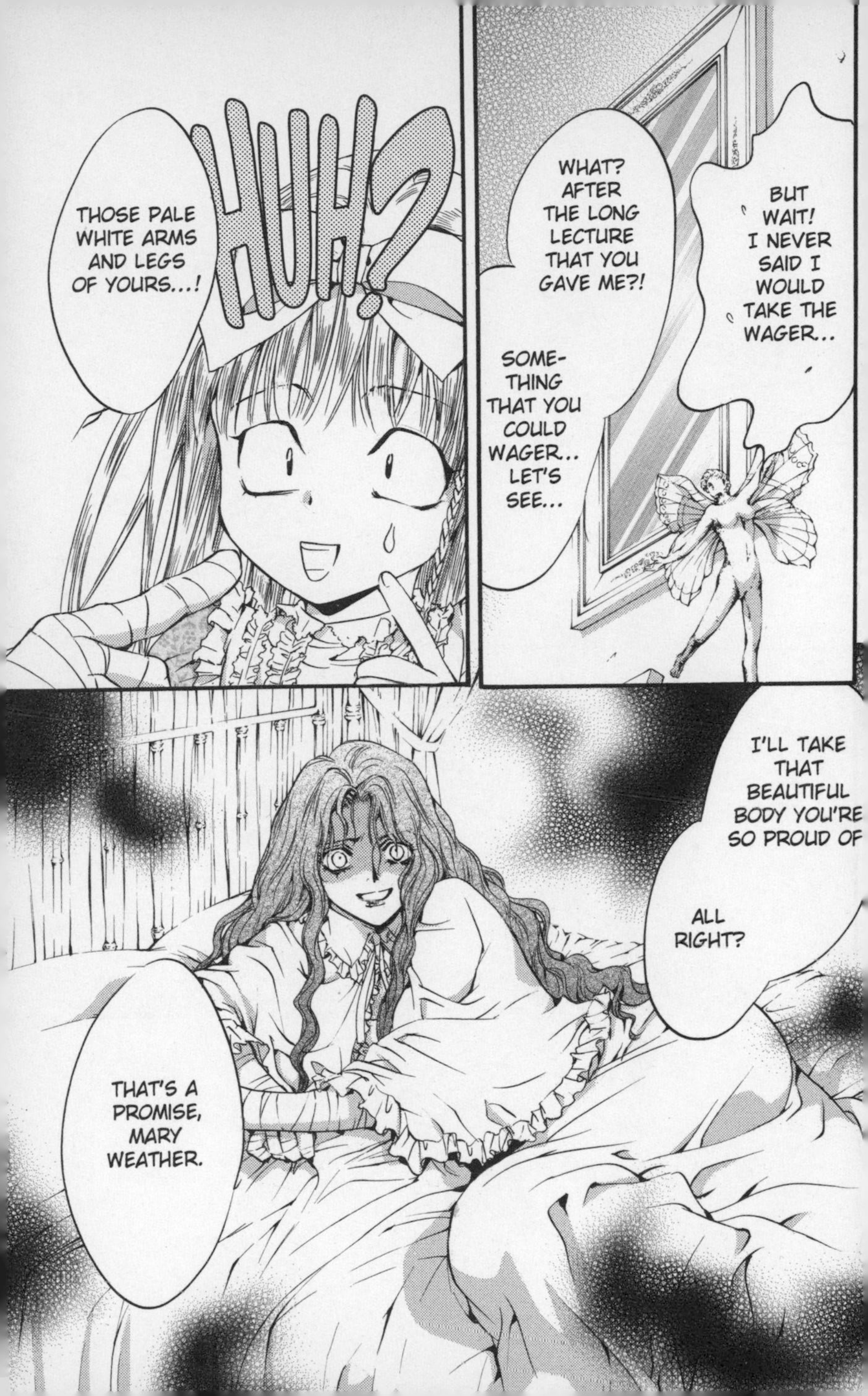
BUT WAIT! I NEVER SAID I WOULD TAKE THE WAGER...
WHAT? AFTER THE LONG LECTURE THAT YOU GAVE ME?!
SOME-THING THAT YOU COULD WAGER... LET'S SEE...
HUH?
THOSE PALE WHITE ARMS AND LEGS OF YOURS...!
I'LL TAKE THAT BEAUTIFUL BODY YOU'RE SO PROUD OF
ALL RIGHT?
THAT'S A PROMISE, MARY WEATHER.

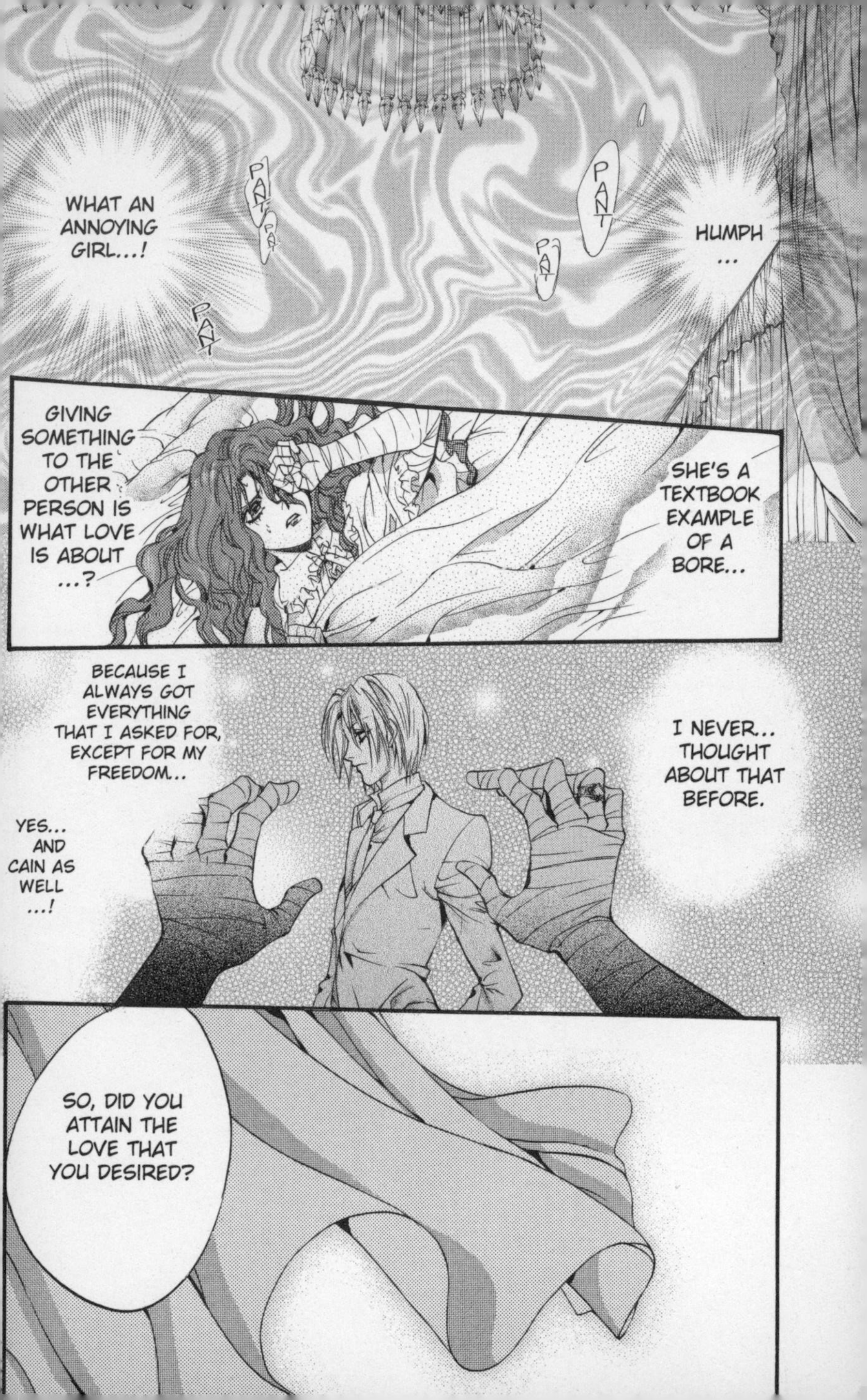
HUMPH ...
PANT
PANT
WHAT AN ANNOYING GIRL...!
PANT PANT
PANT
SHE'S A TEXTBOOK EXAMPLE OF A BORE...
GIVING SOMETHING TO THE OTHER PERSON IS WHAT LOVE IS ABOUT ...?
I NEVER... THOUGHT ABOUT THAT BEFORE.
BECAUSE I ALWAYS GOT EVERYTHING THAT I ASKED FOR, EXCEPT FOR MY FREEDOM...
YES... AND CAIN AS WELL ...!
SO, DID YOU ATTAIN THE LOVE THAT YOU DESIRED?

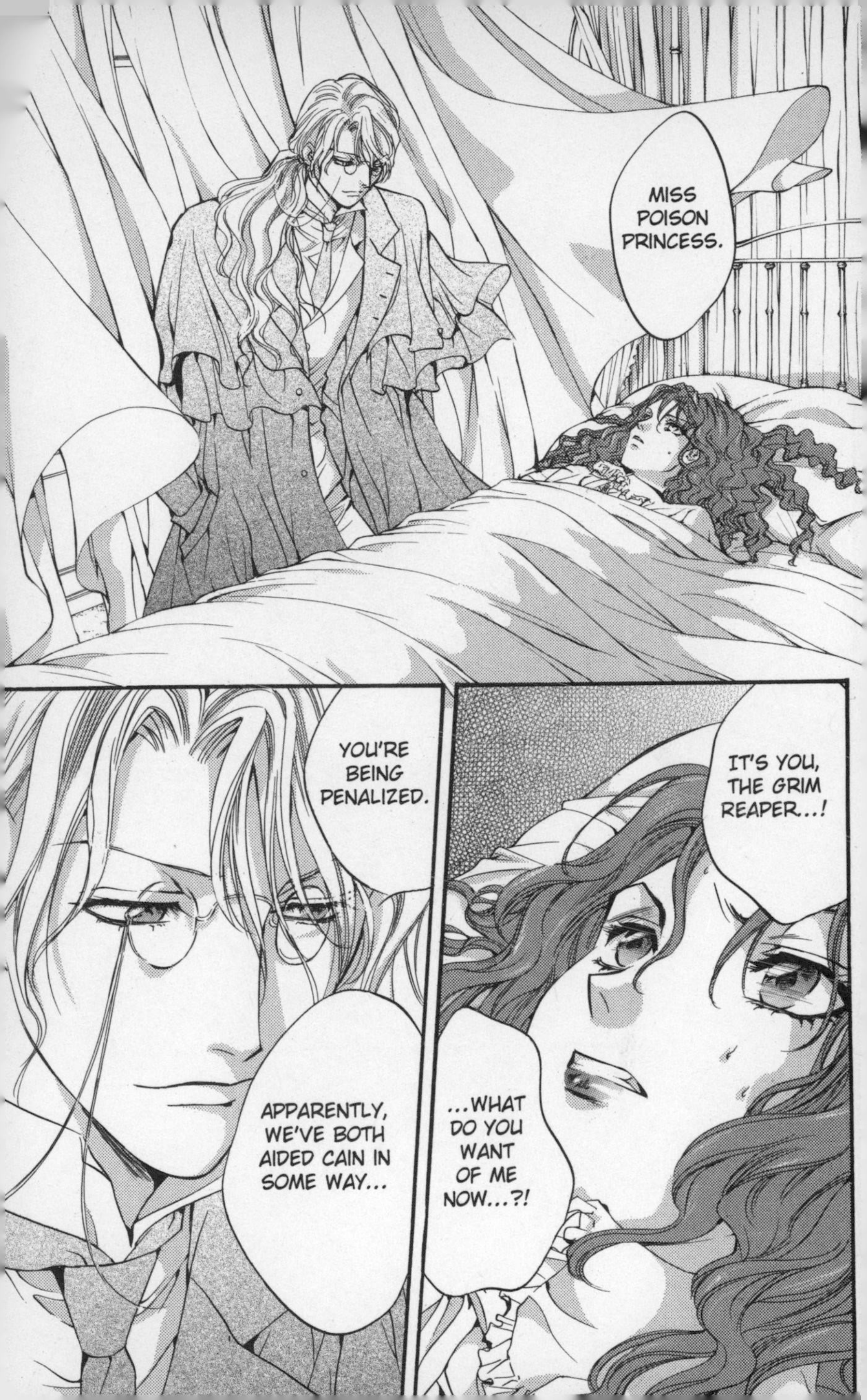
MISS POISON PRINCESS.
IT'S YOU, THE GRIM REAPER...!
...WHAT DO YOU WANT OF ME NOW...?!
YOU'RE BEING PENALIZED.
APPARENTLY, WE'VE BOTH AIDED CAIN IN SOME WAY...

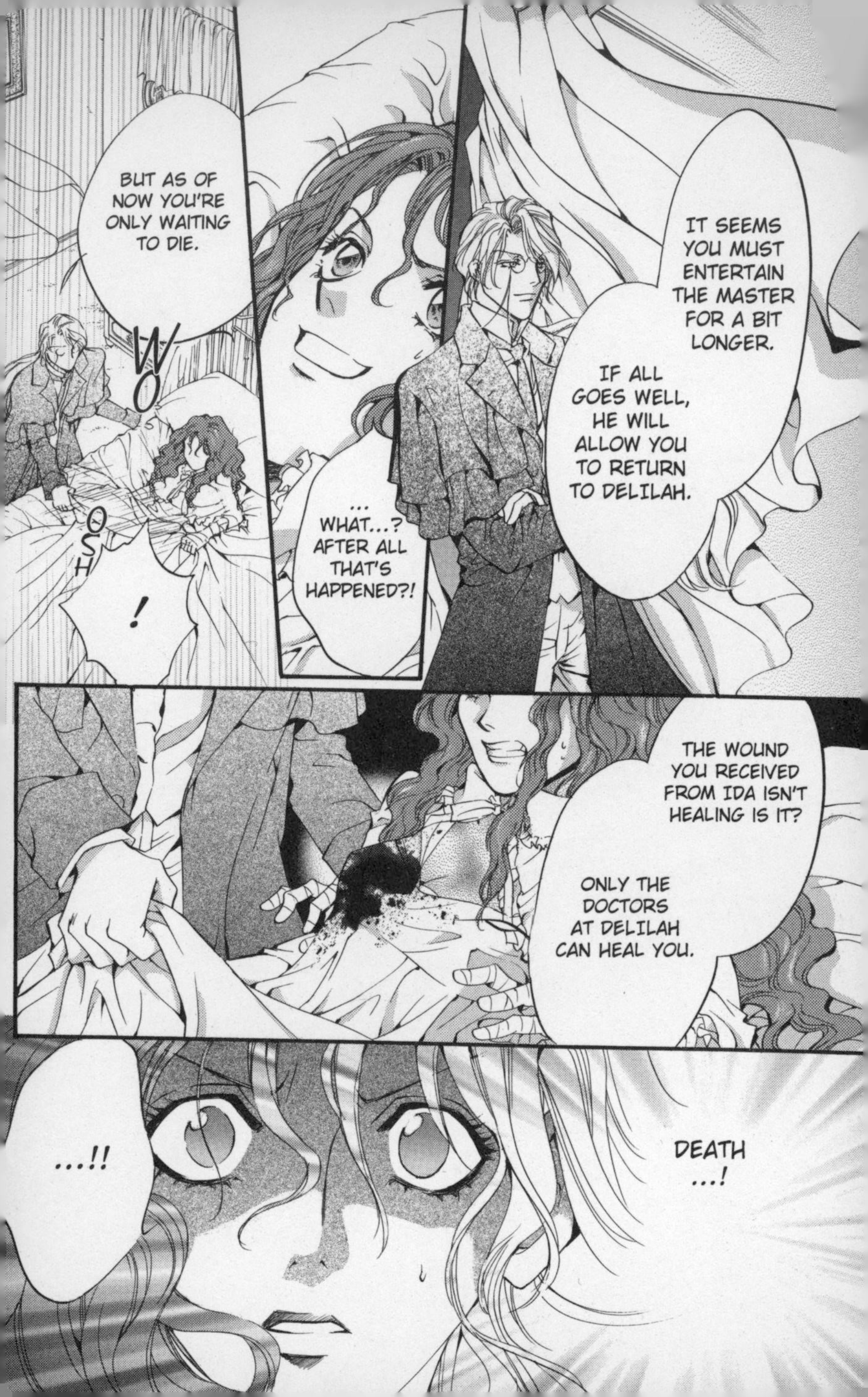
IT SEEMS YOU MUST ENTERTAIN THE MASTER FOR A BIT LONGER.
IF ALL GOES WELL, HE WILL ALLOW YOU TO RETURN TO DELILAH.
... WHAT...? AFTER ALL THAT'S HAPPENED?!
BUT AS OF NOW YOU'RE ONLY WAITING TO DIE.
WOOSH
!
THE WOUND YOU RECEIVED FROM IDA ISN'T HEALING IS IT?
ONLY THE DOCTORS AT DELILAH CAN HEAL YOU.
DEATH ...!
...!!

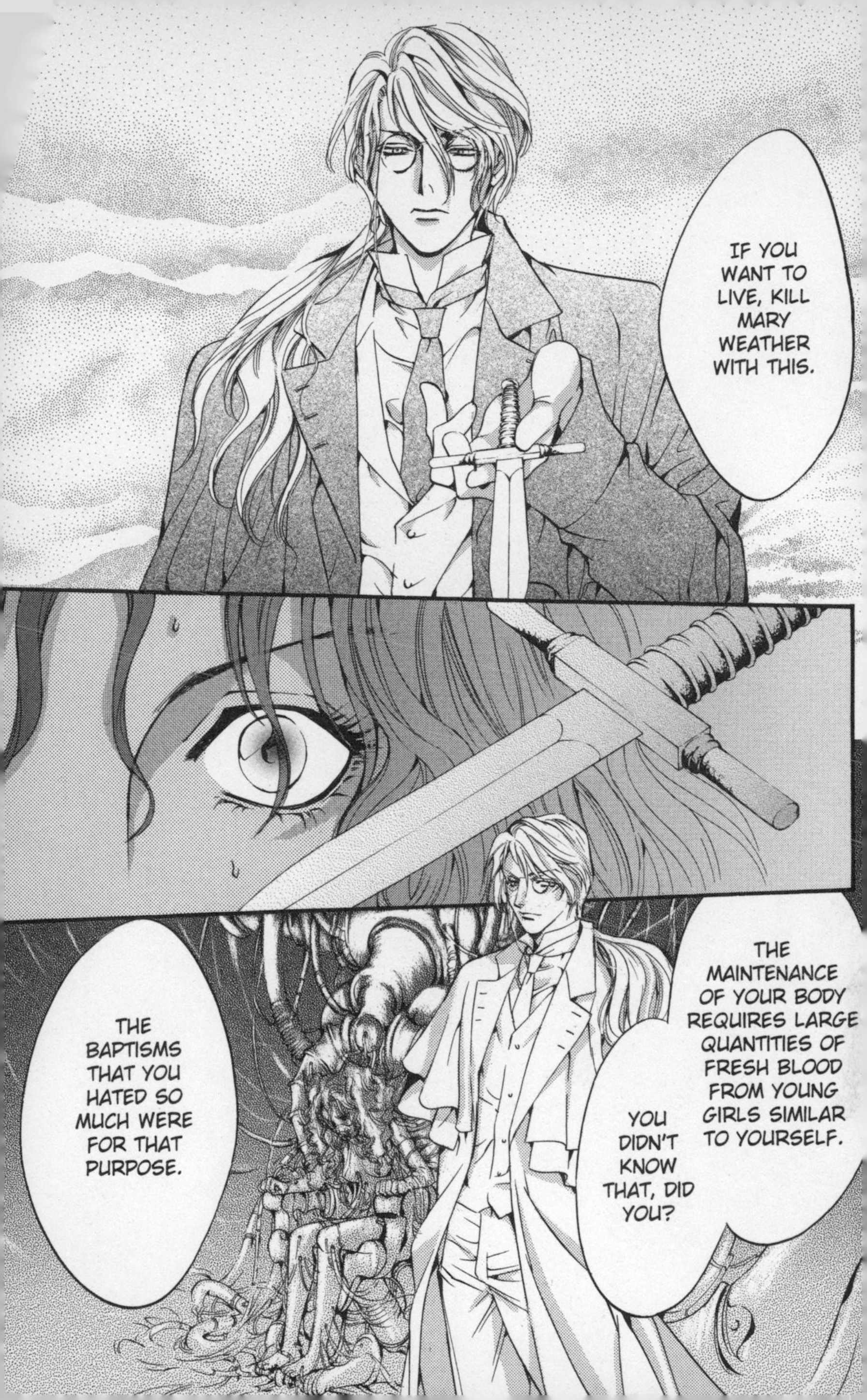
IF YOU WANT TO LIVE, KILL MARY WEATHER WITH THIS.
THE MAINTENANCE OF YOUR BODY REQUIRES LARGE QUANTITIES OF FRESH BLOOD FROM YOUNG GIRLS SIMILAR TO YOURSELF.
YOU DIDN'T KNOW THAT, DID YOU?
THE BAPTISMS THAT YOU HATED SO MUCH WERE FOR THAT PURPOSE.

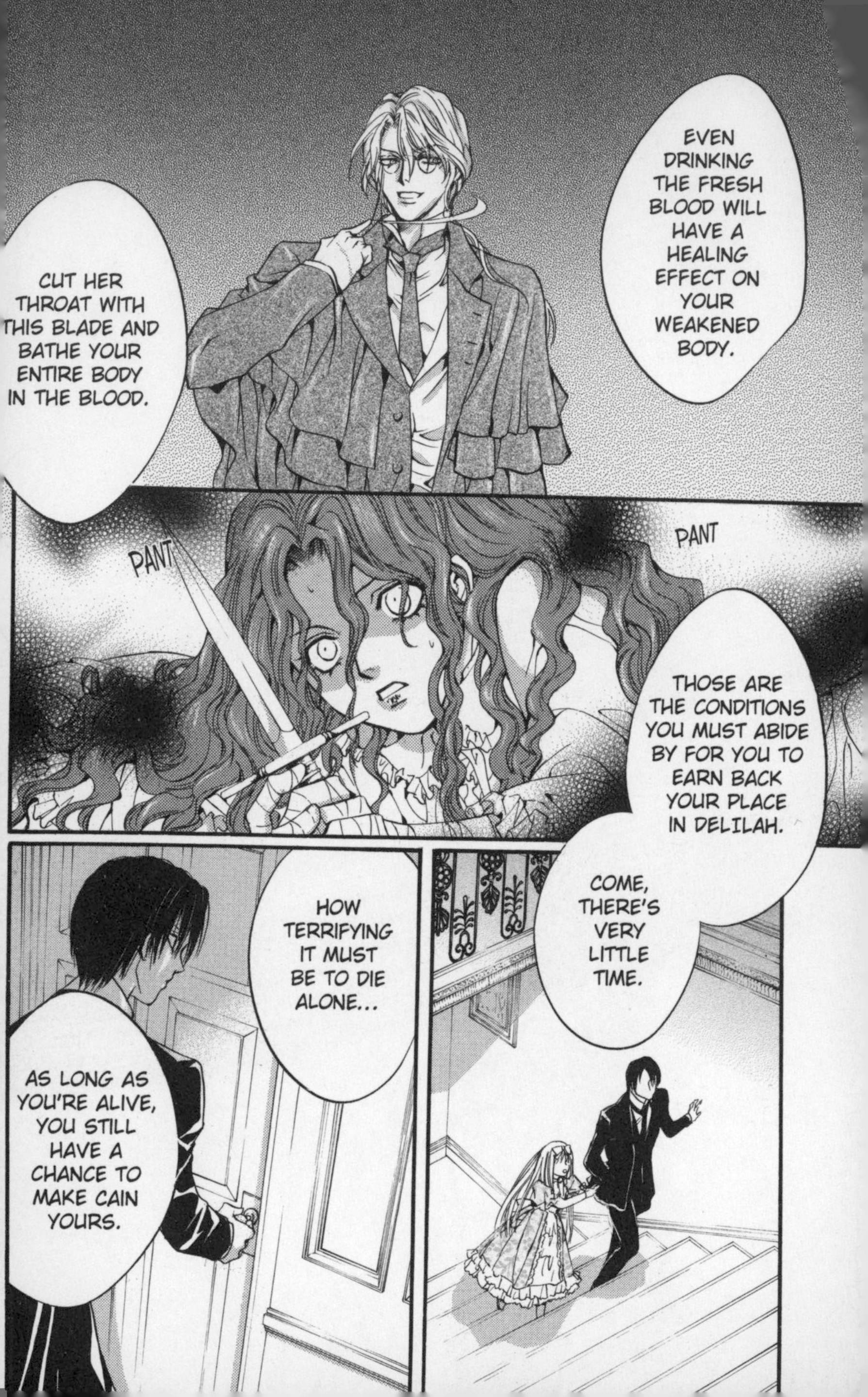
EVEN DRINKING THE FRESH BLOOD WILL HAVE A HEALING EFFECT ON YOUR WEAKENED BODY.
CUT HER THROAT WITH THIS BLADE AND BATHE YOUR ENTIRE BODY IN THE BLOOD.
PANT
PANT
THOSE ARE THE CONDITIONS YOU MUST ABIDE BY FOR YOU TO EARN BACK YOUR PLACE IN DELILAH.
COME, THERE'S VERY LITTLE TIME.
HOW TERRIFYING IT MUST BE TO DIE ALONE...
AS LONG AS YOU'RE ALIVE, YOU STILL HAVE A CHANCE TO MAKE CAIN YOURS.

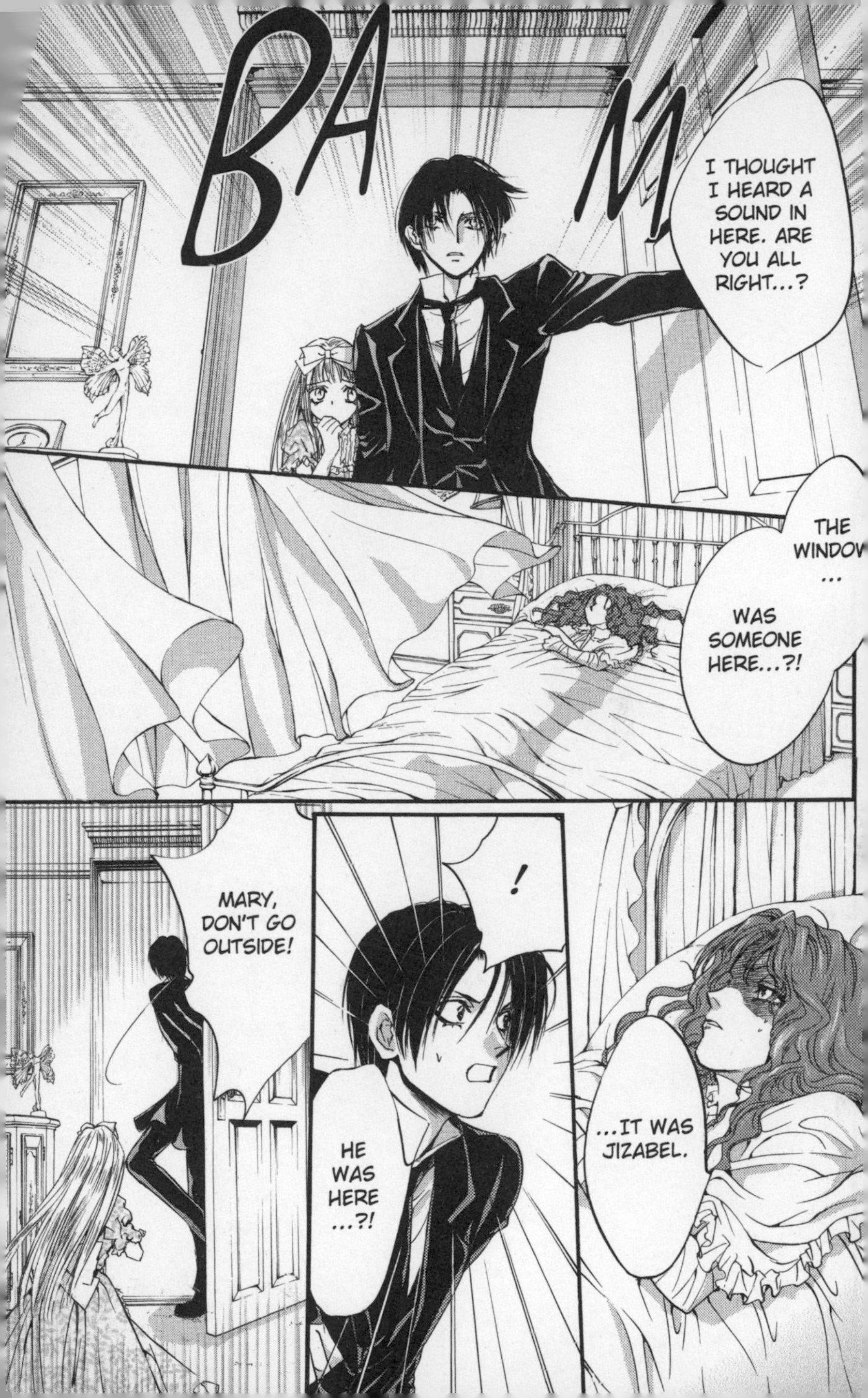
BAM
I THOUGHT I HEARD A SOUND IN HERE. ARE YOU ALL RIGHT...?
THE WINDOW...
WAS SOMEONE HERE...?!
...IT WAS JIZABEL.
!
HE WAS HERE...?!
MARY, DON'T GO OUTSIDE!

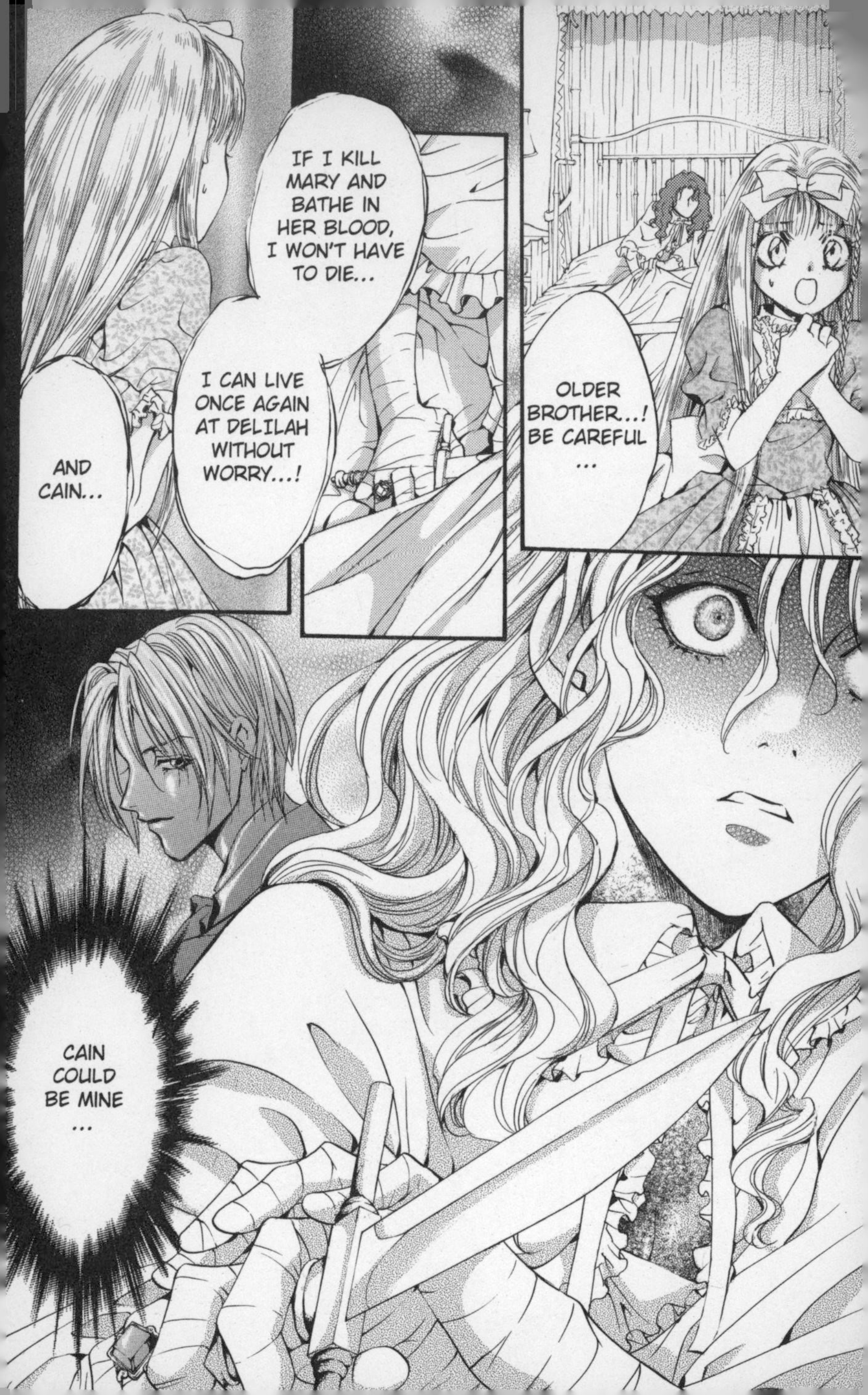
OLDER BROTHER...! BE CAREFUL ...
IF I KILL MARY AND BATHE IN HER BLOOD, I WON'T HAVE TO DIE...
I CAN LIVE ONCE AGAIN AT DELILAH WITHOUT WORRY...!
AND CAIN...
CAIN COULD BE MINE ...

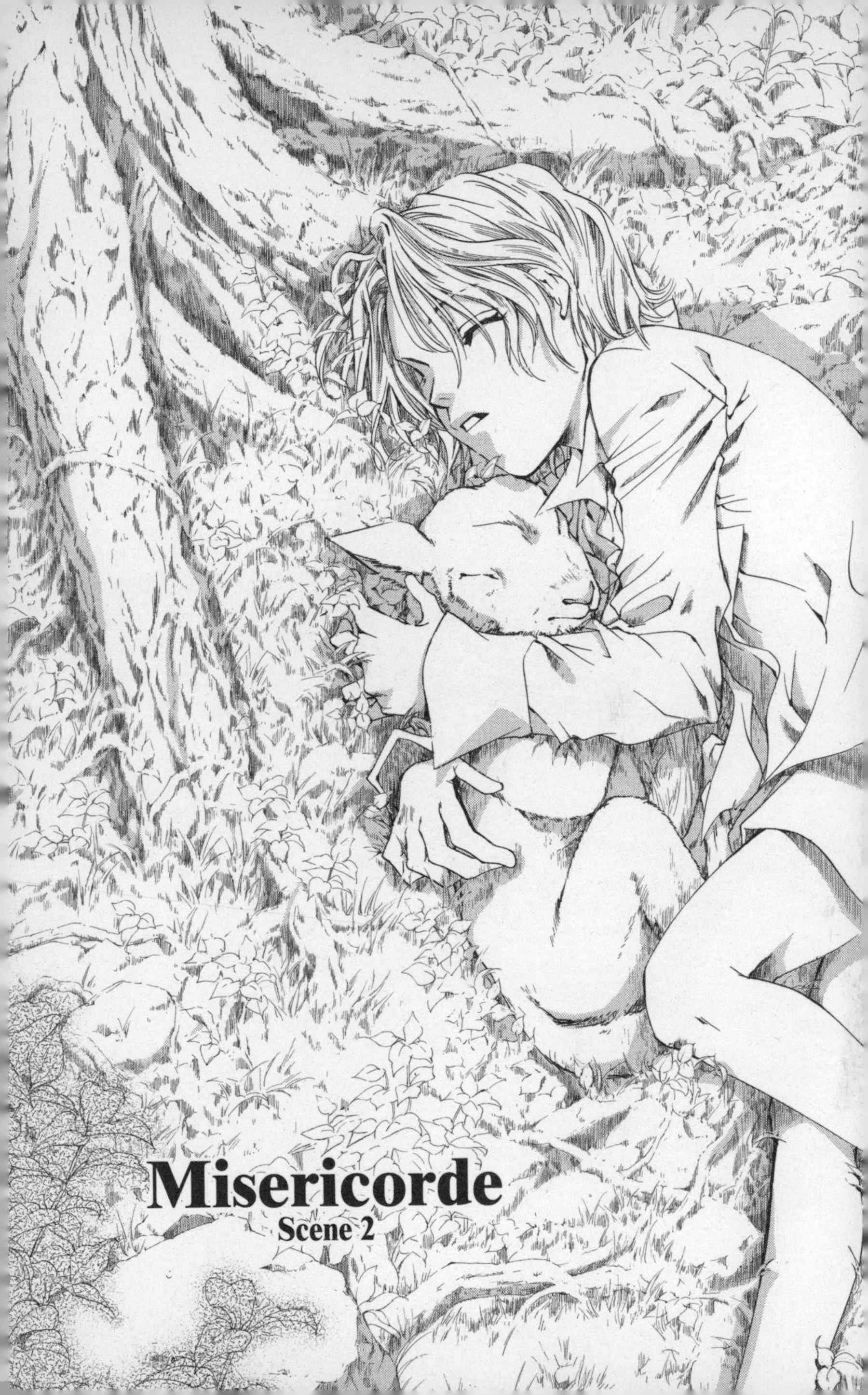
Misericorde
Scene 2

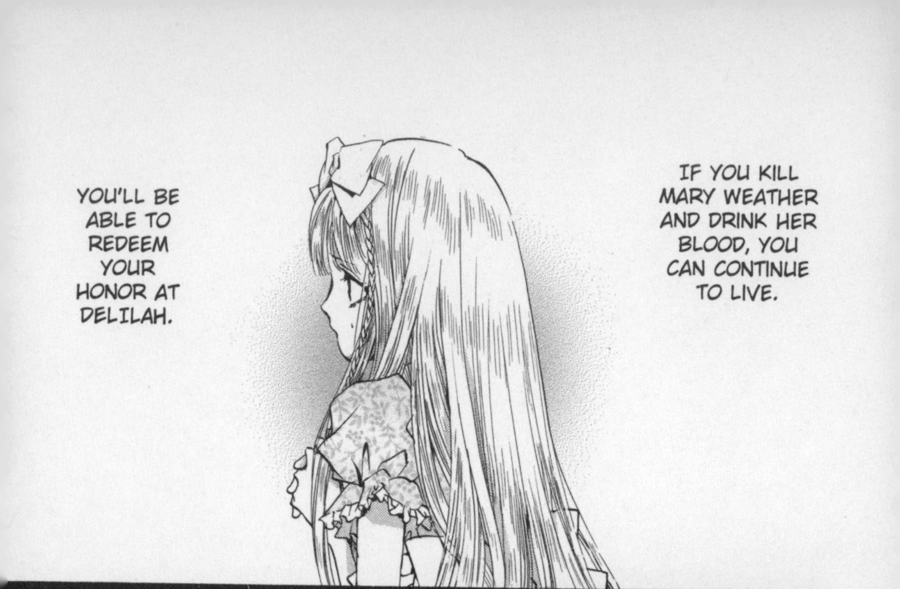
IF YOU KILL MARY WEATHER AND DRINK HER BLOOD, YOU CAN CONTINUE TO LIVE.
YOU'LL BE ABLE TO REDEEM YOUR HONOR AT DELILAH.

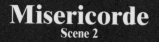

Misericorde
Scene 2

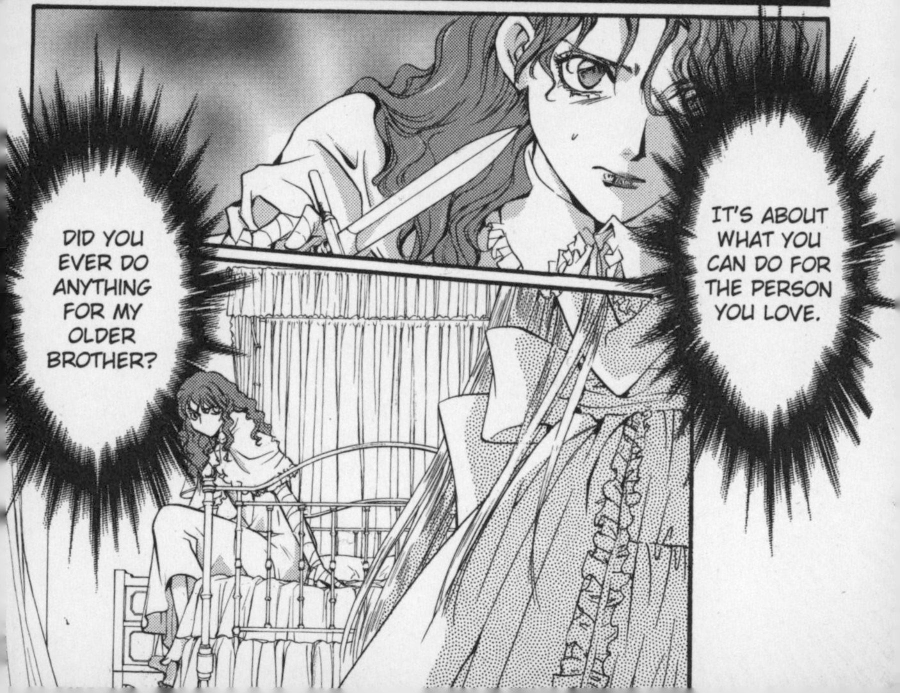
IT'S ABOUT WHAT YOU CAN DO FOR THE PERSON YOU LOVE.
DID YOU EVER DO ANYTHING FOR MY OLDER BROTHER?

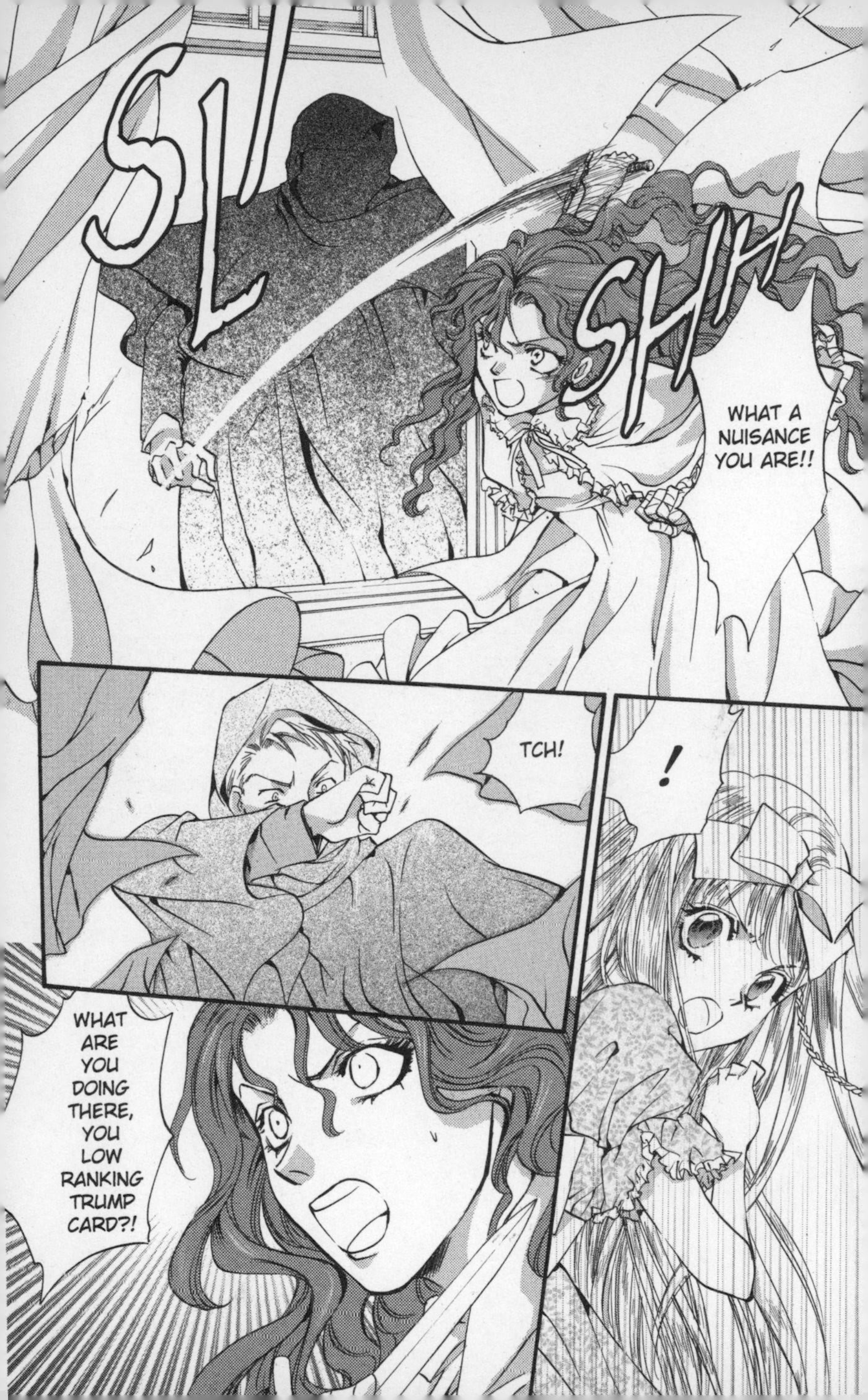
SLISHH
WHAT A NUISANCE YOU ARE!!
!
TCH!
WHAT ARE YOU DOING THERE, YOU LOW RANKING TRUMP CARD?!

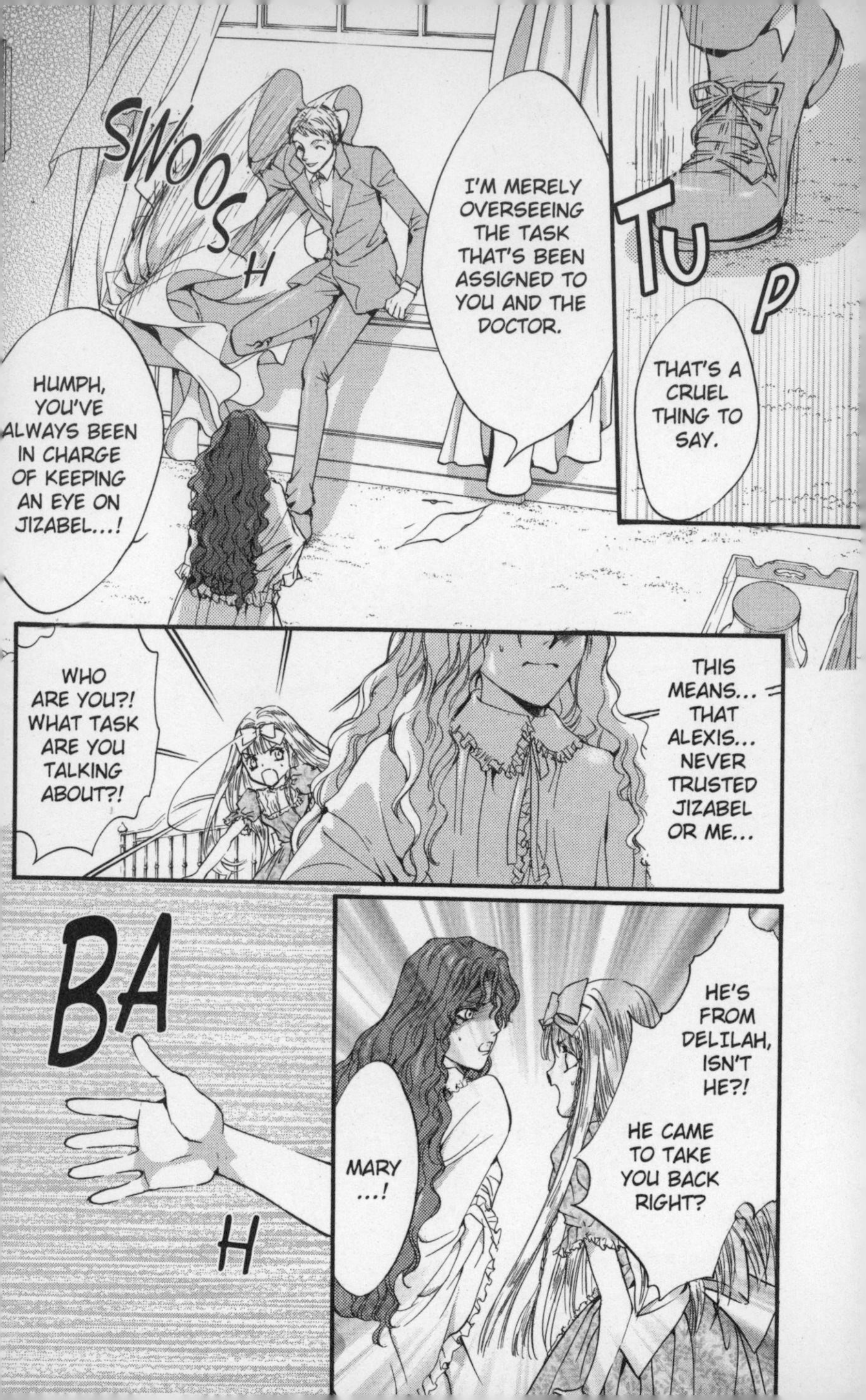
TUP
THAT'S A CRUEL THING TO SAY.
SWOOSH
I'M MERELY OVERSEEING THE TASK THAT'S BEEN ASSIGNED TO YOU AND THE DOCTOR.
HUMPH, YOU'VE ALWAYS BEEN IN CHARGE OF KEEPING AN EYE ON JIZABEL...!
THIS MEANS... THAT ALEXIS... NEVER TRUSTED JIZABEL OR ME...
WHO ARE YOU?! WHAT TASK ARE YOU TALKING ABOUT?!
HE'S FROM DELILAH, ISN'T HE?!
HE CAME TO TAKE YOU BACK RIGHT?
MARY ...!
BAH

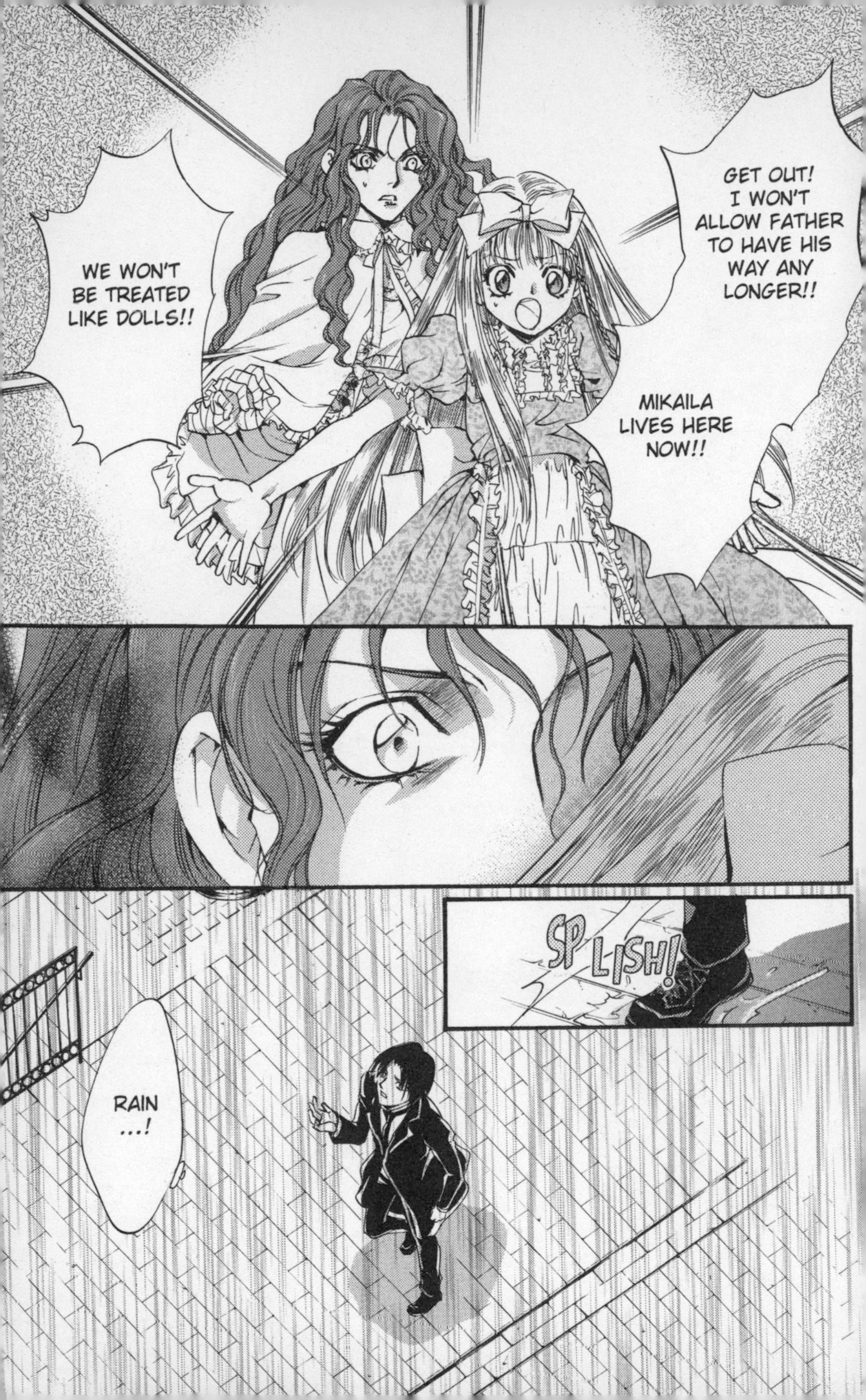
GET OUT! I WON'T ALLOW FATHER TO HAVE HIS WAY ANY LONGER!!
MIKAILA LIVES HERE NOW!!
WE WON'T BE TREATED LIKE DOLLS!!
SPLISH!
RAIN ...!

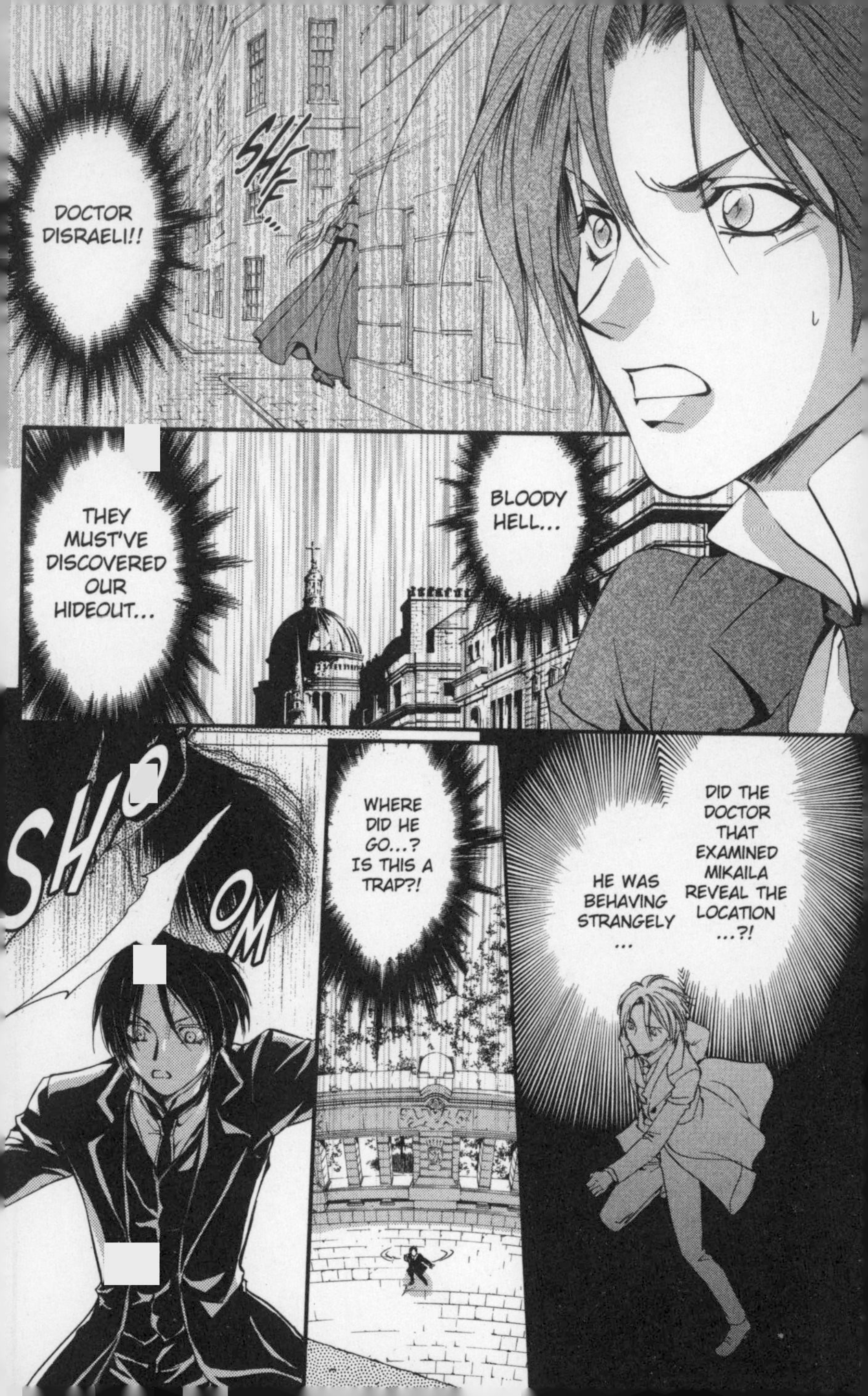
SHF...
DOCTOR DISRAELI!!
BLOODY HELL...
THEY MUST'VE DISCOVERED OUR HIDEOUT...
DID THE DOCTOR THAT EXAMINED MIKAILA REVEAL THE LOCATION ...?!
HE WAS BEHAVING STRANGELY ...
WHERE DID HE GO...? IS THIS A TRAP?!
SHOOM

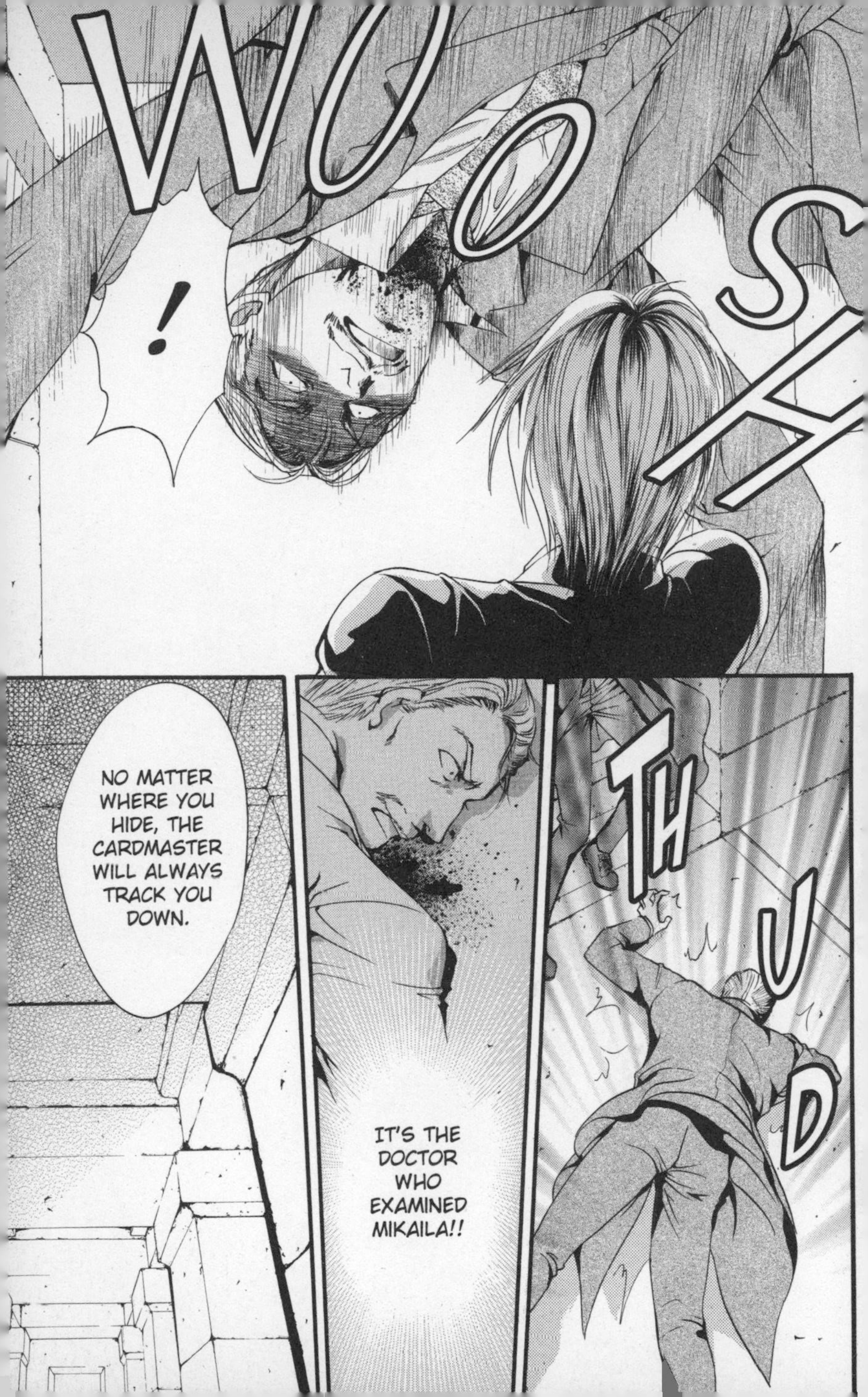
WOOSH
!
THUD
IT'S THE DOCTOR WHO EXAMINED MIKAILA!!
NO MATTER WHERE YOU HIDE, THE CARDMASTER WILL ALWAYS TRACK YOU DOWN.

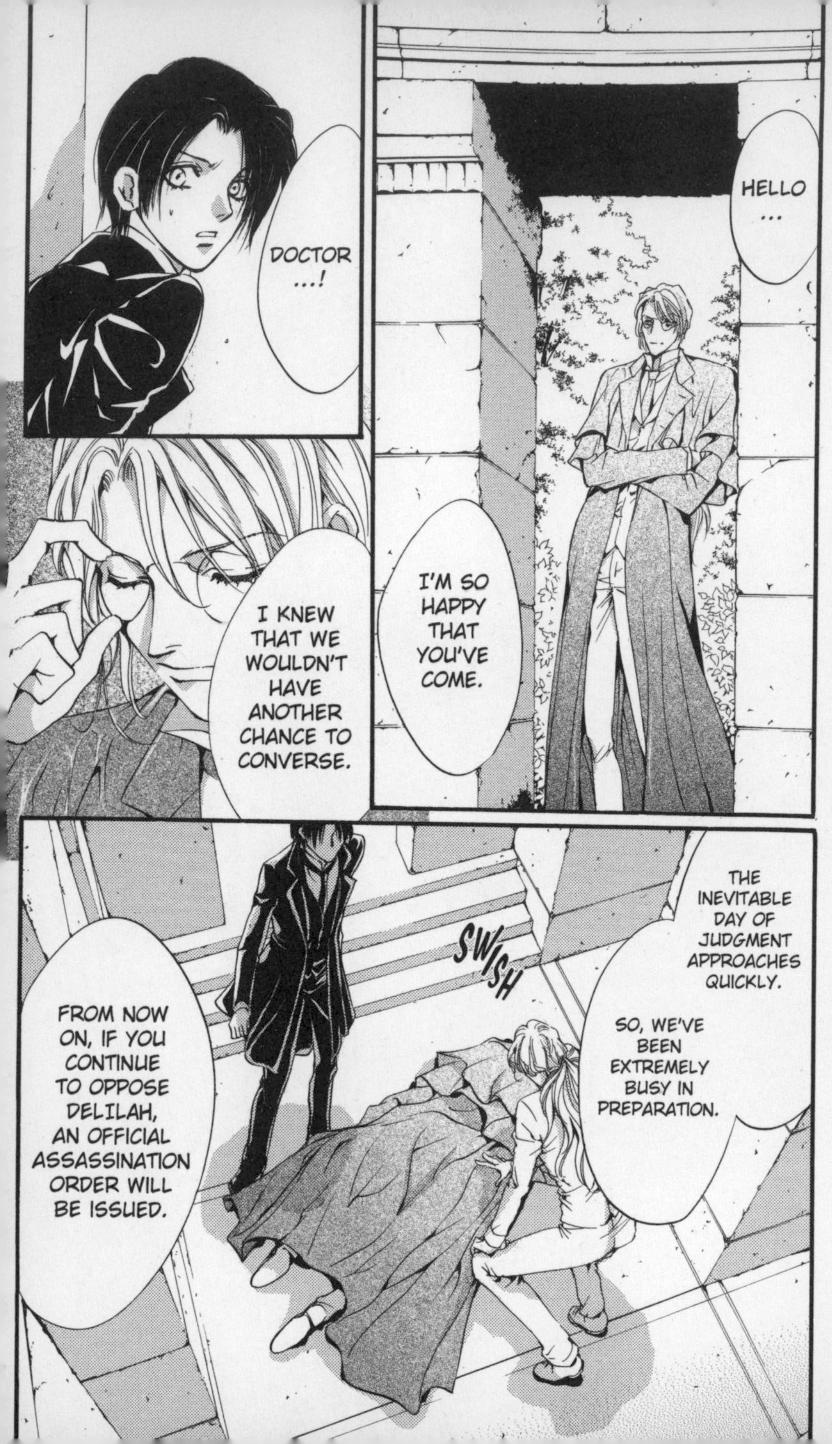
HELLO ...
I'M SO HAPPY THAT YOU'VE COME.
DOCTOR ...!
I KNEW THAT WE WOULDN'T HAVE ANOTHER CHANCE TO CONVERSE.
THE INEVITABLE DAY OF JUDGMENT APPROACHES QUICKLY.
SO, WE'VE BEEN EXTREMELY BUSY IN PREPARATION.
SWISH
FROM NOW ON, IF YOU CONTINUE TO OPPOSE DELILAH, AN OFFICIAL ASSASSINATION ORDER WILL BE ISSUED.

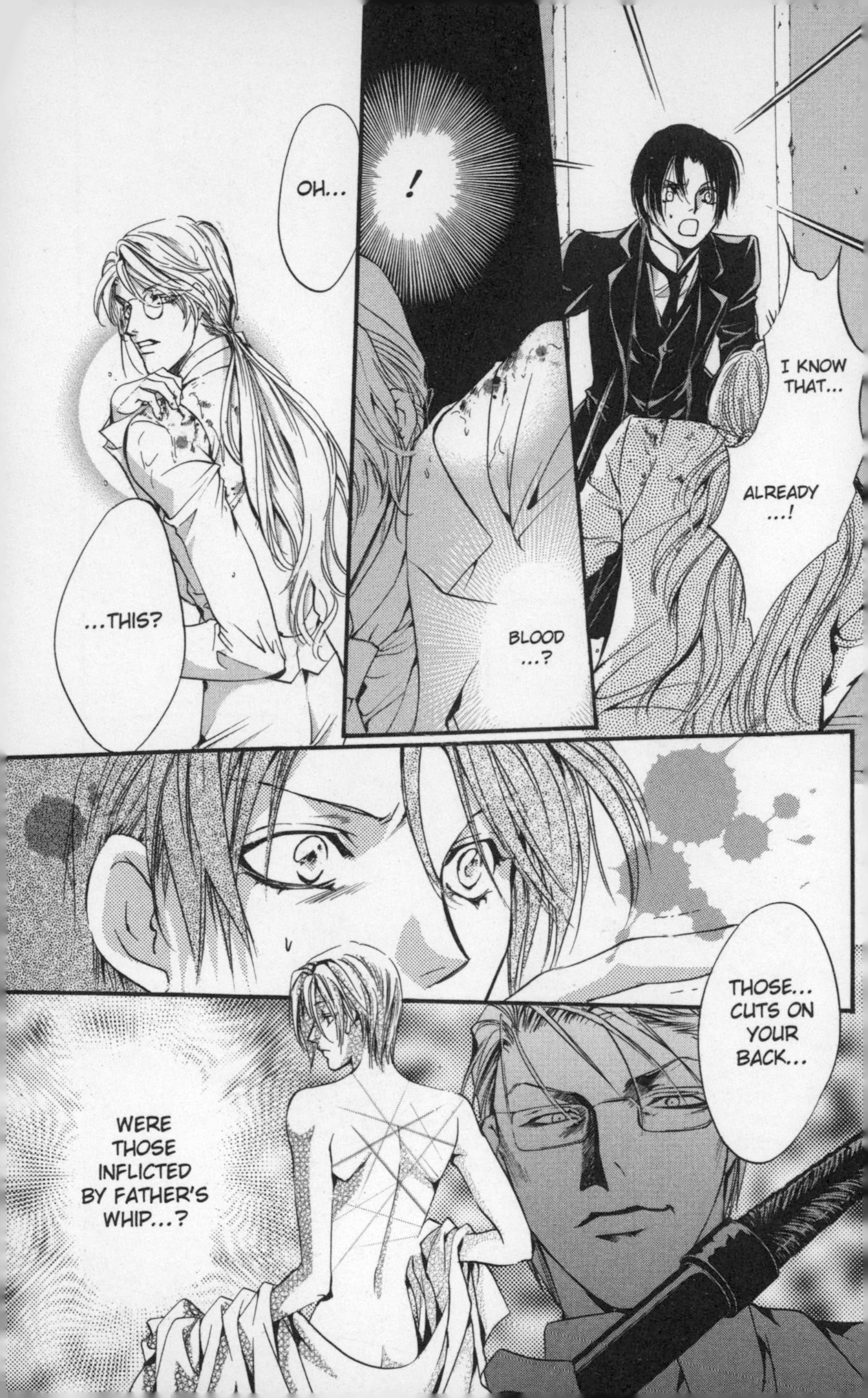
I KNOW THAT...
ALREADY ...!
!
BLOOD ...?
OH...
...THIS?
THOSE... CUTS ON YOUR BACK...
WERE THOSE INFLICTED BY FATHER'S WHIP...?

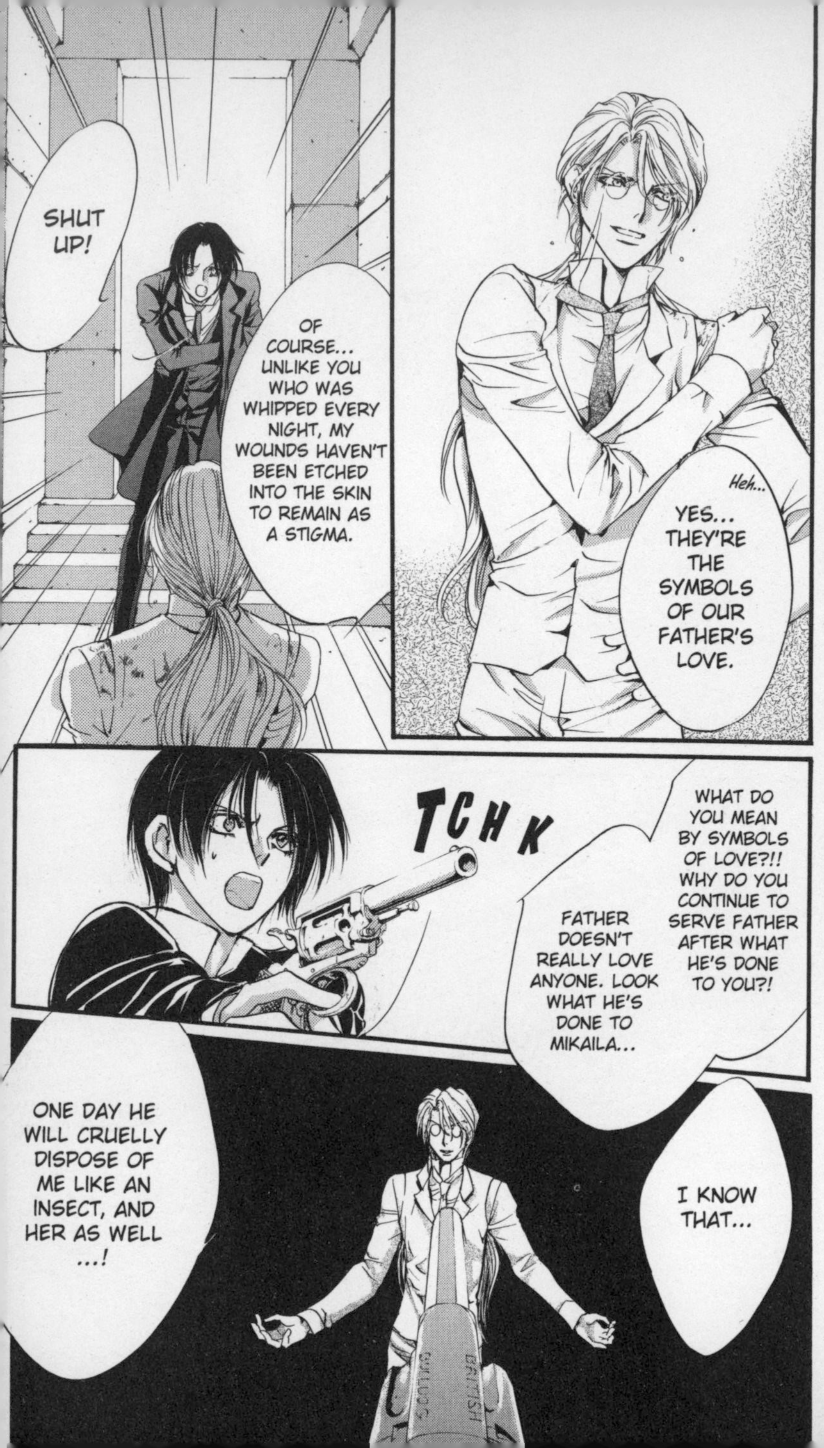
Heh...
YES... THEY'RE THE SYMBOLS OF OUR FATHER'S LOVE.
OF COURSE... UNLIKE YOU WHO WAS WHIPPED EVERY NIGHT, MY WOUNDS HAVEN'T BEEN ETCHED INTO THE SKIN TO REMAIN AS A STIGMA.
SHUT UP!
TCHK
WHAT DO YOU MEAN BY SYMBOLS OF LOVE?!! WHY DO YOU CONTINUE TO SERVE FATHER AFTER WHAT HE'S DONE TO YOU?!
FATHER DOESN'T REALLY LOVE ANYONE. LOOK WHAT HE'S DONE TO MIKAILA...
I KNOW THAT...
ONE DAY HE WILL CRUELLY DISPOSE OF ME LIKE AN INSECT, AND HER AS WELL ...!

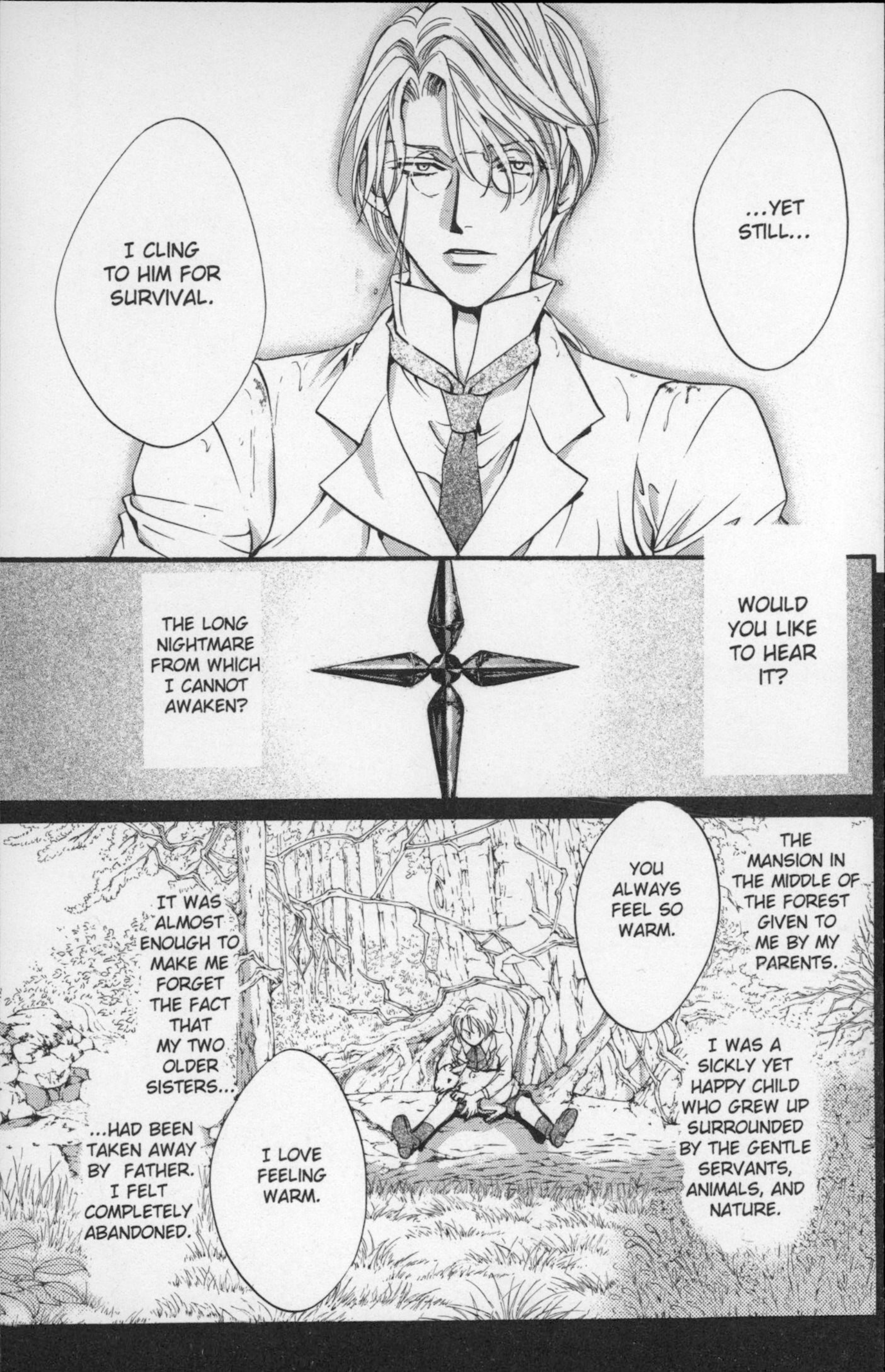
...YET STILL...
I CLING TO HIM FOR SURVIVAL.
WOULD YOU LIKE TO HEAR IT?
THE LONG NIGHTMARE FROM WHICH I CANNOT AWAKEN?
THE MANSION IN THE MIDDLE OF THE FOREST GIVEN TO ME BY MY PARENTS.
YOU ALWAYS FEEL SO WARM.
I WAS A SICKLY YET HAPPY CHILD WHO GREW UP SURROUNDED BY THE GENTLE SERVANTS, ANIMALS, AND NATURE.
IT WAS ALMOST ENOUGH TO MAKE ME FORGET THE FACT THAT MY TWO OLDER SISTERS...
I LOVE FEELING WARM.
...HAD BEEN TAKEN AWAY BY FATHER. I FELT COMPLETELY ABANDONED.

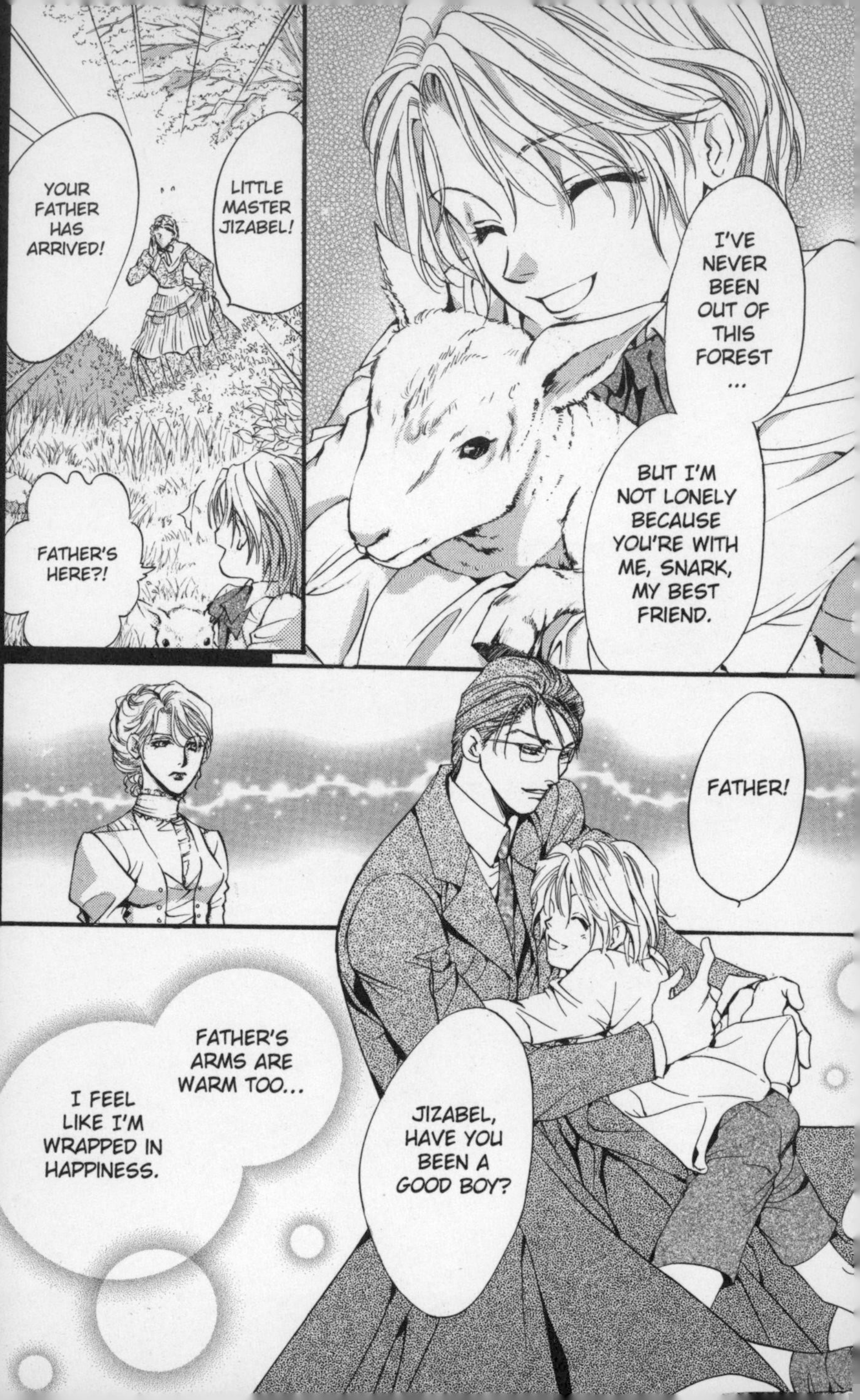
I'VE NEVER BEEN OUT OF THIS FOREST ...
BUT I'M NOT LONELY BECAUSE YOU'RE WITH ME, SNARK, MY BEST FRIEND.
LITTLE MASTER JIZABEL!
YOUR FATHER HAS ARRIVED!
FATHER'S HERE?!
FATHER!
JIZABEL, HAVE YOU BEEN A GOOD BOY?
FATHER'S ARMS ARE WARM TOO...
I FEEL LIKE I'M WRAPPED IN HAPPINESS.

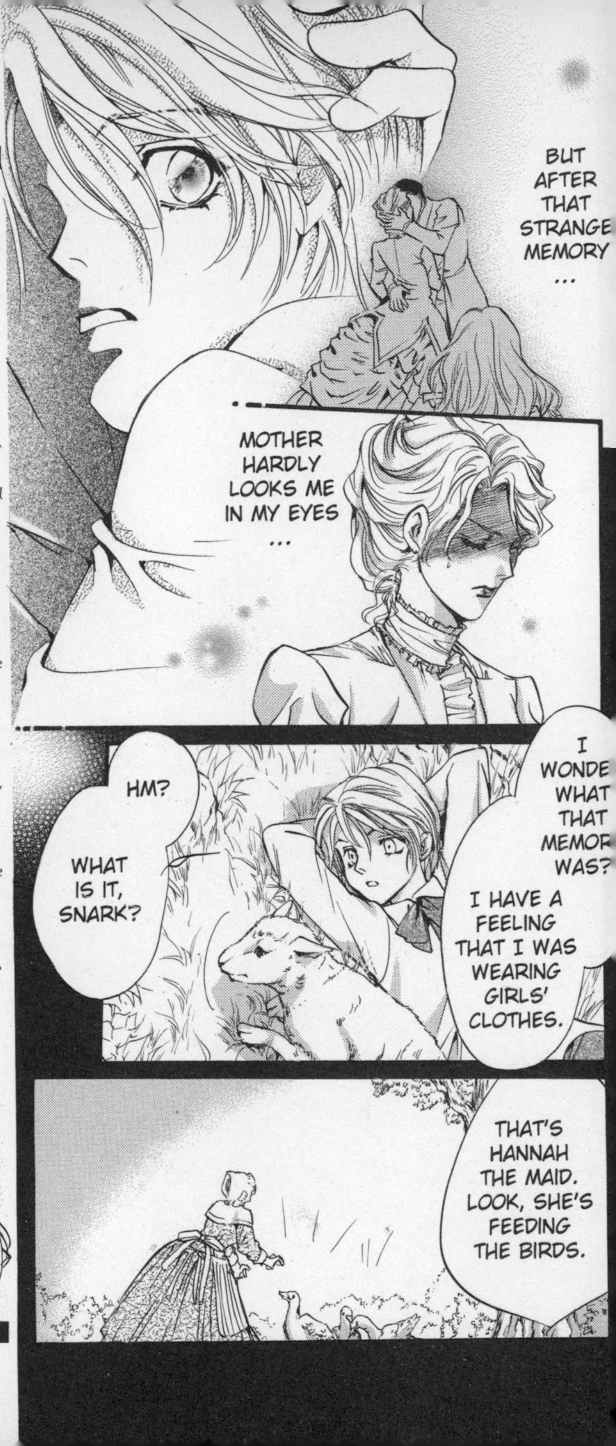
BUT AFTER THAT STRANGE MEMORY ...
MOTHER HARDLY LOOKS ME IN MY EYES ...
I WONDE WHAT THAT MEMOR WAS?
I HAVE A FEELING THAT I WAS WEARING GIRLS' CLOTHES.
HM?
WHAT IS IT, SNARK?
THAT'S HANNAH THE MAID. LOOK, SHE'S FEEDING THE BIRDS.

The Doctor's past is finally revealed... After reviewing my old notes that were haphazardly written, I realized that it could be done as a much shorter episode than I had originally thought. There were also plans to make a short story or a special episode out of it too. But I realized that this story would be pointless unless it was told to Cain, that's why I decided to confine the story to one chapter. And I generally don't like to do special episodes. This way I don't have to waste time using a lot of pages to tell the story. Plus... I hate stories about animals suffering. Which is actually why I wanted to do a story like that... But afterwards I felt really bad... The name Snark comes from Lewis Carroll's poem "The Hunting Of The Snark." In the book "Alice In Wonderland."

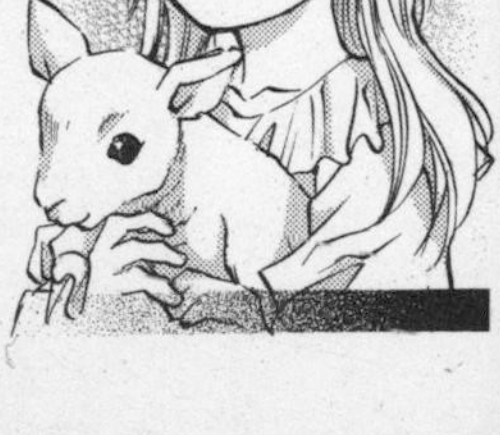

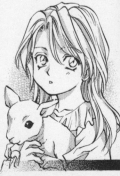

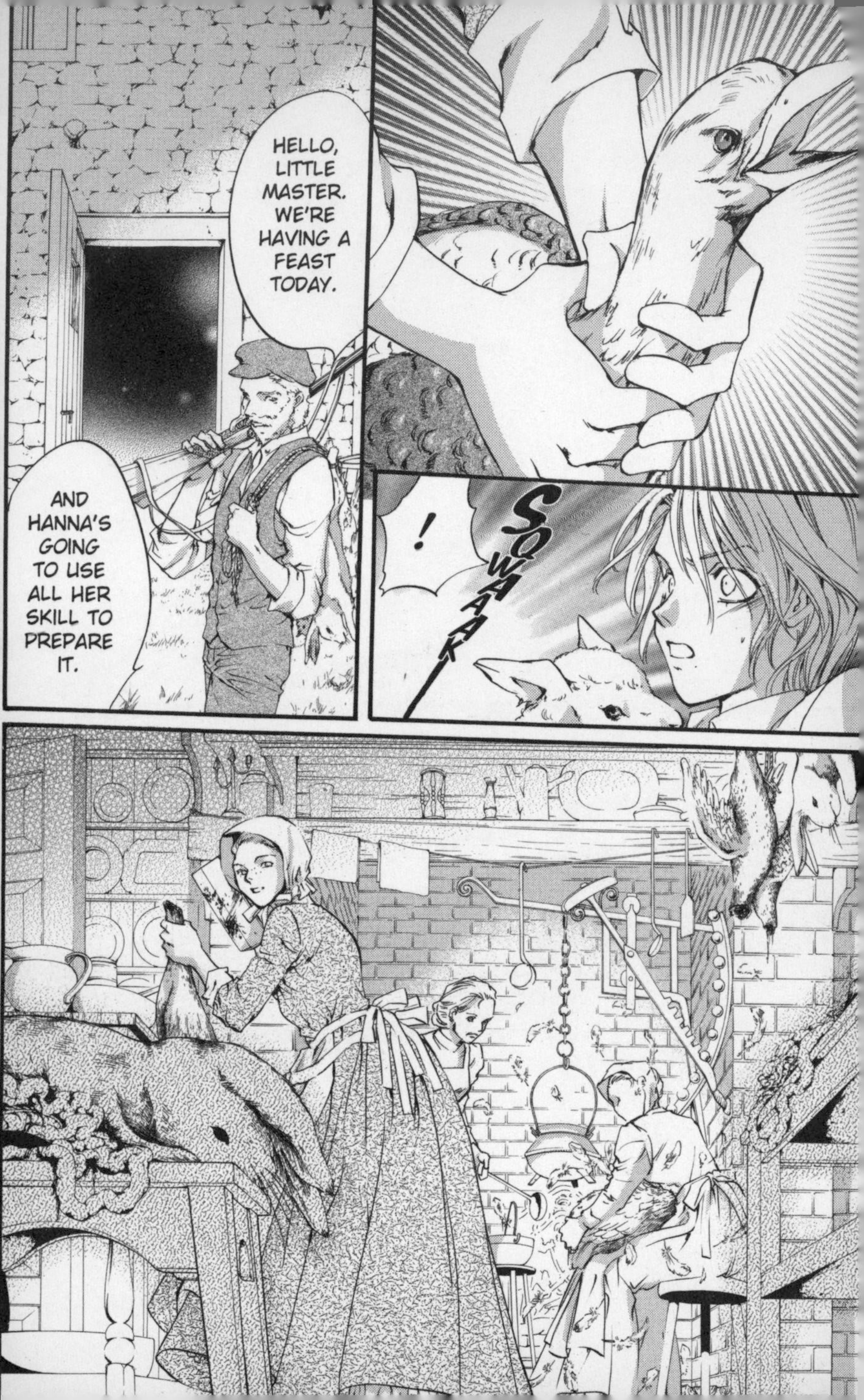
!
SQWAAAK
HELLO, LITTLE MASTER. WE'RE HAVING A FEAST TODAY.
AND HANNA'S GOING TO USE ALL HER SKILL TO PREPARE IT.

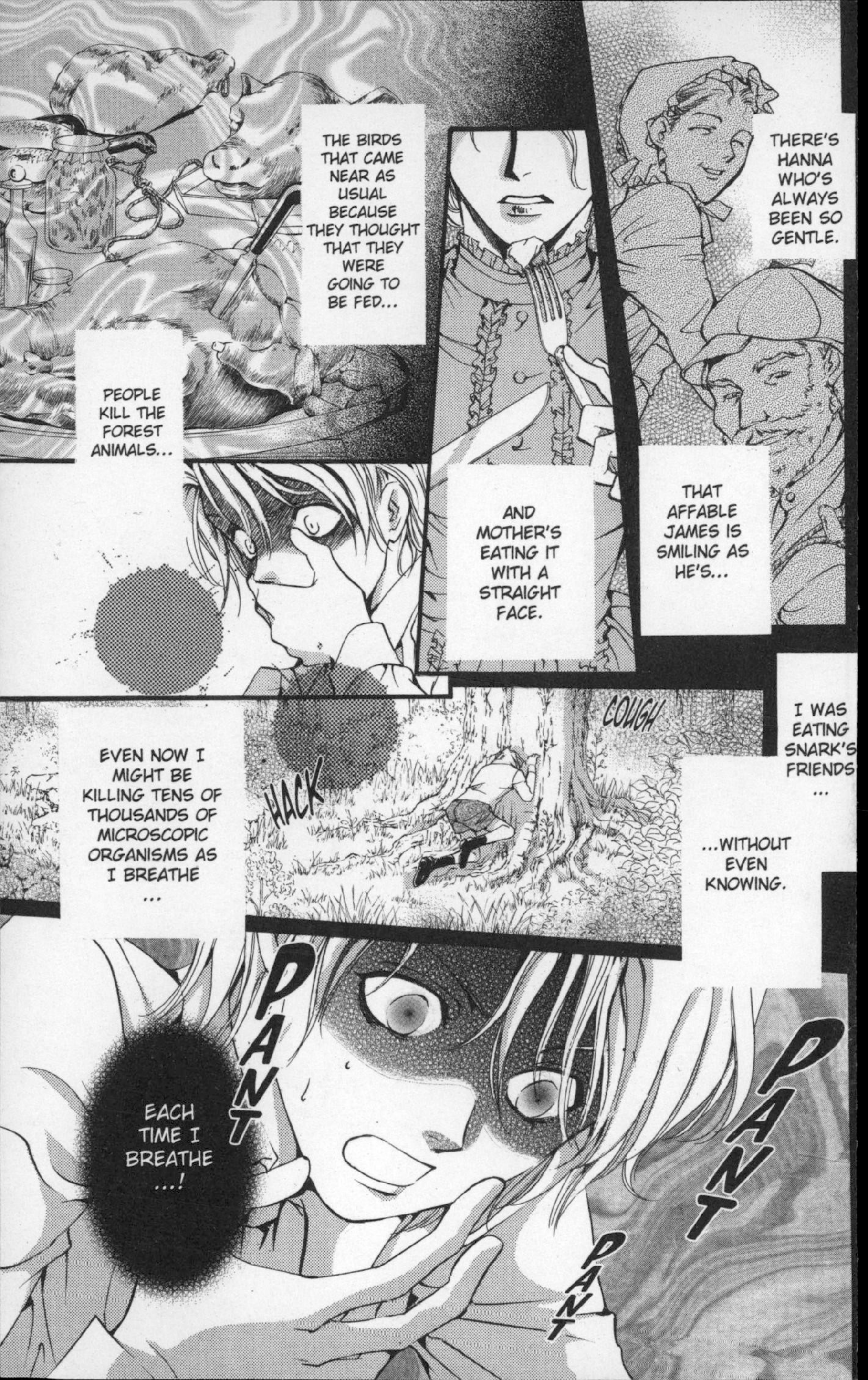
THERE'S HANNA WHO'S ALWAYS BEEN SO GENTLE.
THAT AFFABLE JAMES IS SMILING AS HE'S...
THE BIRDS THAT CAME NEAR AS USUAL BECAUSE THEY THOUGHT THAT THEY WERE GOING TO BE FED...
AND MOTHER'S EATING IT WITH A STRAIGHT FACE.
PEOPLE KILL THE FOREST ANIMALS...
I WAS EATING SNARK'S FRIENDS ...
...WITHOUT EVEN KNOWING.
COUGH
HACK
EVEN NOW I MIGHT BE KILLING TENS OF THOUSANDS OF MICROSCOPIC ORGANISMS AS I BREATHE ...
PANT
PANT
PANT
EACH TIME I BREATHE ...!
PANT

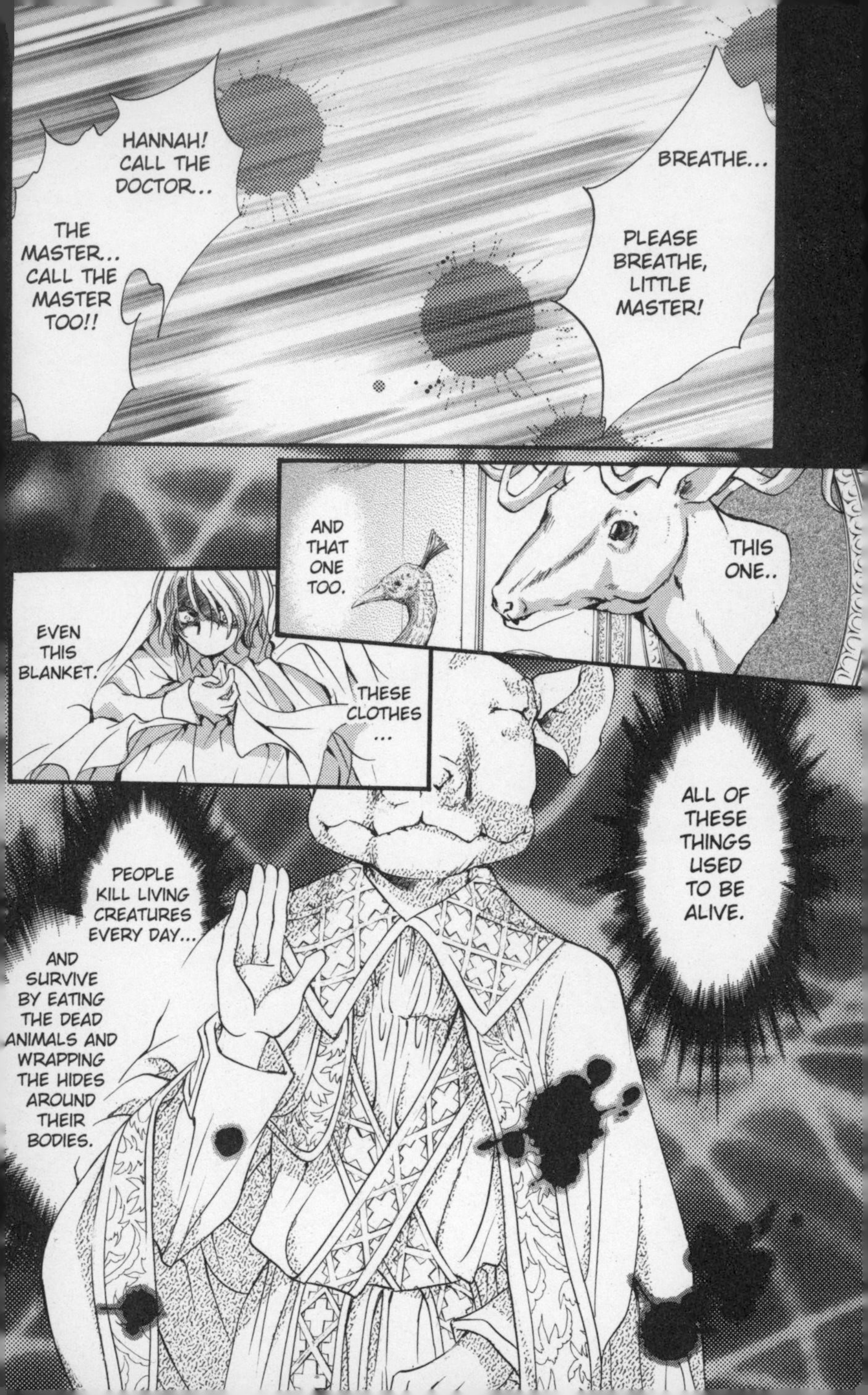
BREATHE...
PLEASE BREATHE, LITTLE MASTER!
HANNAH! CALL THE DOCTOR...
THE MASTER... CALL THE MASTER TOO!!
THIS ONE..
AND THAT ONE TOO.
THESE CLOTHES ...
EVEN THIS BLANKET.
ALL OF THESE THINGS USED TO BE ALIVE.
PEOPLE KILL LIVING CREATURES EVERY DAY...
AND SURVIVE BY EATING THE DEAD ANIMALS AND WRAPPING THE HIDES AROUND THEIR BODIES.

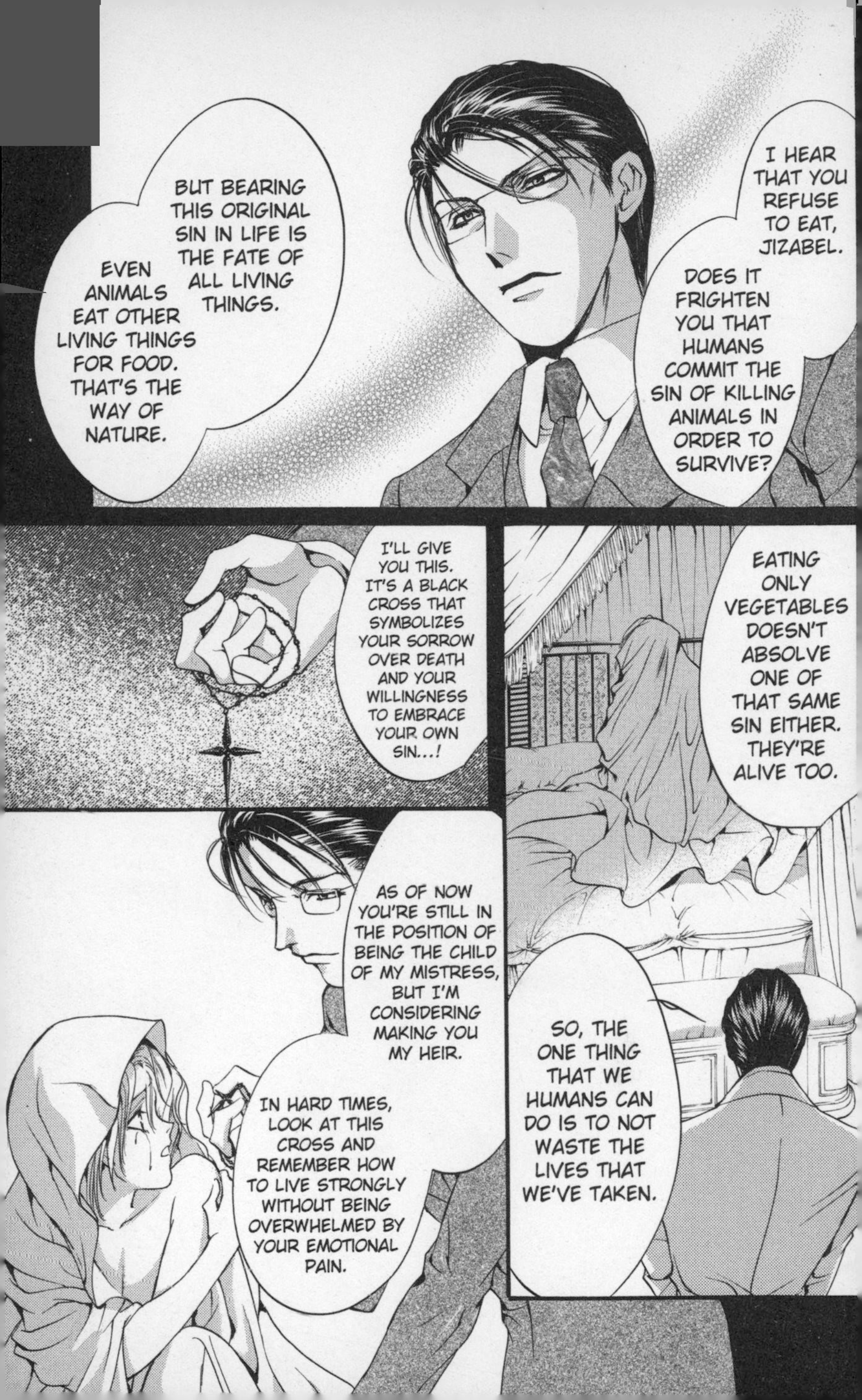
I HEAR THAT YOU REFUSE TO EAT, JIZABEL.
DOES IT FRIGHTEN YOU THAT HUMANS COMMIT THE SIN OF KILLING ANIMALS IN ORDER TO SURVIVE?
EVEN ANIMALS EAT OTHER LIVING THINGS FOR FOOD. THAT'S THE WAY OF NATURE.
BUT BEARING THIS ORIGINAL SIN IN LIFE IS THE FATE OF ALL LIVING THINGS.
EATING ONLY VEGETABLES DOESN'T ABSOLVE ONE OF THAT SAME SIN EITHER. THEY'RE ALIVE TOO.
SO, THE ONE THING THAT WE HUMANS CAN DO IS TO NOT WASTE THE LIVES THAT WE'VE TAKEN.
I'LL GIVE YOU THIS. IT'S A BLACK CROSS THAT SYMBOLIZES YOUR SORROW OVER DEATH AND YOUR WILLINGNESS TO EMBRACE YOUR OWN SIN...!
AS OF NOW YOU'RE STILL IN THE POSITION OF BEING THE CHILD OF MY MISTRESS, BUT I'M CONSIDERING MAKING YOU MY HEIR.
IN HARD TIMES, LOOK AT THIS CROSS AND REMEMBER HOW TO LIVE STRONGLY WITHOUT BEING OVERWHELMED BY YOUR EMOTIONAL PAIN.

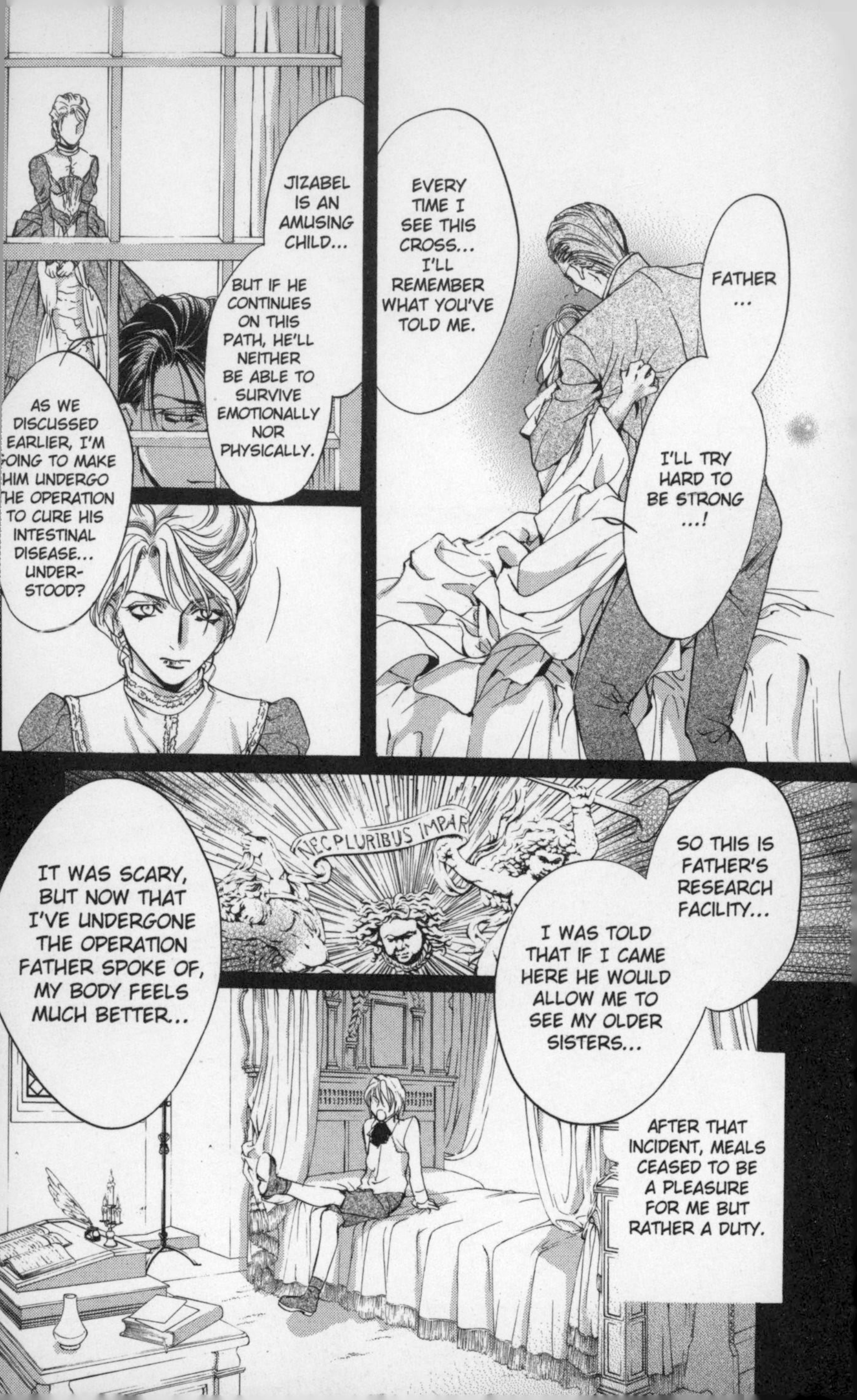
FATHER ...
EVERY TIME I SEE THIS CROSS... I'LL REMEMBER WHAT YOU'VE TOLD ME.
I'LL TRY HARD TO BE STRONG ...!
JIZABEL IS AN AMUSING CHILD...
BUT IF HE CONTINUES ON THIS PATH, HE'LL NEITHER BE ABLE TO SURVIVE EMOTIONALLY NOR PHYSICALLY.
AS WE DISCUSSED EARLIER, I'M GOING TO MAKE HIM UNDERGO THE OPERATION TO CURE HIS INTESTINAL DISEASE... UNDER-STOOD?
NEC PLURIBUS IMPAR
SO THIS IS FATHER'S RESEARCH FACILITY...
I WAS TOLD THAT IF I CAME HERE HE WOULD ALLOW ME TO SEE MY OLDER SISTERS...
IT WAS SCARY, BUT NOW THAT I'VE UNDERGONE THE OPERATION FATHER SPOKE OF, MY BODY FEELS MUCH BETTER...
AFTER THAT INCIDENT, MEALS CEASED TO BE A PLEASURE FOR ME BUT RATHER A DUTY.

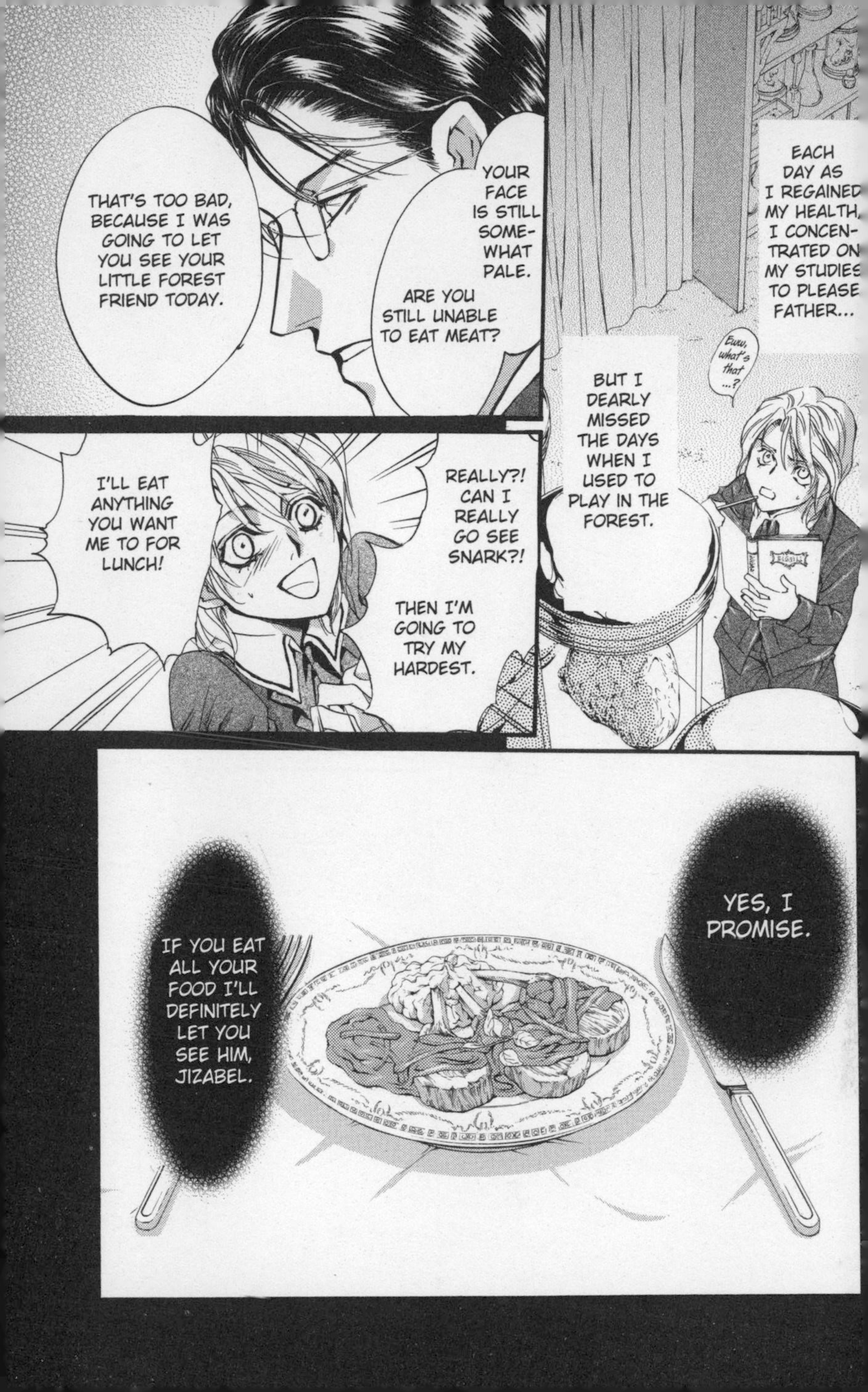
EACH DAY AS I REGAINED MY HEALTH, I CONCENTRATED ON MY STUDIES TO PLEASE FATHER...
Eww, what's that ...?
BUT I DEARLY MISSED THE DAYS WHEN I USED TO PLAY IN THE FOREST.
YOUR FACE IS STILL SOME-WHAT PALE.
ARE YOU STILL UNABLE TO EAT MEAT?
THAT'S TOO BAD, BECAUSE I WAS GOING TO LET YOU SEE YOUR LITTLE FOREST FRIEND TODAY.
REALLY?! CAN I REALLY GO SEE SNARK?!
THEN I'M GOING TO TRY MY HARDEST.
I'LL EAT ANYTHING YOU WANT ME TO FOR LUNCH!
YES, I PROMISE.
IF YOU EAT ALL YOUR FOOD I'LL DEFINITELY LET YOU SEE HIM, JIZABEL.

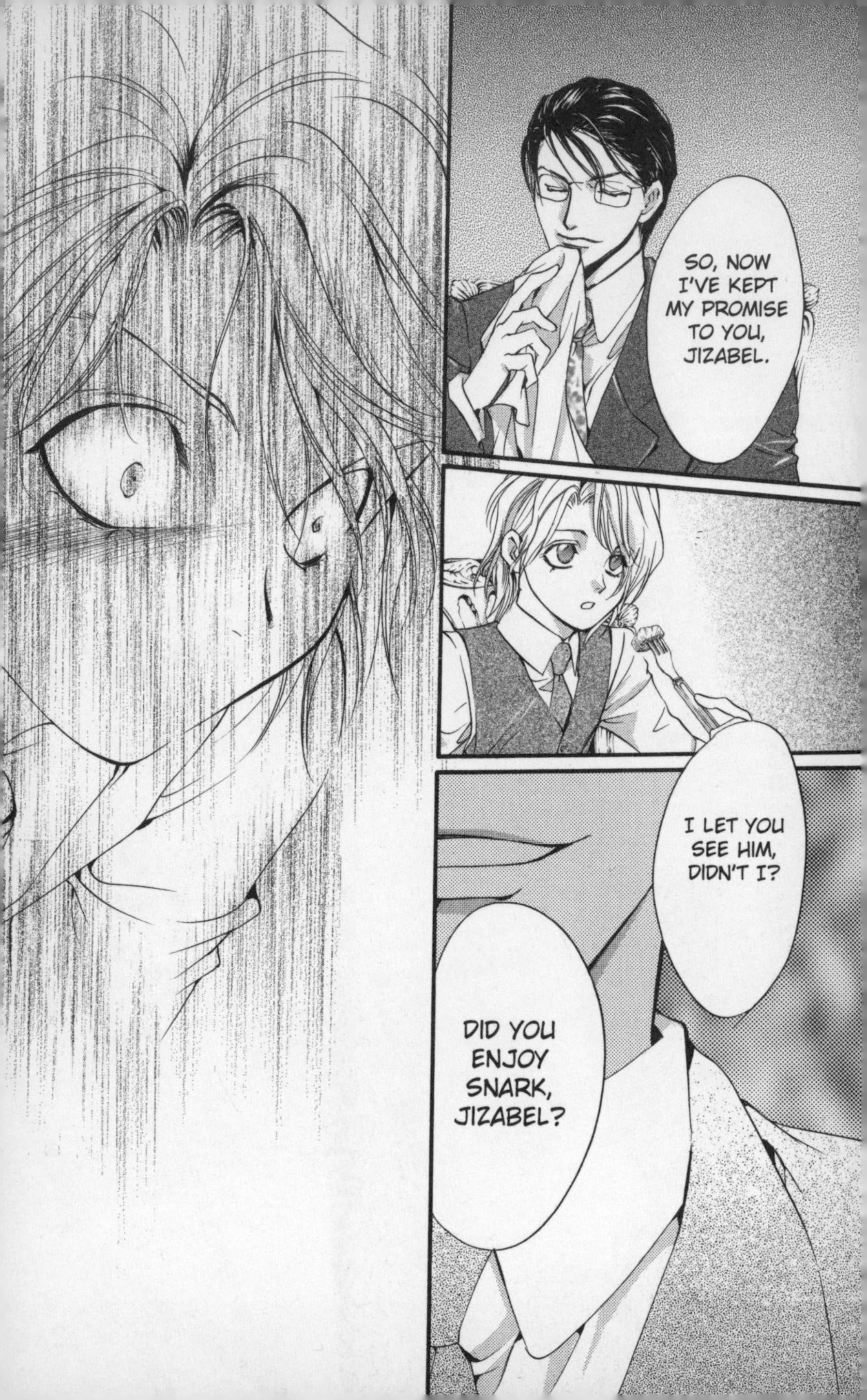
SO, NOW I'VE KEPT MY PROMISE TO YOU, JIZABEL.
I LET YOU SEE HIM, DIDN'T I?
DID YOU ENJOY SNARK, JIZABEL?

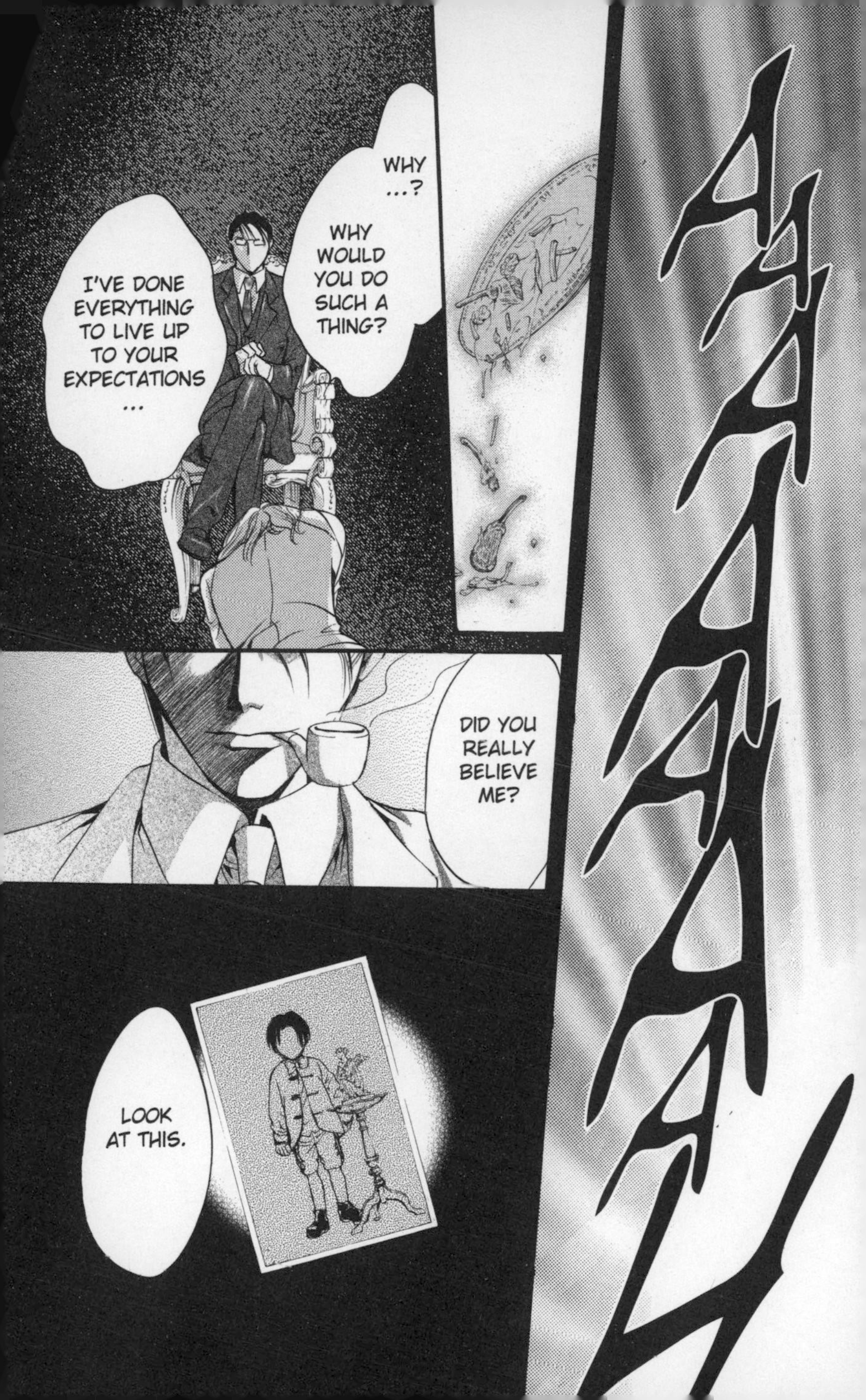
WHY ...?
WHY WOULD YOU DO SUCH A THING?
I'VE DONE EVERYTHING TO LIVE UP TO YOUR EXPECTATIONS ...
DID YOU REALLY BELIEVE ME?
LOOK AT THIS.

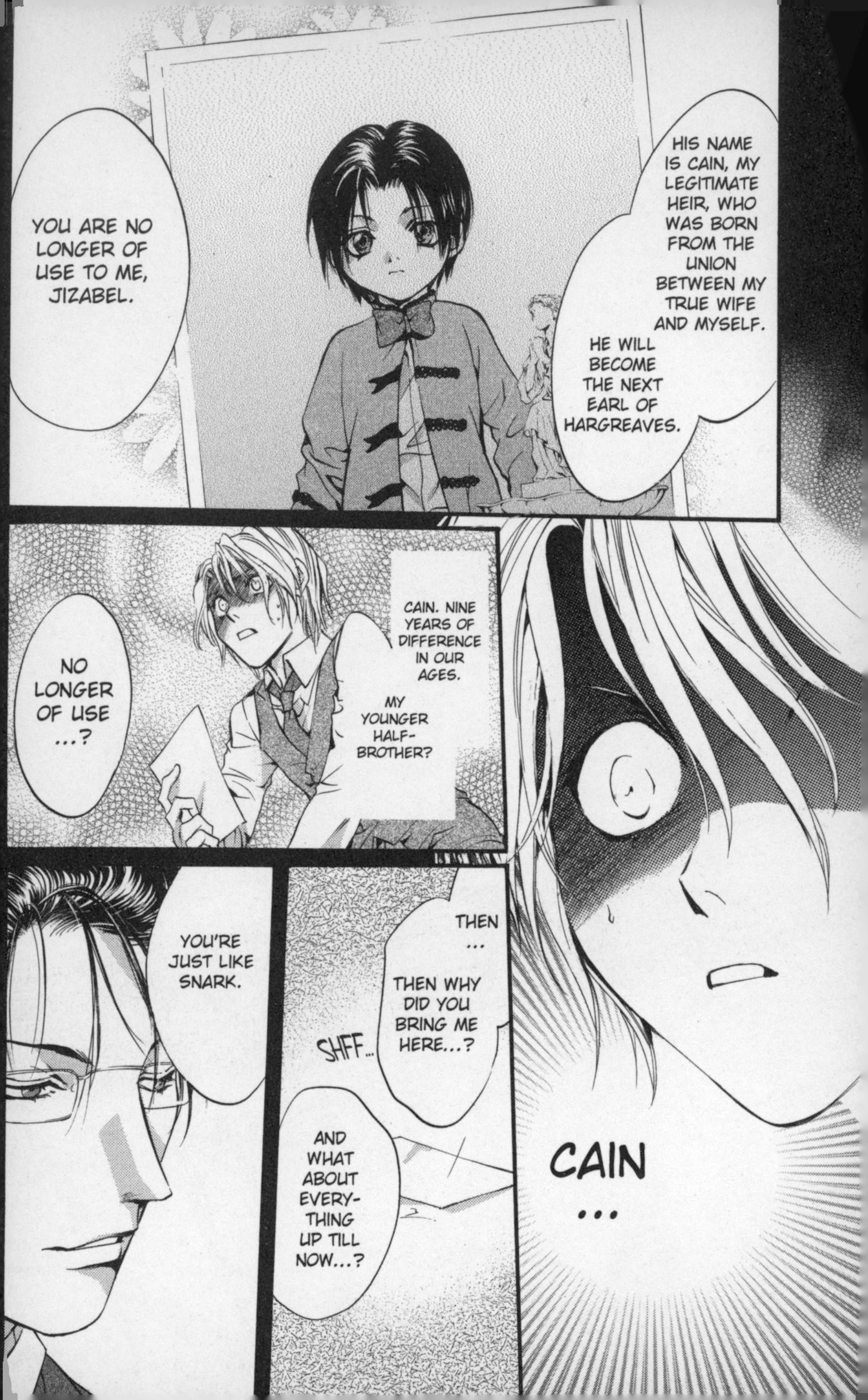
HIS NAME IS CAIN, MY LEGITIMATE HEIR, WHO WAS BORN FROM THE UNION BETWEEN MY TRUE WIFE AND MYSELF.
HE WILL BECOME THE NEXT EARL OF HARGREAVES.
YOU ARE NO LONGER OF USE TO ME, JIZABEL.
CAIN ...
CAIN. NINE YEARS OF DIFFERENCE IN OUR AGES.
MY YOUNGER HALF-BROTHER?
NO LONGER OF USE ...?
THEN ...
THEN WHY DID YOU BRING ME HERE...?
SHFF...
AND WHAT ABOUT EVERY-THING UP TILL NOW...?
YOU'RE JUST LIKE SNARK.

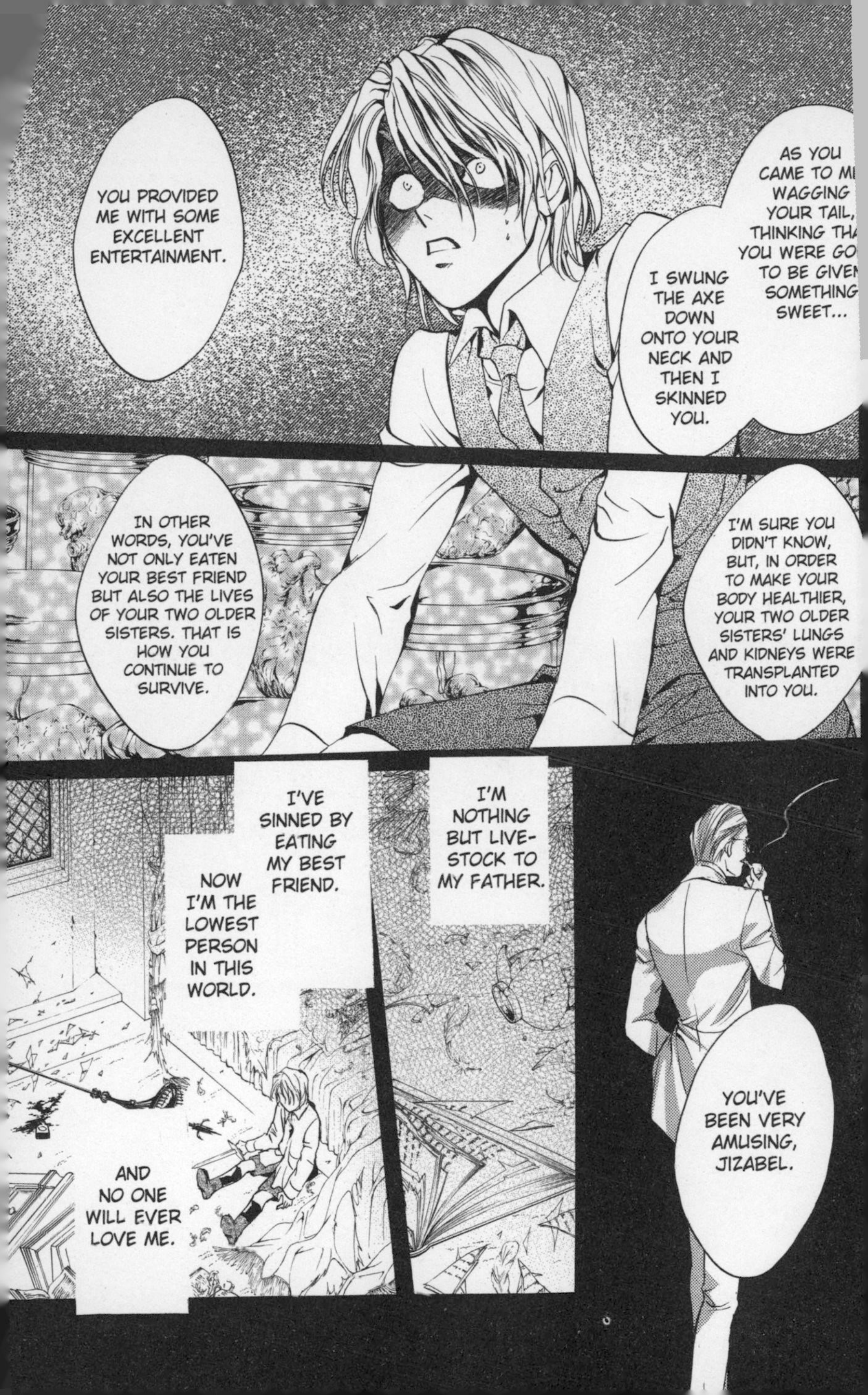
AS YOU CAME TO ME WAGGING YOUR TAIL, THINKING THA YOU WERE GO TO BE GIVE SOMETHING SWEET...
I SWUNG THE AXE DOWN ONTO YOUR NECK AND THEN I SKINNED YOU.
YOU PROVIDED ME WITH SOME EXCELLENT ENTERTAINMENT.
I'M SURE YOU DIDN'T KNOW, BUT, IN ORDER TO MAKE YOUR BODY HEALTHIER, YOUR TWO OLDER SISTERS' LUNGS AND KIDNEYS WERE TRANSPLANTED INTO YOU.
IN OTHER WORDS, YOU'VE NOT ONLY EATEN YOUR BEST FRIEND BUT ALSO THE LIVES OF YOUR TWO OLDER SISTERS. THAT IS HOW YOU CONTINUE TO SURVIVE.
YOU'VE BEEN VERY AMUSING, JIZABEL.
I'M NOTHING BUT LIVE-STOCK TO MY FATHER.
I'VE SINNED BY EATING MY BEST FRIEND.
NOW I'M THE LOWEST PERSON IN THIS WORLD.
AND NO ONE WILL EVER LOVE ME.

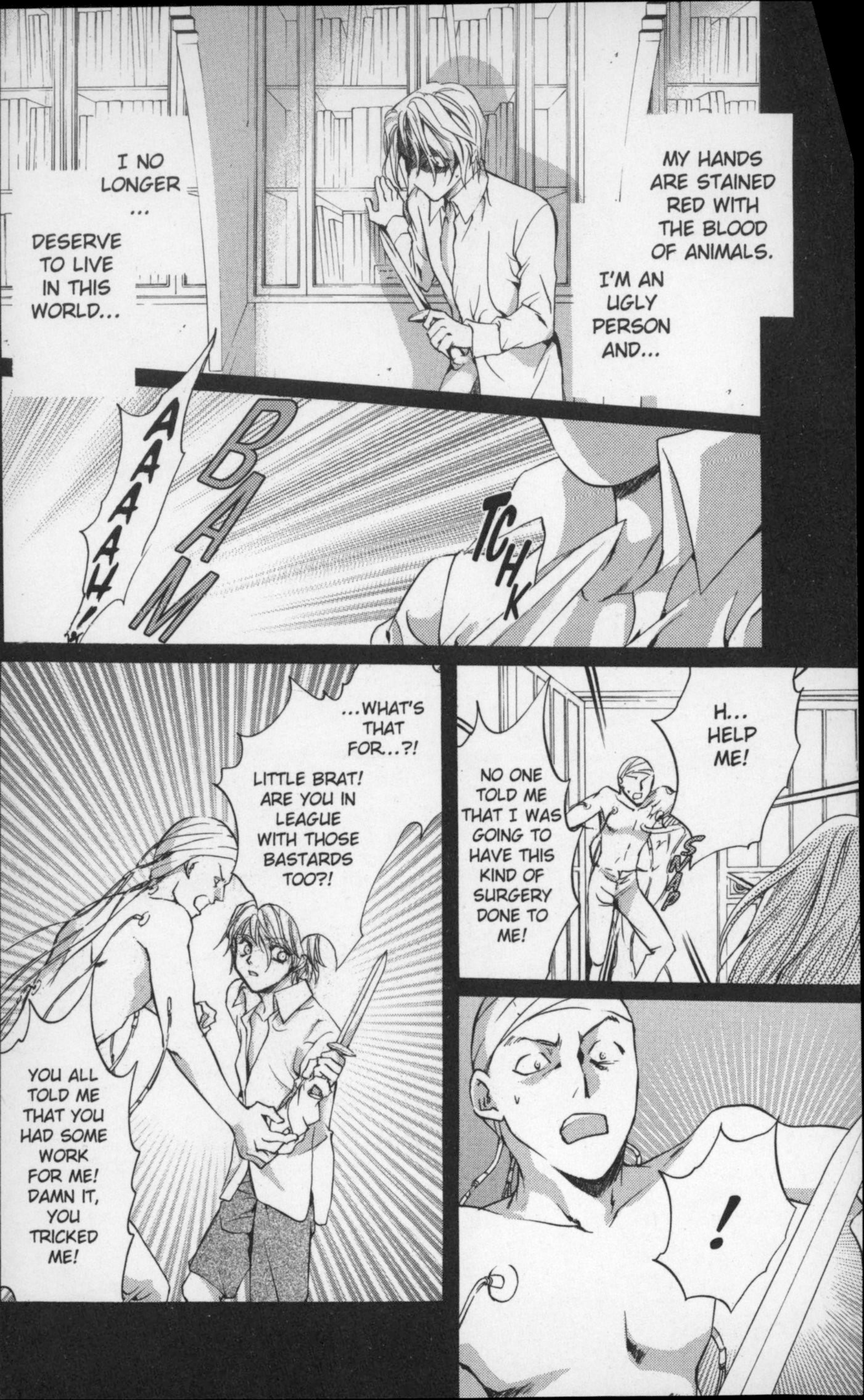
MY HANDS ARE STAINED RED WITH THE BLOOD OF ANIMALS.
I'M AN UGLY PERSON AND...
I NO LONGER ...
DESERVE TO LIVE IN THIS WORLD...
TCHK
BAAM
AAAAAH!
H... HELP ME!
NO ONE TOLD ME THAT I WAS GOING TO HAVE THIS KIND OF SURGERY DONE TO ME!
!
...WHAT'S THAT FOR...?!
LITTLE BRAT! ARE YOU IN LEAGUE WITH THOSE BASTARDS TOO?!
YOU ALL TOLD ME THAT YOU HAD SOME WORK FOR ME! DAMN IT, YOU TRICKED ME!

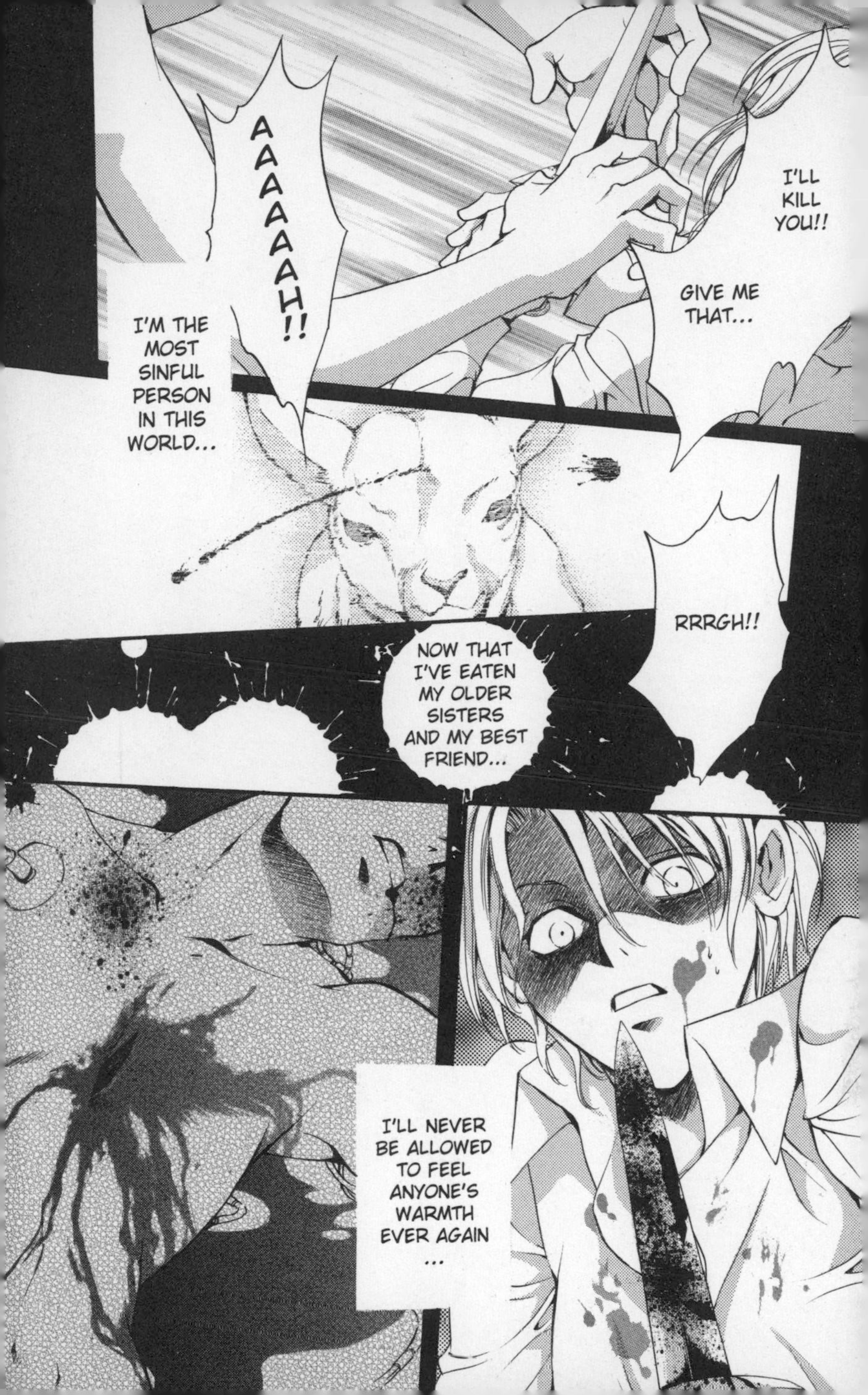
I'LL KILL YOU!!
GIVE ME THAT...
AAAAAAH!!
RRRGH!!
I'M THE MOST SINFUL PERSON IN THIS WORLD...
NOW THAT I'VE EATEN MY OLDER SISTERS AND MY BEST FRIEND...
I'LL NEVER BE ALLOWED TO FEEL ANYONE'S WARMTH EVER AGAIN ...

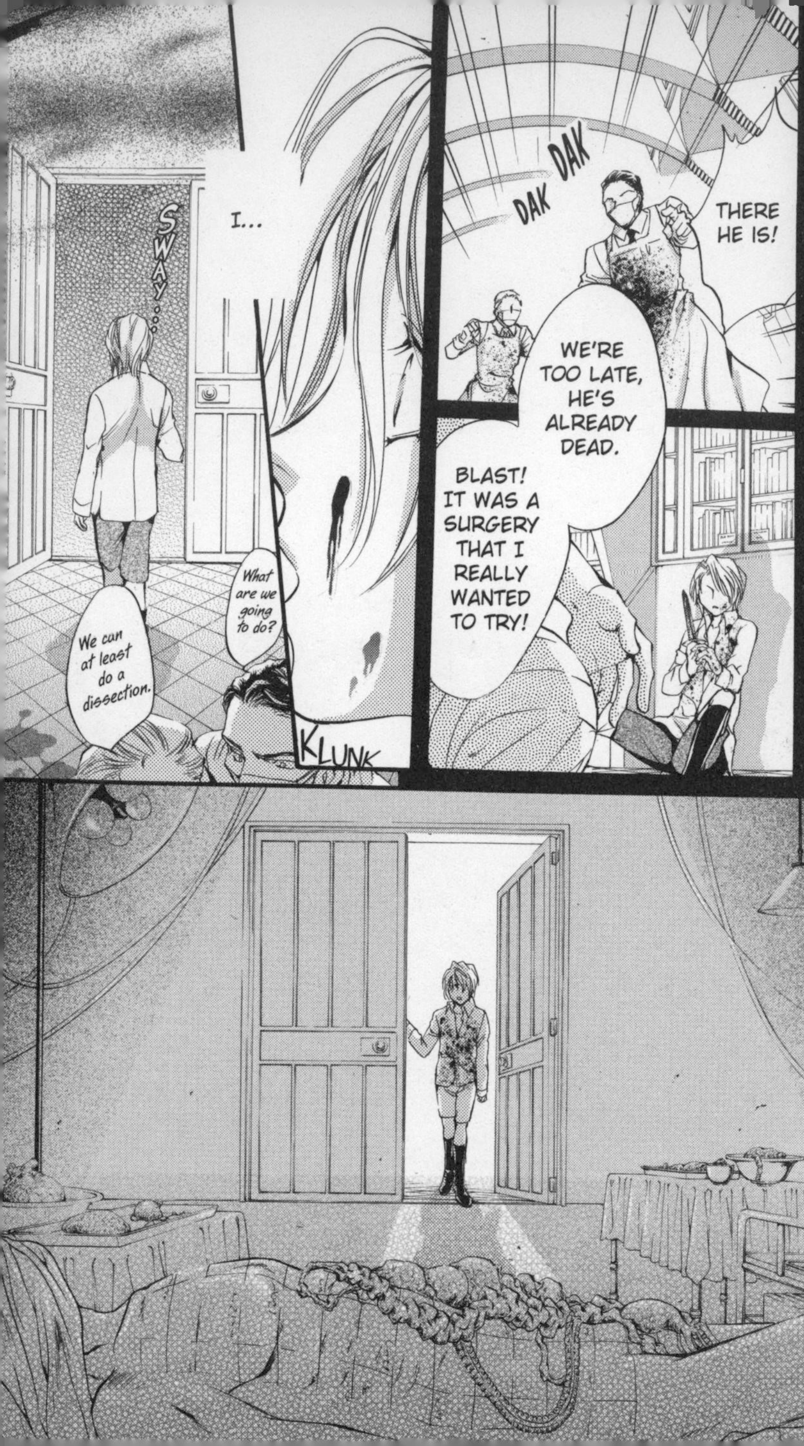
THERE HE IS!
DAK DAK
WE'RE TOO LATE, HE'S ALREADY DEAD.
BLAST! IT WAS A SURGERY THAT I REALLY WANTED TO TRY!
I...
What are we going to do?
KLUNK
SWAY...
We can at least do a dissection.

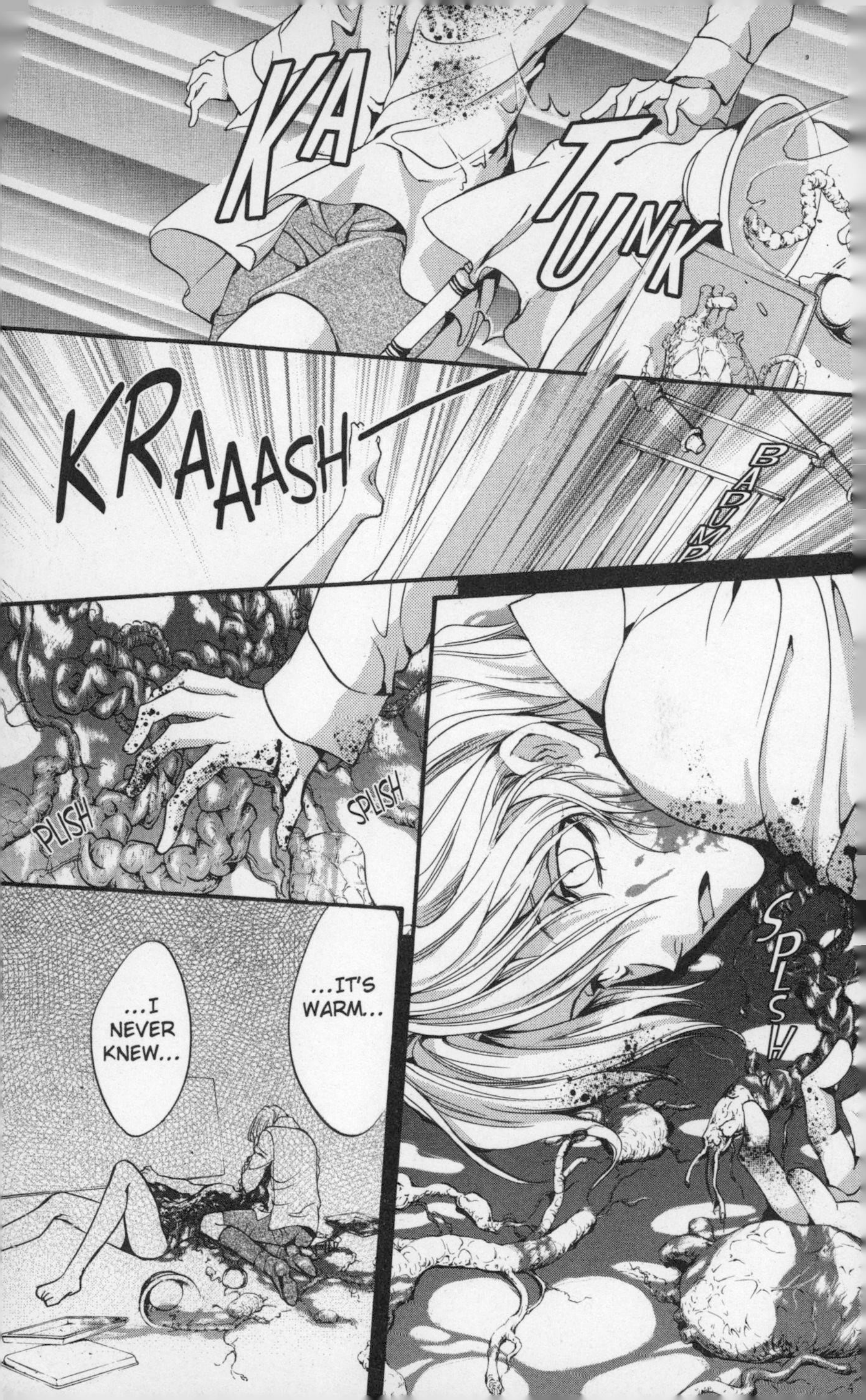
KA
TUNK
KRAAASH
BADUMP
SPLSH
SPLISH
PLISH
...IT'S WARM...
...I NEVER KNEW...

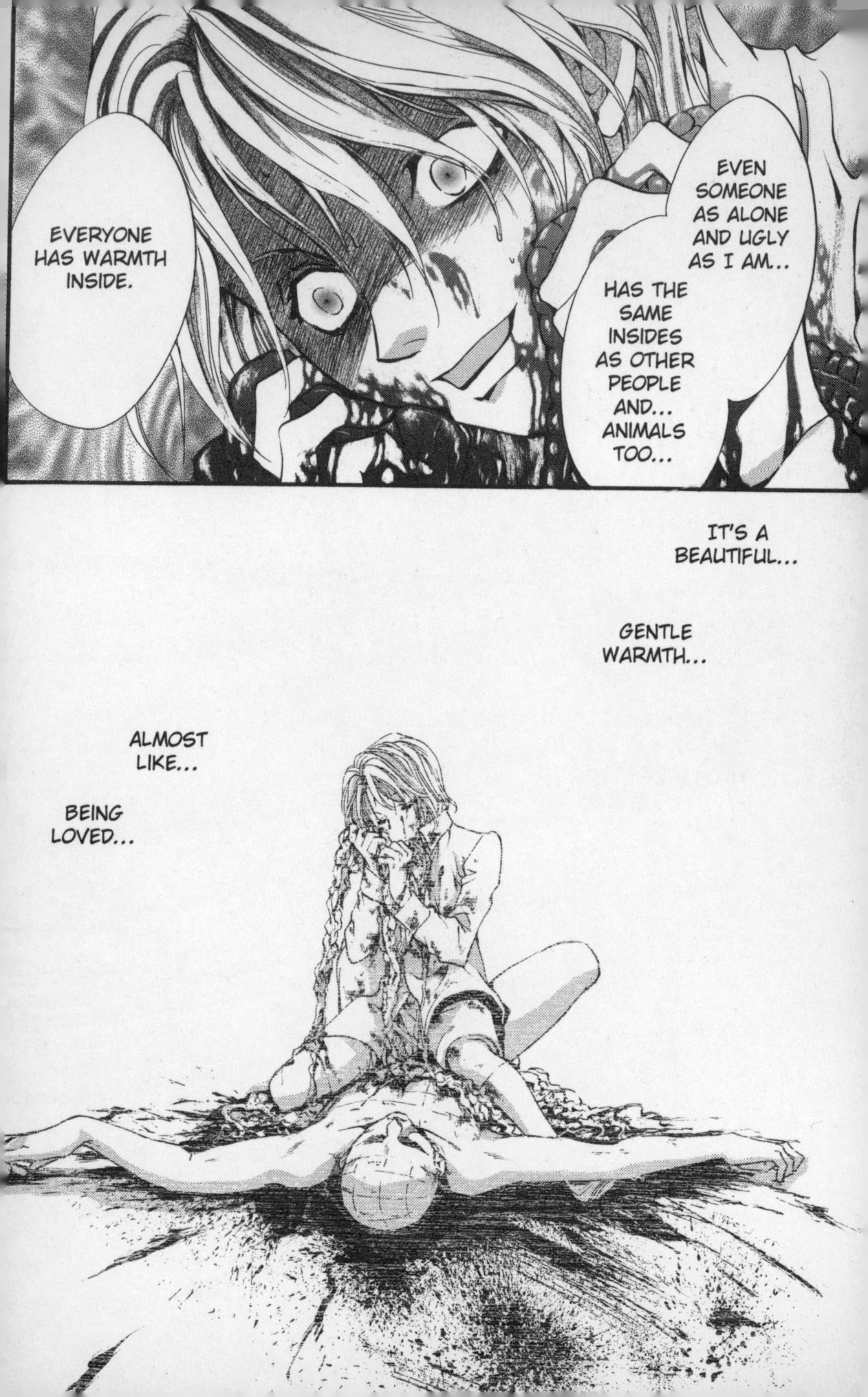
EVEN SOMEONE AS ALONE AND UGLY AS I AM..
HAS THE SAME INSIDES AS OTHER PEOPLE AND... ANIMALS TOO...
EVERYONE HAS WARMTH INSIDE.
IT'S A BEAUTIFUL...
GENTLE WARMTH...
ALMOST LIKE...
BEING LOVED...

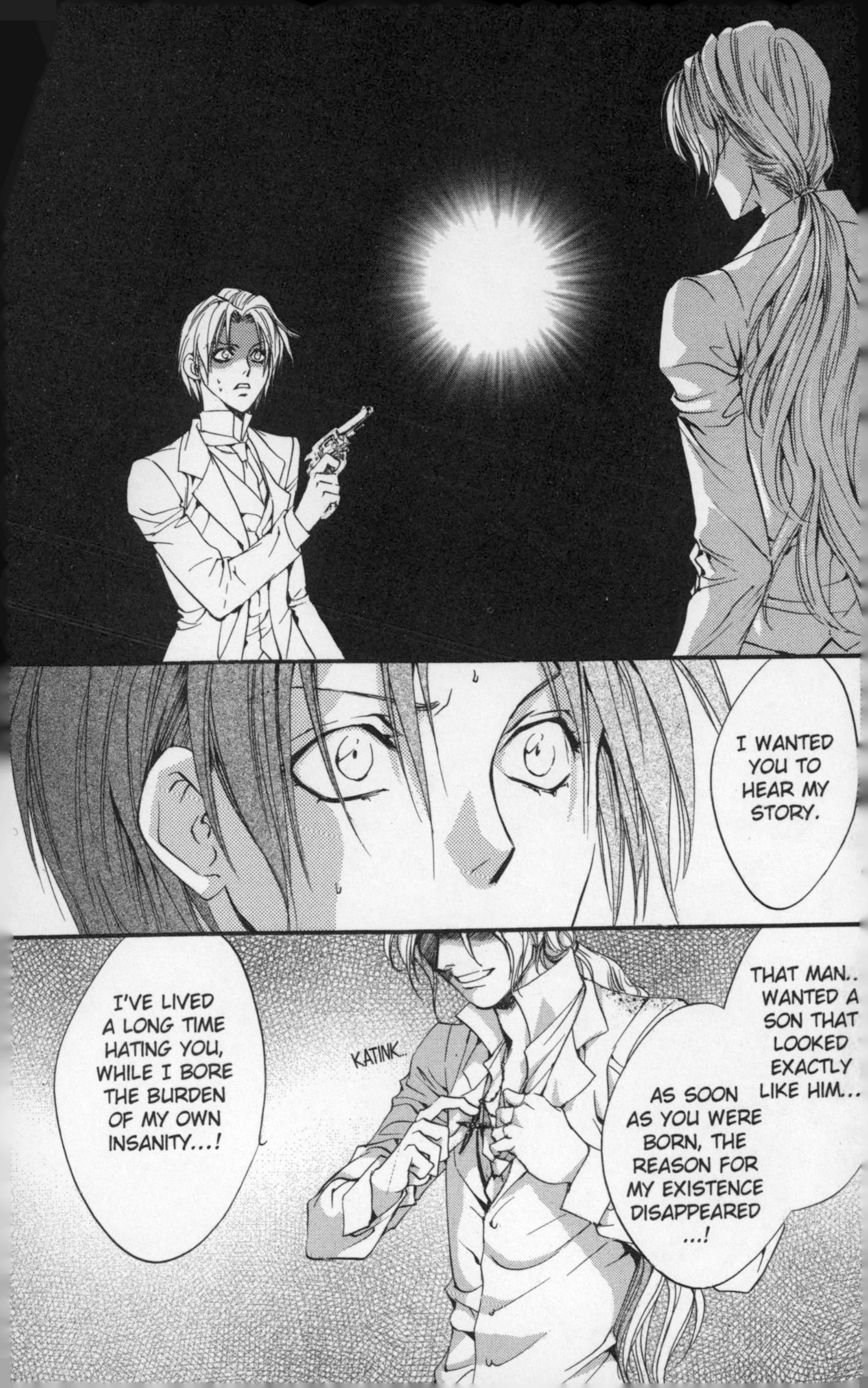
I WANTED YOU TO HEAR MY STORY.
THAT MAN.. WANTED A SON THAT LOOKED EXACTLY LIKE HIM...
AS SOON AS YOU WERE BORN, THE REASON FOR MY EXISTENCE DISAPPEARED ...!
KATINK..
I'VE LIVED A LONG TIME HATING YOU, WHILE I BORE THE BURDEN OF MY OWN INSANITY...!

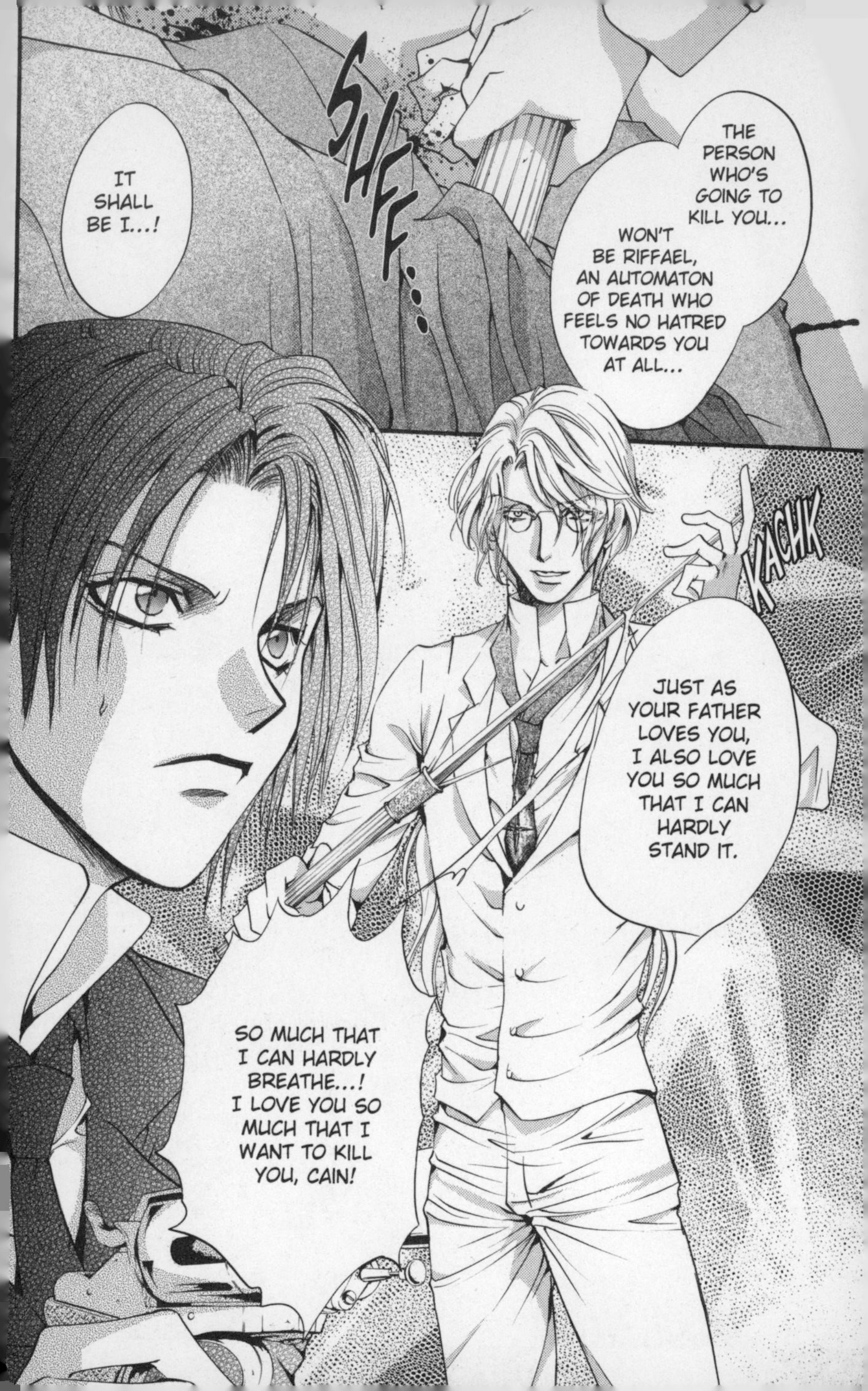
THE PERSON WHO'S GOING TO KILL YOU...
WON'T BE RIFFAEL, AN AUTOMATON OF DEATH WHO FEELS NO HATRED TOWARDS YOU AT ALL...
SHFF...
IT SHALL BE I...!
KACHK
JUST AS YOUR FATHER LOVES YOU, I ALSO LOVE YOU SO MUCH THAT I CAN HARDLY STAND IT.
SO MUCH THAT I CAN HARDLY BREATHE...! I LOVE YOU SO MUCH THAT I WANT TO KILL YOU, CAIN!

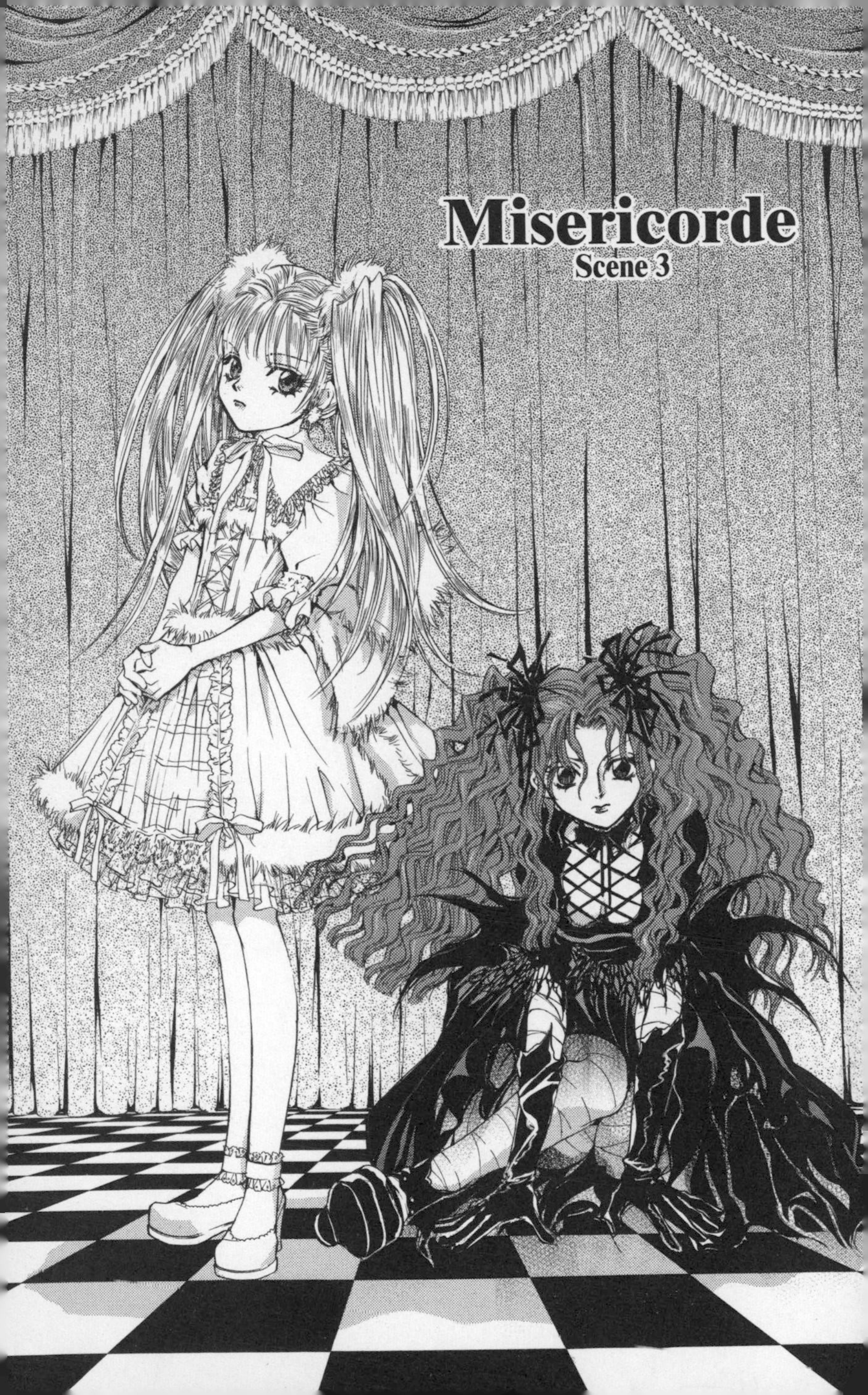
Misericorde
Scene 3

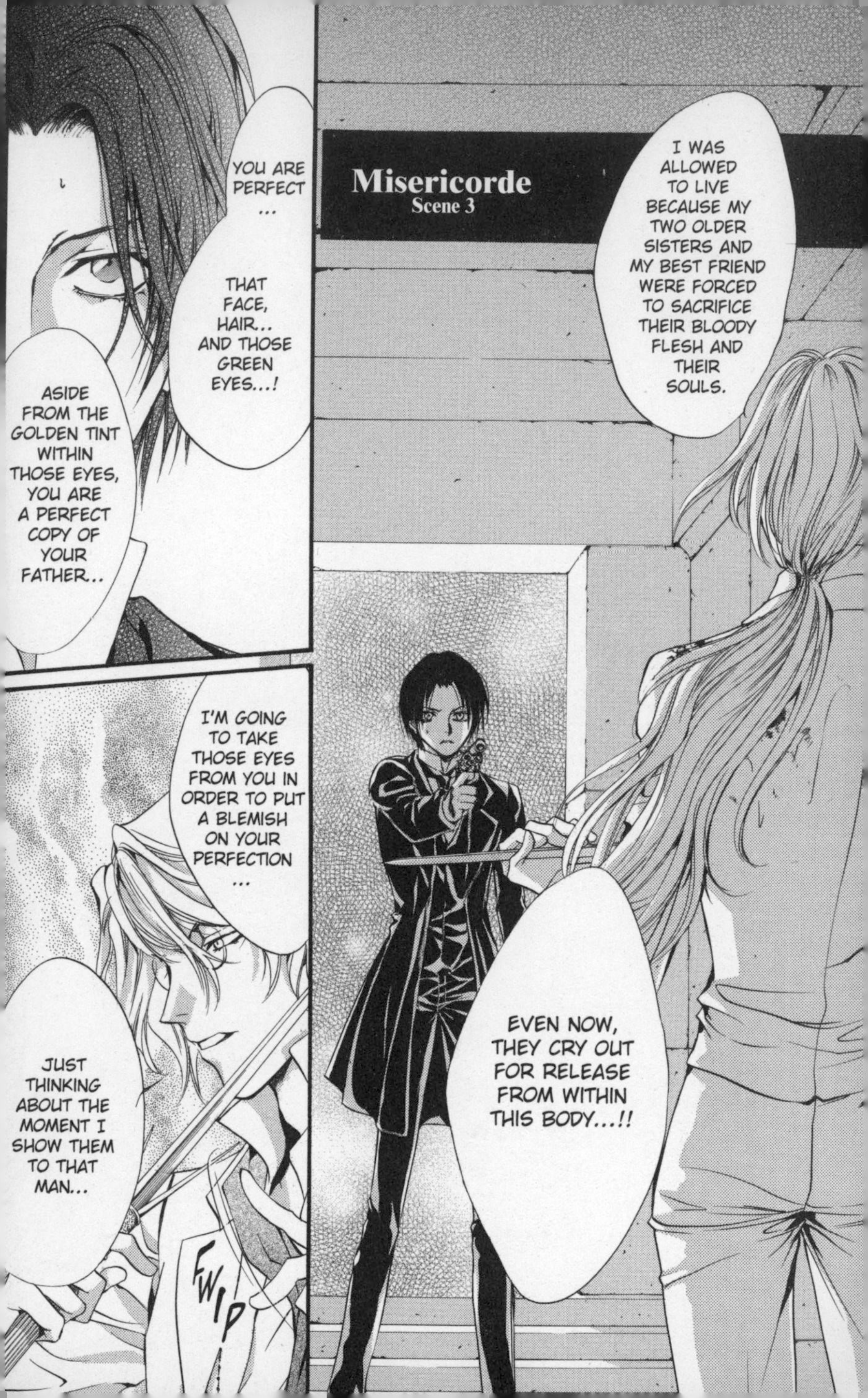
Misericorde
Scene 3
I WAS ALLOWED TO LIVE BECAUSE MY TWO OLDER SISTERS AND MY BEST FRIEND WERE FORCED TO SACRIFICE THEIR BLOODY FLESH AND THEIR SOULS.
EVEN NOW, THEY CRY OUT FOR RELEASE FROM WITHIN THIS BODY...!!
YOU ARE PERFECT ...
THAT FACE, HAIR... AND THOSE GREEN EYES...!
ASIDE FROM THE GOLDEN TINT WITHIN THOSE EYES, YOU ARE A PERFECT COPY OF YOUR FATHER...
I'M GOING TO TAKE THOSE EYES FROM YOU IN ORDER TO PUT A BLEMISH ON YOUR PERFECTION ...
JUST THINKING ABOUT THE MOMENT I SHOW THEM TO THAT MAN...
FWIP

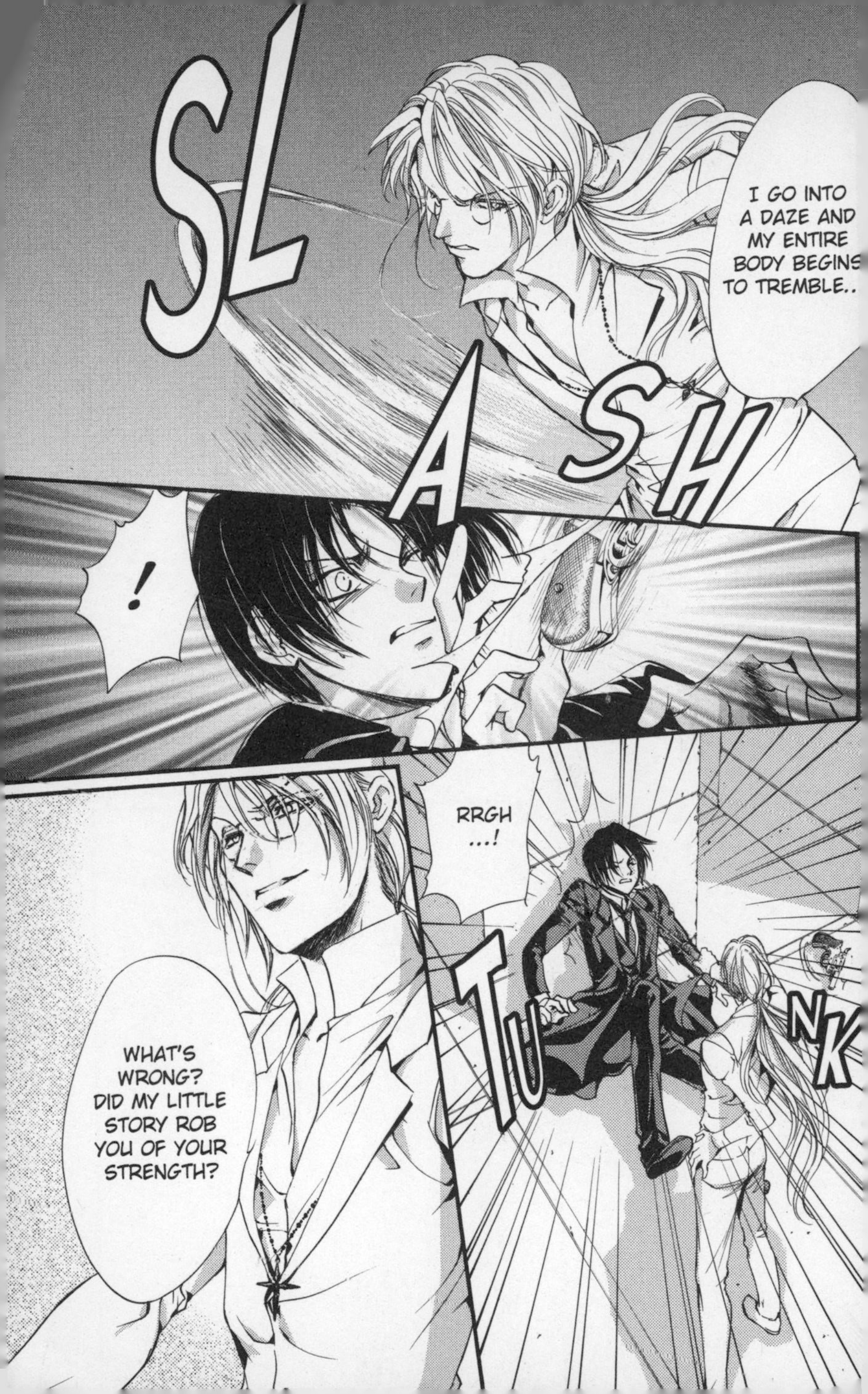
I GO INTO A DAZE AND MY ENTIRE BODY BEGINS TO TREMBLE..
SLASH
!
RRGH ...!
TUNK
WHAT'S WRONG? DID MY LITTLE STORY ROB YOU OF YOUR STRENGTH?

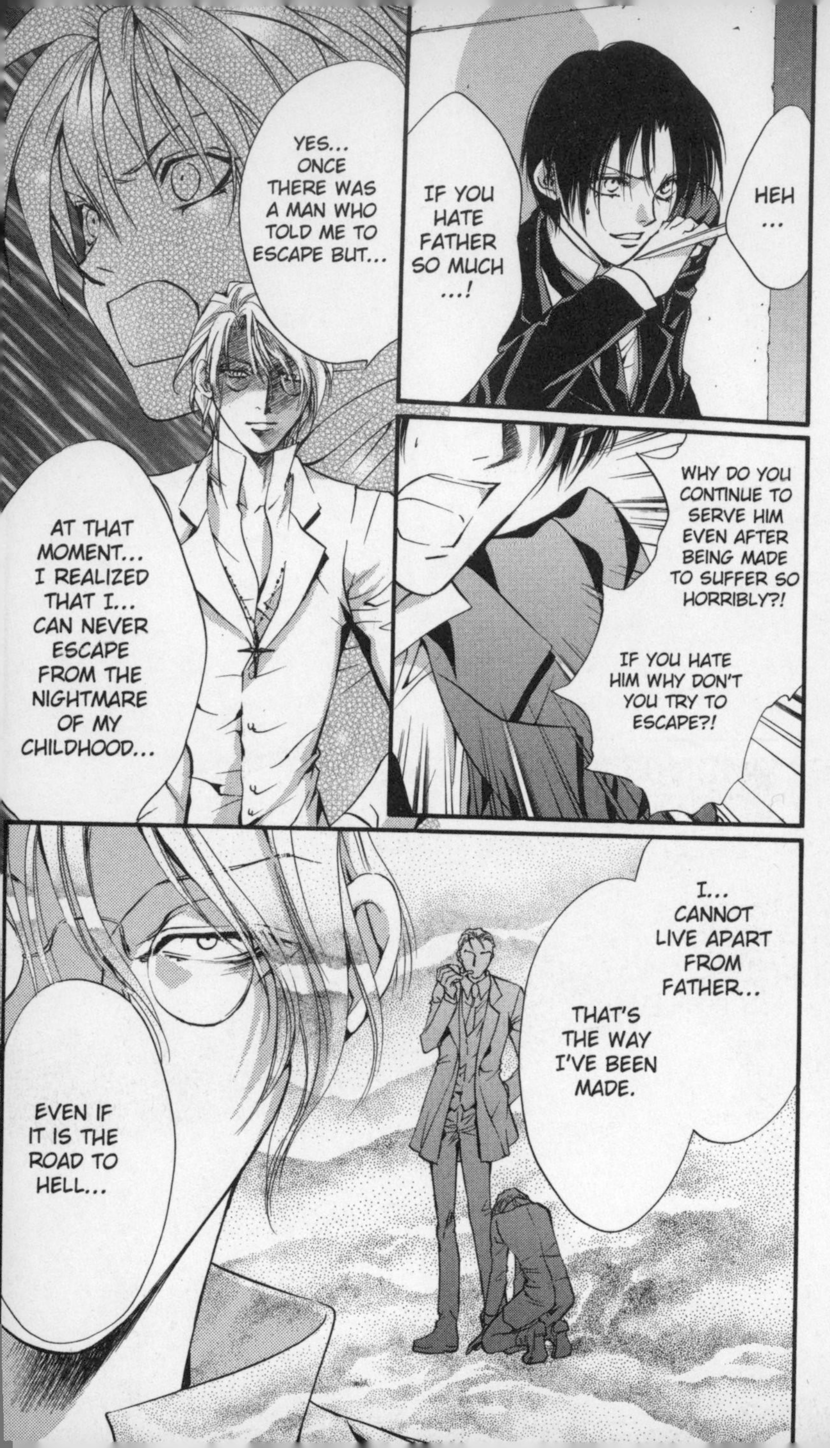
HEH...
IF YOU HATE FATHER SO MUCH...!
WHY DO YOU CONTINUE TO SERVE HIM EVEN AFTER BEING MADE TO SUFFER SO HORRIBLY?!
IF YOU HATE HIM WHY DON'T YOU TRY TO ESCAPE?!
YES... ONCE THERE WAS A MAN WHO TOLD ME TO ESCAPE BUT...
AT THAT MOMENT... I REALIZED THAT I... CAN NEVER ESCAPE FROM THE NIGHTMARE OF MY CHILDHOOD...
I... CANNOT LIVE APART FROM FATHER..
THAT'S THE WAY I'VE BEEN MADE.
EVEN IF IT IS THE ROAD TO HELL...

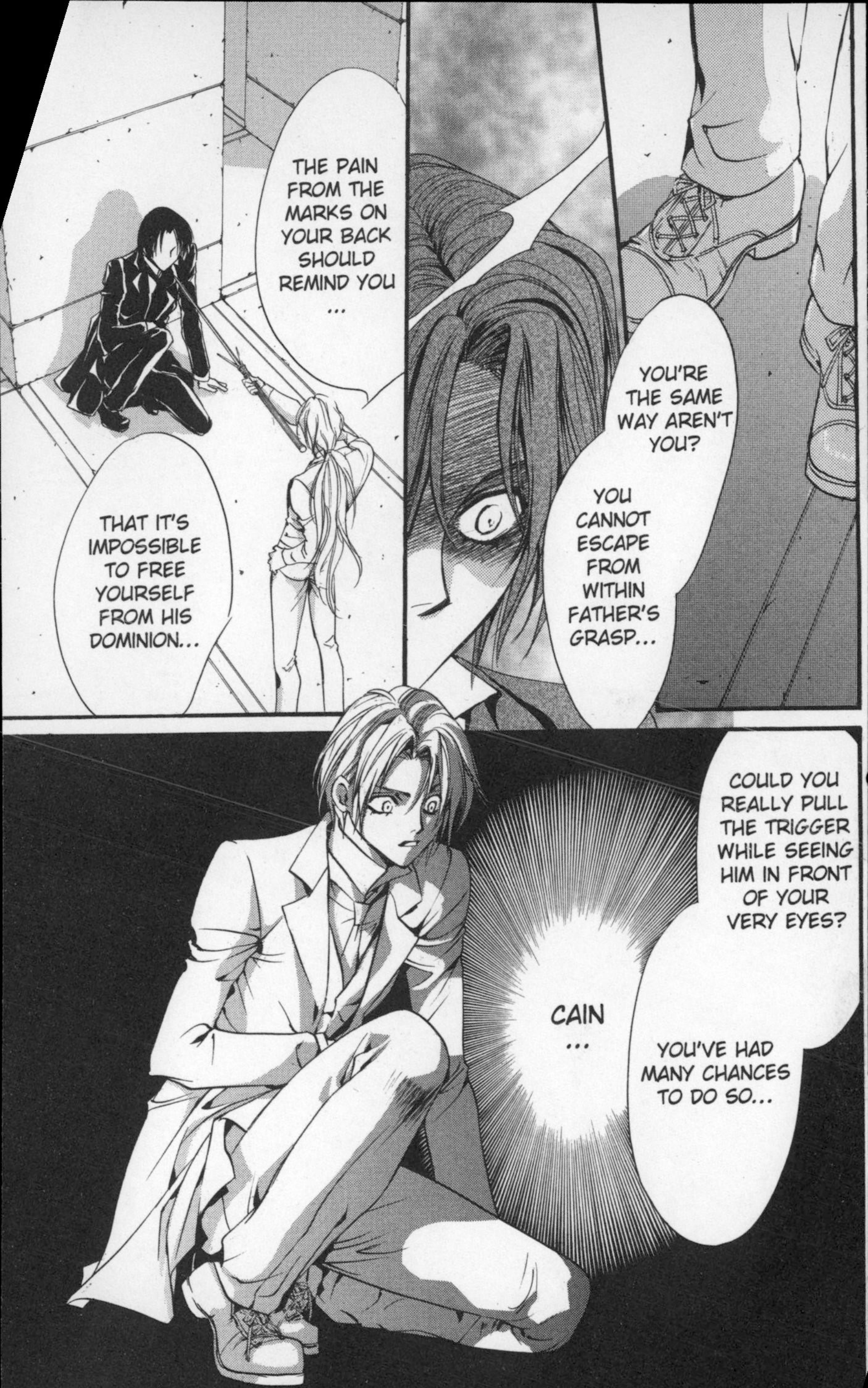
YOU'RE THE SAME WAY AREN'T YOU?
YOU CANNOT ESCAPE FROM WITHIN FATHER'S GRASP...
THE PAIN FROM THE MARKS ON YOUR BACK SHOULD REMIND YOU ...
THAT IT'S IMPOSSIBLE TO FREE YOURSELF FROM HIS DOMINION...
COULD YOU REALLY PULL THE TRIGGER WHILE SEEING HIM IN FRONT OF YOUR VERY EYES?
YOU'VE HAD MANY CHANCES TO DO SO...
CAIN ...

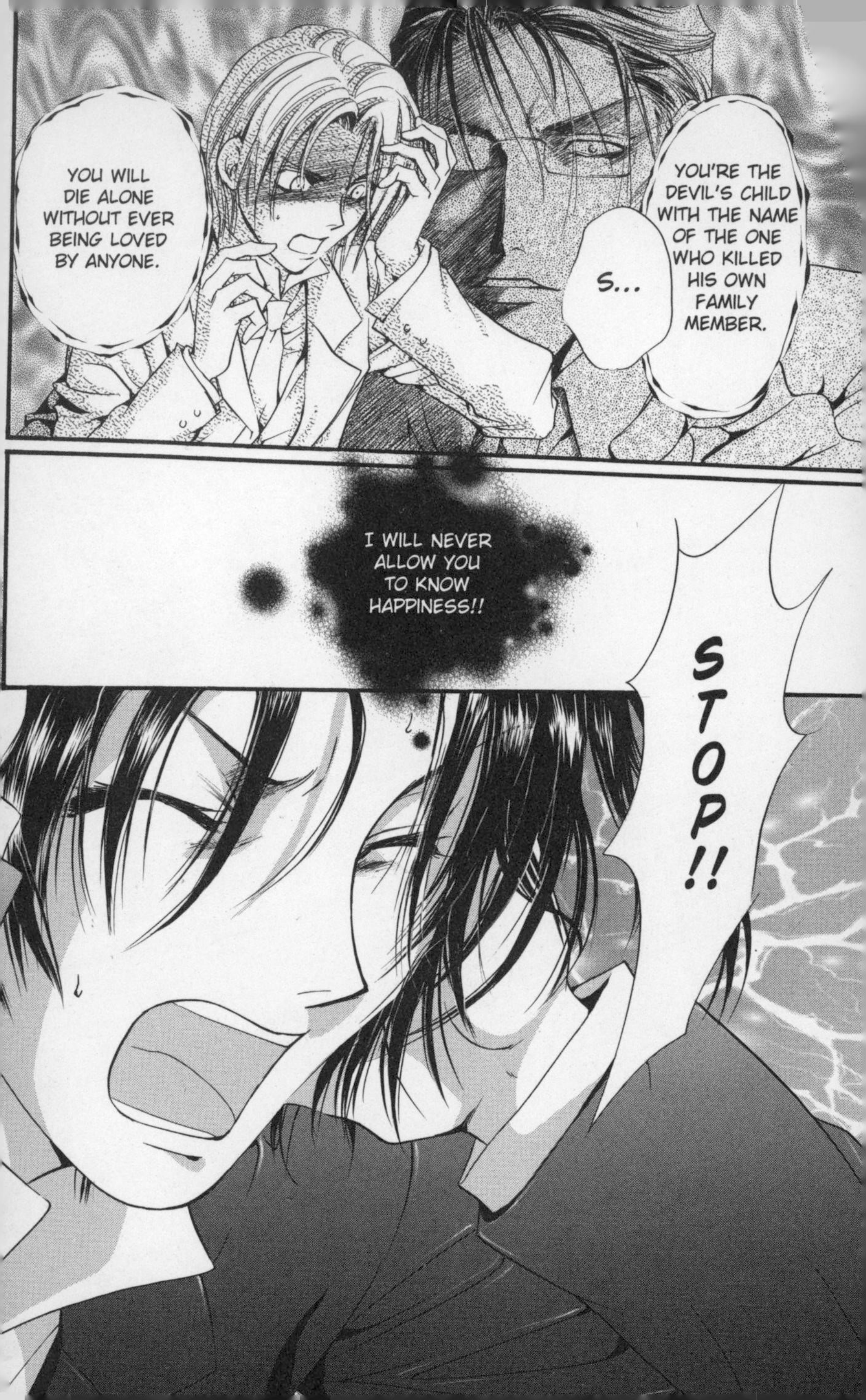
YOU'RE THE DEVIL'S CHILD WITH THE NAME OF THE ONE WHO KILLED HIS OWN FAMILY MEMBER.
S...
YOU WILL DIE ALONE WITHOUT EVER BEING LOVED BY ANYONE.
I WILL NEVER ALLOW YOU TO KNOW HAPPINESS!!
STOP!!

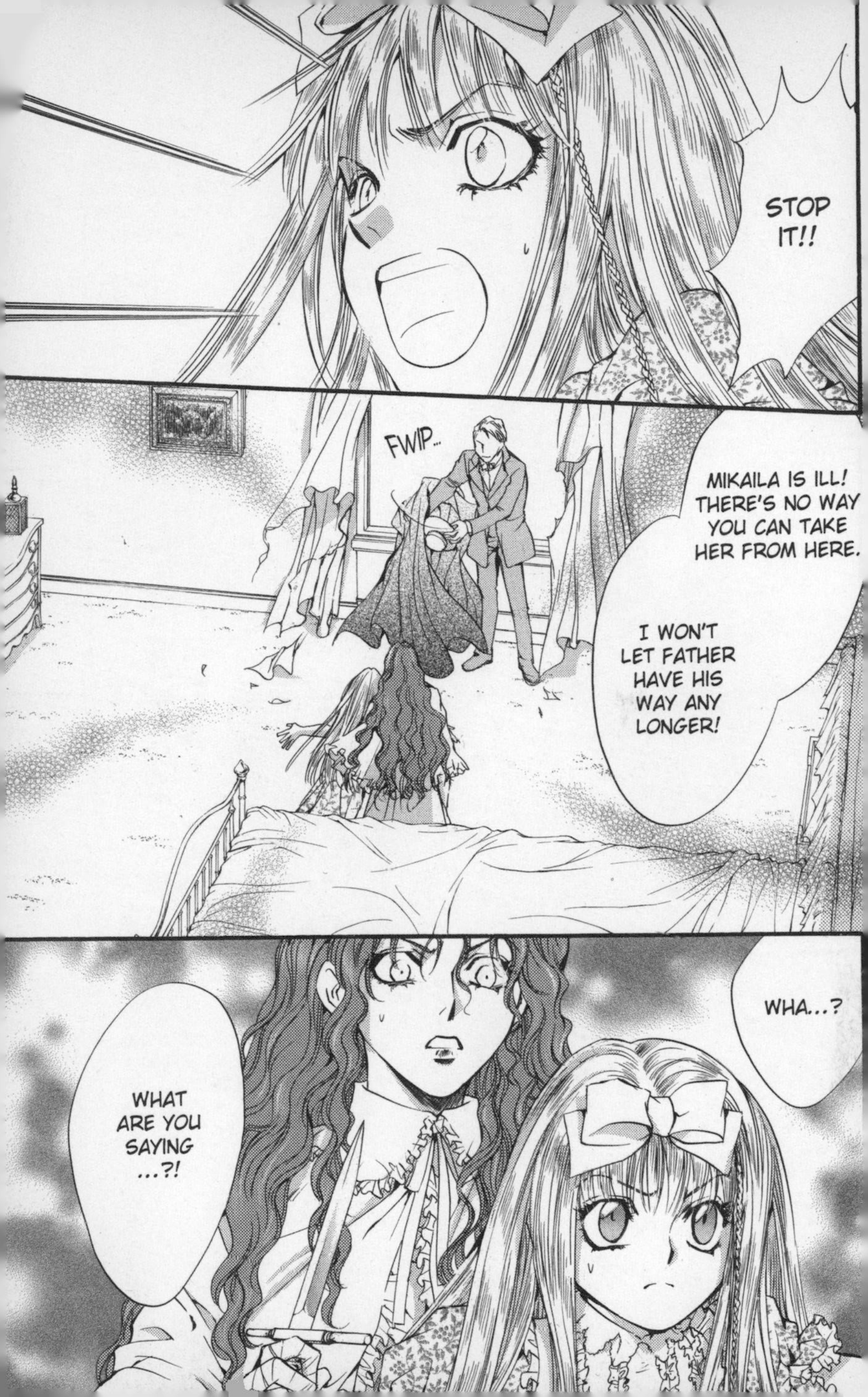
STOP IT!!
MIKAILA IS ILL! THERE'S NO WAY YOU CAN TAKE HER FROM HERE.
I WON'T LET FATHER HAVE HIS WAY ANY LONGER!
FWIP...
WHA...?
WHAT ARE YOU SAYING ...?!

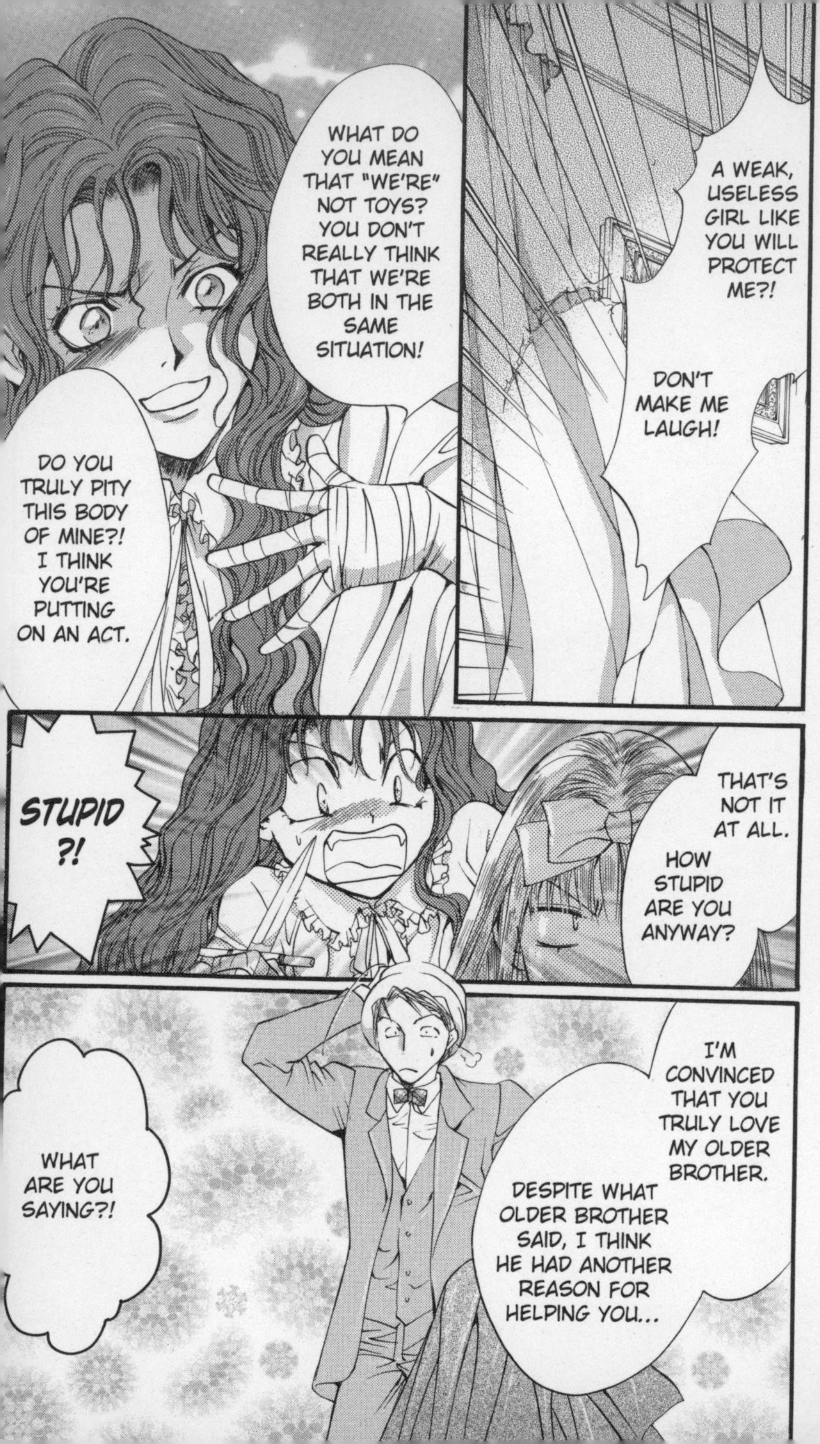
A WEAK, USELESS GIRL LIKE YOU WILL PROTECT ME?!
DON'T MAKE ME LAUGH!
WHAT DO YOU MEAN THAT "WE'RE" NOT TOYS? YOU DON'T REALLY THINK THAT WE'RE BOTH IN THE SAME SITUATION!
DO YOU TRULY PITY THIS BODY OF MINE?! I THINK YOU'RE PUTTING ON AN ACT.
THAT'S NOT IT AT ALL.
HOW STUPID ARE YOU ANYWAY?
STUPID ?!
I'M CONVINCED THAT YOU TRULY LOVE MY OLDER BROTHER.
DESPITE WHAT OLDER BROTHER SAID, I THINK HE HAD ANOTHER REASON FOR HELPING YOU...
WHAT ARE YOU SAYING?!

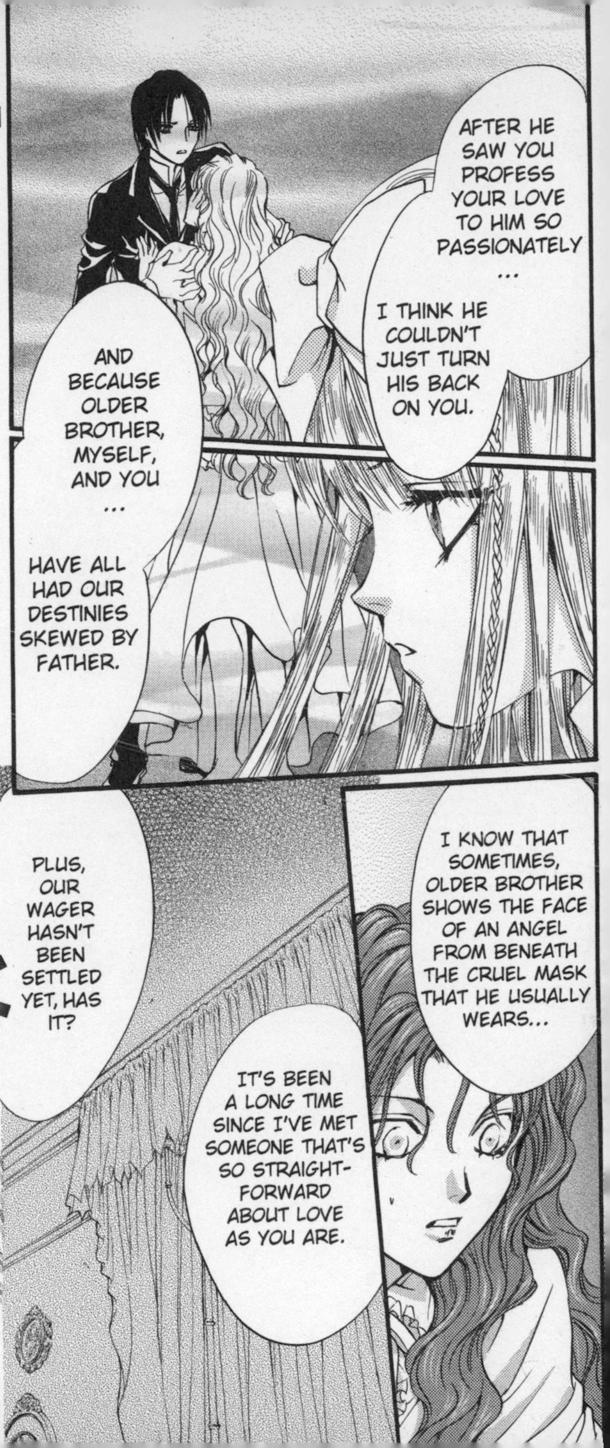
AFTER HE SAW YOU PROFESS YOUR LOVE TO HIM SO PASSIONATELY...
I THINK HE COULDN'T JUST TURN HIS BACK ON YOU.
AND BECAUSE OLDER BROTHER, MYSELF, AND YOU...
HAVE ALL HAD OUR DESTINIES SKEWED BY FATHER.
I KNOW THAT SOMETIMES, OLDER BROTHER SHOWS THE FACE OF AN ANGEL FROM BENEATH THE CRUEL MASK THAT HE USUALLY WEARS...
IT'S BEEN A LONG TIME SINCE I'VE MET SOMEONE THAT'S SO STRAIGHT-FORWARD ABOUT LOVE AS YOU ARE.
PLUS, OUR WAGER HASN'T BEEN SETTLED YET, HAS IT?

This is the arsonist... he doesn't have a name. I wanted him to look like an easygoing airhead but he's actually quite a villain. His outfit was taken from certain outdoor fashions that were shown in fashion magazines of the period. I don't think it would look good on Cain... I don't know... it's just that Cain always wears black so maybe he's just not very fashionable. It's much more fun to think up dresses for girls. Even though all the frills are a lot of work to draw.

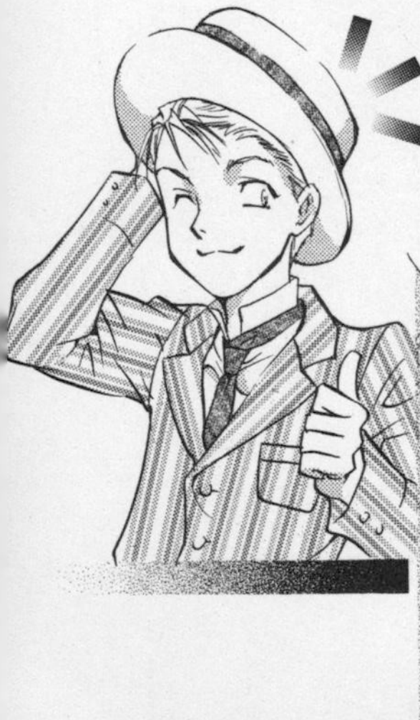

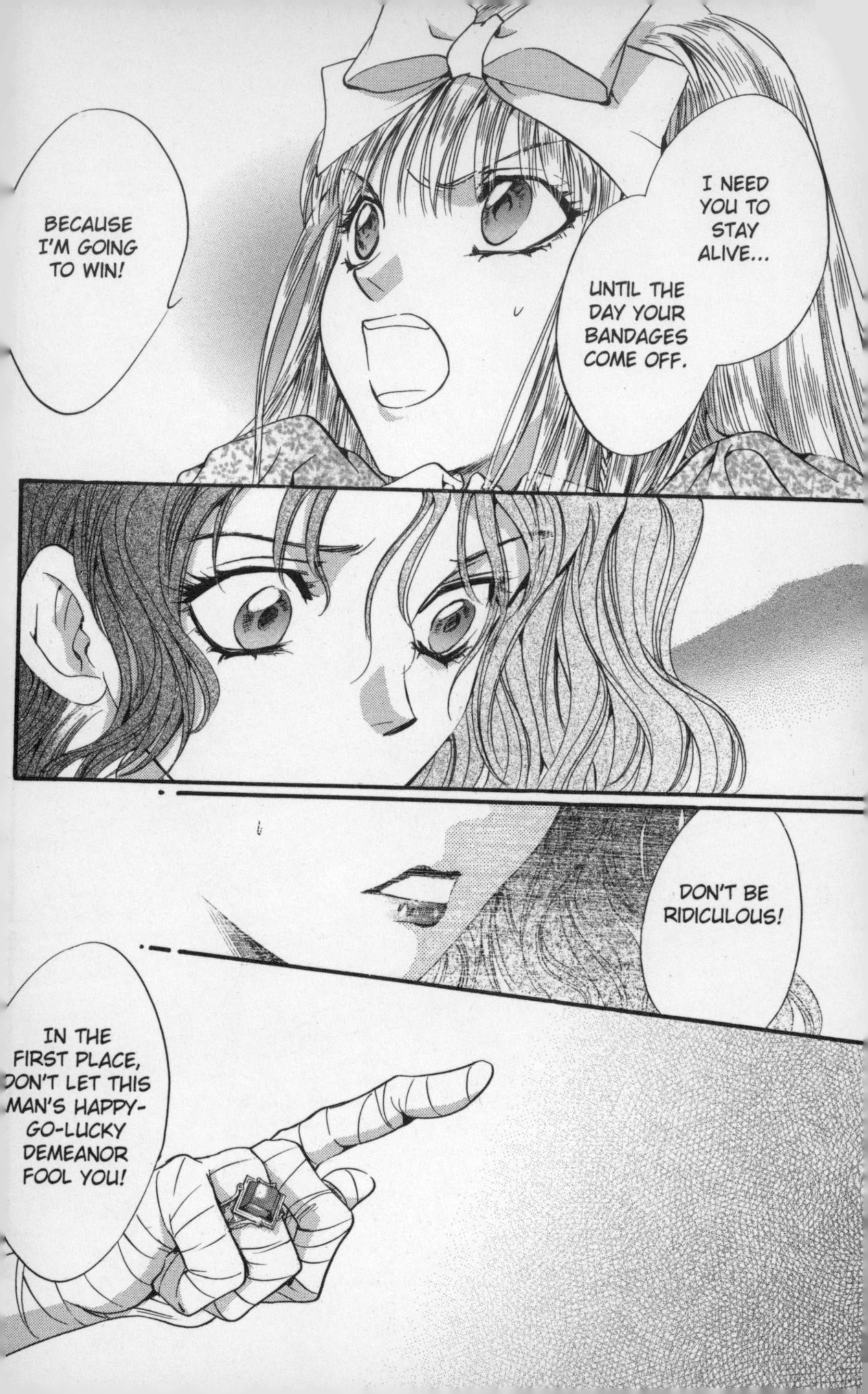
I NEED YOU TO STAY ALIVE...
UNTIL THE DAY YOUR BANDAGES COME OFF.
BECAUSE I'M GOING TO WIN!
DON'T BE RIDICULOUS!
IN THE FIRST PLACE, DON'T LET THIS MAN'S HAPPY-GO-LUCKY DEMEANOR FOOL YOU!

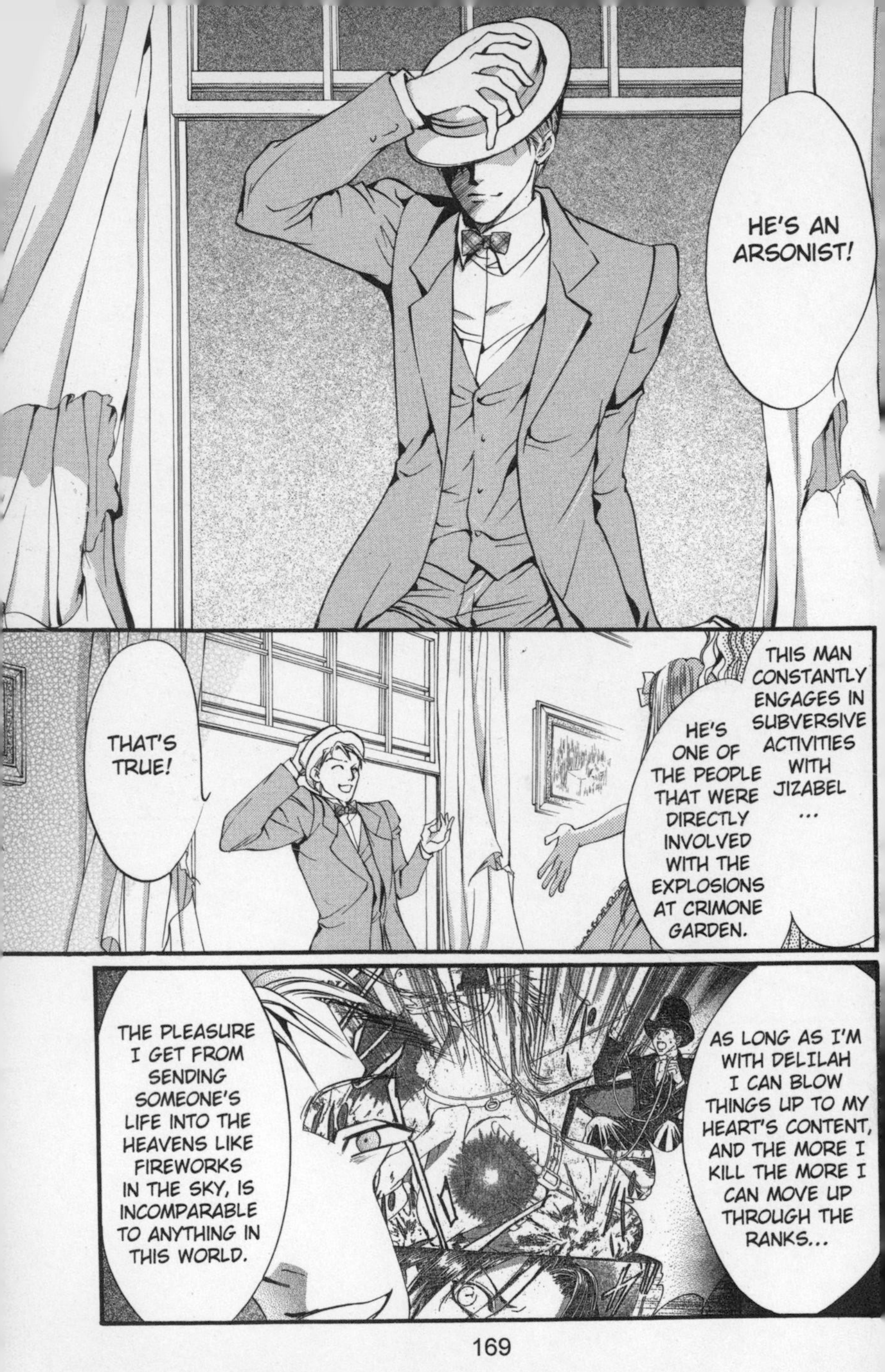
HE'S AN ARSONIST!
THIS MAN CONSTANTLY ENGAGES IN SUBVERSIVE ACTIVITIES WITH JIZABEL...
HE'S ONE OF THE PEOPLE THAT WERE DIRECTLY INVOLVED WITH THE EXPLOSIONS AT CRIMONE GARDEN.
THAT'S TRUE!
AS LONG AS I'M WITH DELILAH I CAN BLOW THINGS UP TO MY HEART'S CONTENT, AND THE MORE I KILL THE MORE I CAN MOVE UP THROUGH THE RANKS...
THE PLEASURE I GET FROM SENDING SOMEONE'S LIFE INTO THE HEAVENS LIKE FIREWORKS IN THE SKY, IS INCOMPARABLE TO ANYTHING IN THIS WORLD.

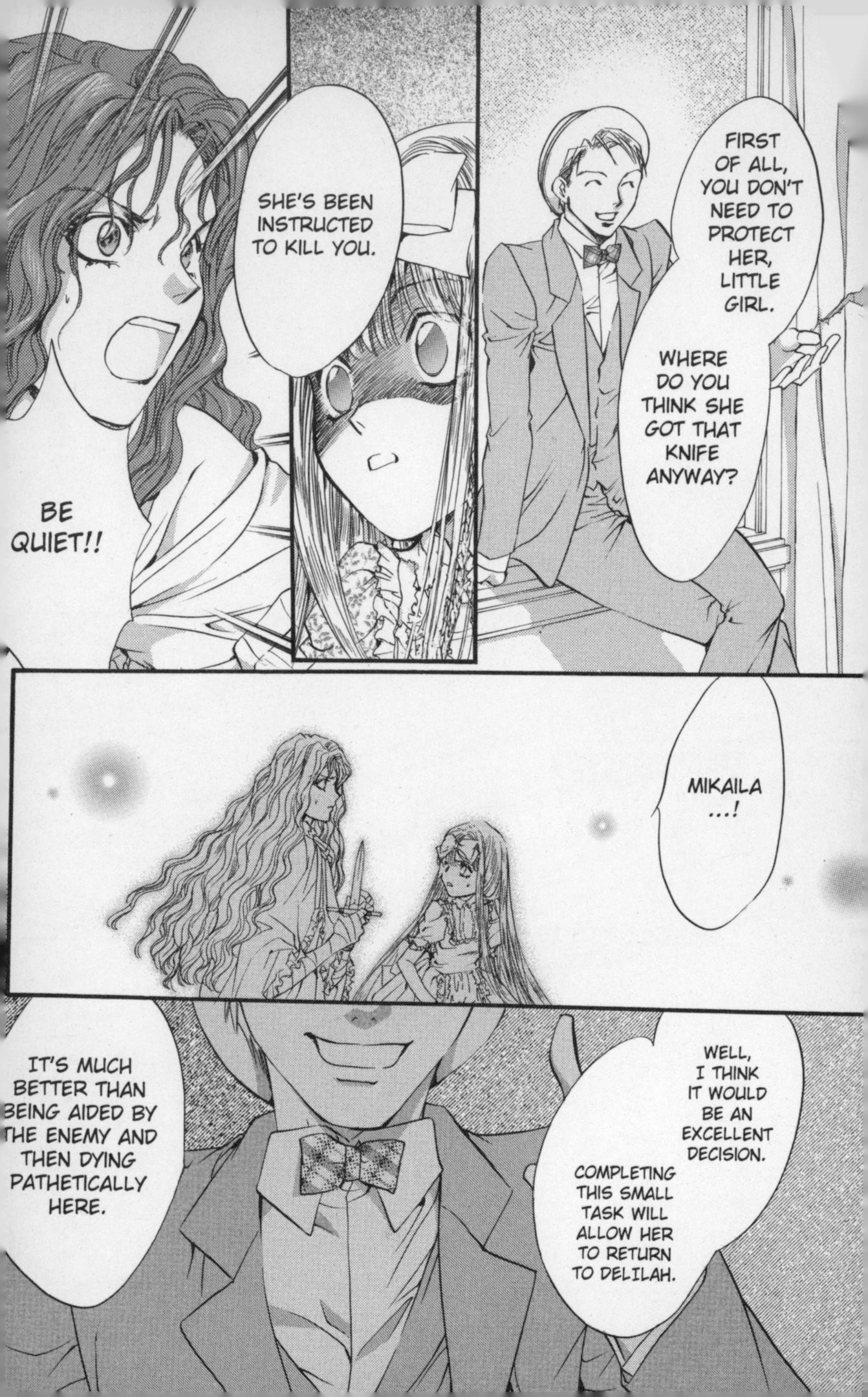
FIRST OF ALL, YOU DON'T NEED TO PROTECT HER, LITTLE GIRL.
WHERE DO YOU THINK SHE GOT THAT KNIFE ANYWAY?
SHE'S BEEN INSTRUCTED TO KILL YOU.
BE QUIET!!
MIKAILA ...!
WELL, I THINK IT WOULD BE AN EXCELLENT DECISION.
COMPLETING THIS SMALL TASK WILL ALLOW HER TO RETURN TO DELILAH.
IT'S MUCH BETTER THAN BEING AIDED BY THE ENEMY AND THEN DYING PATHETICALLY HERE.

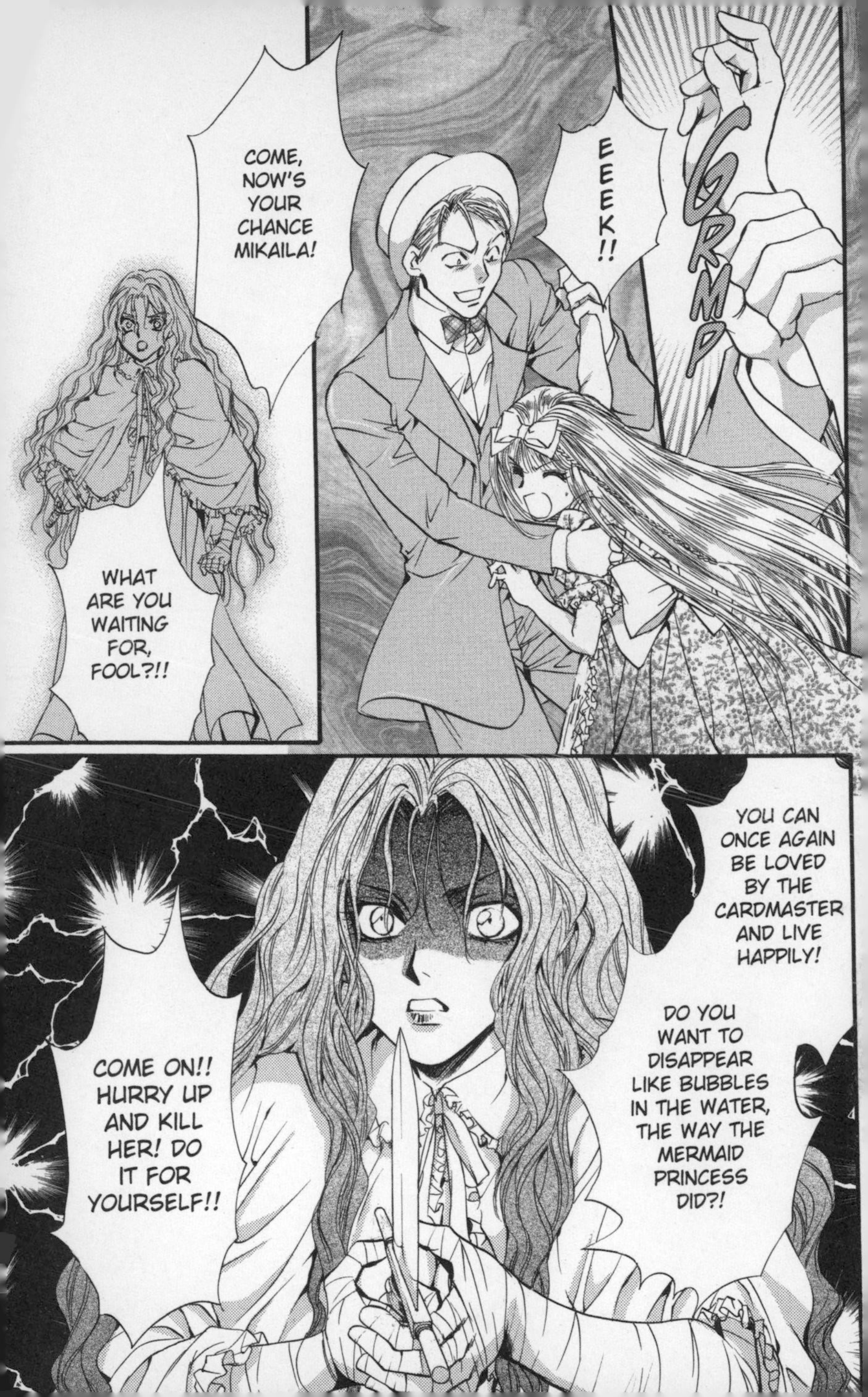
EEEK!!
GRMP
COME, NOW'S YOUR CHANCE MIKAILA!
WHAT ARE YOU WAITING FOR, FOOL?!!
YOU CAN ONCE AGAIN BE LOVED BY THE CARDMASTER AND LIVE HAPPILY!
DO YOU WANT TO DISAPPEAR LIKE BUBBLES IN THE WATER, THE WAY THE MERMAID PRINCESS DID?!
COME ON!! HURRY UP AND KILL HER! DO IT FOR YOURSELF!!

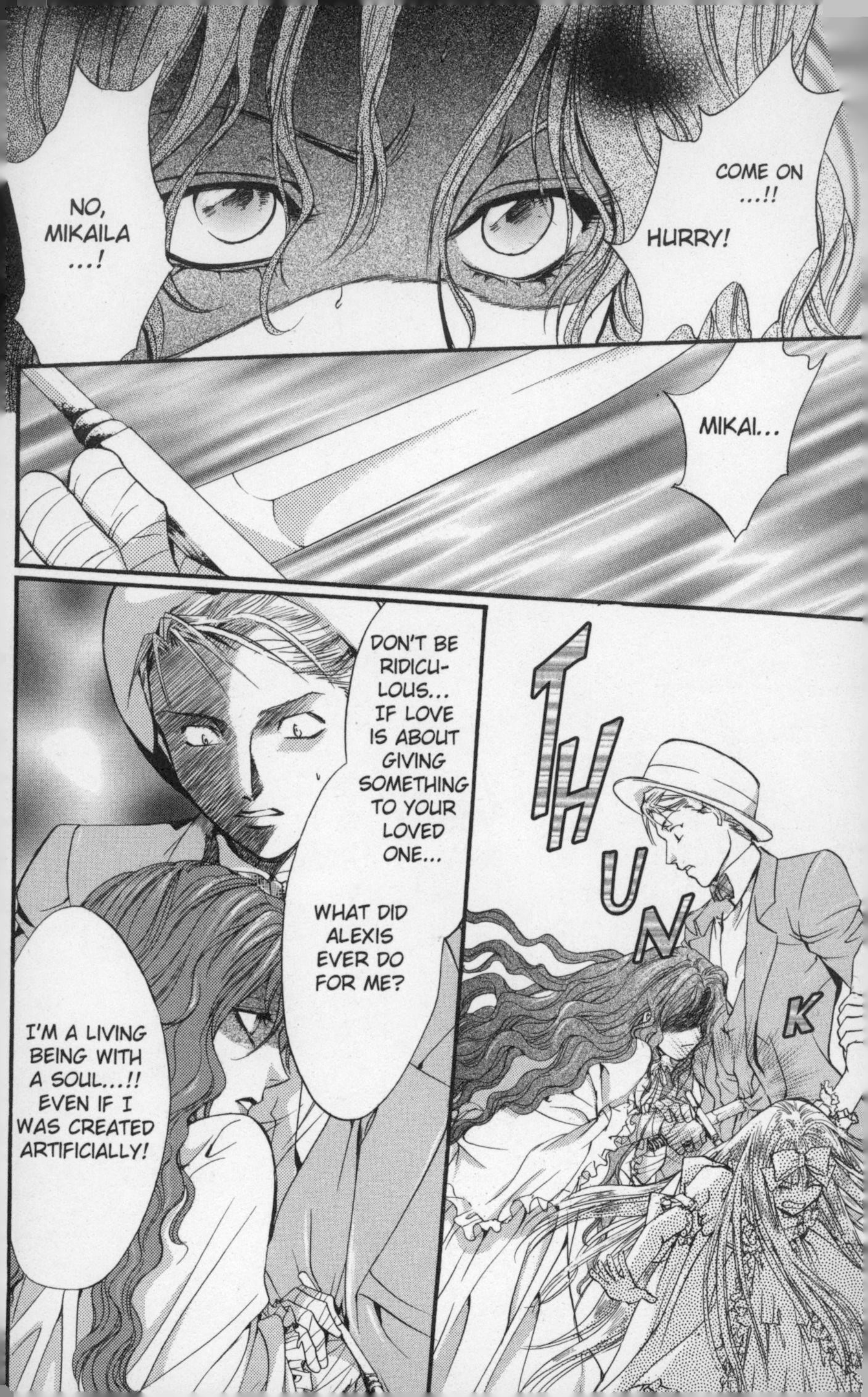
COME ON ...!!
HURRY!
NO, MIKAILA ...!
MIKAI...
THUNK
DON'T BE RIDICULOUS... IF LOVE IS ABOUT GIVING SOMETHING TO YOUR LOVED ONE...
WHAT DID ALEXIS EVER DO FOR ME?
I'M A LIVING BEING WITH A SOUL...!! EVEN IF I WAS CREATED ARTIFICIALLY!

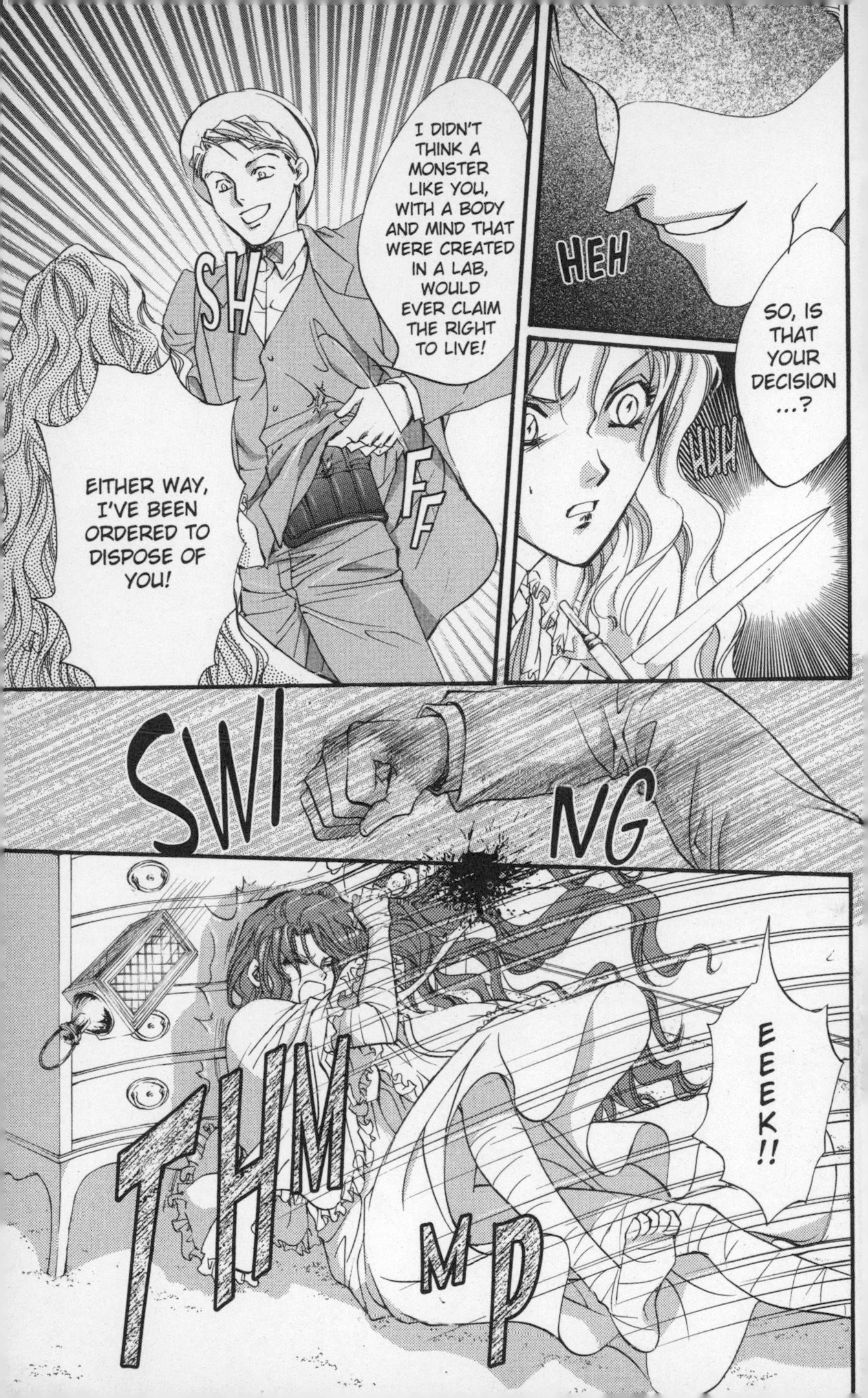
HEH
SO, IS THAT YOUR DECISION ...?
HUH
I DIDN'T THINK A MONSTER LIKE YOU, WITH A BODY AND MIND THAT WERE CREATED IN A LAB, WOULD EVER CLAIM THE RIGHT TO LIVE!
SHFF
EITHER WAY, I'VE BEEN ORDERED TO DISPOSE OF YOU!
SWING
EEEK!!
THMMP

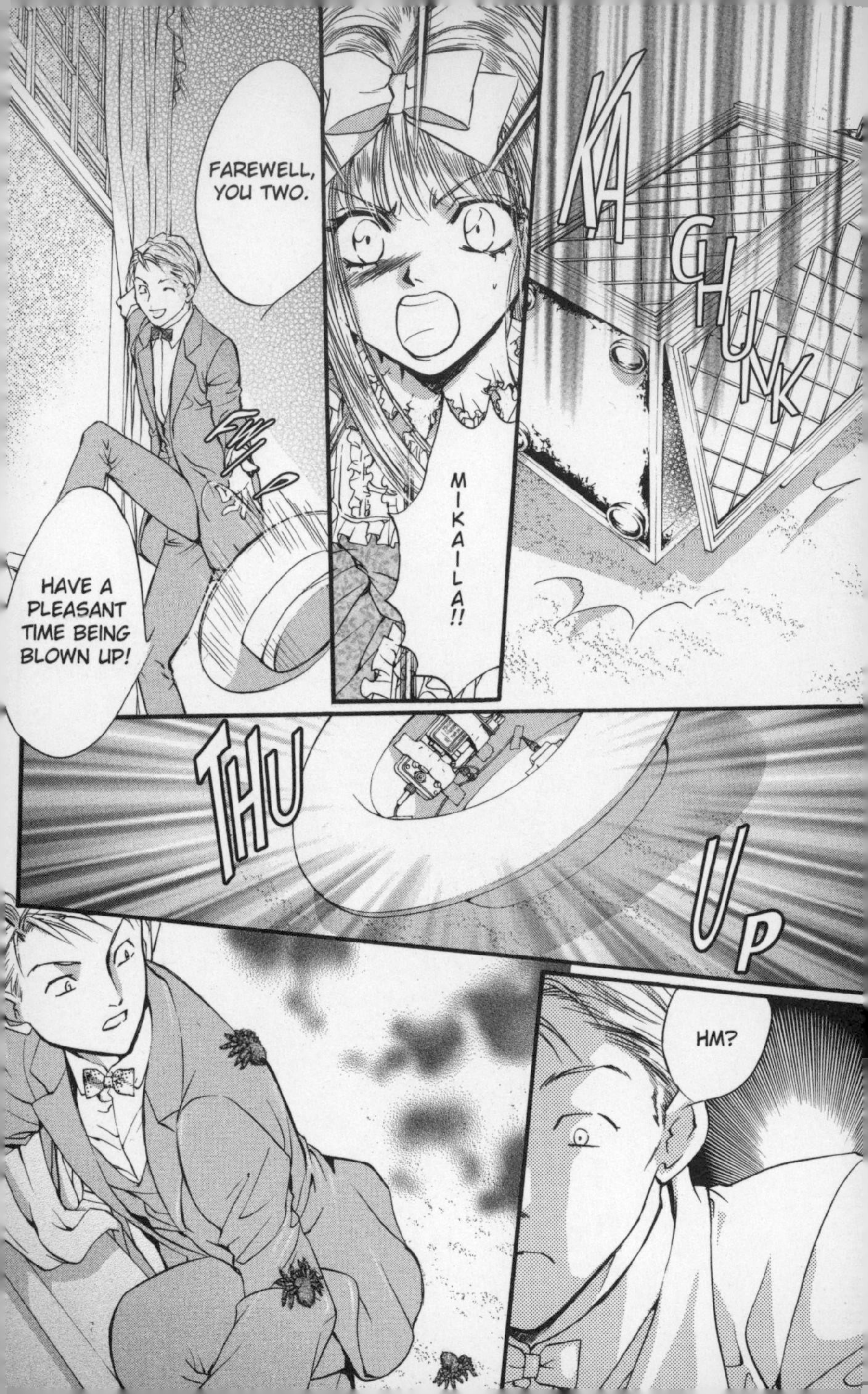
KA
CHUNK
MIKAILA!!
FAREWELL, YOU TWO.
HAVE A PLEASANT TIME BEING BLOWN UP!
THU
UP
HM?

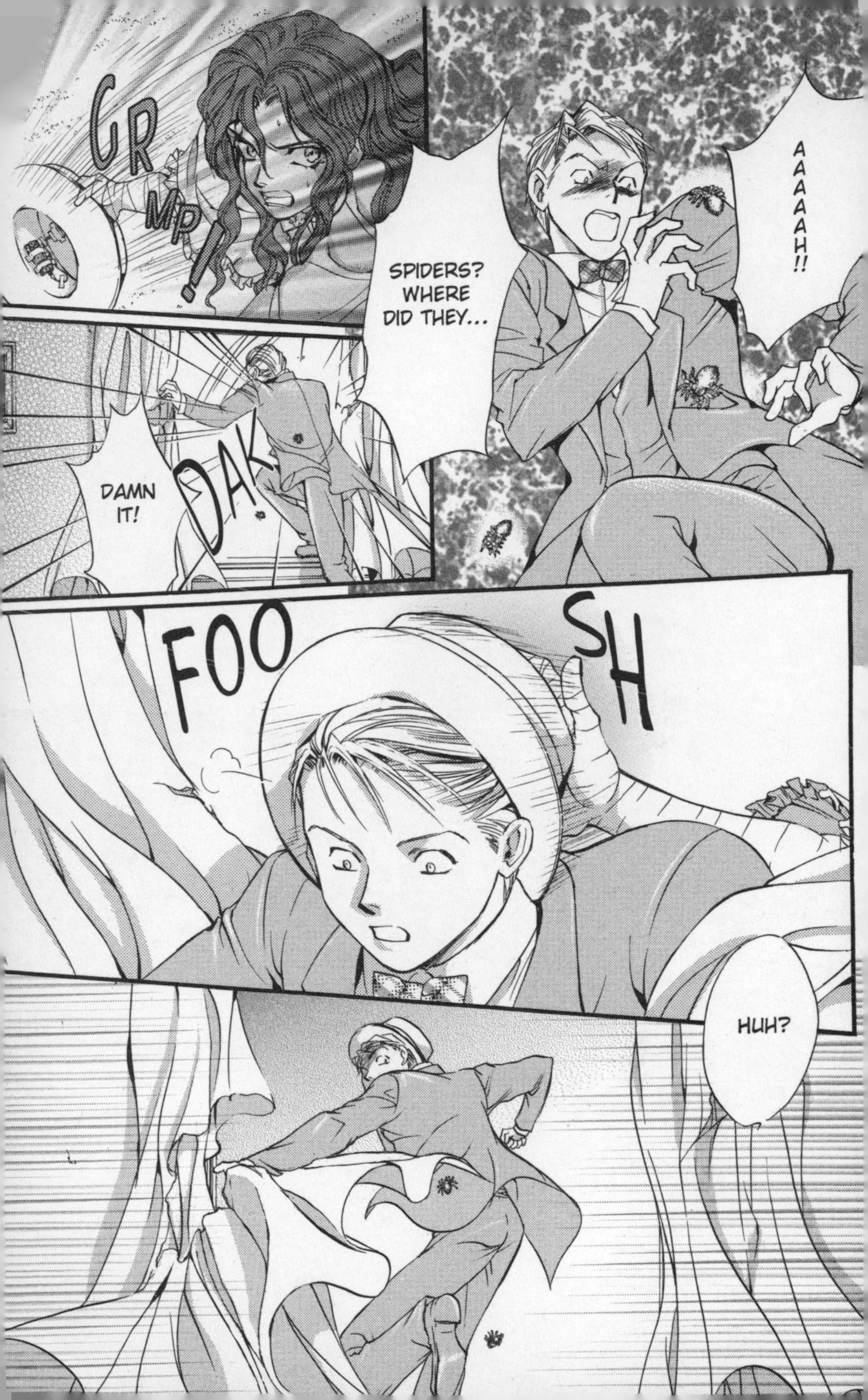

AAAAAAH!!
SPIDERS? WHERE DID THEY...
GRMP!!
DAMN IT!
DAK
FOOSH
HUH?

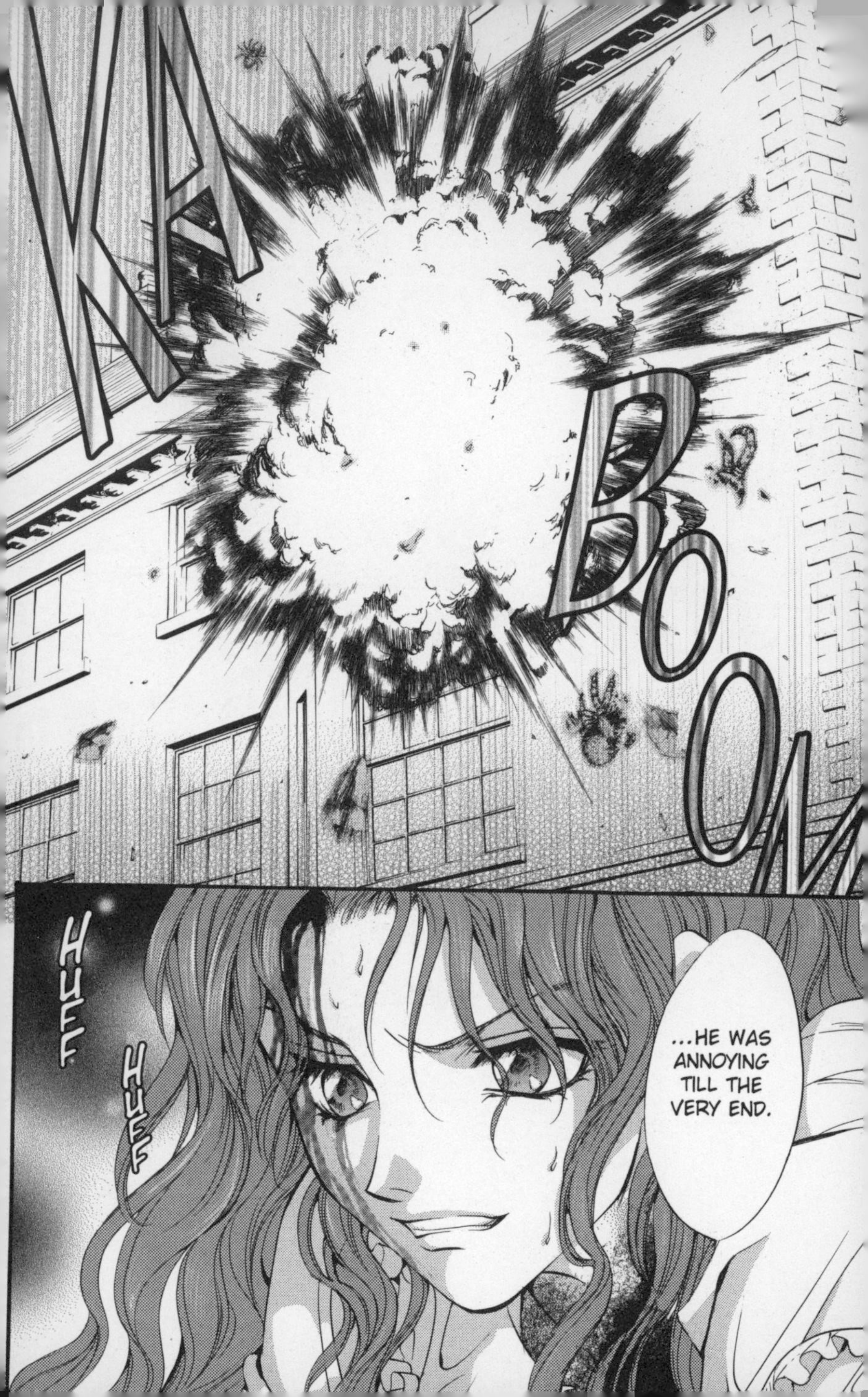
KA
BOOM
HUFF
HUFF
...HE WAS ANNOYING TILL THE VERY END.

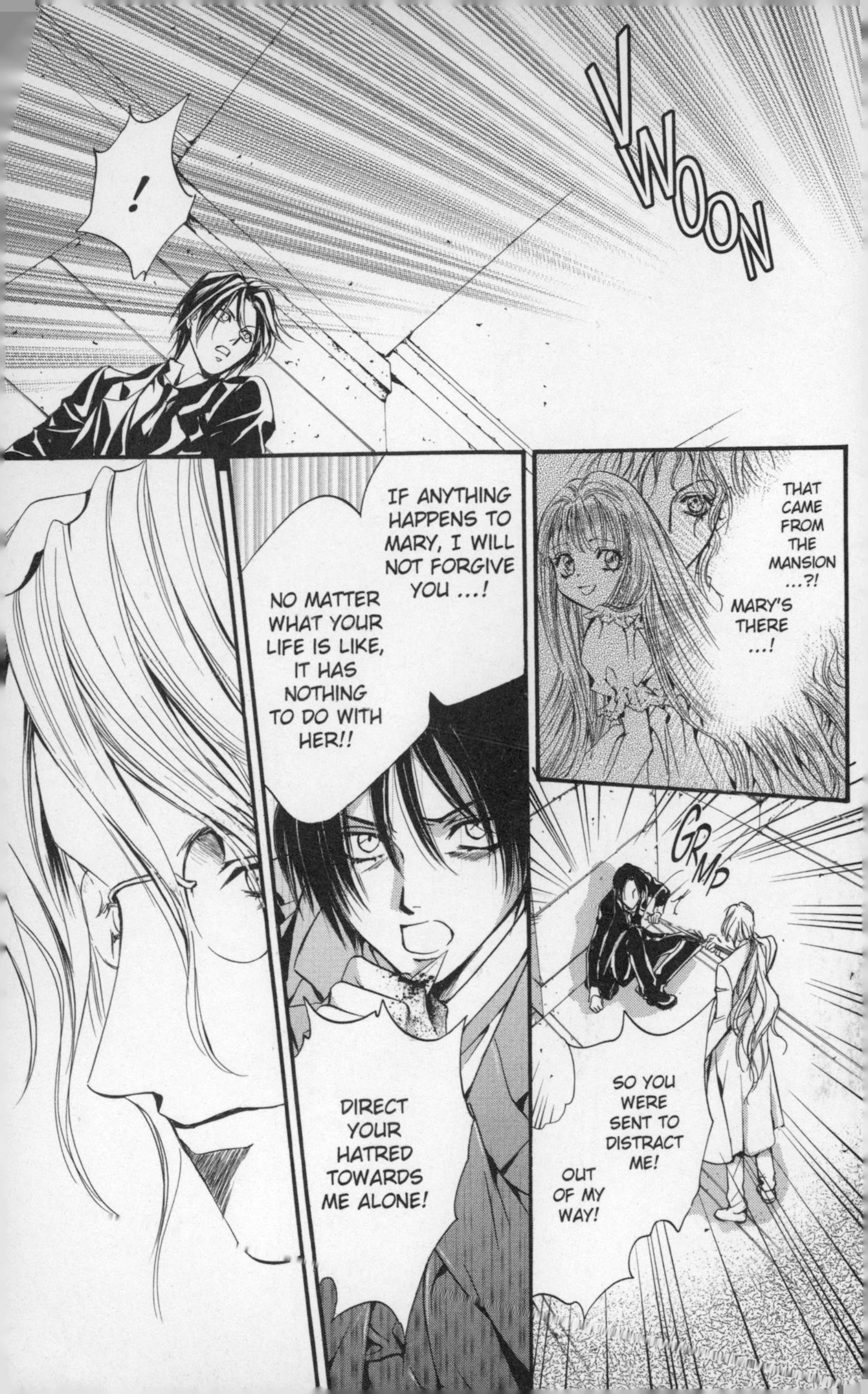
VWOON
!
THAT CAME FROM THE MANSION ...?!
MARY'S THERE ...!
GRMP
SO YOU WERE SENT TO DISTRACT ME!
OUT OF MY WAY!
IF ANYTHING HAPPENS TO MARY, I WILL NOT FORGIVE YOU ...!
NO MATTER WHAT YOUR LIFE IS LIKE, IT HAS NOTHING TO DO WITH HER!!
DIRECT YOUR HATRED TOWARDS ME ALONE!

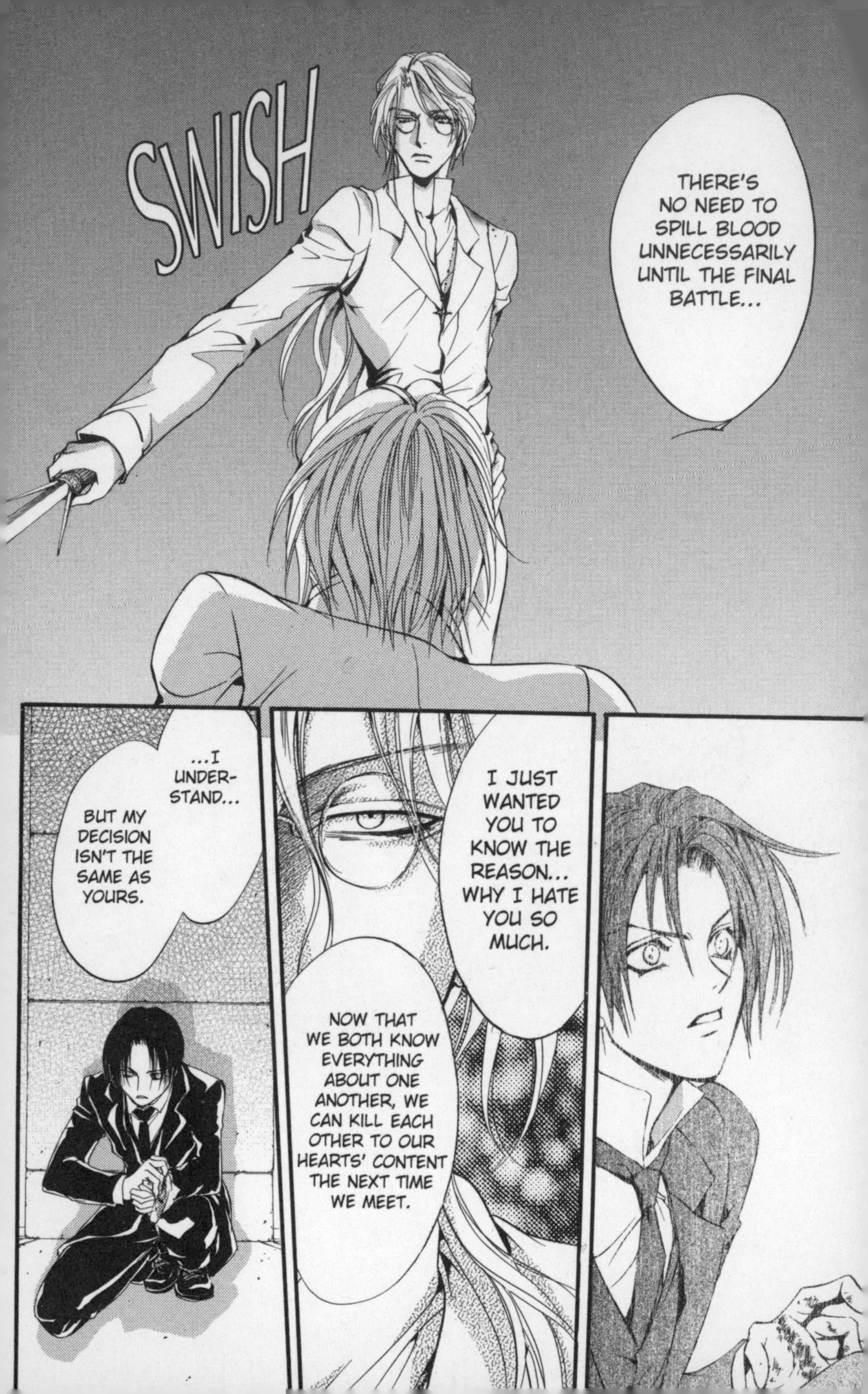
THERE'S NO NEED TO SPILL BLOOD UNNECESSARILY UNTIL THE FINAL BATTLE...
SWISH
I JUST WANTED YOU TO KNOW THE REASON... WHY I HATE YOU SO MUCH.
NOW THAT WE BOTH KNOW EVERYTHING ABOUT ONE ANOTHER, WE CAN KILL EACH OTHER TO OUR HEARTS' CONTENT THE NEXT TIME WE MEET.
...I UNDER-STAND...
BUT MY DECISION ISN'T THE SAME AS YOURS.

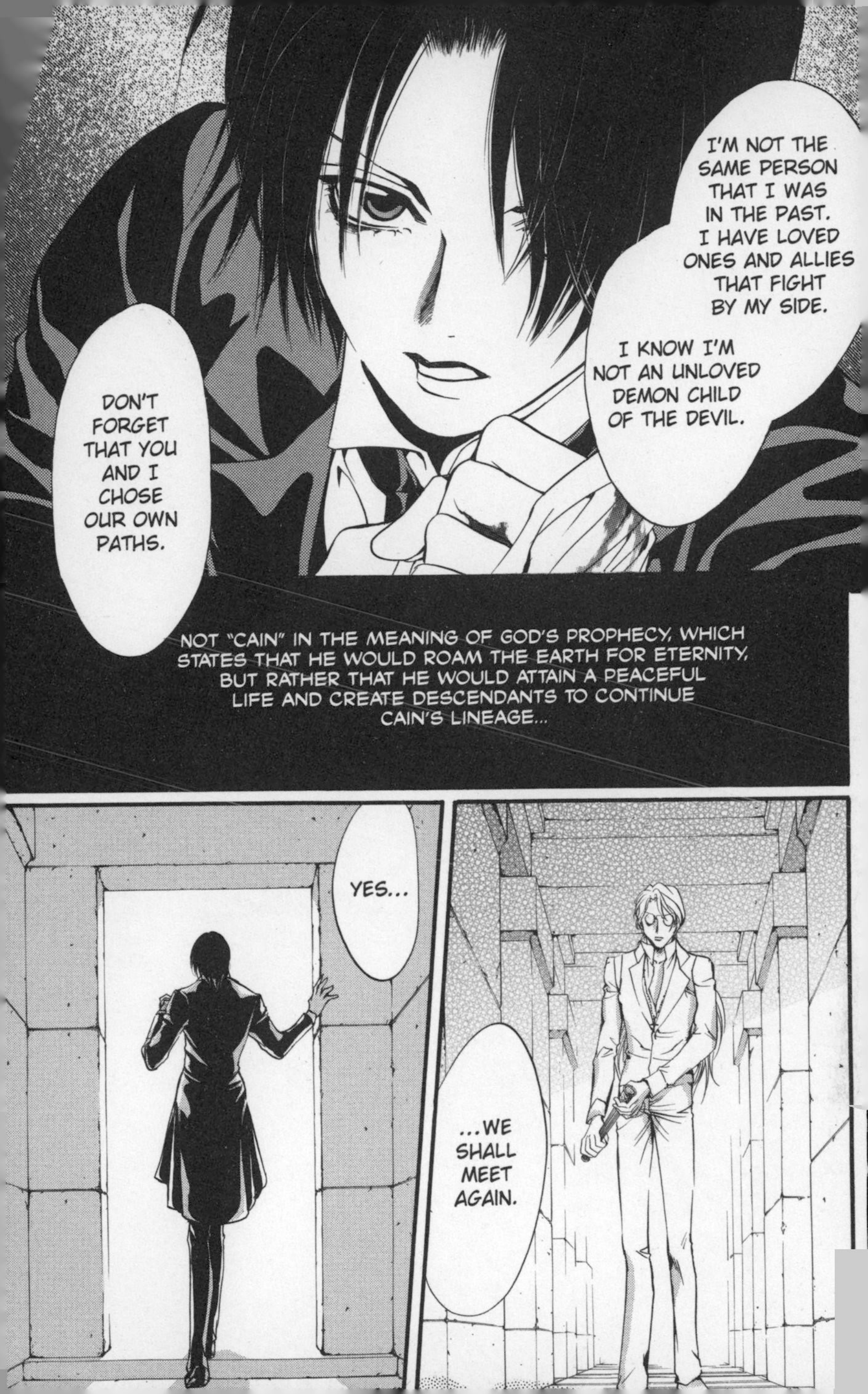
I'M NOT THE SAME PERSON THAT I WAS IN THE PAST. I HAVE LOVED ONES AND ALLIES THAT FIGHT BY MY SIDE.
I KNOW I'M NOT AN UNLOVED DEMON CHILD OF THE DEVIL.
DON'T FORGET THAT YOU AND I CHOSE OUR OWN PATHS.
NOT "CAIN" IN THE MEANING OF GOD'S PROPHECY, WHICH STATES THAT HE WOULD ROAM THE EARTH FOR ETERNITY, BUT RATHER THAT HE WOULD ATTAIN A PEACEFUL LIFE AND CREATE DESCENDANTS TO CONTINUE CAIN'S LINEAGE...
...WE SHALL MEET AGAIN.
YES...

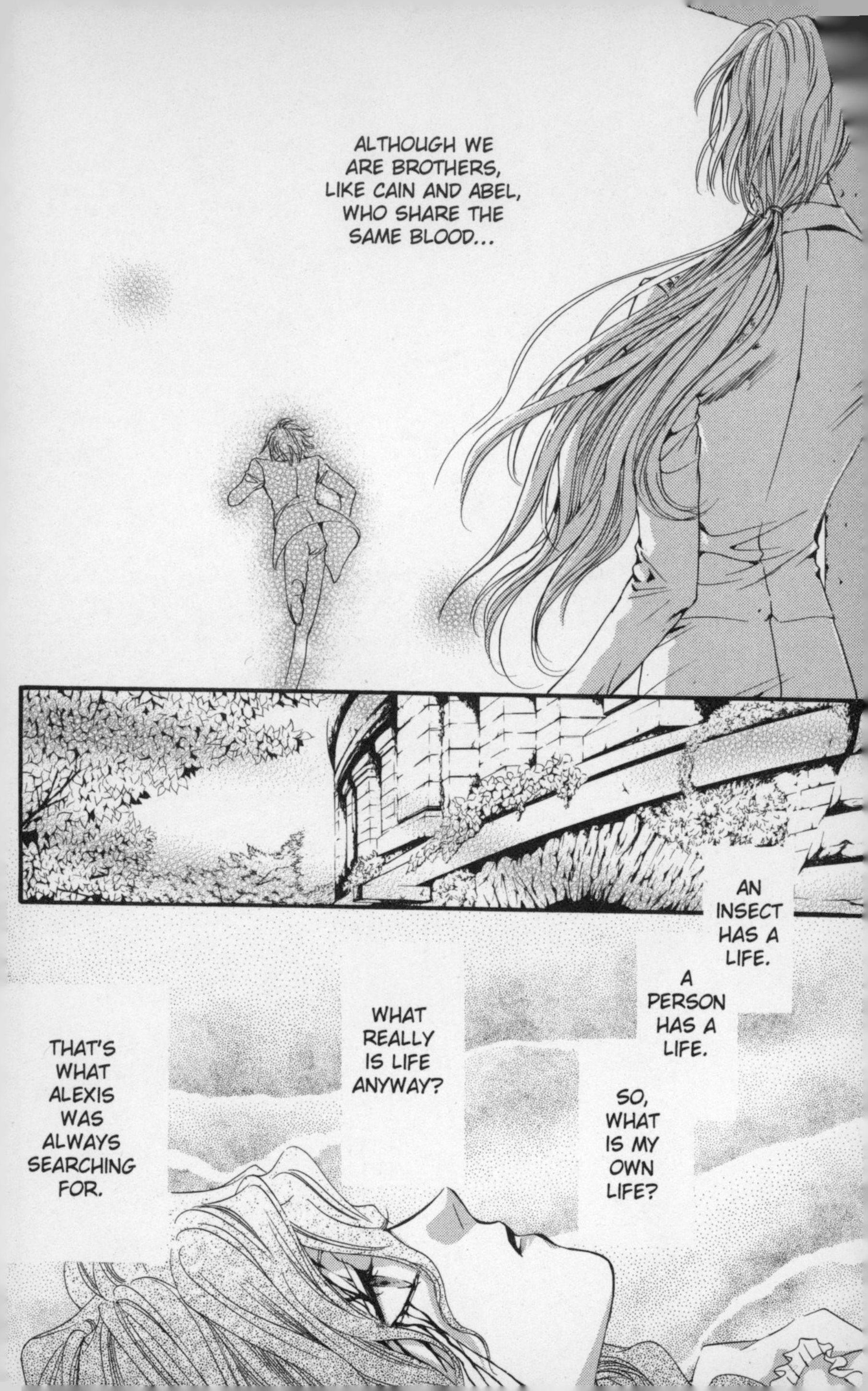
ALTHOUGH WE ARE BROTHERS, LIKE CAIN AND ABEL, WHO SHARE THE SAME BLOOD...
AN INSECT HAS A LIFE.
A PERSON HAS A LIFE.
SO, WHAT IS MY OWN LIFE?
WHAT REALLY IS LIFE ANYWAY?
THAT'S WHAT ALEXIS WAS ALWAYS SEARCHING FOR.

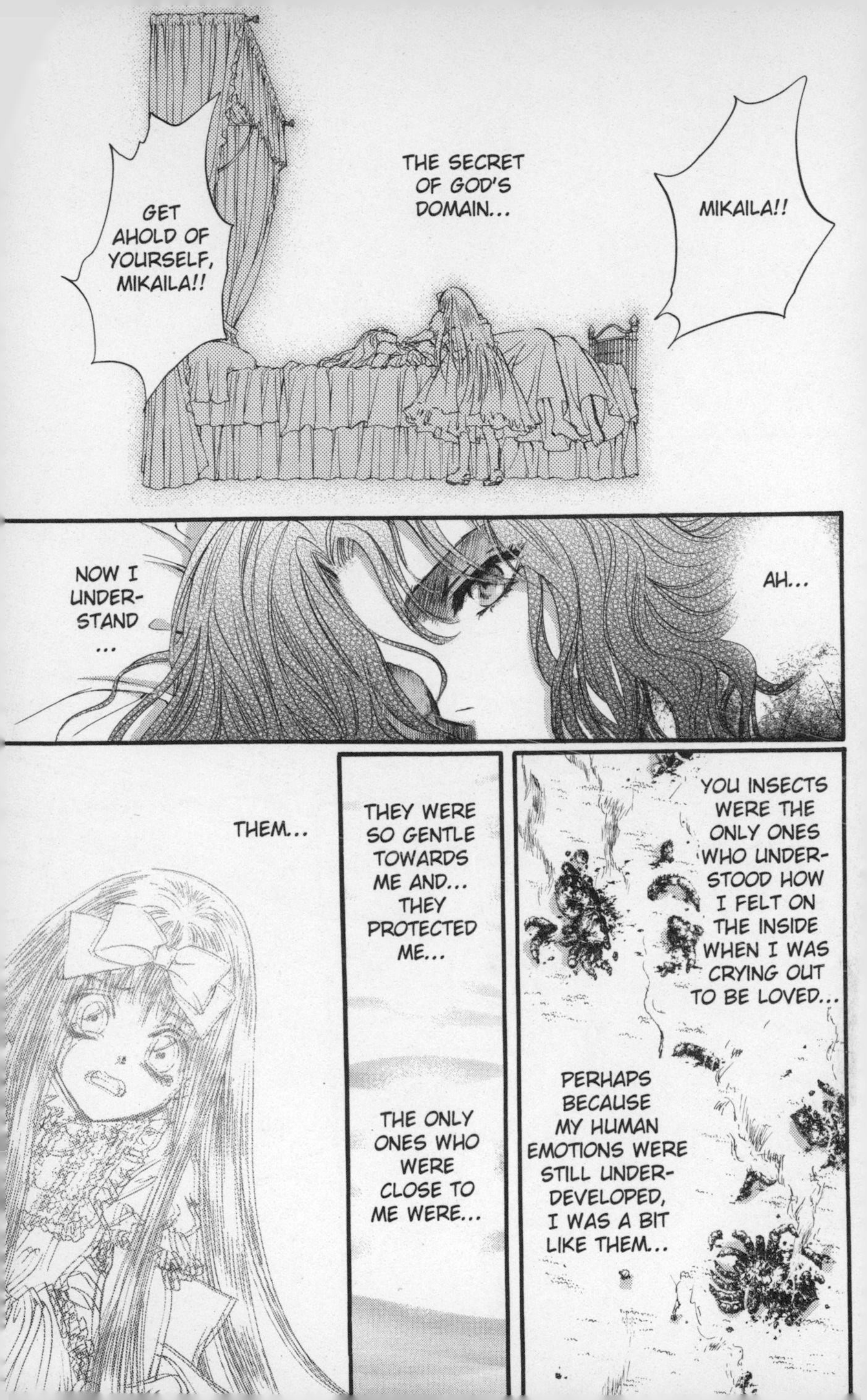
MIKAILA!!
THE SECRET OF GOD'S DOMAIN...
GET AHOLD OF YOURSELF, MIKAILA!!
AH...
NOW I UNDERSTAND...
YOU INSECTS WERE THE ONLY ONES WHO UNDERSTOOD HOW I FELT ON THE INSIDE WHEN I WAS CRYING OUT TO BE LOVED...
PERHAPS BECAUSE MY HUMAN EMOTIONS WERE STILL UNDERDEVELOPED, I WAS A BIT LIKE THEM...
THEY WERE SO GENTLE TOWARDS ME AND... THEY PROTECTED ME...
THE ONLY ONES WHO WERE CLOSE TO ME WERE...
THEM...

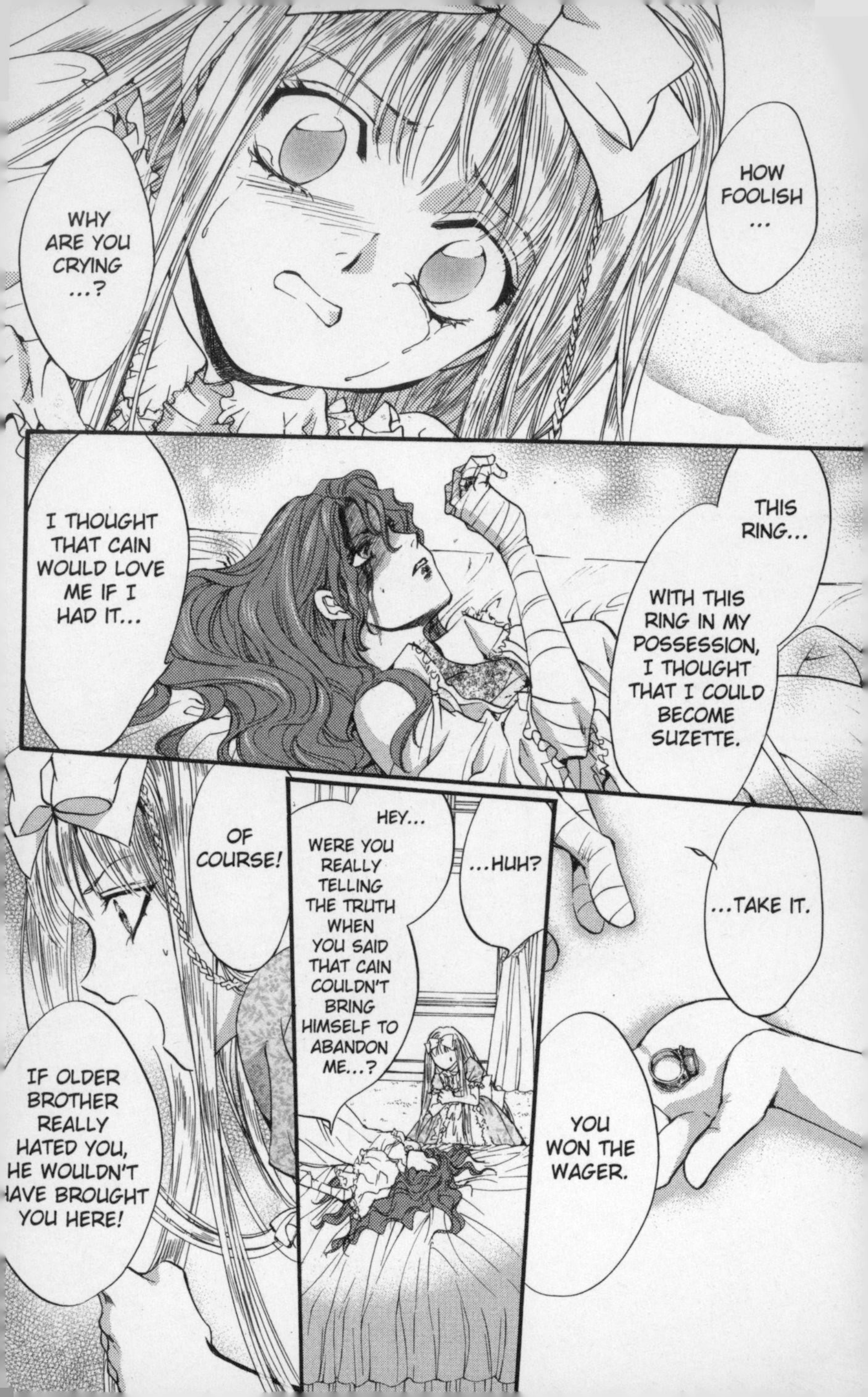
HOW FOOLISH ...
WHY ARE YOU CRYING ...?
THIS RING...
WITH THIS RING IN MY POSSESSION, I THOUGHT THAT I COULD BECOME SUZETTE.
I THOUGHT THAT CAIN WOULD LOVE ME IF I HAD IT...
...TAKE IT.
YOU WON THE WAGER.
...HUH?
HEY...
WERE YOU REALLY TELLING THE TRUTH WHEN YOU SAID THAT CAIN COULDN'T BRING HIMSELF TO ABANDON ME...?
OF COURSE!
IF OLDER BROTHER REALLY HATED YOU, HE WOULDN'T HAVE BROUGHT YOU HERE!

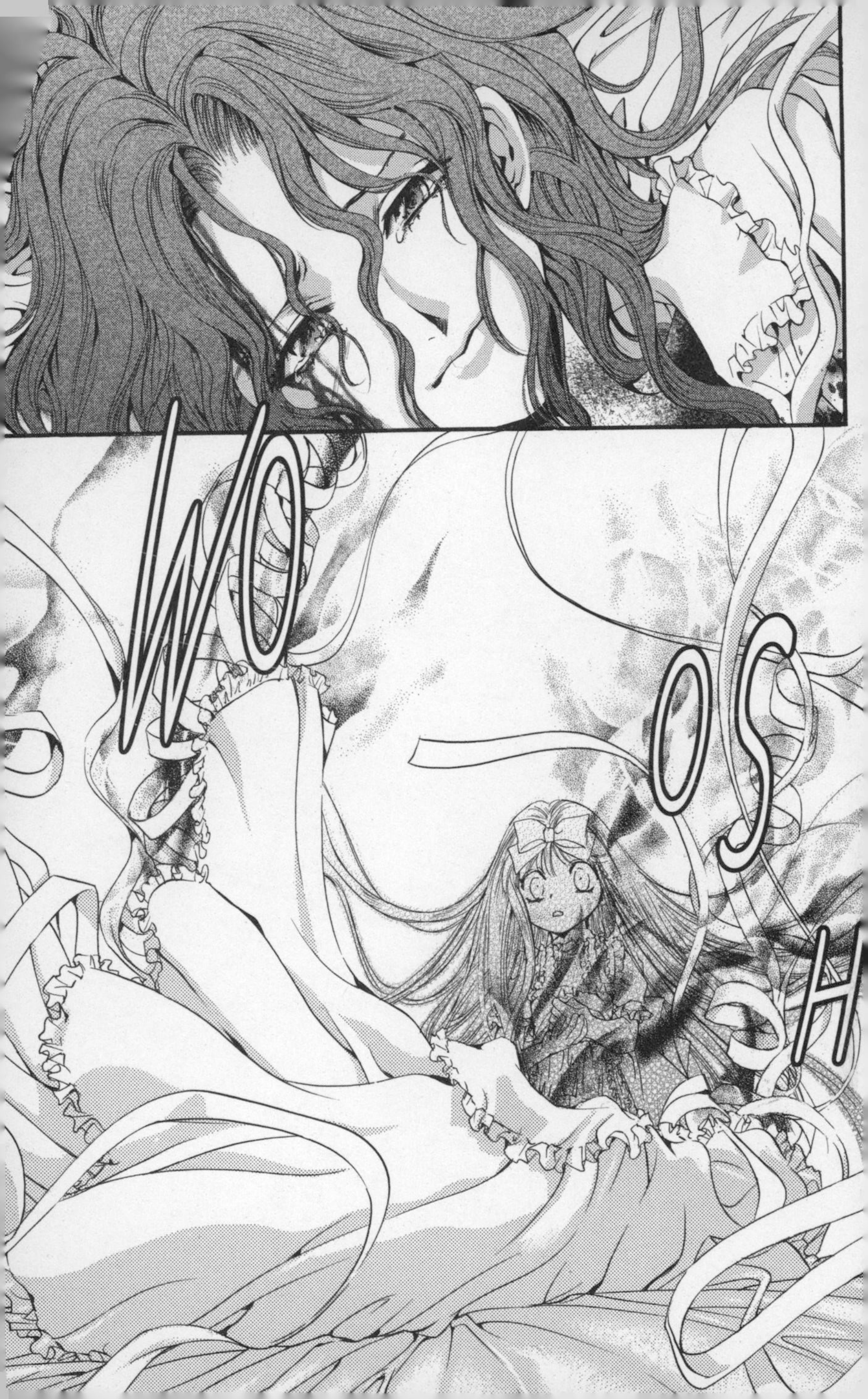
WOOSH

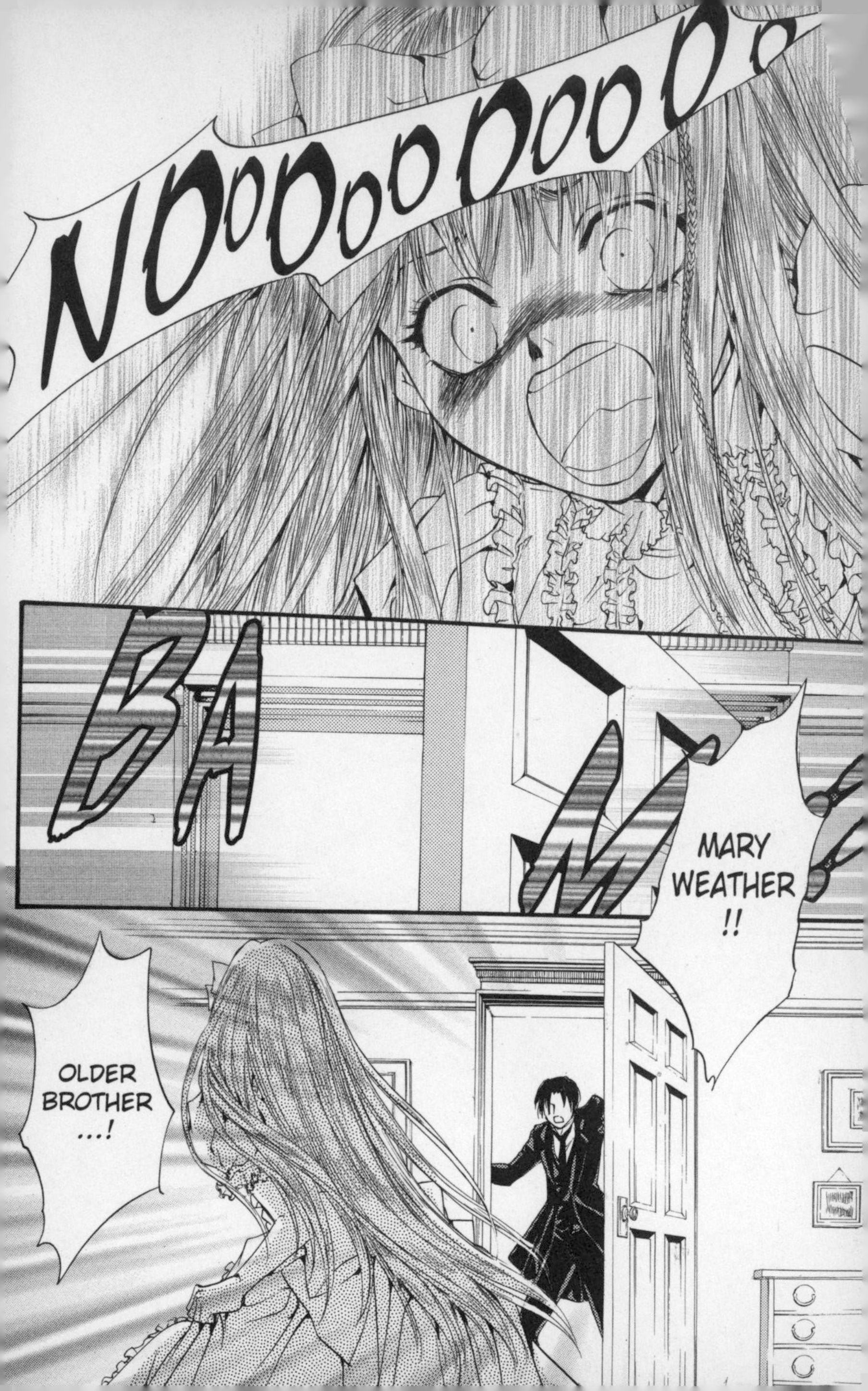
NOOOOOOOOOOOOO
BAM
MARY WEATHER !!
OLDER BROTHER ...!

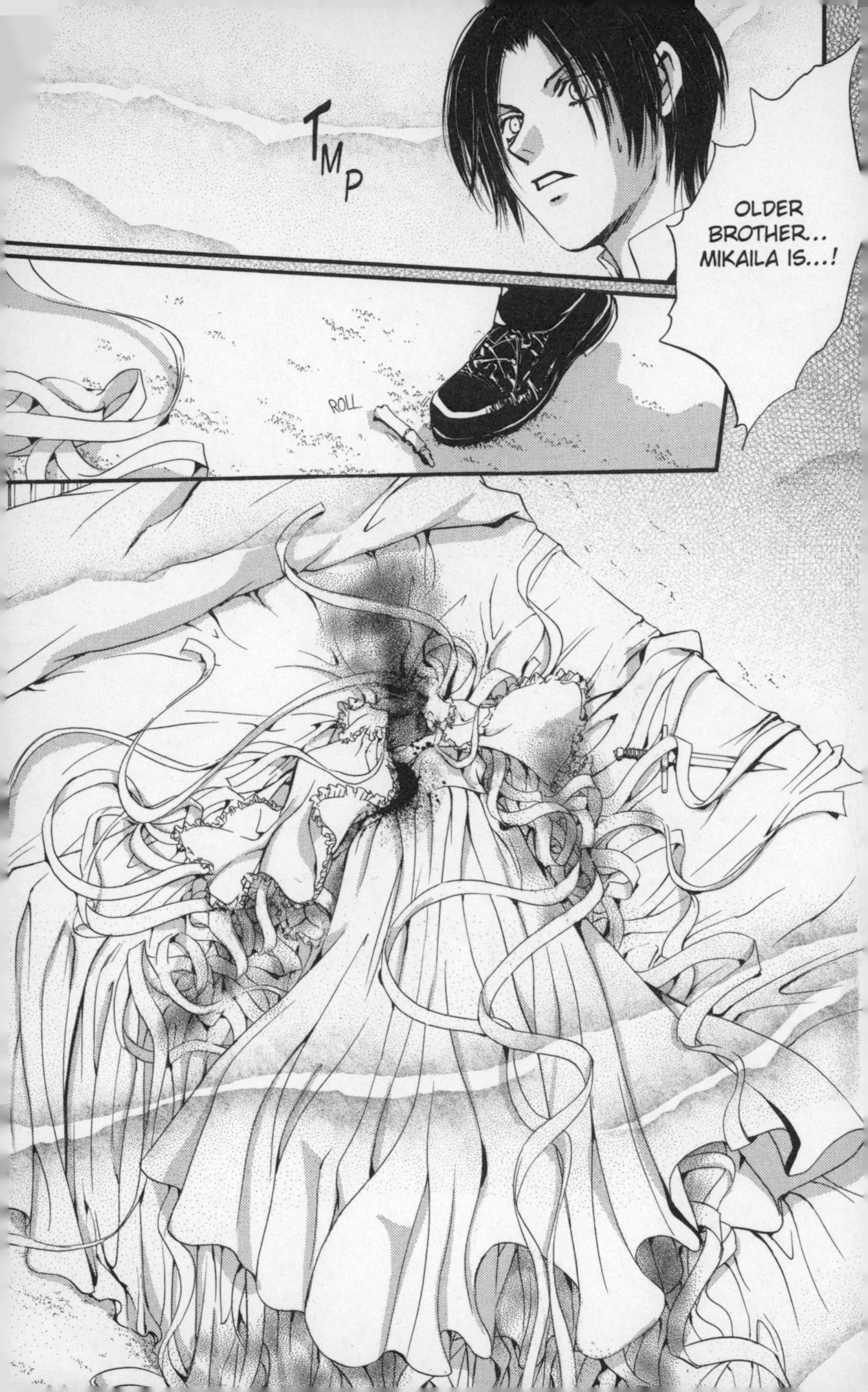
OLDER BROTHER... MIKAILA IS...!
TMP
ROLL

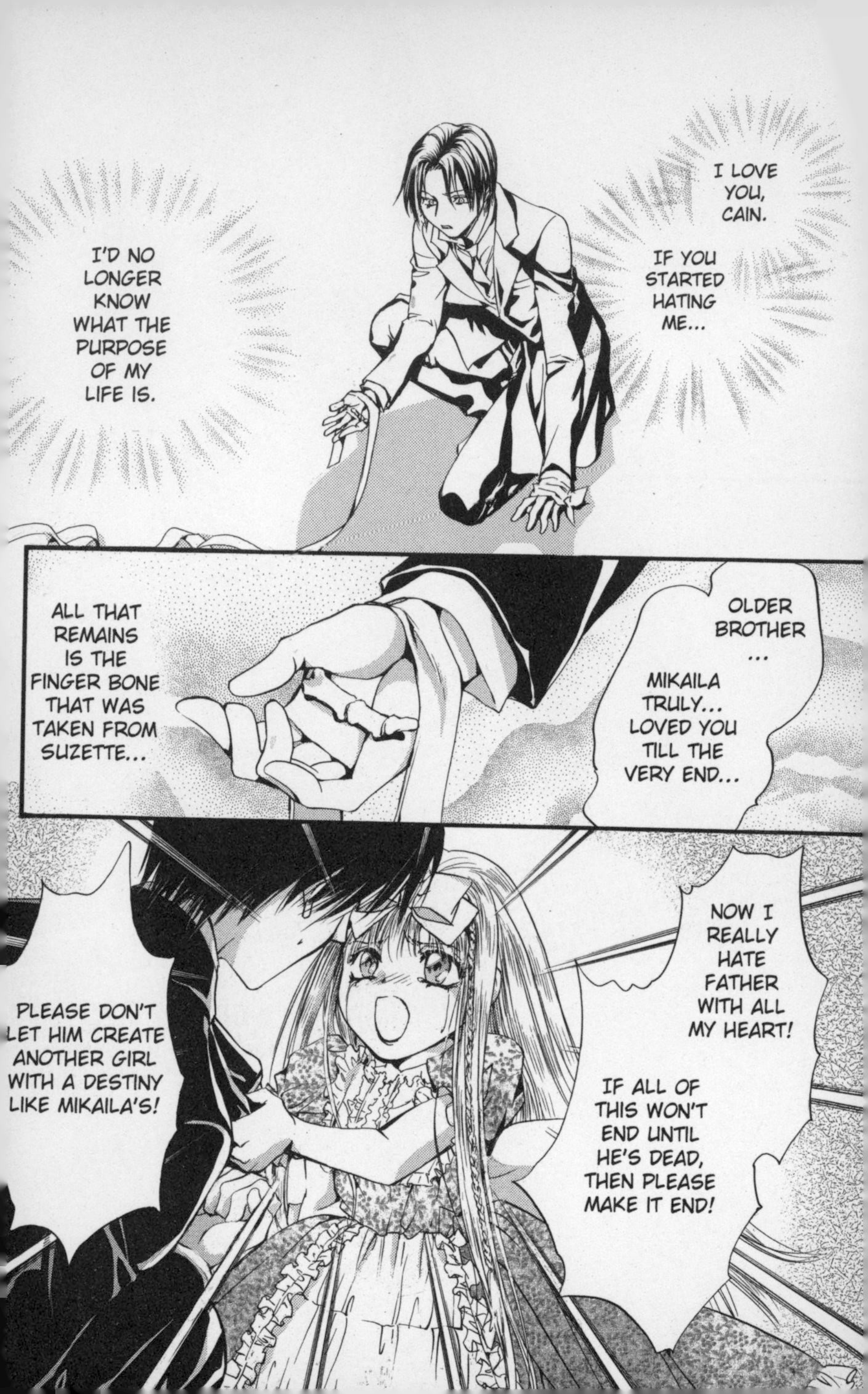
I LOVE YOU, CAIN.
IF YOU STARTED HATING ME...
I'D NO LONGER KNOW WHAT THE PURPOSE OF MY LIFE IS.
OLDER BROTHER ...
MIKAILA TRULY... LOVED YOU TILL THE VERY END...
ALL THAT REMAINS IS THE FINGER BONE THAT WAS TAKEN FROM SUZETTE...
NOW I REALLY HATE FATHER WITH ALL MY HEART!
IF ALL OF THIS WON'T END UNTIL HE'S DEAD, THEN PLEASE MAKE IT END!
PLEASE DON'T LET HIM CREATE ANOTHER GIRL WITH A DESTINY LIKE MIKAILA'S!

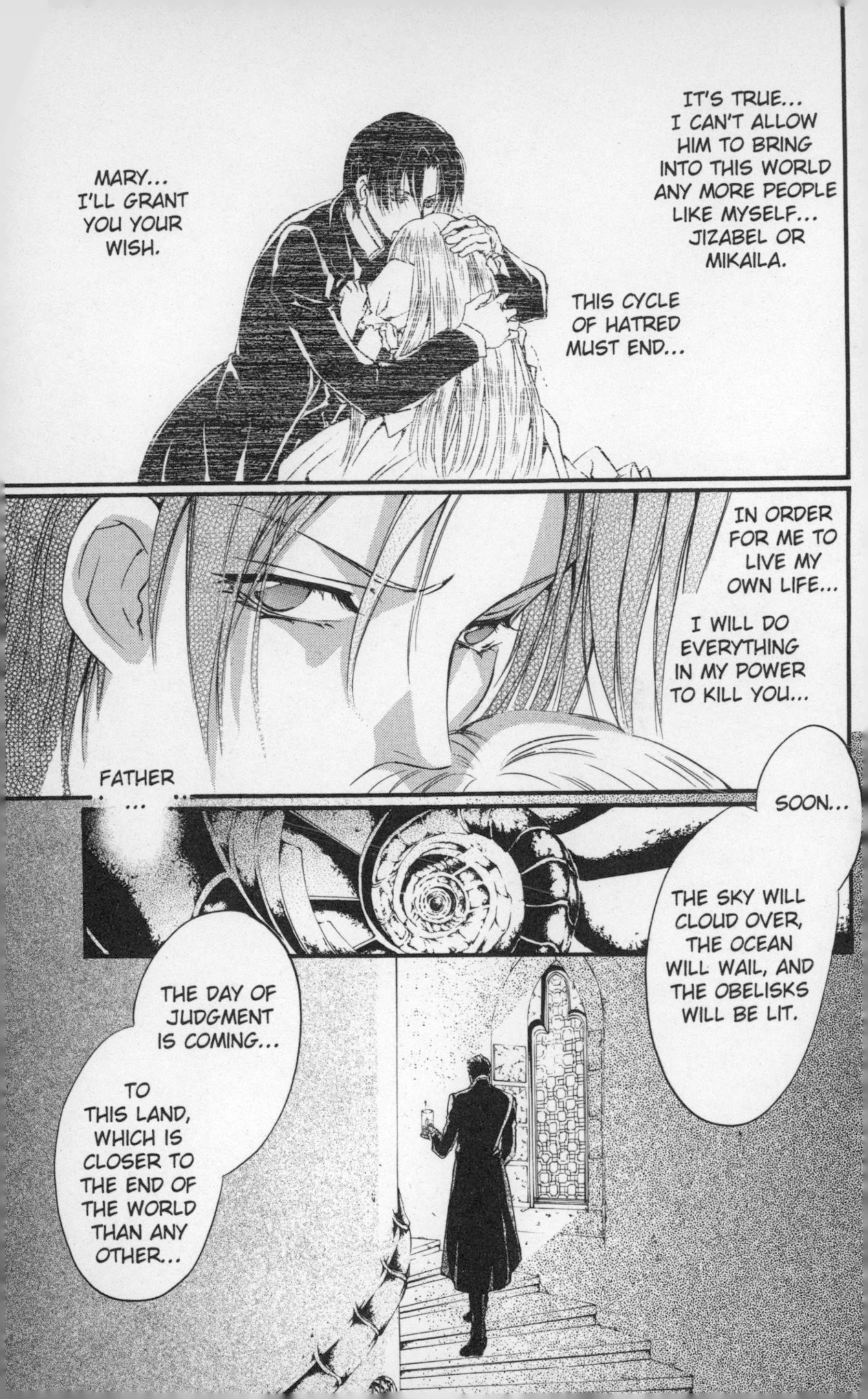
IT'S TRUE... I CAN'T ALLOW HIM TO BRING INTO THIS WORLD ANY MORE PEOPLE LIKE MYSELF... JIZABEL OR MIKAILA.
THIS CYCLE OF HATRED MUST END...
MARY... I'LL GRANT YOU YOUR WISH.
IN ORDER FOR ME TO LIVE MY OWN LIFE...
I WILL DO EVERYTHING IN MY POWER TO KILL YOU...
FATHER...
SOON...
THE SKY WILL CLOUD OVER, THE OCEAN WILL WAIL, AND THE OBELISKS WILL BE LIT.
THE DAY OF JUDGMENT IS COMING...
TO THIS LAND, WHICH IS CLOSER TO THE END OF THE WORLD THAN ANY OTHER...

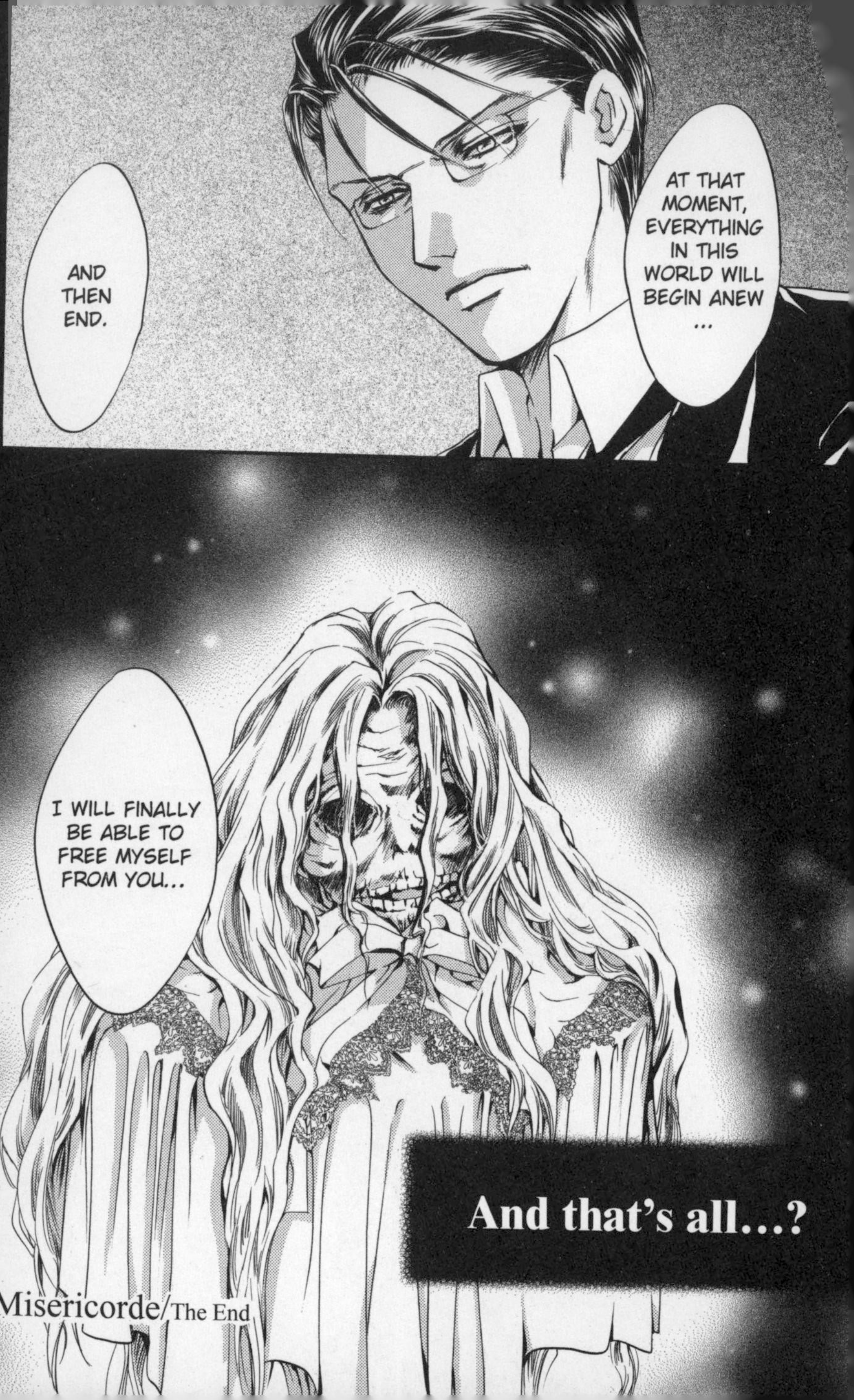
AT THAT MOMENT, EVERYTHING IN THIS WORLD WILL BEGIN ANEW ...
AND THEN END.
I WILL FINALLY BE ABLE TO FREE MYSELF FROM YOU...
And that's all...?
Misèricorde/The End

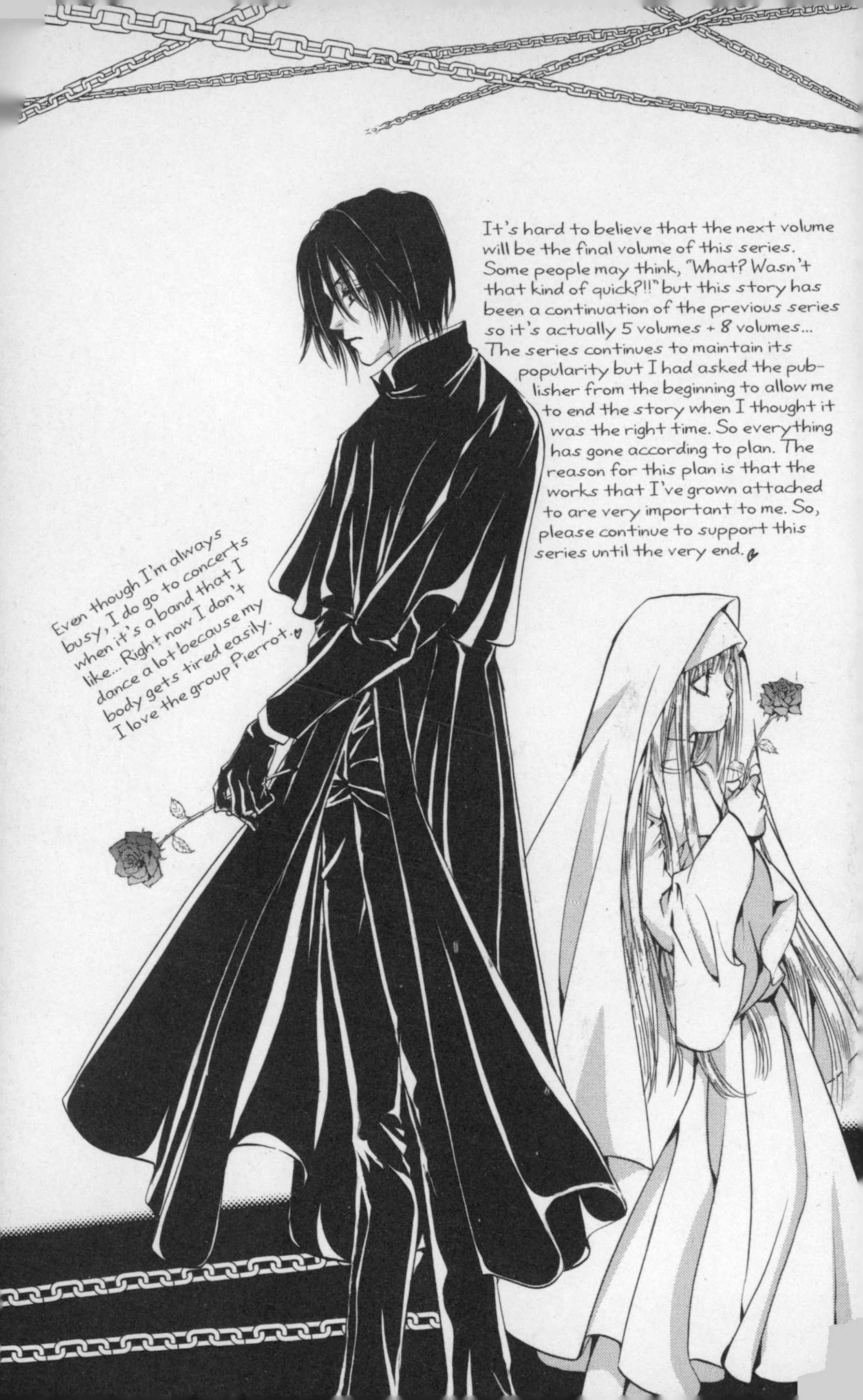
It's hard to believe that the next volume will be the final volume of this series. Some people may think, "What? Wasn't that kind of quick?!!" but this story has been a continuation of the previous series so it's actually 5 volumes + 8 volumes... The series continues to maintain its popularity but I had asked the publisher from the beginning to allow me to end the story when I thought it was the right time. So everything has gone according to plan. The reason for this plan is that the works that I've grown attached to are very important to me. So, please continue to support this series until the very end.
Even though I'm always busy, I do go to concerts when it's a band that I like... Right now I don't dance a lot because my body gets tired easily. I love the group Pierrot.

THE TRUE MEANING OF THE GODFATHER'S LAST WORDS HAVE BEEN DISCOVERED?

THE SKULL...OF AN EMBRYO...?!

WHAT IS HAPPENING TO LONDON...?

THE WINGS OF DEATH DESCEND UPON GREATER LONDON.

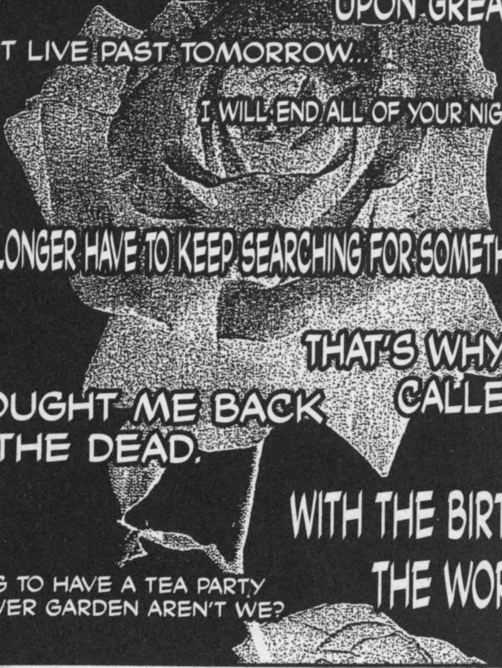

WILL NOT LIVE PAST TOMORROW...

I WILL END ALL OF YOUR NIGHTMARES FOR YOU.

E WILL NO LONGER HAVE TO KEEP SEARCHING FOR SOMETHING AND BE IN PAIN.

THAT'S WHY I AM CALLED THE OWL.

HE BROUGHT ME BACK FROM THE DEAD.

WITH THE BIRTH OF CHAOS, THE WORLD WILL END.

E'RE GOING TO HAVE A TEA PARTY
THE FLOWER GARDEN AREN'T WE?

Godchild Vol.8

The final chapter

Godless

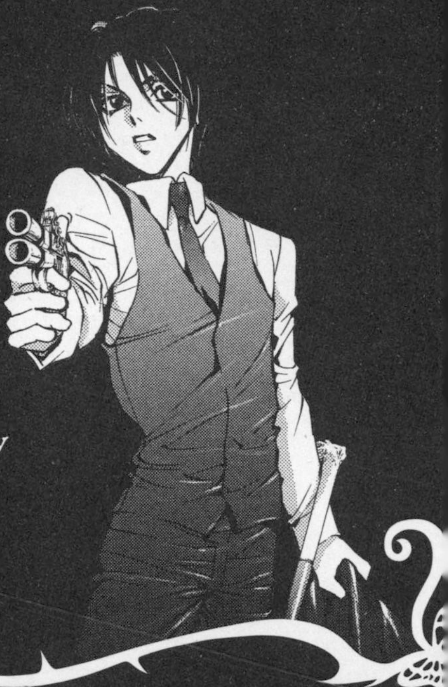

Creator: Kaori Yuki

Date of Birth: December 18

Blood Type: B

Major Works: *Angel Sanctuary* and *The Cain Saga*

Kaori Yuki was born in Tokyo and started drawing at a very early age. Following her debut work *Natsufuku no Erie* (Ellie in Summer Clothes) in the Japanese magazine *Bessatsu Hana to Yume* (1987), she wrote a compelling series of short stories: *Zankoku na Douwatachi* (Cruel Fairy Tales), *Neji* (Screw), and *Sareki Ôkoku* (Gravel Kingdom).

As proven by her best-selling series *Angel Sanctuary* and *The Cain Saga*, her celebrated body of work has etched an indelible mark on the gothic comics genre. She likes mysteries and British films, and is a fan of the movie *Dead Poets Society* and the show *Twin Peaks*.

Read Kaori Yuki's entire Earl Cain Series

Series 1: *The Cain Saga*: Forgotten Juliet
Series 2: *The Cain Saga*: The Sound of a Boy Hatching
Series 3: *The Cain Saga*: Kafka
Series 4: *The Cain Saga*: The Seal of the Red Ram, Volumes 1 & 2
Series 5: *Godchild*, Volumes 1-8

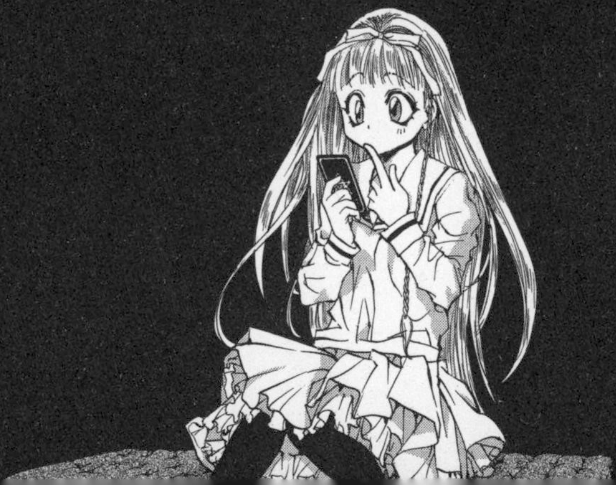

GODCHILD, vol. 7
The Shojo Beat Manga Edition

STORY & ART BY KAORI YUKI

Translation/Akira Watanabe
Touch-up Art & Lettering/James Gaubatz
Design/Courtney Utt
Editor/Joel Enos

Editor in Chief, Books/Alvin Lu
Editor in Chief, Magazines/Marc Weidenbaum
VP of Publishing Licensing/Rika Inouye
VP of Sales/Gonzalo Ferreyra
Sr. VP of Marketing/Liza Coppola
Publisher/Hyoe Narita

Printed in Canada

Published by VIZ Media, LLC
P.O. Box 77010
San Francisco, CA 94107

Shojo Beat Manga Edition
10 9 8 7 6 5 4 3 2 1
First printing, November 2007

PARENTAL ADVISORY
GODCHILD is rated T+ for Older Teen and is
recommended for ages 16 and up. This volume
contains graphic violence and adult themes.
ratings.viz.com

store.viz.com

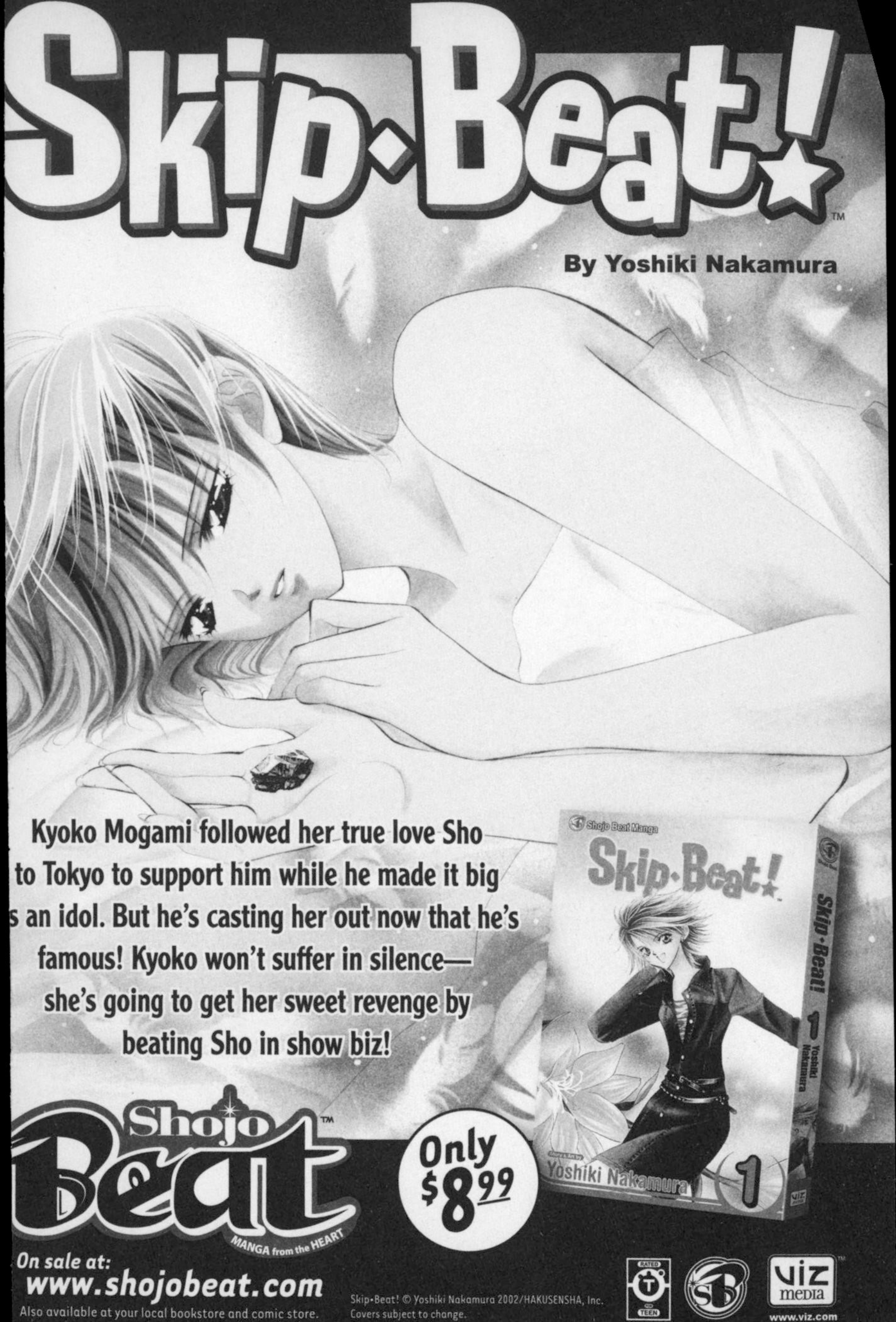
Skip·Beat!™
By Yoshiki Nakamura
Kyoko Mogami followed her true love Sho to Tokyo to support him while he made it big as an idol. But he's casting her out now that he's famous! Kyoko won't suffer in silence— she's going to get her sweet revenge by beating Sho in show biz!
Shojo Beat Manga
Skip·Beat!
Yoshiki Nakamura
1
Shojo Beat™
MANGA from the HEART
Only $8.99
On sale at:
www.shojobeat.com
Also available at your local bookstore and comic store.
Skip•Beat! © Yoshiki Nakamura 2002/HAKUSENSHA, Inc.
Covers subject to change.
RATED T TEEN
VIZ media
www.viz.com

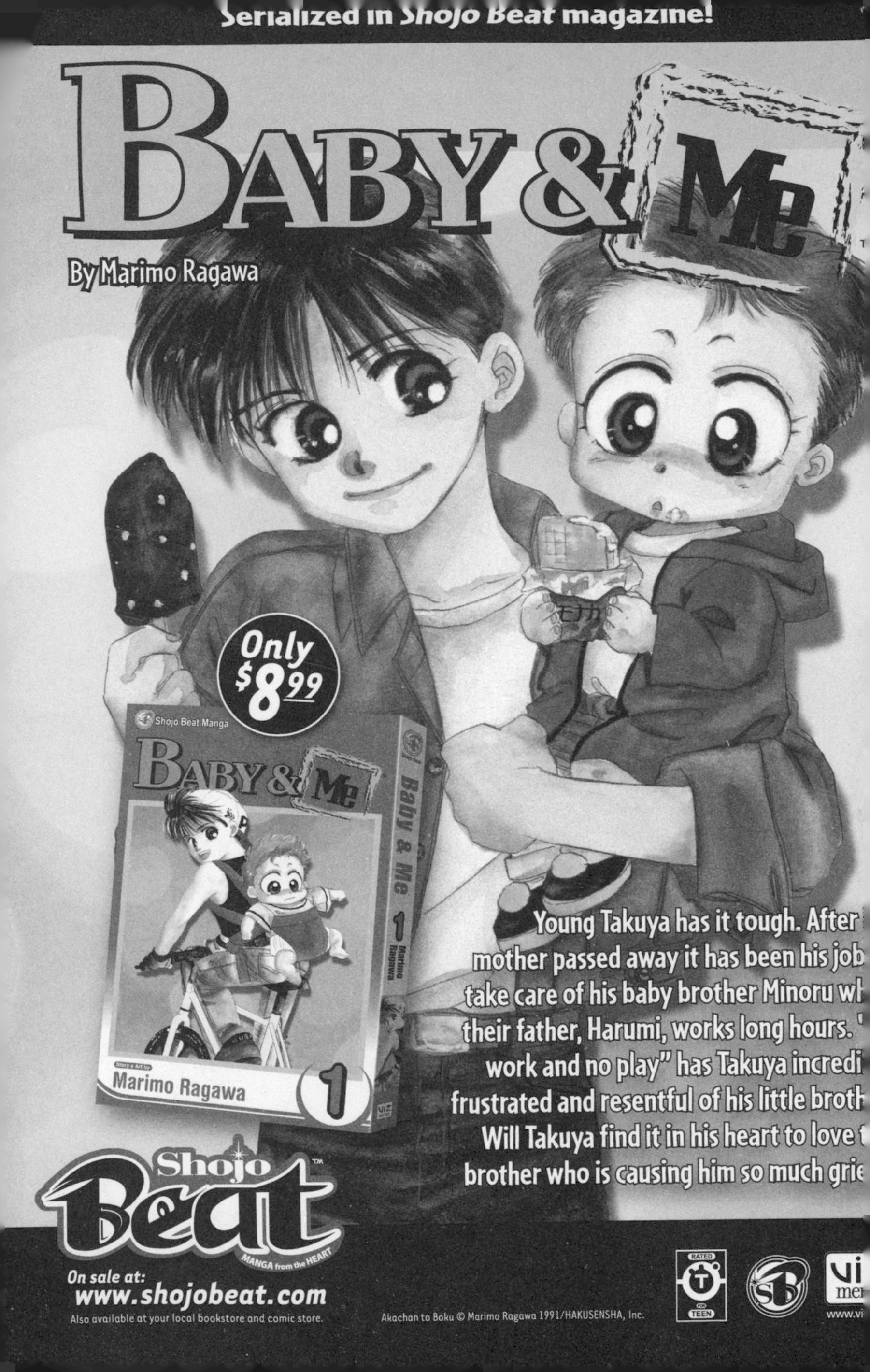
Serialized in Shojo Beat magazine!
BABY & Me
By Marimo Ragawa
Only $8.99
Shojo Beat Manga
Baby & Me
1
Marimo Ragawa
Young Takuya has it tough. After
mother passed away it has been his job
take care of his baby brother Minoru wh
their father, Harumi, works long hours. "
work and no play" has Takuya incredi
frustrated and resentful of his little broth
Will Takuya find it in his heart to love t
brother who is causing him so much grie
Shojo Beat
MANGA from the HEART
On sale at:
www.shojobeat.com
Also available at your local bookstore and comic store.
Akachan to Boku © Marimo Ragawa 1991/HAKUSENSHA, Inc.
RATED T FOR TEEN

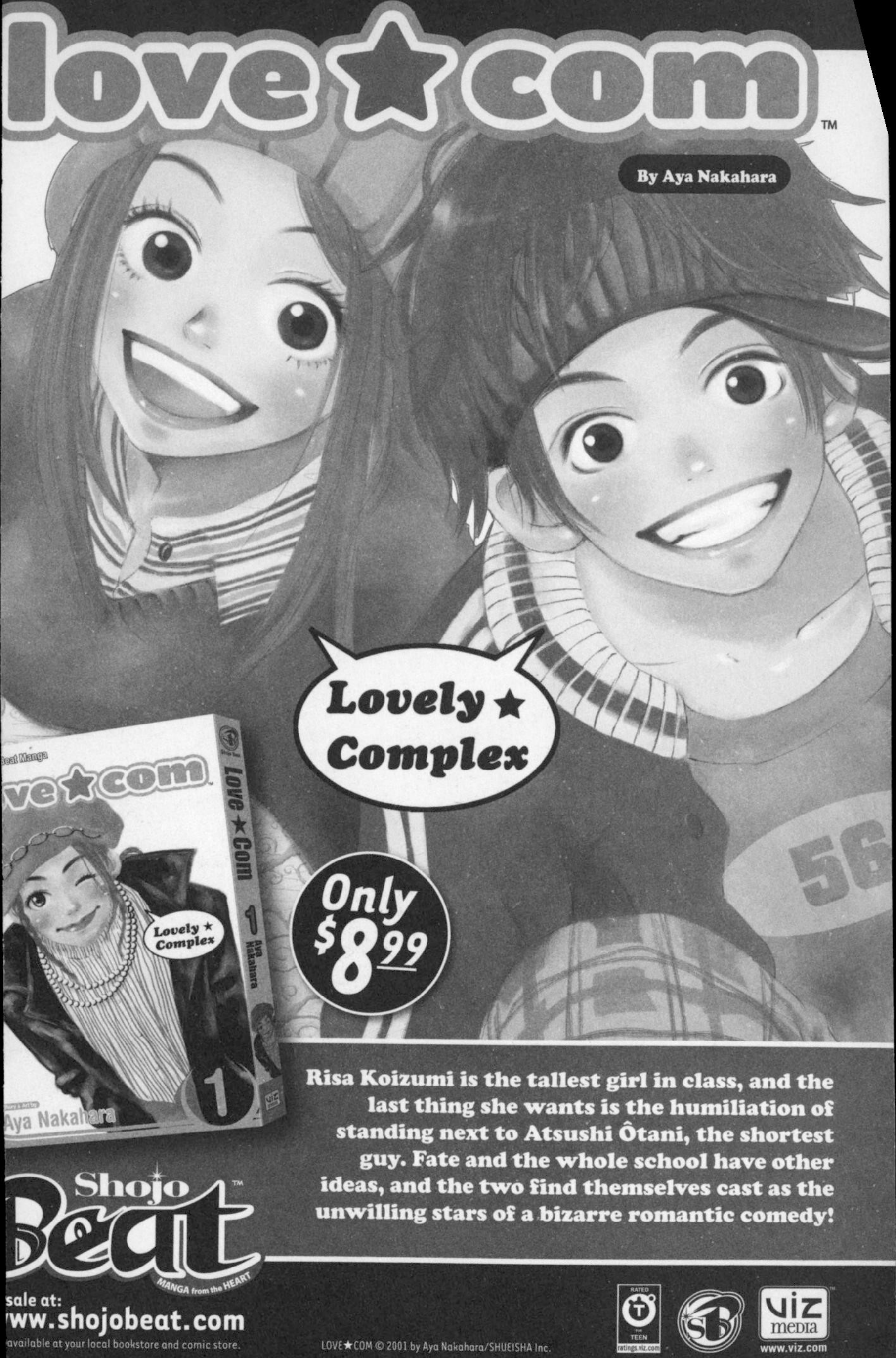

love★com™
By Aya Nakahara
Lovely★ Complex
Love★Com 1 Aya Nakahara
Only $8.99
Risa Koizumi is the tallest girl in class, and the last thing she wants is the humiliation of standing next to Atsushi Ôtani, the shortest guy. Fate and the whole school have other ideas, and the two find themselves cast as the unwilling stars of a bizarre romantic comedy!
Shojo Beat™ MANGA from the HEART
sale at:
www.shojobeat.com
available at your local bookstore and comic store.
LOVE★COM © 2001 by Aya Nakahara/SHUEISHA Inc.
RATED T TEEN ratings.viz.com
viz media
www.viz.com

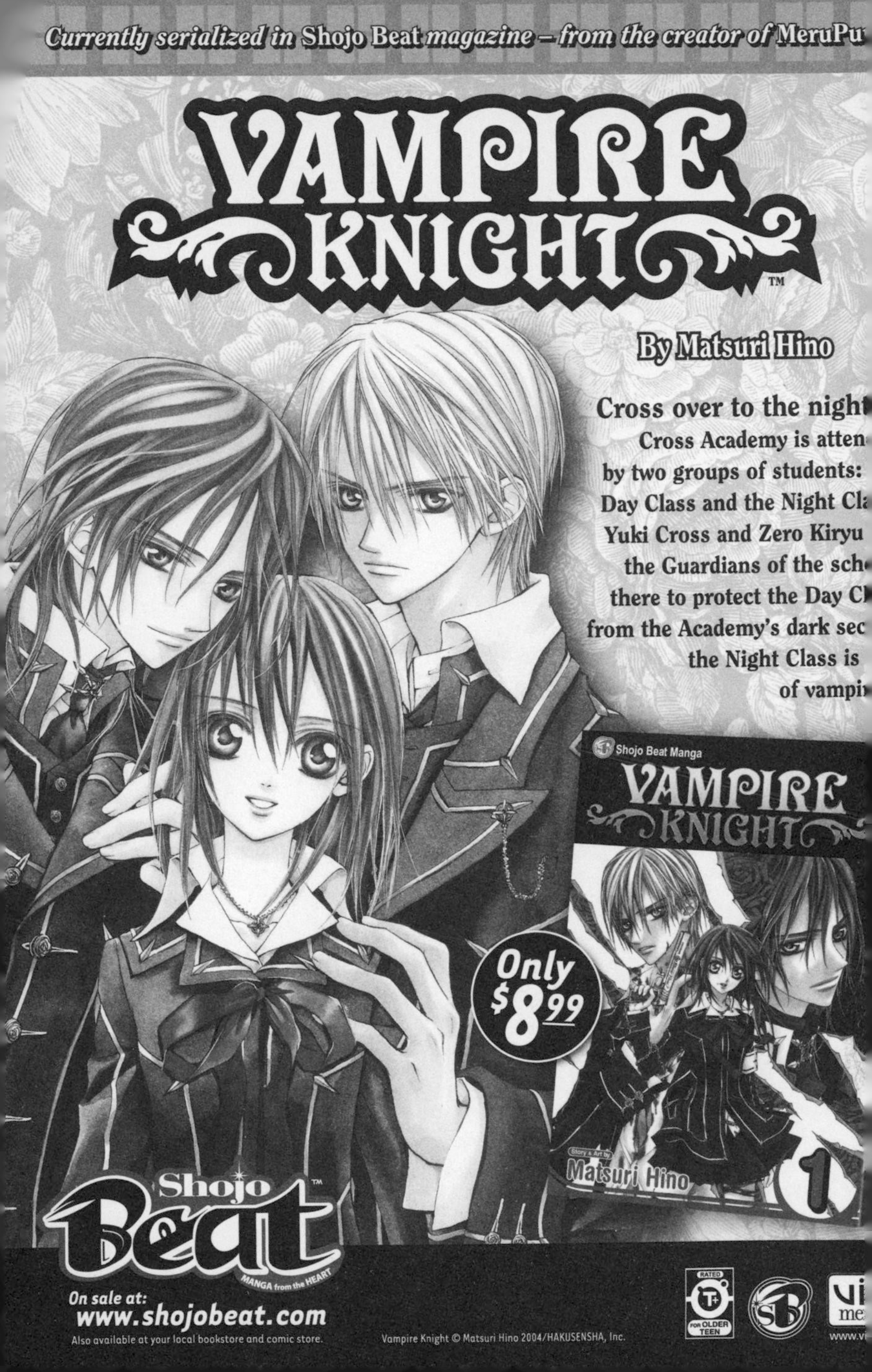
Currently serialized in Shojo Beat magazine – from the creator of MeruPu
VAMPIRE KNIGHT™
By Matsuri Hino
Cross over to the nigh
Cross Academy is atten
by two groups of students:
Day Class and the Night Cl
Yuki Cross and Zero Kiryu
the Guardians of the sch
there to protect the Day C
from the Academy's dark sec
the Night Class is
of vampi
Shojo Beat Manga
VAMPIRE KNIGHT
Story & Art by
Matsuri Hino
1
Only $8.99
Shojo Beat™
MANGA from the HEART
On sale at:
www.shojobeat.com
Also available at your local bookstore and comic store.
Vampire Knight © Matsuri Hino 2004/HAKUSENSHA, Inc.
RATED T+ FOR OLDER TEEN

Tell us what you think about Shojo Beat Manga!

Our survey is now available online. Go to:

shojobeat.com/mangasurvey

Help us make our product offerings better!

THE REAL DRAMA BEGINS IN...

Shojo Beat

MANGA from the HEART

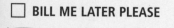